Trinidad ᴗarnival:

A Quest for National Identity

Peter van Koningsbruggen

CARIBBEAN

First published 1997 by
MACMILLAN EDUCATION LTD
London and Basingstoke
*Associated companies and representatives in Accra, Banjul,
Cairo, Dar es Salaam, Delhi, Freetown, Gaborone, Harare,
Hong Kong, Johannesburg, Kampala, Lagos, Lahore, Lusaka,
Mexico City, Nairobi, São Paulo, Tokyo*

ISBN 0–333–65172–3

10	9	8	7	6	5	4	3	2	1
06	05	04	03	02	01	00	99	98	97

Printed in Hong Kong

A catalogue record for this book is available from the
British Library.

Cover photograph courtesy of the author

Warwick University
Caribbean Studies

Series Editors: Alistair Hennessy and Gad Heuman

Behind the Planter's Back – Lower Class Response to Marginality in Beguia Island, St Vincent   0–333–47460–0
Neil Price

The Bloodstained Tombs – The Muharram Massacre in Trinidad, 1884
Kelvin Singh   0–333–47177–6

The Commonwealth Caribbean in the World Economy
Ramesh Ramsaran   0–333–49867–4

Europe and the Caribbean
Editor: Paul Sutton   0–333–48785–0

Explanation in Caribbean Migration – Perception and the Image: Jamaica, Barbados, St Vincent
Elizabeth M. Thomas-Hope   0–333–53503–0

Financing Development in the Commonwealth Caribbean
Editors: Delisle Worrell, Compton Bourne,
        Dinesh Dodhia   0–333–55204–0

From Dessalines to Duvalier – Race, Colour and National Independence in Haiti 3rd Edition   0–333–65026–3
David Nicholls

Hindu Trinidad – Religion, Ethnicity and Socio-Economic Change
Steven Vertovec   0–333–53505–7

In Miserable Slavery – Thomas Thistlewood in Jamaica, 1750–86
Douglas Hall   0–333–48030–9

Intellectuals in the Twentieth-Century Caribbean
Editor: Alistair Hennessy
Vol 1: Spectre of the New Class – The Commonwealth Caribbean
                                                            0–333–53509–X
Vol 2: Unity in Variety – The Hispanic and Francophone Caribbean
                                                            0–333–56939–3

The Jamaican People 1880–1902
Patrick Bryan   0–333–55125–7

Labour in the Caribbean – From Emancipation to Independence
Editors: Malcolm Cross and Gad Heuman   0–333–44729–8

Land and Development in the Caribbean
Editors: Jean Besson and Janet Momsen   0–333–45406–5

The Literate Imagination – Essays on the Novels of Wilson Harris
Editor: Michael Gilkes   0–333–49518–7

The Powerless People – The Amerindians of the Corentyne River
Andrew Sanders   0–333–45096–5

Teachers, Education and Politics in Jamaica, 1892–1972
Harry Goulbourne   0–333–47331–0

Trinidad Ethnicity
Kevin Yelvington   0–333–56601–7

The Autobiography of a Runaway Slave (Esteban Montejo)
(Miguel Barnet: Introduction: Alistair Hennessy)   0–333–53507–3

Caribbean Revolutions and Revolutionary Theory – Cuba, Nicaragua and Grenada
Brian Meeks   0–333–57759–0

Across the Dark Waters – Ethnicity and Indian Identity in the Caribbean
D. Dabydeen and B. Samaroo   0–333–53508–1

The Fractured Blockade – West European-Cuban Relations During the Revolution
Alistair Hennessy and George Lambie   0–333–58365–5

French and West Indian: Martinique, Guadeloupe and French Guiana Today
Richard Burton and Fred Reno   0–333–56602–5

*Noises in the Blood – Orality, Gender and the 'Vulgar' Body of Jamaican
Popular Culture*
Carolyn Cooper   0–333–57824–4

The United States and the Caribbean
Anthony Maingot   0–333–57231–9

Woman Version – Theoretical Approaches to West Indian Fiction by Women
Evelyn O'Callaghan   0–333–57837–6

Caribbean Economic Policy and South-South Co-operation
Ramesh F. Ramsaran   0–333–58677–8

Frontiers of Caribbean Literature
Frank Birbalsingh   0–333–60062–2

The Killing Time – The Morant Bay Rebellion in Jamaica
Gad Heuman   0–333–49400–8

Ethnicity in the Caribbean – Essays in Honor of Harry Hoetink
Gert Oostindie   0–333–64561–8

Caribbean Transactions – West Indian Culture in Literature
Renu Juneja   0–333–62552–8

Trinidad Carnival: A Quest for National Identity
Peter van Koningsbruggen   0–333–65172–3

Narratives of Exile and Return
Mary Chamberlain   0–333–64826–9

'Tiger in the Stars'
Clem Seecharan   0–333–68098–7

Series preface

Politics and culture are being determined, as never before, by the elusive notion of identity. In the Caribbean this is nowhere more apparent than in Trinidad. To the heterogeneity of its people of varied ancestry from Africa, India, China, the Middle East and Europe as well as Amerindians, living with the legacies of Spanish, French and British colonial rule and the looming presence of the United States, must now be added the cacophony of post-modernism and the babble of ethereal super-highways dependent on ever-changing information technologies. To affirm distinctiveness and to resist homogenization are imperatives which determine both cultural expression and political action in the search for a sense of community and nationhood.

The uniqueness of Trinidad, marking it off from Brazil, the obvious comparison (and one made in this book), is that by studying carnival in historical perspective it is possible to trace how a festival of the French planter-elite, with limited appeal, was transformed into a national symbol. This book analyses the long historical process of synthesis. It will doubtless stimulate controversy: no study of carnival can avoid stirring up an academic hornet's nest or offending susceptibilities, whether these be racial, political, social, moral, gender, or those of a group excluded from a festival which claims to represent the national culture.

Trinidad is unique also among small nations because of its creativity and its diverse cultural vitality. Such vitality rarely stems from consensus but is rather a consequence of conflicts and disagreements within a divided but mutually respecting society. In Trinidad these can be aired in carnival which acts as a forum for public debates – a 'festival of ticklish affairs' in the author's expressive phrase. After the abolition of slavery carnival became a festival of the people, spontaneous, rumbustious, saturnalian and afrocentric in spirit. In the colonial period those responsible for law and order were prepared to suppress the wider aspects, as in the 1880s. Nor was the Asian Muslim festival of Hosein exempt, as Kelvin Singh has shown in *Bloodstained Tombs: the Muharram Massacre, 1884* in this series.

Although carnival was to become a model elsewhere for West Indians, these carnivals lacked the historical conditioning factors which made the Trinidad case exceptional – that cultural and ethnic mélange and the festivities of Catholicism. The contrast with neighbouring Guyana is striking. Although it had a comparable ethnic mix the Guyanese had to live with the legacies of Dutch Calvinism and its British puritannical equivalents.

The author argues that carnival, with its symbolism and ambiguous potential, dramatizes divergent values without expressing preferences. It is thus, to use his phrase, 'a form of meta-comment on Trinidad within the performance of a kind of collective psycho-drama'. However, as with most expressions of a distinctive national identity there is the danger, under modern conditions, that it will succumb to market forces and the insidious new colonialism of the satellite dish and pap culture. Of all anglophone countries in the Caribbean, Trinidad has been the most Americanized: its music was packaged and popularized earlier in the century by American recording companies, and American mores and money were introduced during the 'Rum and Coca Cola' years of the American occupation of the Chaguaramas base in the Second World War. With oil money tastes for American artefacts could be indulged but at the end of the oil boom tourism became the new dollar earner. Carnival was now threatened with co-option by politicians and by the Tourist Board, much as it had been co-opted by the Creole middle class for its own social reasons earlier.

How the tensions between the demands of the tourist industry – the titillation of foreigners avid for exotic spectacle – and those of national identity will be resolved is one of the problems left for the reader to ponder in this comprehensive and thought-provoking analysis of the growth of national consciousness. Peter van Koningsbruggen's book is the fifth in the series to address the problems and culture of a society which Trinidadian themselves claim to be not only the most vibrant in the Caribbean but on the wider world stage as well, with carnival as the 'greatest show on earth'.

Alistair Hennessy

Contents

Acknowledgements

This book is the translation of a revised version of my 1993 dissertation on the Trinidad Carnival. I am very grateful to Harry Hoetink and Gert Oostindie for their expert assistance and advice in preparing the revised version for publication. I also owe a debt of thanks to Frank Bovenkerk and Arie de Ruijter for their encouragement and support in making my work accessible to a wider audience. The English translation was made possible by a generous grant from the Nederlandse Organisatie voor Wetenschappelijk Onderzoek (Dutch Council for Scientific Research). I have pleasant recollections of working with the translator, Peter Mason. His skill with language and with translation, combined with a thorough knowledge of the social sciences, greatly benefited the metamorphosis from Dutch into English. I would also like to thank Paula van Duivenvoorde, Petra Nesselaar and Jan Withagen from the University of Utrecht for their support in preparing the manuscript of this book on the word processor, and Shirley Hamber and Janey Fisher from Macmillan for taking care of the editorial side.

Finally, I am deeply indebted to Alistair Hennessy, series editor of the Warwick Caribbean Series for the extremely conscientious and unfailingly sympathetic way in which he commented on my manuscript and advised and assisted me.

Peter van Koningsbruggen

*'I have tried too in my time to be a philosopher,
but I don't know how,
cheerfulness was always breaking in.'*

Oliver Edwards (1711–91)

Introduction

Why should we assume that a people portray themselves only in ideal terms in their stylized public enactments? Does not art explore the range of the crucial values and motives of a group?... It therefore seems useful to see these festivities as enactments of the polarities of conflicting attitudes and alternative life-styles.

(Abrahams 1983: 107–8)

This study focuses on carnival on the Caribbean island of Trinidad, and especially on the role this festival plays in the progression towards national identity. One can speak of such an identity when the historical experience of a nation is conceived and handed down as a common experience (Hoetink 1973: 148).[1]

The island (4828 sq km, population 1 039 100), which constitutes a single state with the neighbouring island of Tobago (300 sq km, population 40 700), has been independent from the United Kingdom since 1962 (CSO 1986).[2] The shared experience of history, however, is hindered by the extremely heterogeneous composition of its population. It is a hybrid of both distinct and overlapping 'races', ethnicities, classes, cultures and religions, the product of years of colonial rule.[3] During those years, every initiative or development towards national unity was weighed up against or had to make way for the geo-political power interests and economic greed of the colonizers and the groups that supported them. In ideological terms, this situation has resulted in an erratic mosaic of ideas, beliefs and experiences among the people of Trinidad about their origin (Africa, Asia, Europe), historical consciousness, self-esteem, and the image that they have of their society. Together with the heterogeneity mentioned above, this forms the basis for separate political organizations, associations, schools, religious and social movements, rituals and celebrations.[4]

Unlike the many intra-group festivals of the island, carnival has developed, especially since World War II, into a cultural event which is largely divorced from religious, social and political particularism. This makes the festival an appropriate instrument to dramatize in symbolic form both the illusion of communality and its absence. It can be characterized in the same way as the staged exhibition of folk dancing in the Quebec City Winter Carnival, which is described by Handler (1988: 13) as 'a piece of "native" nationalist anthropology, a self-conscious representation or objectification of authentic national culture', or, as he formulates it elsewhere, '.... of what is *imagined* to be Québécois culture' (Handler 1988: 11, emphasis added). In *Nationalism and the Politics of Culture in Quebec* Handler writes (1988: 8–13) that his book is about 'the metaphors of boundedness, continuity, and homogeneity that both nationalist ideology and social-scientific discourse presuppose in their understanding of nations as entities. It is an attempt to disentangle social-scientific analysis from what I will call the interpenetration of nationalist and social-scientific discourse' (for a similar social constructionist approach see Segal's article (1994) on nationalism in Trinidad and Tobago). Handler calls his book an ethnography of these two mutually sustaining discourses. In his search for a suitable context in which the people of Quebec express their ideas about national identity and culture ('the nationalist discourse'), he ends up with the folkdance spectacle as a crucial example.

The present work is primarily concentrated on this 'discourse', the Trinidadian carnival as 'a piece of "native" nationalist anthropology'. Seen in this light, and to prevent any unnecessary confusion between the two discourses, I shall limit the 'social-scientific' definition of 'national identity' to the one provided above at the beginning of this introduction, especially as this book focuses on the *developmental process* leading up to (something like) national identity.

This function of carnival as a national cultural event is the result of almost two centuries of history, in which specific events which were initially confined to specific social groups gradually became the common property of society at large and were transformed into national symbols. In a nutshell: what was at first a festival belonging to the socio-cultural domain of the French Creole planter elite was transferred to that of the black lower class after the abolition of slavery (1834); with the increased interest and participation of the Creole middle class from the beginning of the twentieth century, it has turned into a festival of national importance.

If the early nineteenth-century carnival revels of the plantocracy that introduced the festival to Trinidad are left out of account for a moment, we can detect a trend in the development of the festival which corresponds to a large extent to the three stages proposed by Menezes (see Oliven 1984: 10) through which popular culture has to pass before it can become a generally accepted or dominant culture. The first is the rejection of those elements of popular culture which are regarded as offensive or disorderly; this action is taken by the state repressive apparatus (such as the police).

The second stage is characterized by domestication. The scientific apparatus, as Menezes calls it, of the dominant class is set to work to separate the dangerous components of popular culture from those which are conceived in a purely decorative or exotic fashion. The third stage, that of recuperation, is one of simultaneous action by the ideological apparatus and the 'culture industry' to transform the components of popular culture into cultural expressions of the dominant class, which are arranged and assigned a place in museums and exhibitions, offered as exotic items for sale to tourists, or serve as ideological instruments for educational and other purposes. A significant role is played in this entire process by state intervention and the role of the mass media in the creation of public opinion.

This model, which Menezes (Oliven 1984) proposed in connection with the Brazilian carnival, may have its analytical uses, but the cultural reality of the festival situation in Trinidad diverges considerably from it on a number of essential points. A complicating factor is the fact that the dominant position in relation to carnival has not always been held by the same class. This position was occupied by the white colonial elite during the nineteenth century and a part of the twentieth; after a transitional period of a few decades, and definitively after independence in 1962, this position has been taken over by the Creole middle class, which has political control of the island. The stage of rejection and suppression of carnival is dominated by the white elite's opposition to the 'black bacchanal', while the Creole middle class blew hot and cold, as its motives coincided often but not always with those of the white elite. During the domestication stage, there was a gradual transition as power passed from the white elite (which was pulling out of the social and political arena – some of its members returned to their country of origin), to the Creole middle class. The latter is virtually in sole control during the final recuperative stage.

These are not the only reasons for modifying the three-stage model in the case of Trinidad, for the model also overstates the social and cultural distinction between the dominant and the lower class. It assumes that the former only appropriates cultural concepts and symbols in order to win the support of marginal or subaltern groups and so legitimize its own political power, and that the carnival it takes over is merely transformed into a consumer and tourist article and a symbol of national identity. All of these intentions or motives undoubtedly apply in the case of the Creole middle class, but its position within the social stratification of Trinidad does not correspond to the image of an autonomous class. In fact, it is precisely its special position which explains the dynamic significance of the present-day carnival as a vehicle in the process of nation-building.

Traditionally, the Creole middle class has always occupied a problematic intermediate position. On the one hand, its members looked down on members of the black lower class and avoided social identification with them. On the other hand, they tried to secure social recognition from the white upper class, even though the latter barred them from the major economic and political sectors. They embraced the values and norms of the white elite, but were only incorporated to a lesser degree, if at all, in its social world. At the same time, however, they entertained disguised or open sympathies for the cultural values of the black lower class and thus for carnival. In this sense, their growing interest in carnival can be seen as a sign of an emergent reappraisal of a part of their own cultural heritage rather than as the adoption of cultural elements which originally only belonged to the subordinate class.

This ambiguous orientation of the Creole middle class can be seen as the crystallization of the social and ideological fissure affecting the whole of Trinidad society to a greater or lesser extent. There is a complex of conflicting value orientations that dominates social discourse. Though the Creole middle class provides little or nothing in the way of cultural scenario, carnival, whose organizational framework is provided by this class, can be regarded as a dramatization of this discourse. The ideological ambiguity gives the festival its dynamic political and social content, thereby preventing it from turning into a pure tourist attraction. However, carnival does not just reflect the dominant discourse in a passive, symbolic way; it also makes an active essential contribution to that discourse. The image of Trinidad presented by carnival provokes reactions and conflicts, as Trinidad society is shocked at its own appearance. Carnival is a controversial event which animates social discourse. Every year, the carnival period provokes social discussion, bringing into the open the question of that society's identity. Carnival is the mirror of society, in the same way that Greek tragedy, according to Turner (1982: 104), is a 'social metacommentary' (the terminology is Geertz's) on Greek society (1974: 26). This mirror is active: not only does it reflect, but it promotes reflexivity. In Turner's words, it is a mirror:

> ... that probed and analyzed the axioms and assumptions of the social structure, isolated the building blocks of the culture, and sometimes used them to construct novel edifices, Cloud Cuckoolands or Persian courts that never were on land or sea, but were, nevertheless, possible variants based on rules underlying the structures of familiar sociocultural life or experienced social reality.

A summary of the contents of the chapters of the present book may help to make the significance of carnival for Trinidad even clearer:
Chapter 1 deals with the history of the nineteenth-century carnival in Trinidad, with the events which give the festival its final form and content. While at first the festival was mainly an affair of the Catholic, French-Creole planter elite, after the abolition of slavery in 1834 it quickly developed

into a popular festival, with sexual and violent aspects which increasingly aroused the contempt and suspicion of the establishment. Towards the end of the century, carnival gradually became open to participation by the members of the middle and upper class, and a process got under way which has provided the festival with its present-day national allure.

Chapter 2 shows how the contours of carnival as we know it today began to take shape. For the main part, this development was given direction by people from the lower classes of African (born in Africa) and Creole (born in the West Indies) origin. The restrictions proclaimed by the government on the conduct of the festival stimulated the people's imagination, and they created new forms and alternatives to satisfy the deeply rooted need for certain cultural expressions. The three most important manifestations of carnival stem from this process and form the pillars of today's national festival: calypso music, the steelband and the masquerade.

Chapter 3 begins with a description of the origin and development of the Creole middle class from a perspective which explains its increasing receptivity to carnival. In the pursuit of its own identity, this class slowly came to regard carnival as a part of its own cultural heritage. After World War II typical middle-class 'virtues', such as a concern for respectability and the imitation of features of the North American show in particular, were added to carnival. They betray a growing socio-political dominance and an awakening national consciousness on the part of the middle class, resulting in independence in 1962. The large Indian community has been almost totally excluded from this process, in which the struggles for 'racial' and national identity were inextricably blurred. Focusing on the position of this group exposes the real situation: a society organized, if not divided, by 'race' and class. The Creole middle class determines to a large extent the national profile of Trinidad and Tobago, symbolized in popular form by carnival as the celebrations come more and more under the control and patronage of the authorities. The contemporary carnival arouses feelings of all kinds among every sector of the population. It invites Trinidadians to celebrate, criticize and call into question their own society. Festival and society reflect one another *ad infinitum*.

Chapter 4 is an attempt to provide a picture of Trinidad as one big stage for carnival and revellers. The conclusion is that Trinidad society is dominated by highly diverse values, the product of its colonial past.

Chapter 5 contains a discussion of a conflict model for Caribbean values developed by Peter Wilson (1969; 1973). Based on an 'emic' reputation/respectability value dichotomy, it brings order into the confusion of contesting values and orientations. It provides deeper insight into the social structure and organization of society and into the nature, significance and mutual implication of typical Caribbean oppositions which also determine the internal dynamics of carnival.

Wilson's model can be reduced to two general cultural-ideological hypotheses on society. From this perspective **Chapter 6**, based on a number of events, contains an account of mutually contradictory beliefs, opinions and points of view, which are connected with the notion of culture as it is experienced by various social classes and groups. Some themes prove to be directly linked with carnival, others are only marginally so, if at all. Nevertheless, the connecting link between the themes is that they form part of the annually recurring 'broad social discussion' instigated by the festival.

Presentation 1   The carnival festival programme

From about five weeks before carnival:

• The calypso tents, the theatres where the calypso singers perform the latest carnival songs, open their doors to the public. This marks the beginning of the calypso competition.

• The prospective revellers can bespeak the costume of their choice in the mas camps, the workshops where the costumes for the various masquerade bands are tailored. Each mas camp has its own band. The purchase of a costume means membership of a band during the carnival parades.

• The steelbands start their daily rehearsals in the panyards, semi-public rehearsal areas, to prepare for the steelband contest. Each band (consisting of 80 to 100 players) has a panyard as its base.

• Hotels, clubs and private individuals organize fêtes, especially in the weekends, where dancing to the sounds of the latest calypso hits begins at around ten o'clock at night. These parties carry on throughout the entire carnival season.

From about three weeks before carnival:

• Qualification contests are held all over the country for the steelband, calypso and masquerade competitions. During these preliminaries, the jury chosen by the organizing body, the National Carnival Commission, selects participants for the finals in accordance with a number of clearly defined criteria.

Saturday before carnival: National Panorama Finals

• Ten to twelve steelbands take part in the final in Queens Park Savannah, a big park near the centre of Port of Spain, where the main carnival events are held. The show begins at 19:00 hours and goes on until late. The jury announces the Panorama Steelband of the Year at dawn.

In **Chapter 7** a number of components of carnival are described to show how boundaries between what were originally class-related socio-cultural spheres within the festival become blurred and disappear. This situation makes it possible to arrive at an exchange and confrontation of opposite orientations in a completely original way. It is not the social, political or organizational dominance of the Creole middle class but its cultural ambivalence which has saved the festival from the general levelling process which has affected other areas of society as a result of 'middle-classization'.

Sunday before carnival: Dimanche Gras Show

- Large-scale spectacle in Queens Park Savannah, beginning at 20:00 hours. The show includes the final of the King and Queen of the Bands: the showpieces of the masquerade bands, often fantastic and bizarre mobile constructions, at the centre of which is the *masquerader*. These 'costumes' extravagantly illustrate the band's carnival theme. The most important event in this show, however, is the calypso final. The jury selects the Calypso Monarch of the Year from eight candidates. The show goes on until around 02:00 hours.

Carnival Monday: Jouvert Morning

- The opening of carnival itself, very early in the morning of Lundi Gras. Starting around 03:00 hours, thousands of carnival revellers occupy the inner streets of Port of Spain. The glitter and glamour of the Dimanche Gras Show, which has just finished, make way for chaotic carnival scenes which recall the 'forbidden bacchanal' of the nineteenth century. This part of the festival ends at around 11:00 hours. After a couple of hours of relative peace, the revellers and steelbands reappear in the streets.

Carnival Tuesday: Mardi Gras

- Masquerade bands, accompanied by steelbands and music floats, proceed through the streets of Port of Spain on their way to the Savannah, where they will be on display to the public and the jury in a well-organized fashion and in full regalia. The Band of the Year is chosen, as well as the Road March of the Year, the calypso melody which has been heard most often in the accompaniment of the bands in the procession. This part of carnival occupies the entire day.
- When the last masquerade band leaves the stage of the Grand Stand in the Savannah at around 19:00 hours, the closing stage of carnival, *Las Lap*, begins, accompanied by spontaneous drinking and dancing parties in the streets. At the stroke of midnight King Carnival makes way for Ash Wednesday.

Carnival therefore retains its function as a forum for the national discourse on Trinidad's search for its own identity. The concluding **Chapter 8** draws on a number of theoretical approaches, polemically at times, to clarify the significance of the Trinidad carnival for the island itself. Today's carnival is not an innocent tourist attraction, despite the claims of certain critics. Contesting values are brought together in a single carnival festival, managed but not entirely dominated by the Creole middle class. It is the non-partisan nature of the festival which accounts for its capacity to provide a metacommentary on society.

As this summary of contents shows, in the first instance considerable space is devoted to the history of carnival without its being immediately clear what form the festival will eventually assume. The various components of carnival are then discussed, though not following the chronological order of their appearance. In order to gain a proper understanding of the whole, it is worth providing the reader at this stage with a general outline of the programmatic structure of the carnival festival as it is celebrated today (see Presentation 1).

Notes

1   The context in which Hoetink sets this definition of national identity is explained at the beginning of Chapter 6.

2   Tobago, which has formed a constitutional unit with Trinidad since 1889, is left out of account in the present study. The carnival celebrated on the island of Tobago, where 93.5 per cent of the population is of African origin, follows the Trinidadian model, and the islanders take part in the national carnival competition held every year in the capital, Port of Spain, in Trinidad.

3   The ethnic composition of the population of Trinidad is as follows: 40.8 per cent negroes, 40.7 per cent Indians, 16.3 per cent coloureds, 0.9 per cent whites, 0.5 per cent Chinese, 0.8 per cent others.

4   Segal (1994: 223) points out that:

> In representations of the nation, present-day Trinidadian society is populated by collective characters from the colonial past, each of whom is defined both by ancestry (or 'race') and an affixed position in the plantation economy. ... [T]he often perceived 'pluralism' of Trinidadian society is an effect of a particular memorialization of the past, rather than of some unusual degree of social heterogeneity within contemporary society.

1 | The history of the Trinidad carnival in the nineteenth century

While at first the festival was mainly an affair of the Catholic, French-Creole planter elite, after the abolition of slavery in 1834 it quickly developed into a popular festival, with sexual and violent aspects, which increasingly aroused the contempt and suspicion of the establishment. The government's attempts to put an end to the disorderly festivities of the Jamet carnival reached a climax with the Canboulay uprisings in the years 1881–4. In this chapter we consider to what extent Jamet carnival and Canboulay uprising set processes of social and cultural emancipation in motion which have influenced or determined the further development of the festival to the present day. The chapter concludes with some theoretical comments on this question.

The development of carnival

Before the party began (1498–1797)

After Christopher Columbus had discovered Trinidad and thereby brought it under Spanish control during his third voyage to the New World in 1498, almost three centuries passed before the island came to assume any importance in the Spanish colonial empire, which had been severely weakened in the meantime. This interest came too late, because Trinidad passed into English hands in 1797. The island did not have much gold or precious stones, and the main reason for the Spanish Crown to take occasional note of Trinidad was its strategic position so close to the South American mainland, where it was supposed that the highly coveted El Dorado would some day be found. When the Dutch plundered the main town and fortification of San Josef, this seriously neglected outpost of the Spanish empire was defended by a mere twenty-eight soldiers (Hill 1972: 6). In 1662 the Spanish governor wrote to Madrid that the colonists had no knives, axes, picks or agricultural tools, and he complained that no Spanish ship had put in at Trinidad for thirty years (Brereton 1981: 3). Meagre conditions and a stagnation in population growth persisted without any significant fluctuations until 1783 (see table 1.1).

Table 1.1   Demographic structure in 1783

Whites	Coloureds	Slaves	Indians	Total
126	245	310	2000	2681

Source: Pearse 1971: 528

The year 1783 marked a turning-point. It heralded the development of present-day Trinidad society, and it shaped the history from which carnival was to emerge. The growing presence and power of the French and the British in the Caribbean at the end of the eighteenth century made it more and more difficult for the Spanish to hold on to Trinidad. During this period, Europe was primarily interested, not in gold, but in the development of crops such as tobacco, cacao, spices and sugar for the expanding European markets. This activity required immigrants from the mother country, and Spain was not in a position to supply them. The flow of wealth from the New World to Spain itself had already created a labour shortage, and the population of Spain – eight million at the end of the eighteenth century (Vogt 1975: 53) – was insufficient to allow large-scale emigration to the colonies.

These were the main reasons for the promulgation in 1783 of the *Cédula de Población* by the liberal regime of the Spanish Bourbons, who had grown less mercantilist over the years. This law made it possible for foreign immigrants to settle on Trinidad, provided they were Catholics, subjects of a friendly nation, swore an oath of allegiance to Spain and accepted the laws of that country (Williams 1982: 41). As a result of the combination of these terms, the composition of the population in the region and the effects of the international political situation, a spectacular immigration got under way, consisting chiefly of French planters and their slaves from Saint Domingue, Martinique, Guadeloupe, Dominica, St Lucia, Grenada and elsewhere. The French Revolution and the Napoleonic era spelled considerable unrest and uncertainty within the traditional colonial societies of the French West Indies. Power was successively seized by various conflicting factions, there was a fear of slave revolts, and in the background the menace of a Franco-English war which might have repercussions further afield. These considerations prompted many people to emigrate. It was attractive to start afresh on the virtually uncultivated but fertile island of Trinidad, because the *Cédula* laid down that every white immigrant and every member of his family would receive some 30 acres of land, plus half that again for every slave he brought with him (Black *et al.* 1976: 42). Although people of mixed descent only received half of the amount of land that was granted to their white counterparts, plus allocations for each slave on the same basis, the Spanish government also conferred on them the formal status of planters and slave owners. The prospect of civil rights which would make them equal to whites before Spanish law was dangled before their eyes, a position which it was impossible to obtain in the non-Spanish West Indies (Brereton 1981: 14).

By the time the British took Trinidad from the Spanish, the immigrant planters had cultivated some 85 000 acres of land and acquired a reasonable level of prosperity (Hill 1972: 7). The composition of the population had changed drastically within a period of fourteen years, in which an enormous growth had taken place (see table 1.2).

Table 1.2 Demographic structure in 1797

	Whites	Coloureds	Slaves	Indians	Total
Spanish	150	200	300	1 127	1 777
French	2 250	4 700	9 700	—	16 650
Total	2 400	4 900	10 000	1 127	18 427

Source: Pearse 1971: 529

The scanty inhabitants of the island before 1783 had been predominantly Spanish or Indian, but a few years later the demographic structure of Trinidad had changed completely. It was now dominated by a sizeable African and French group, which was culturally orientated towards the French West Indies. There is no evidence to suggest that carnival existed on the island in any form before 1783, and it is unlikely in any case in view of the small number of islanders. At any rate, it is only possible to trace continuity in the Trinidad carnival from the period in which a white,

French-Creole elite formed the core of society. It is not without importance that the first steps towards a (planters') carnival took place under a (Spanish) regime which did not regard such activity as strange or menacing.

The planter elite celebrates (1797–1834)

From the beginning of the nineteenth century, then, there was a French plantocracy in the newly won British colony, which could maintain the life-style of a rural aristocracy. Balls, concerts, dinners, hunting parties and *fêtes champêtres* were organized mainly in the carnival season, which extended from Christmas to Ash Wednesday. House visits, walks or rides in a carriage, music and dance, fun and pranks were the main ingredients which contributed to an authentic carnival atmosphere.

In view of the changes which took place in the celebration of carnival over the years, it is important to note the mixed character of Trinidad society at this time. One of the consequences of the liberal Spanish admittance policy was that all kinds of opportunists and adventurers were attracted to the island. The well-to-do planter caste regarded them as 'the riffraff of the Southern Caribbean' (Hollis 1941: 82). The British conquest of the island did not put an end to the flow of immigrants; the diversity of races and cultures steadily increased. However the original Amerindian inhabitants, the Carib in Tobago and the Arawak in Trinidad, were subjected and enslaved by the Spanish conquerors and colonists. By the middle of the nineteenth century, this population group was either practically extinct or assimilated. The population statistics for the period 1783–1831 yield the following picture (table 1.3):[1]

Table 1.3   *Demographic structure, 1783–1831*

Year	Total	Whites	Coloureds	Indians	Chinese	Slaves
1783	2 763	126	295	2 032	—	310
1797	17 712	2 151	4 474	1 078	—	10 009
1800	22 850	2 359	4 408	1 071	—	15 012
1805	30 076	2 434	5 801	1 733	—	20 108
1810	31 143	2 487	6 269	1 659	—	20 728
1815	38 348	3 219	9 563	1 147	—	24 329
1820	41 348	3 707	13 965	910	29	22 738
1828	42 262	3 310	14 980	727	12	23 230
1831	41 675	3 319	16 285	762	7	21 302

Source: West Indian Census, 1941, p ix. From Braithwaite 1975: 87

Within thirty years – by 1810 – the number of slaves had more than doubled from 10 009 to 20 728 (Williams refers to a doubling from 10 000 to 22 000 in the period 1797–1808; 1982: 68). They were joined by freed negro slaves from the United States, coloureds from Venezuela, Chinese immigrants, Corsicans, Scots, Swiss, Germans and Italians. This ethnic mix was exceptional, even by contemporary Caribbean standards. It gave Trinidad '... the cosmopolitan, almost Levantine atmosphere which it has never lost and Port of Spain was becoming a restless Caribbean Alexandria where people of different cultures came together and where the texture of life was quite unlike that of Kingston, Bridgetown, Fort-de-France, or even Havanna' (Wood 1986: 44). However, this did not mean that the hierarchical distinction based on 'race', religion or nationality had disappeared. On the contrary, under British administration measures were adopted to guarantee a stricter differentiation by colour than had been the case under Spanish rule. Whites belonged to the elite at the top of the social ladder, and people of mixed origin, who would have been their equals under Spanish law, were degraded to second-class citizens. The position of the slaves remained unchanged, although they grew daily more aware that their liberation would not be long in coming. The British were particularly afraid of the growing dissatisfaction of the latter two social groups, which might result in explosive tensions. Hill (1972: 10) says:

> 'Carnival, the traditional leveler of social distinctions, was incompatible with such a society. It had either to die from neglect or to change its character substantially. The former contingency became the hopeful prediction of the upper class over half a century; the latter is what actually happened'.

It is true that carnival in general does have this function as leveller of social distinctions, but this does not necessarily mean that it is irreconcilable with early nineteenth-century Trinidad society. The relation between carnival and social conflict is more complex than just this levelling. Carnival can also function as a mechanism which reinforces class and ethnic boundaries. Through role-changing and other means, carnival can bring to light an opposition in society which is experienced as irreducible, thereby representing this opposition afresh as beyond dispute and as generally characteristic of the society involved (Devisch 1978: 12). (Incidentally, it is remarkable how many Trinidadian writers see carnival as nothing more than a 'leveller of social distinctions'. Their historiography is motivated by an ideological finality which coincides with the current dominant nationalist view that carnival simply promotes unity in the plural society of Trinidad.)

The first description of carnival in which it is presented as a kind of rite of reversal, an important transcultural aspect of the festival, can be found in the Port-of-Spain Gazette for 19 March 1881, in which an anonymous writer discusses the origin of Canboulay or Cannes Brulées. His description (cited in Hill 1972: 11) of the heyday of carnival (around 1820) is as follows:

> ... tout le beau monde se masquait, ou se déguisait. Les déguisement les plus à la mode étaient, pour les Dames, le joli et riche costume de 'mulatresse' de l'époque, et, pour les Messieurs, celui de 'nègre de jardin', en créole 'negue jadin', c'est à dire, esclaves noirs attachés à la culture. Nos mères et nos grand'mères, au carnaval, ont meme dansé le 'belair' au son du tam-tam africain, dont les sons n'écorchaient pas leurs fines oreilles rosées, et nos pères et grand'pères, le 'bamboula', le 'ghouba', et le 'calinda'.... Parfois aussi, les 'nègres de jardin', formés en ateliers, se portaient le soir aux Cannes Brulées. Leur marche splendide, aux flambeaux, par les rues de la ville, était la reproduction de ce qui se passait aux champs lorsque l'incendie avait dévoré une plantation. Les ateliers des plantations voisines y étaient conduits, par quarts, de nuit comme de jour, pour convertir en sucre, avant qu'elles aient le temps de s'aigrir, les 'Cannes Brûlées'.[2]

This is the very first explicit record of the contribution of elements of slave culture to the Trinidad carnival. An account of the festivities of the planter elite also provides information on the existence of slave dances such as Belair, Bamboula, Ghouba and Calinda. The Canboulay torch procession is a parody of a dramatic event in plantation life, when slaves were herded together with the cracking of whips and driven towards the spot where a fire had broken out. Occasionally these fires were deliberately caused by slaves in retaliation for the behaviour of their masters or overseers (De Verteuil 1984: 63). After Emancipation in 1834, the freed negroes turned this custom into a sort of memorial ceremony, which they held on the night of 1 August, the date of their liberation from slavery. Fifteen years later we find Canboulay as the rebellious opening of the three main days of carnival on Sunday night. It is not clear from the history whether the ritual really shifted from 1 August to the opening of carnival. The Canboulay procession could also have arisen as a lower-class imitation of the 'nègre jardin' band, as the white elite conceived it within carnival (De Verteuil 1984: 62–3; Brereton 1979; Hill 1972; Pearse 1971). This possibility is interesting as a case of double role-reversal: white slavers imitate the behaviour of negro slaves with exaggerated pomp and circumstance, which is later imitated and mocked by the freed slaves as the behaviour of their former masters.

The abolition of slavery: carnival to the people (1834)

Before the abolition of slavery, carnival was an affair of the white elite and, within their own circle, of people of mixed origin. All the same, there was still some scope for the slaves to hold their rituals and festivals. The strict demarcation, particularly between the white elite and the negroes, did not impede influences in both directions on the form and content of the festivities. For the English, Christmas was the traditional starting signal for a period of amusement and pleasure, and to a certain extent the slaves were granted the same recreation. There was mutual contact, not only because the services provided by the slaves sometimes obliged them to attend the festivals of the whites, but also because a master might stage the amusements of the slaves outside or inside his house as a form of theatre. To prevent liberty of this kind from getting out of hand, it was traditional practice to impose a state of emergency in the British colonies during the Christmas period. Military inspections and parades were intended to underline the social order and the prestige of the elite, and at the same time carnival enabled the free population to take on assumed social roles and to appear masked on the street, thereby overstepping the same social barriers (Pearse 1971: 534–8). Some of the later carnival bands of freed slaves are a distant reflection of these military parades (D.R. Hill 1993: 32). The annual mustering of troops was regarded as the prelude to a light-hearted and carefree season rather than as a menacing premonition of imminent bloody revolution (Hill 1972: 13).

There is plenty of evidence on the entertainments of the white elite in the sources, but we are less well informed about what took place within the communities of negro slaves. When after 1834 the ex-slaves took carnival over from the whites in the streets of Port of Spain, the latter took their celebrations indoors into the salons and ballrooms, and the character of the festival was virtually immediately determined by a mixture of mythico-religious performances, fights, songs and dances of African and European origin. The eruptive character of these events indicates that the years of slavery were also a period of cultural incubation. V.S. Naipaul (1985: 136–7) has described the atmosphere as follows:

> In the slave plantations of the Caribbean Africans existed in two worlds. There was the world of the day; that was the white world. There was the world of the night; that was the African world, of spirits and magic and the true gods. And in that world ragged men, humiliated by day, were transformed – in their own eyes, and the eyes of their fellows – into kings, sorcerers, herbalists, men in touch with the true forces of the earth and possessed of complete power. A king of the night, a slave by day, might be required at night never to exert himself; he would be taken about by his fellows in a litter.... To the outsider, to the slave-owner, the African night world might appear a mimic world, a child's world, a carnival. But to the African – however much in daylight, he appeared himself to mock it – it was the true world: it turned white men to phantoms and plantation life to an illusion.

After Emancipation, carnival passed into the hands of the lower classes and changed into a noisy, wild and disorderly amusement, viewed with increasing disdain by the well-to-do and with suspicion by the authorities. The rebellious aspects of the festival provoked numerous measures which were intended to prevent excessive boisterousness, but they were never so far-reaching that the festival had to be done away with, in order to avoid the opposite effect. This wavering attitude on the part of the government was due not only to fear of a genuine revolt; it was also necessary to take the position of the coloured middle class into account. The carnival season was an important opportunity for all kinds of festivities for them too. Although any association with the masses in the streets was avoided, there was hostility to any government intervention, and a readiness to use carnival as an instrument for attacking the governor and the white upper class if tensions ran too high (Pearse 1971: 541). Nevertheless, during the first post-emancipation years, the dismissive but mild reports in the Trinidadian papers and other media did not yet add up to a negative assessment of carnival. Even Charles Day, who calls the negro a savage, ten times worse than the autochthonous Indian population of the island, in the preface to his book *Five Years in the West Indies*, offers a picture of carnival in 1848 that does not call for its complete abolition. It is worth quoting a few passages from his report (1852, cited in Hill 1972: 18–19), because it provides such an accurate account of the mid-century carnival:

> The maskers parade the streets in gangs of from ten to twenty, occasionally joining forces in procession. The primitives were negroes, as nearly naked as might be, bedaubed with a black varnish. One of this gang had a long chain and padlock attached to his leg, which chain the others pulled. What this typified, I was unable to learn; but as the chained one was occasionally thrown down on the ground, and treated with a mock bastina doing it probably represented slavery. Each mask was armed with a good stout quarter-staff, so that they could overcome one-half more police than themselves, should occasion present itself. Parties of negro ladies danced through the streets, each clique distinguished by boddices [sic] of the same colour. Every negro, male and female, wore a white flesh-coloured mask, their woolly hair carefully concealed by handkerchiefs; this, contrasted with the black bosom and arms, was droll in the extreme. The ladies who aimed at the superior civilization of shoes and stockings, invariably clothed their pedal extremities in pink silk stockings and blue, white or yellow kid shoes, sandled up their sturdy legs. For the men the predominating character was Pulichinello [sic]; every second negro, at least, aiming at playing the continental Jack-pudding. Pirates too were very common, dressed in Guernsey frocks, full scarlet trousers, and red wollen [sic] cap, with wooden pistols for arms.... Turks also there were, and one Highlander.... There were also two grand processions, having triumphant 'wans' [sic], one of which was to commemorate the recent marriage of a high law-officer; the other ... - represented the Sovereign pair of England.... The best embodiments were the Indians of South America, daubed with red ochre;

personified by the Spanish peons from the Main, themselves half-Indian.... Many of these had red Indian quivers and bows, as well as baskets.... One personation of Death... stalked about with part of a horse's vertebra attached to him and a horse's thigh bone in his hand.... I noticed that whenever a black mask appeared, it was sure to be a white man. Little girls dressed *à la jupe*, in the *vrai creole* negro costume, looked very interesting. All parties with the assistance of bands of execrable music, made a tremendous uproar....

These are colourful carnival scenes which were unlikely to disturb public order excessively. Day's summary of the disguises and costumes reveals their European and Creole origins. The Pulinchinello or Punchinello, a figure derived from Italian puppet theatre, is the model for a number of diverse costumes which make their appearance in the late nineteenth-century carnival. Turks, pirates, the Highlanders and Death are all taken from European tradition. The latter two figures can be regarded as precursors of the military bands and devil bands. The figure of the Red Indian is taken over by the negroes a few years later, acquiring a very warlike character and a repertoire of songs and speeches to go with it (Hill 1972: 19). It is noteworthy that Day reports white participation in the 1848 carnival, which may indicate that, fourteen years after Emancipation, the festival was still not entirely in the hands of the former negro slaves: '... whenever a black mask appeared, it was sure to be a white man.' All in all, there is no suggestion in Day's report of institutionalized conflicts or fights between the bands, as there was to be on a serious scale twenty-five years later.

Below the diameter of decency

Two elements in Day's report are of crucial importance for an understanding of the development towards that stage of the Trinidad carnival. The first is the reference to 'primitives ... bedaubed with a black varnish', pulling a chain fastened to the leg of one of them with a padlock, which was thrown down on the ground from time to time to undergo a mock bastinado. This certainly refers to slavery, but the scene itself has more in common with Canboulay, in which the freed negroes relived and commemorated the time of terrible oppression in a ritualized form. The second element is contained in the remark that: 'Each mask was armed with a good stout quarter-staff, so that they could overcome one-half more police than themselves, should occasion present itself.' This is the first reference to the formidable hardwood fighting-stick, which was later to become the favourite weapon of the Canboulay bands (Hill 1972: 25). At this time – around 1848 – the Calinda, a combination of stick-fighting and dancing to accompany this sport, was also very popular.[3] Between five and twenty stick-fighters formed a band, which went out on the street to combat rival bands during carnival (Crowley 1956: 194–5). Each band had its own champion, who was encouraged during the fight with special Calinda songs performed by the chantwelle, a sort of artistic leader, while the rest of the band members provided choral accompaniment. Sometimes the fighter was a Calinda singer as well (Elder, 1966, calls him a 'battling troubadour'). These were usually eulogies of the accomplishments of the band, and provocative texts with the rival as their target. The Calinda songs can be regarded as the prototype of the Calypso, and their belligerent tradition is continued in the Calypso repertoire (Brereton 1979: 167–8; Hill 1972: 27).

As ritual and/or play,[4] Canboulay and Calinda ('stick-fighting') can be viewed as elements of a relatively innocent carnival activity, but it is evident from their nature that, if circumstances demanded, the carnivalesque aggression and rebellion could be transmuted into forms of violence which an orderly society would not be prepared to tolerate. This was the case from around 1860; Canboulay and Calinda increasingly abandoned their traditional significance and fused to become a dangerous instrument of violence in the hands of a sizeable urban proletariat, organized in a number of bands, which existed all year round and were particularly active during carnival. Canboulay now meant a fight between rival bands in Port of Spain, San Fernando and the other cities, which had little of the 'sportive' and regulated character of the earlier fights. Sticks, bottles and stones were now the weapons in the hands of the male and female members of a band and their followers. Finally, in 1881, this development acquired a class character when the rival bands united in their struggle against the police.

In order to understand this development, it is necessary to consider the living conditions of the former slaves and other groups from the lowest levels of society in Port of Spain. The city expanded considerably during the twenty years between 1860 and the so-called Canboulay revolt of 1881; the population increased from 16 457 to 29 468, 40 per cent of whom were born outside Trinidad (Pearse 1971: 550), mainly from the small British islands such as Barbados, Grenada and St Vincent (Rohlehr 1983: 52). The grid-like plan of the town with its rectangular blocks of streets and houses, the front dominated by respectable homes and shops, goes back to the time of the Spanish. The backstreets area consisted mainly of wooden barracks with separate plots, divided up into rooms accommodating whole families. The outskirts of Port of Spain were (and largely still are) characterized by a spontaneous accumulation of irregular settlements, some of whose residents had found work in town. There was hardly any privacy in the barracks community of the time, and life went on in the common yard in the middle. People were boxed in so tightly, competing for scarce items such as water and the use of a toilet, that tensions were bound to arise, and they had to be dealt with quickly because of this enforced living together. In conditions like these, inevitably marked by clashes and conflicts, people learned to stick up for themselves; they needed a quick tongue to stand up to and deliver criticism. This atmosphere of constant competition led to a hierarchy of rivals, between whom a degree of relaxation of tension sometimes arose during the traditional pastime of dance, song and stick-fighting. At other times, dissatisfaction turned into hostility towards the outside world, in particular towards other backstreet communities in town, and bitter conflicts were fought out between them by select groups.

The position of these yards, right behind the houses of the middle and upper classes, entailed a continual interaction between the two worlds. The barracks residents were confronted with the lifestyle and cultural norms of the privileged. They were thus aware of the gulf separating them, but this was to some extent bridged by the fact that the women in particular did household chores for the rich and often played a large part in raising their children. Moreover, men from the middle class had liaisons with the barracks women and it was not uncommon for them to be patrons of yard bands or even stick-fighters, known as jacketmen because of the associations of their clothing with the upper class (Brereton 1979: 166; Pearse 1971: 550–1).

From around 1860 the yard bands increasingly came to dominate carnival. In fact, they changed its form and content to such an extent that it entered history under a special name: Jamet (or Jamette) carnival. The word 'Jamet' comes from *diamètre* or *diamèt*, one of the terms in use at the time to refer to those members of society who lived 'below the diameter of respectability' (Pearse 1971: 546), in other words in the underworld. In *Savacou* (De Verteuil 1984: 60–2), Brereton describes the Jamet carnival as follows:

> The festival was almost entirely taken over by the jamets, who had created in the backyards of Port of Spain their own sub-culture.... Yard 'bands' were formed ... The big Carnival bands were a combination of several yard bands. The jamets, who were the band members, were the singers, drummers, dancers, stickmen, prostitutes, pimps, and 'bad johns' in general. They boasted their skill and bravery, verbal wit, talent in song, dance and drumming, their indifference to the law, their sexual prowess, their familiarity with jail, and sometimes their contempt for the Church.
>
> Probably the most objectionable feature of the diametre Carnival was its obscenity. Bands of prostitutes roamed the streets making indecent gestures and singing 'lewd' songs. There were also traditional masks, with explicit sexual themes....
>
> Bands ... used the days of Carnival to pay off old grudges or to increase their prestige at the expense of other bands.... Such affrays were, of course, illegal and numerous arrests were made each Carnival. Yet the street fights continued until the early 1880's.

Political satire as a weapon

The government issued a series of provisions to regulate the orgy. From 1840 on, the wearing of masks came in for the greatest censure. Disguise of this kind was not only a seductive instrument in brief affairs of the heart, but it also provided anonymity during street riots (Wood 1986: 244). In 1858 governor Keate, a man who had a reputation as a *bon vivant* himself, attempted to prohibit the wearing of masks for ever. The police were instructed to arrest everyone wearing a mask. This met with such popular resistance that the police were forced to withdraw. The resistance seemed to assume an organized form when, after the police defeat, a group of three or four thousand negroes provocatively marched past the police station armed with axes, clubs and machetes. The protest was not confined to the lower class. The middle class was equally up in arms against Keate's ban, because no one believed that it was simply intended to keep disorderly behaviour in check. They saw it as an attempt to anglicize the colony; the 'foreign' carnival and its relation to the Catholic church, which both formed a part of the tradition and culture of this group as well, were obstacles to such an endeavour. But there were doubts about taking excessively strict action even in the highest echelons of society; it was the done thing to condemn carnival, but hard-handed intervention was to be avoided, all the more as it was believed that the wild bacchanal would soon die a natural death (De Verteuil 1984: 73). A report in the *Gazette* of that year, however (Pearse 1971: 544), makes it clear that Canboulay had come to stay:

> In our towns... commencing with the orgies on Sunday night, we have the fearful howling of a parcel of semi-savages emerging God knows where from, exhibiting hellish scenes and the most demoniacal representations of the days of slavery as they were 40 years ago: then using the mask the two following days as a mere cloak for every species of barbarism and crime....

There were rumours that Keate intended to ban the 1860 carnival completely, but things never went that far. It cannot be ruled out that the clash between the authorities and the carnival revellers, together with the failure of the policy of the sitting governor, formed the main pretext for the increase of satire and an undertone of political protest in carnival during the 1860s. The masquerades made fun of prominent public figures, such as the governor, the Minister of Justice, and the Attorney General. The 1869 carnival included a comic cricket match (cricket was still a sport for the few), which was by no means complimentary to the Trinidad team. There were also parodies of the civil service, newspaper editors and figures from the medical world. In short, practically every group or profession from the upper classes was satirized and ridiculed. These caricatures were the only elements of this 'degenerating' carnival which were appreciated by members of these classes. They were probably not aware that behind these apparently innocent performances lay bitterness and aggression towards them, which were soon to surface in less entertaining spectacles (Wood 1986: 246–7).

The Canboulay revolt – from festival to rebellion (1881–4)

A law promulgated in 1868 banned the carrying of torches, but it was not until 1884 that the nocturnal Canboulay torch procession of the dreaded Jamets finally came to an end. The 1870s are marked by a wavering policy on the Jamet carnival, which was mainly due to the weak authority of the head of police, the historian L.M. Fraser (De Verteuil 1984: 64). The elite and the well-to-do bourgeoisie displayed an increasing aversion to and irritation at the excesses of the carnival festivities. An example of their resentment is found in the *San Fernando Gazette* of 18 September 1875 (Broek 1985: 293):

> Hardly anything else is so dangerous to our society.... Hordes of men and women, youthful in years but matured in every vice that perverts and degrades humanity, dwell together in all the rude licentiousness of barbarian life: men without aim, without occupation and without any recognised mode of existence – women, wanton, perverse, and depraved beyond expression.

The clamour for action grew louder. The *Port of Spain Gazette* of 17 February 1877 (De Verteuil 1984: 66) had this to say:

> To everybody who has not taken leave of his senses, the reasons for putting a stop to this outrageous practice are self-evident; while, on the other side, we are not aware of any ground on which its continuance can be defended... the suppression by force, if necessary, of our beastly Carnival, would contribute much more towards the refinement of vulgar tastes than all the learning and labour of our primary schools put together for a year.... The thing should not be allowed to go further. It were better to deny recreation to outlawed ruffians than to have pollution and obscenity exhibited naked before the eyes of our wives and daughters. We dismiss it as unworthy of a thought that any sane person would be found to construe a forcible suppression of the scandal as an invasion of the rights and privileges of the lower classes of the Community....

In 1877 the weak Fraser was replaced by the militant Captain Baker, who was determined to put a stop to the excesses of carnival. He aimed to bring the organized bands under control if total elimination proved impossible. The 1878 and 1879 carnivals were held under close police supervision, which prevented the popular stick-fight (Calinda) from being performed in town. Strengthened in his resolve by the 1868 legal prohibition on the carrying of torches, Baker decided to crush the 1880 Canboulay procession. The unannounced police action came as such a surprise to the Jamets that they surrendered their sticks, torches and drums without any resistance. The 1880 carnival proceeded in an orderly fashion, and the fulsome praise of his measures in the papers led the head of police himself to believe that the problems connected with the festival had been settled for once and for all (De Verteuil 1984: 65–70).

Rumour has it that Baker and his friends made a wager in the bar of the Marine Club that at the next carnival he would definitively clear the streets of stick-fighters and torch-bearers (see for example, Hill 1983: 15). Perhaps drinking had made him over-confident, because there were signs of a massive resistance which would not be easy to break. The wager was confirmed in public and added fuel to the tenacious reports that Baker planned to put a stop to the whole carnival. This was one of the factors which prompted the bands to forget their mutual conflicts and to form a common front. Despite the wishes of the governor, or rather in the absence of clear instructions to the head of police, Captain Baker once again attempted to remove the torches and other illegal attributes from the Canboulay procession on the night of Sunday 27 February 1881. This time, however, he ran up against an organized and determined resistance (De Verteuil 1984: 80–1):

> ... And as the band danced, swayed and sung its way onward, a woman who was gyrating in front of the Nègre-Jardin dancers suddenly spied the Captain at the corner. She ran back to the band, screaming out to them: 'Messieurs, Cap'n Baker au coin à la rue avec tous l'hommes' (Captain Baker and all his men at the corner). The band stopped, replenished with oil and lit their flambeaux. They raised their sticks, they shouted a song and marched down Duke street. The excitement and the panic grew.... The fight was hot. The stones and bottles rattled like musket shots against the fences, making a sort of harmony with the shouting and the sound of thwacking sticks.

The revolt was crushed, but the outcome remained undecided. Thirty-eight of the 150 police officers were wounded, while forty to fifty of the participants received injuries, and acts of vandalism were carried out in the streets of the town (Brereton 1979: 171; De Verteuil 1984: 89). Feelings ran high as a result of the clash. The rumour spread that if the police intended to put in another appearance in the streets on Monday night, the rebels would set the whole of Port of Spain ablaze. The authorities viewed the situation with concern and decided to take drastic measures to prevent a serious general uprising. On the orders of the governor, the police were confined to barracks and reinforced with fifty soldiers and forty-three volunteers who were enrolled as policemen on the spot (Pearse 1971: 547). The town council of Port of Spain called upon the governor, Sir Sanford Freeling, to make a concessionary gesture to ward off the feared civil disturbances. He set out for the Eastern Market on Monday afternoon to address the excited carnival revellers (De Verteuil 1984: 91):

> My friends, I have come down this afternoon to have a little talk with you. [Cheers]. I wish to tell you that it is entirely a misconception on your part, to think that there is any desire on the part of the Government to stop your amusement. [Cheers]

He also assured the crowd that he would not let slip any opportunity to celebrate in person. The only reason for the ban on torches was to prevent fire during the dry season. He was well aware of how important the carnival masquerade was for everyone and he underlined his pride as governor of Trinidad: 'I shall give orders that the Police shall not molest or interfere with you, if you keep within the law. I trust that you will continue to enjoy yourselves without any disturbance. There shall be no interference with your masquerade' (De Verteuil 1984: 92).

Freeling's speech was received with approval and resulted in a calm celebration of carnival on Monday and Tuesday, at least in Port of Spain. The police did not appear in the streets until the morning of Ash Wednesday. They were the target of mockery and ridicule because of the loss of face. The carnival uprising acquired a political dimension when the English Party, a strong political group whose principles included law and order, used the incidents to detach the governor from the more liberal camp. It was claimed that Captain Baker was hired by this conservative party to provoke riots with his brutal actions and thereby to force the governor to alter his concessionary policy (De Verteuil 1984: 97).

However that may be, the governor's actions can be seen as a first initiative towards restoring the relations between the authorities and the people with their specific way of celebrating carnival. The newspapers were now also unanimous in their condemnation of the action of Captain Baker and were full of praise for the way in which the governor had handled the situation. Although the prosperous bourgeoisie also claimed in public to detest many aspects of carnival at the time, they held just as negative a view of the violent intervention by the authorities. It seemed as if they were (tacitly) aware of the fact that carnival was an intrinsic part of a popular culture towards which they entertained feelings of sympathy in the last resort, and with which in a certain sense they felt more affinity than with the intentions and exercise of power of a 'high-handed and ex-patriate government' (Brereton 1979: 172). This subtle relation was to accompany and shape the process of rejection and acceptance of carnival right up to the present.

Drastic measures

The 1882 carnival was held without any incidents worthy of note. There was no fighting between rival bands, even though the Canboulay procession took place on a larger scale than ever before. However, things went wrong again in 1883. This time the uprising was not confined to a tug of war between the bands and the police, but ordinary citizens were molested and private homes and shops were plundered and vandalized. It was above all immigrants from other British West Indian islands who were regarded as the instigators of the violence. Around 1881 they accounted for one-third of the total population of Port of Spain, which was estimated at 30 000 (Rohlehr 1983: 53). They were associated in a band called Newgates, and their only aim seemed to be to go around without masks and beat up as many French-speaking people in masks as they could. The police were barely able to keep the eruption of violence under control. It was even claimed that the police force had urged the Newgates to use violence in order to discredit the existing bands as an act of retaliation for the loss of prestige in the two previous years. Another interpretation is that Baker had encouraged the traditional bands to attack the Newgates in order to play a strong card into the hand of the anti-carnival faction within the government (Brereton 1979: 172). At any rate, it was obvious to the governor that Canboulay and the belligerent bands had to be stopped. In 1884 he issued a prohibition on public torch processions, drumming, and groups of ten or more armed with sticks or other weapons. The playing of any musical instrument was also banned except between the hours of six o'clock in the morning of Carnival Monday and twelve o'clock at night on Carnival Tuesday (Brereton 1979: 173).

As the 1884 carnival approached, rumours spread of all kinds of wild actions which the troublemakers were planning as a reaction to the drastic government measures. It was said that there were plans afoot to poison the town's reservoir, destroy telephone lines, and blow up the gunpowder magazine. Panic broke out. Hundreds of civilians were recruited as special agents and provided with long staves by the government. The police, army and marines on board HMS *Dido* in the harbour of Port of Spain were kept on standby (De Verteuil 1984: 110). The preparations were so stringent and comprehensive that they probably deterred rioters from provocation and revolt. At any rate, the situation in Port of Spain remained calm and no attempt to hold a Canboulay procession was made. Outside the capital, however, there was considerable disturbance. Serious riots broke out in San Fernando and Princes Town in the south of Trinidad. When bands as many as 500 strong attacked with sticks, stones and bottles, the police responded by opening fire: two band members were killed and five seriously wounded. It was supposed that key figures from the most notorious Port of Spain bands had provoked the riots in the south now that they were prevented from doing so in their own town (Brereton 1979: 173).

Bloodbath in San Fernando

De Verteuil's (1984) book on the period 1881–8 in Trinidad is entitled *The Years of Revolt*, and it certainly was a tumultuous period in the island's history. This was not only due to the events connected with the carnival. The members of the Indian community, who had been imported to Trinidad after Emancipation as contract labourers, and who numbered 48 820 by 1881 (31.8 per cent of the total population), were also involved in a serious clash with the government. At the heart of this conflict was a festival too: the Shia Muslim celebration of Muharram, better known in the island as the Hosein or Hosay festival or procession. The authorities felt that the violent form assumed by this procession was too much of a threat to public order. It is worth devoting some attention to this festival here because it sets the carnival revolt within a broader social context and refutes the suggestion that it was an isolated event without a place in the general fabric of society. A calypso singer of the time nicknamed Beau Wulfe (cited in De Leon 1988: 68) summed up the two events thus:[5]

> *The Canboulay fracas was a free-for-all battle,*
> *With lots of French Creoles, but mostly foreign people,*
> *Caused by drum-beating, and other instruments*
> *Said to be outlawed by the British Government*
> *Captain Baker was prepared to be violent,*
> *But the revellers were adamant and refused to relent*
> *But the slaughtering of Indians on Hosay Day,*
> *Was worse than that of the Canboulay.*

The Hosein festival is still very popular today. It is regarded by some as the Indian counterpart to the predominantly Creole 'bacchanal' (a conventional positive way of referring to the carnival in Trinidad). It also attracts growing interest from participants outside the Indian community and from tourists. Today its main centre is St James, a suburb of Port of Spain. Wood (1986: 151–2) provides a summary of the similarities in content, which he takes to be a possible explanation for the popularity of the two festivals. The underlying religious significance has vanished in both cases; both festivals have developed to become occasions for unbridled behaviour; they were both dominated by lower-class activities in the nineteenth century and may be taken to have exercised a certain therapeutic effect on socio-cultural tensions and ill feeling; both carnival and Hosein are processions, with large-scale movements which have a more exciting effect on the public than events tied down to a single spot; finally, perhaps the most important similarity lies in the strong element of competition that is a feature of both festivals and which (in my opinion) makes them ideal potential instruments for mutual conflict and rebelliousness *vis-à-vis* the authorities and government bodies.

The Hosein festival was celebrated every year from around 1850. Though originally a Muslim festival to commemorate the murder of Mohammed's grandsons Hosein and Hassan, it soon lost its religious character, and both Hindus and Muslims enthusiastically took part in it. Besides the addition of rough elements from the Creole community who were out to riot, negroes also assumed a more respectable position in the event as drummers, for which they were paid in cash or rum. Wood (1986: 153) regards this as '... a ray of hope in race relations when members of one group go to the public festivities of another, not to disrupt them but to join in the fun'. The Indians, in turn, flocked to Arima for the annual Santa Rosa da Lima festival, which had gradually changed in the course of the previous century from a religious ceremony in honour of the 'Patroness of the Americas' to a betting race. Wood (1986: 151) regards it as a characteristic of Hinduism 'to overlap tolerantly into the preserves of others.' (A recent example is the originally Catholic procession in Saparia in the south of Trinidad. The black image of Maria, 'La Divina Pastora', brought from Venezuela by Capuchin monks, is revered at the same time by the Hindus under the name 'Saparia Mai'. Nevertheless, this is not a case of a 'tolerant overlapping'; there are disputes every year on who the image belongs to, or rather, which community – the Christians or the Hindus – is entitled to the money that the faithful give to the image during the procession.)

Around 1880 Hosein had turned into a genuinely national festival for the Indians in Trinidad, and it was the ideal opportunity for them to demonstrate their growing power (De Verteuil 1984: 136). The festival centred on a colourful procession in which the tazias (replicas of the tombs of the martyrs Hassan and Hosein, grandchildren of the prophet) were carried, surrounded by well-trained moon-dancers and accompanied by the beating of drums (*tassa*) and the stick-fighting game Gutkar (Jha 1985: 5). In the end, the tazias were thrown into a plantation pond, a river or the sea.

The cordial rivalry between the residents of various plantations (the best tazia, the best tassa drummer, the leading position in the procession, the first to reach the water) gradually tended to some extent towards street fighting like that which characterized carnival. The fear of a genuine uprising grew in the 1870s, stimulated by a reduction in wages and a speeding up of the work rhythm in 1880. A commentary in the *Port of Spain Gazette*, organ of planter and commercial interest, of 1 March 1884 betrays the attempt to create a mood in which intervention would be justified (De Verteuil 1984: 165):

> Let us not forget that these Asiatics now form one-third of our population and that as fanatics of an effete superstition and a most corrupt form of ethics, they must as a matter of self-preservation, be kept in subjection to our laws.

In the wake of the police activities connected with the carnival revolt, the government considered the time ripe for intervention in the Hosein festivities now that they had got out of hand. Besides, it would be a case of unacceptable injustice to ban Creole carnival revellers from carrying torches and from playing drums if the Indians were allowed to do whatever they liked (Singh 1988: 15).

The *Trinidad Recorder* of 14 November 1883 expresses the general feelings of the press at the time in connection with serious Hosein disturbances in Port of Spain:

> On Saturday last about three in the afternoon, Queen Street presented one of those sights which we do not remember seeing even on our sadly celebrated carnival days. It was 'Hosein' day, and the coolies from various parts of the country were in town.... It appears that these coolies following fast in the footsteps of our fighting masqueraders, now form themselves into separate bands.

Curiously enough, the commentary ended with a remark which could have been taken straight from a contemporary paper on Hosein or carnival as they are celebrated today: 'What can foreigners think of us, when contemplating in broad day-light such scenes as the one we have tried to describe above?' (De Verteuil 1984: 153).

In 1884 the Indians were no longer allowed to hold their celebrations in the streets of Port of Spain and San Fernando, capital of the vast sugar districts of the Naparimas, and they were also banned from all public highways outside these towns. The Indian community simply refused to accept these restrictions. When on 30 October 1884 large numbers of them tried to march into San Fernando, the police opened fire, killing at least sixteen and wounding over a hundred (Singh 1988: 1). This bloodbath did not deter the government from its determined resolve to regulate the Hosein festival in an orderly manner. The festival had been successfully 'tamed' before the end of the century, and this was probably why the rebellious Creole elements had pulled out of it – the result intended by the government measure of 1884 (Brereton 1979: 184). De Verteuil (1984: 199–200) concludes:

> The Indian 'revolt' in Trinidad was focussed on a religious rite but expressed a general attitude of rebellion inclusive of the world of work. Thus the

authorities in Trinidad were perhaps not so far wrong when they preferred
to regard it almost entirely in terms of a power struggle.

Singh (1988: 8, 30–1) writes that 'in the normal course of its social evolution,
the Muharram celebration would probably have emerged as a national
festival serving, like the carnival, as a major integrative social mechanism
in what was conspicuously a plural society.'

After the events of 1884, Canboulay was definitively banned from
carnival and the fights between the notorious yard bands declined. The
festival still had to be cleaned up of all kinds of offensive obscenities, or at
least of what the bourgeoisie regarded as such. Brereton (1979: 174) suggests:

> ... it probably reflects the far more casual approach to sex which
> characterised the masses as compared to the 'respectable' classes. Privacy
> and delicacy were impossible in the physical conditions under which they
> lived, and masques like Pissenlit[6] were probably harmless tomfoolery to
> them.

In the last decade of the nineteenth century, measures were taken to eradicate
most of what were considered to be obscenities. The throwing of projectiles
(including flour) at the spectators was prohibited. Those who wanted to
disguise themselves as pierrots had to register with the police beforehand.
Travesty and obscenities in word and deed were no longer tolerated. The
paving of the streets and the collecting of used bottles were measures to
counter the use of traditional warlike weapons (Pearse 1971: 548). Around
the turn of the century, this all helped to make the festival more accessible
for the 'respectable classes'.

Some theoretical remarks

The above account of the Trinidad carnival in the nineteenth century makes
it clear that this stage in the development of the festival is characterized by
a complex combination of partly amorphous cultural events and anarchistic
expressions of social discontent and rebelliousness. The same combination
can be found in later periods, but in a much less pronounced form. This
justifies a brief theoretical intermezzo focusing on the role of violence or
rebellion in carnival as a transcultural phenomenon. Can we point to 'margins'
of carnival in this connection, and can they be marked?

Carnival rebellion in the service of the status quo?

Alonso's (1990) fascinating study of the meaning of protest and inversion
in the Jamet carnival sharply delineates the rebellious and revolutionary

potential of the festival. First, she claims (74–5) that the nineteenth-century Trinidadian version shows the shortcomings of Turner's analysis of carnival, which is widely approved by many investigators of this genre. Obviously under the influence of the work of Gluckman, Turner (1969) states that 'liminal' phenomena like carnival are characterized by the disappearance or levelling of differences in rank and status. Hierarchical relations are replaced by communitas as a situation of essential and general human togetherness; in this sense, liminality is conceived as an anti-structure. The communitas of liminality and the hierarchy of structure are complementary modalities of social relations which, despite their apparent opposition, depend on one another in a dialectical (or functional) manner. It is their mutual interaction which maintains social equilibrium.

Alonso (1990: 76–7) has difficulty in applying the Turnerian model because it is based on an uncontroversial and non-contradictory moral order to which everyone is supposed to subscribe. This does not apply to nineteenth-century Trinidad, with its extremely heterogeneous demographic composition and its linguistic and cultural differences. Alonso (1990: 78–9) also objects to Turner's notion that rituals of symbolic inversion in carnival, which invert the social relations of everyday life, are a reassertion of the existing social structure and moral order.[7] She points to the permanent fear of blacks felt by the white elite. Carnival, 'an offense against decency and civilization', according to the *Port of Spain Gazette* from 1833, was in the eyes of this elite the embodiment of chaos, a chaos which evoked the fear for their lives which once characterized the attitude of planters towards their slaves. The Canboulay revolt, and the large-scale protest against the authorities and the white elite which sometimes erupted in armed confrontations between police and lower-class blacks, refute the claim – at least as far as Trinidad is concerned – that carnival reinforces the social structure and contributes to the maintenance of the moral order.

Alonso convincingly demonstrates that carnival can produce a degree of rebellion which is experienced as threatening by the establishment, but she then goes on to emphasize that the carnivalesque rebelliousness, the 'subversive discourse of carnival', as she calls it (1990: 117), cannot lead to a genuine revolution. There is something in carnival that stifles a potentially revolutionary effect. Carnival is subversive, but not revolutionary. It is only by viewing carnival as a game instead of as a ritual that it becomes possible to indicate clearly the limitations of this cultural phenomenon's capacity for genuine social change. As Handelman (1979: 165) explains, though ritual and game have many elements in common, they constitute two distinct modes of expression whose relations to everyday discourse are radically different:

Both play and ritual are framed domains which alter perception and experience. The passage to either is predicated upon a transformation of cognition which is meta-communicative, and which bypasses paradoxes about the nature of reality which such alteration connotes.... The meta-message, 'this is play', which transforms cognition, is one of 'make believe'. Modelled upon everyday life, it inverts this reality to question and to doubt the validity of ongoing existence.... play communicates the arbitrariness of ordinary experience. By contrast, the bypass to ritual is predicated upon a premise of 'let us believe'. Thus communication within the ritual frame is sanctified, is imbued with moral worth, is made 'true' and is made absolute. The meta-message of the ritual frame supersedes paradox.

According to Alonso (1990: 117–18), carnival is game, and as such it is ambiguous: 'It both "counts" and does not count in the "real" world. To be revolutionary, a discourse must overtly define an alternative order for the whole society.' Although games can contain the seeds of revolution, they remain seeds, not the tree. However, this does not mean that the game reinforces the establishment or that carnival maintains social equilibrium. 'Carnivalesque discourse challenges official discourse but does not become its replacement. Still, carnivalesque discourse poses enough of a threat that official discourse takes up the challenge.' Alonso's resolute option for the festival as game certainly does throw light on the scope of the violence that played such a prominent part in the nineteenth-century Trinidad carnival, but at the same time it pushes the importance of ritual for a more comprehensive analysis of carnival too far into the background, as we shall see in the course of this study. It is Handelman (1977: 188) himself who emphasizes both the complementary and the contrastive relation between play and ritual: 'The experience of play can prepare one for ritual, and that of ritual for play.' He claims that it is this dramatic succession or alternation of play and ritual, and not the specific relation of each of them to the social context, that requires closer examination.

Carnivalesque violence or class conflict

In his *Popular Culture in Early Modern Europe* (1978: 203–4), the historian Peter Burke writes:

> Riots may be regarded as an extraordinary form of popular ritual. Of course riots and rebellions are not just rituals; they are attempts at direct action, not symbolic action. However, rebels and rioters employed ritual and symbol to legitimise their action.

In a nutshell, this is the problem which will be tackled in the remaining pages of this chapter: the relation between aggression and group solidarity, carnivalesque violence and class conflict. The tumult of the Jamet carnival, climaxing in the Canboulay uprising, cannot be dismissed as a few carnival processions which got out of hand, and whose participants could soon be brought back in line. The question arises to what extent there was a class conflict at stake and to what extent the phenomenon as a whole has set into motion processes of social and cultural emancipation. What specific role can be assigned to the carnival festival in all this?

In fact, carnival overflows its banks when (with a heavy loss of rituals of reversal as its main instrument) the character of political protest gains the upper hand to such an extent that the event turns into a popular revolt, even if it still retains clear elements that are characteristic of folklore or carnival. A development of this kind can be traced in the evolution of the Trinidad carnival from an elite festival which reinforced the status quo to an anarchistic Jamet bacchanal, erupting in outright (Canboulay) uprisings.

Pearse (1971: 552) comes close to this view when he claims that the festival, an ideal opportunity for licentious behaviour and a reversal of roles and values, found itself in a social vacuum once it ceased to be an important component of elite culture. While form and content were soon determined by an accumulation of folklore of all kinds of groups on the island, the 'organization' came under the control of organized criminal gangs, which eventually led to the Canboulay conflicts. Brereton (1979: 174) considers that it can be labelled without exaggeration as a 'class action'. The decision to put an end to the two most popular manifestations of the Jamets, Canboulay and fighting between bands, was taken by the authorities under pressure from the upper and middle class. The Jamets or the lower classes ceased their internal conflicts and united against the government's attempts to interfere with their own festival. De Verteuil (1984: 71) cites Brereton, but also suggests that this is merely a classic case of mob manipulation by a couple of leaders. He tries, in vain in my opinion, to bring these two points of view together by citing Albert Soboul on the French Revolution: 'les masses populaires urbaines ont fourni à la bourgeoisie révolutionnaire la force indispensable pour abattre le Gouvernement'.[8] Pearse (1971: 551) refers more circumspectly to a 'class character, with the disappearance of band rivalries in united action against the police.' He probes deeper into the implications and consequences of two decades of Jamet carnival and draws two conclusions. The first is that the colonial administration was aware of the importance of carnival with the concomitant licentiousness and reversals of roles and values on a few predetermined days each year. By breaking the power of the Jamet bands and purging carnival of its worst excesses, the government more or less brought carnival under control. The second conclusion is much more interesting (1971: 552); namely that:

> ... police intervention on Canboulay night brought to a head several different
> types of existing hostility to the administration, causing new social groups

to identify themselves nominally with 'the People' and the people's festival, so that Carnival began to be a symbol for a national sentiment shared by a broad section of the community, and in opposition to the administration, manned largely by British (i.e. 'foreign') officials.

The most important part of Pearse's conclusion is that, as a result of increasing tensions and conflicts between 'the People' with its carnival, on the one hand, and the establishment, on the other, social groups came to identify with 'the People' who had never done so before. This was a remarkable development in a society with an extremely heterogeneous ethnic composition, divided by highly diverse and diffuse social, cultural, linguistic and religious orientations.

Within the conglomerate that was connected with the Trinidad carnival around 1860, the core group consisted of former slaves and their descendants, some with a more or less shared cultural baggage because of the length of their residence on the islands, others who had come as immigrants from Barbados and other islands, and a relatively large group of 'Free Africans' who could still claim Africa as their country of birth. There was also a group of colonists, labourers and craftsmen of mixed descent who did not have a slave background. In addition, there were Spanish-speaking journeymen from Venezuela, whose cultural background (Hispano-Afro-Indian) reinforced the tradition of the Spanish colonists and their descendants that already existed on the island (Brereton 1979: 152; Pearse 1971: 549).

Although it is impossible to assign a shared culture to this mixed community, all of these groups did have a number of points in common. They were completely excluded from participation in political or civic life; their customs and practices were to a large extent held in low esteem by the middle and upper classes; and they occupied the lowest economic positions. The living conditions in the slums of Port of Spain, based on the structure of the barracks courtyards to which all of these groups were condemned, produced a sort of subculture, dominated by singers, drummers, dancers, stick-fighters, prostitutes, pimps and 'badjohns' in general, who entered history under the common denominator of Jamets. This 'class' of largely unemployed men and women was organized in a loose fashion in the bands, whose main activities were gambling, drinking and above all fighting. Fighting was primarily in-fighting, though clashes with the police frequently occurred. Franz Fanon (1967: 42), a theoretician of violence in society, has claimed that colonial oppression is the source of *intra-class* aggression of this kind,: '... for the last resort of the native is to defend his personality vis-à-vis his brother.' In the 1880s, however, the bands united in a common struggle against the authorities. There was a growth of *inter-class* aggression, in which carnival probably functioned as the focus of the Afro-Creole subculture in Trinidad (Brereton 1979: 169).

To sum up, the major concepts for an interpretation of the nineteenth-century Trinidad carnival are aggression and ritual (Johnson 1983: 183). A high level of unemployment, appalling accommodation, overpopulation, illness, youth vagrancy and prostitution, created a situation in which tensions, conflicts and aggression were bound to flourish. More than religion or any other rituals or festivals, carnival was the more-or-less shared frame of reference for the groups who were uprooted in so many ways. It offered a ritualized outlet for aggression, so that actual violence could be reduced to a minimum, while still making it possible to vent (repressed) emotions.

It should be emphasized that the majority of the working class did not belong to the Jamets and probably did not approve of their way of life either. However, as Brereton (1979: 174) puts it, 'each Carnival, the jamets came out in their glory and the whole Creole working class felt a vicarious pride in their exploits.' It provided this class with an identity and a degree of social consciousness. The ritualized aggression of carnival ensured group cohesion. Though it was of internal importance at first, at a later stage it was turned outside, leading to genuine class conflict. As Wood (1986: 8) puts it: 'Carnival gave the Negro Creoles the chance to express a corporate pride in their own values and at the same time to ridicule the pretensions of the upper class'; or more forcefully (Brereton 1979: 169), 'the festival became an arena in which class antagonisms were worked out. The jamet Carnival was a reversal of all the judgements and values of respectable society.'

Repression leads to new cultural forms

Le Roy Ladurie's 1979 study entitled *Le Carnaval de Romans* offers a fascinating analysis of the way in which carnival can be linked symbiotically with political and social conflict. In the second half of the sixteenth century, the region of Dauphiné was the scene of resistance to tax levies, nobility and government. By right of birth the aristocracy was exempt from tax obligations. This aroused the anger of farmers and citizens who resented the tax burden, but were probably even more annoyed by the fiscal injustice (1981: xvi). The carnival held in the city of Romans in 1580, which culminated in a bloodbath – some thirty dead and a number of executions in the aftermath – marked the climax of this widespread regional revolt. The conflicting parties expressed their feelings and points of view symbolically in a variegated mixture of fun and earnest which took shape in the *reynages* (see Chapter 2, page 41), masquerades, bacchanalia and numerous other carnival rituals. Le Roy Ladurie (1981: 291) records that, when Calixte Lafosse described carnival in Romans in about 1840, 260 years after the people's uprising there, it still enjoyed a great reputation. The *reynages* had vanished, but in their place there were at least twenty singing societies having among their members poets and actors ..., each trying to outdo the other in song and verse. Fine entertainment for the public! They sang in every possible style, in patois ..., in French ..., they sang comedy, tragedy, drama, political rhymes, racy refrains, masterpieces, nonsense. A free show! The best tunes would be sung for several months afterwards, then everything would die down until the next year's songs were readied.

One could find passages like this on the calypso tradition in the tourist folders issued by the Trinidad Tourist Board. Like the carnival in Romans, the Trinidad carnival has evolved from a stormy past to become a festival of satire, lyric, narrative poetry and music, a plurality of cultural expression as 'a sort of comprehensive and poetic description of society, neighbourhoods, professions, age groups, the young, males, and so forth', as Le Roy Ladurie puts it (1981: 292).

However, it would be wrong to suppose that, after the Jamet period and the Canboulay revolts, carnival obediently assumed the standards of taste and respectability of the well-to-do bourgeoisie. The legal restrictions imposed on the festival by the authorities restrained the aspects of pure violence and the most shocking forms of obscenity. This made it possible for other social groups than the lower class to join (once again) in the annual festival gradually on an increasing scale. In 1890 a few businessmen already realized that carnival had commercially attractive facets, schoolboys and shop assistants organized masquerades, and society ladies followed 'their' bands, albeit in carriages which were carefully kept separate from what they regarded as the street rabble (Brereton 1979: 173–4). Despite the fact that they imposed their own standards on calypso and Mas (a popular term for the carnival procession in Trinidad), the main agent in giving the festival its cultural form was still the lower class until late in the twentieth century. This meant the maintenance of a tradition of protest and anarchy, which was to manifest itself on a number of occasions in the future.

Ironically, government measures not only put a stop to certain carnival activities in the nineteenth century, but they also stimulated the creativity of the lower class in looking for alternatives. Restrictions have therefore not led to impoverishment or limitation, but to a change in the cultural content and meaning of the festival. The ban on the African drum provided a challenge to seek assiduously for new forms for the rhythmic accompaniment of song and dance, which was such a fixed component in the West African musical tradition, eventually leading to the birth of the steel band. The prohibition on stick-fighting eliminated the aspect of physical violence, but the verbal confrontation associated with it (the Calinda songs sung by chantwelles) was reinforced and transformed into fighting in which verbal mastery provided the weapons: the Calypso wars which were fought out in many a backyard in Port of Spain. These specific developments of new cultural forms which launched the Trinidad carnival into the twentieth century will be discussed in the following chapter.

Notes

1   There is very little data available on the demographic structure for this period. The statistics are self-contradictory and very unreliable. For instance, Pearse's figures for 1783 and 1797 do not match those of Braithwaite.

2   The passage from Hill may be translated as follows:

> ... the elite of society was masked or disguised. The favourite costume of the ladies was the graceful and costly 'mulatress' of the period, while gentlemen adopted that of the 'garden Negro', in Creole 'negue jadin', or black field slave. At carnival time our mothers and grandmothers have even danced the 'belair' to the African drum, whose sounds did not offend their dainty ears, and our fathers and grandfathers danced the 'bamboula', the 'ghouba', and the 'calinda'.... Sometimes also the 'garden negroes' united in bands, would proceed on evenings to the Cannes Brulees. Their splendid march with torches through the town streets imitated what actually took place on the estates when a plantation was on fire. In such cases labourers on neighbouring estates were conducted there alternately, day and night, to assist in grinding the burned canes before they went sour; hence the cannes brûlees.

3   The origin of stick-fighting is unclear. Hill (1972: 25) considers an African origin likely. Stewart (1986: 301) suggests that it was taken from the Indians in the region. Crowley (1956: 192) points out a relation with England ('... Little John appears in Robin Hood tales as a quarter-staff fighter') and refers to the Bajan stick sport from Barbados and the Indian Gutkar, a stick-fighting dance on Trinidad.

4   In his discussion of the European carnival in *Popular Culture in Early Modern Europe*, Peter Burke (1978: 180) remarks on the difficulty of defining the term 'ritual' in relation to festivals and says '... it will refer to the use of action to express meaning, as opposed to the more utilitarian actions and also to the expression of meaning through words or images'. This definition applies to the term 'ritual' as it is used in this chapter.

5   The writer claims without further comment that the song must have been composed soon after the Canboulay and Hosay incidents. If so, this text is a translation from French or patois, since English was not the language of calypso at the time.

6   See below, Chapter Two.

7   Alonso notes that Turner subsequently modified his views, but does not take this into account in her argument. In Babcock's *The Reversible World*, Turner (1978: 281) writes:

> In complex, industrial societies, characterized by a high degree of social and economic division of labor, the models and paradigms presented in dramas, poems, folk tales, carnivals, literature, and so on do have a chance of influencing those who exercise power over the work structure of society and of modifying that structure ...; they may even revolutionize it, when the originally ludic models are taken up by and help to mobilize the dispossessed and disadvantaged, who, by virtue of their numbers, organization, and motivation, have very real power resources in political arenas.

8   The urban masses have furnished the revolutionary bourgeois with an indispensable force with which to bring down the government.

2 | The development of the Jamet carnival into a national festival

Although for convenience's sake the events described in the previous chapter were placed under the heading of the history of the Trinidad carnival in the nineteenth century, there was in fact hardly any question of a definable complex of activities which can be subsumed under the name of carnival. This was because of the high degree of intermingling of festival, ritual and a degree of rebellion, arising from different, often vague sources. Moreover, they had a spontaneous and impulsive character which may in the long term have encouraged the formation of tradition, but which for the time being stood in the way of a progression towards a recognizable annual series of festivities. Besides, a synthesis between all kinds of cultural and religious manifestations was often the fortuitous outcome of an inconsistent and repressive policy by the authorities, so that fermentation was constantly taking place within the complex cultural mosaic of Trinidad. The social and cultural developments of this emergent society were therefore so hybrid in character that it is only in retrospect that elements can be discerned which were to prove of significance for the eventual shaping of the more or less organized and regulated festival that we know today.

The Canboulay revolts of 1881–4 can be regarded as the most serious test of strength between the government, on the one hand, and revellers and troublemakers, on the other. However, they were also a sign that the case had been settled, in so far as the measures which were taken led to the disappearance of prohibited aspects of the popular demonstrations which well-to-do citizens and the authorities felt to pose a threat to the public order and to be at odds with common decency. Around the turn of the century groups from the higher social strata hesitatingly began to take part in the street festivities. It was also possible to detect the beginnings of a gradual delineation of the contours of a popular festival, which was now to develop in calmer waters to become carnival in its present-day form. This development was mainly directed by members of the lower classes of Africans (born in Africa) and Creoles (born in the West Indies). The government restrictions on the conduct of the festival stimulated their imagination to create new forms and alternatives which could satisfy their deeply rooted need for certain cultural expressions.

This process resulted in the three most important manifestations of carnival, which form the pillars of the contemporary national festival: calypso music, the steelband, and the masquerade. Since the history of the Trinidad carnival in the twentieth century is largely determined by the course of development of these impressive cultural achievements, I shall deal with each of them in turn in the present chapter.

Calypso, steelband and masquerade

The development of calypso, steelband and masquerade shows how cultural aspects of the lower classes gradually gained acceptance and appreciation from wide sectors of the population. This process did not run smoothly. Violence, which was so conspicuously present in the nineteenth-century street carnival, also plays a role now and then in the history of rise of the steelband, for until the end of the 1950s this social phenomenon was closely associated with the street gangs from the backyards of Port of Spain who were spoiling for a fight. The calypso tradition detached itself from this notorious reputation at an earlier stage. Singers from the middle class with a higher level of education or training helped to shape this art form at the beginning of the twentieth century, though without conferring any social prestige on it. The calypso texts, which often adopted a tone of social criticism, repeatedly shocked the establishment, and the government felt so threatened that it considered it necessary to adopt some form of censorship to impose restrictions on this unwelcome voicing of opinion.

All the same, it should not be supposed that, with the exception of a few echoes of the more turbulent times in the nineteenth century, the historical trajectory of calypso, steelband and masquerade can be seen as an irresistible course towards a moment in time when they have become nothing but innocent popular entertainment, tailored to pander to the taste of 'respectable' and 'decent' citizens and tourists. At any rate, that point has not been reached to date. The current level of acceptance does not yet mean the complete elimination of elements of rebelliousness, resistance and protest, no matter how much they are embedded in a smoothly organized annual carnival festival with a number of appropriate activities. However, this is to anticipate what will be dealt with more extensively and clearly in the course of the argument. First of all, I want to focus on the way in which calypso music, steelband and masquerade have passed through a process of growth in the early years of this century to achieve a position in which it has become impossible to imagine making do without them. These developments will be traced separately up to the 1950s, when these cultural manifestations more or less attained their current form. The period from then up to the present day, with which this chapter closes, can thus be dealt with in more general terms, especially as a number of aspects will crop up in the actual description of the carnival, based on four periods of fieldwork. Aspects of ethno-musicological, linguistic or oral literary interest will only be mentioned in passing.

From battling troubadour to calypso monarch

> *Never mind whatever measures are employed,*
> *Kaiso is art and cannot be destroyed.*
> *And centuries to come I'd have them know,*
> *People will still be singing calypso.*
> *Atilla the Hun* (Quevedo 1983:158)

In this verse from a calypso, in which the calypsonian Atilla the Hun reacted to yet another government censorship regulation in the 1930s, the musical style is referred to by the old word *kaiso*. This term is still in fashion; it can be heard among an enthusiastic audience at the performance of a high-quality calypso which corresponds to the classical form. The calypsonian is distinguished by the title *kaisonian*, a prerogative of the few who maintain the original musical tradition practically untainted. Etymological inquiry into the word 'calypso' reveals the musicological problem of tracing the musical form back to its origin, illustrating the cultural diversity from which it has arisen. Research does not actually go beyond a list of explanations, along with the researcher's preference for one of them made on the basis of rather arbitrary arguments. Thus 'calypso' is taken to be a corruption of *carieto* or *arieto*, a dance of the original Carib and Arawak Indian population of Trinidad, which was accompanied by historical songs. Or it is derived from the word *caliso*, a song with topical references, originating in the highlands of Spanish South America. Or it is supposed to come from *carrousseaux*, a patois expression which can be traced back to the archaic French word *carrousse* or *carrousel*, with the same meaning as the English 'carousal'. As for the word *kaiso*, it is a Hausa (West African) word for 'bravo!' to express a strong emotion of approval and encouragement (see for example Hill 1972: 61; 1976: 67; Quevedo

1983: 4; Warner 1983: 8). Quevedo, who was himself the famous calypsonian Atilla the Hun, writes in his posthumously published autobiography *Atilla's Kaiso* (1983: 4):

> In my own experience of over half a century's association with kaiso, carnival, and kaiso tents, the first word which I heard used to describe this song and dance form was 'kaiso'. 'Kaiso' was used to describe the song when sung as well as a means of expressing ecstatic satisfaction over what was in the opinion of the audience a particularly excellent kaiso.

The majority of those who have written on the subject accept *kaiso* as the root of 'calypso', even though this conclusion is sometimes also prompted by the (nationalistic) tendency to derive the traditions of the black population in Trinidad in a simplistic manner from West African culture (see for example Elder 1988; Liverpool 1986; Eastman 1986). The extent to which the calypso is particularly esteemed as a part of the 'pure' African heritage by black intellectuals heavily influenced by the ideology of the Caribbean Black Power movements of the 1970s can be seen from the discussion provoked by the appearance of the work of the famous calypsonian The Roaring Lion (Rafael de Leon). In the book bearing the somewhat pretentious title *Calypso, from France to Trinidad; 800 years of history*, the veteran of the art claims (1988: 1–2):

> ... the calypso has no ties whatsoever with Africa and in fact, there is no evidence to support the claim that it is either a variant of African folk songs or that it was invented by African slaves in Trinidad. This belief is purely speculative.... There is ample data to uphold my theory that the calypso is of French origin, and this is supported by documentary evidence.

Although not a shred of evidence is adduced to support this provocative claim, the flood of criticism with which the Black Power romantics attacked the book was not based on any evidence either; apparently they were concerned to defend the myth of a fully African origin as a doctrine at all costs. It is regrettable that this often prevents a dialogue between experts, while De Leon's analysis of the resemblance between the late medieval French ballad and the calypso, as well as his accurate description of the first calypso tents (theatre-like areas where singers of both sexes performed their latest compositions before a critical audience) is very valuable for acquiring a balanced view.

Songs of praise and mockery

'Kaiso' is the only name that has survived besides 'calypso'. Leaving etymological considerations to one side, its African connotations do justice to the undeniably important contribution of the West African slaves to this

Caribbean musical style. As can be seen from observations by eighteenth-century writers, the songs of praise and blame, often improvised, were brought to the West Indies from the African mother country by these slaves. The same is true of the typical West African litany form, in which the lead singer, accompanied by percussion, sings a couplet of a song and a choir sings the refrain. The theme may be a love affair or a beautiful woman, but the songs are just as likely to contain satire or mockery. Not only did the slaves attack one another in this way, but the target of their ridicule was often their master too. All of these characteristics can still be found in the present-day calypso (Hill 1976: 67–8; Rohlehr 1983: 43–4; 1990: 1–4, 15–18). In her study of Yoruba songs from Trinidad Warner-Lewis (1984) states: 'the *picong* (provocation) and *mépris* (scorn) modes of so many of these Yoruba songs, whether sacred or secular, indicate one source, no doubt a reinforcement, of that satire-cum-boast tradition within the calypso'. Hill (1971: 23) recognizes much of the classical *griot* in the modern calypsonian. Centuries ago they assumed a prestigious position among the nobility of powerful West African states: 'They were the repositories of their country's history, of its music, dances and poetry.' There is indeed a striking similarity to the calypsonian if we consider how the *griots* of the West African Mandingo people describe themselves (Hill 1971: 23): 'We are word-containers. We are the memory of man. By the power of the word we give life to the king's actions for the benefit of the young. History contains no secret for us.'

A variegated medley of dance and music came with the waves of migrations from the entire Caribbean region between the end of the eighteenth century and the middle of the twentieth. In 1881, the year of the notorious Canboulay revolts, 15.7 per cent of the total population of 171 179 consisted of migrants from the rest of the West Indies. This group accounted for 33.87 per cent of the total of 71 000 migrants. The presence of these English-speaking West Indians (one-third of the population of Port of Spain) and their participation in the cultural life of Trinidad were so striking that the old French-speaking inhabitants accused this group in particular of having contributed to the roughness and obscenity of the Jamet carnival (Rohlehr 1983: 52–3). As a result of the lack of data on the precise composition of these migrations – there was no accurate census before 1851 (Wood 1986: 44) – it is impossible to obtain a good picture of the relation between the Creole (West Indian) and the African influence in the calypso. An extra problem is formed by the mutual influence and combination with European musical forms. It was from this cultural mélange, in which dances which were originally distinct from one another, like the Jhouba and the Bel Air, have virtually been absorbed, that the name of a different classical dance emerged – the Calinda – as a general term for a whole complex of dance and ritual activity (D.R. Hill 1993: 25–32). The combination of Calinda with stick-fighting and the role of the chantwelle (from *chanterelle*, originally only used for a female singer – Hill 1976: 68) gave the street gangs a militant character, so that carnivalesque aggression during the turbulent Canboulay period easily degenerated into serious forms of violence. These rival gangs were marked by a high level of ritualization. Linked to a territory and operating in semi-clandestinity, they may well have originally been reconstructions of West African secret societies (Brereton 1979: 166; Matthews 1952: 93–4; Wood 1986: 240–1). All the same, here too the form is a hybrid one, in which African and European traditions which are difficult to trace have combined with one another, or even more strikingly, seem to complement one another with similar expressive elements. For example, Rohlehr (1983: 62) reports that already in the nineteenth century the – sometimes annual – election of a king or queen 'might have been simultaneously a longing for lost tribal chieftainship and an index of how deeply the society at large had begun to assimilate, perhaps from the upper class Carnival of the pre-emancipation period, French notions of royalty and aristocracy.'

In fact, every carnival band was a small kingdom in its own right, with a hierarchy of officers. Hill (1972: 35) describes two rival bands on the former French island of St Lucia in the 1840s. The bands were named after flowers – La Rose and La Marguerite – to which the members showed their devotion through songs of praise. These bands or societies were headed by a king and a queen.

Apart from the question of whether these organizational forms had their roots in French culture, their resemblance to Le Roy Ladurie's account is at least remarkable. In his monograph *Le Carnaval de Romans* (1981: 281–2) he refers to the existence of so-called *reynages*: 'Carnival was inseparable from the founding of a certain number of kingdoms or 'reynages', specific folk gatherings and festivities'. The *reynages* had names like Kingdom of the Sheep, Eagle, Cock, Hare, Capon, and Partridge. The coronation of a king and queen, the appointment of mock officers as a sort of court, burlesque competitions and dances were the kinds of activities they engaged in. The *reynage* 'created a social tool, allowing the lower classes to express themselves, their mockery, and sometimes even their grievances. Plebeian political tendencies that were repressed during the rest of the year came to light during the festivities.' De Leon, the Roaring Lion (1988: 17 and 41) refers to Le Roy Ladurie's work to support his argument that the calypso is a direct successor of the ballad. However, the fact that he demonstrates that the ballad, like the calypso, is not only a love song, but can also serve, in the case of Romans, as an instrument of social and political commentary and protest, is not enough to establish the relationship between the two musical forms. More convincing is the parallel that he demonstrates between the prosody and meter of the two forms of song. A more balanced picture of the French connection, which also helps to defend De Leon's polemic against the sharp criticism of the African romantics, is provided by his famous fellow calypsonian Quevedo (1983: 19). The latter writes:

> The galaxy of kaisos which have been paraded must surely indicate a certain musical affinity between the kaisos from the French-speaking territories with those of Trinidad and should lead to the clear conclusion that the distinctiveness of the Trinidad kaiso may be attributed, in large part, to the stimulus of French influence in our cultural heritage.

By around 1840 the sixteenth-century *reynages* of Romans had become song clubs. In Trinidad the carnival bands with Calinda and stick-fighting have also undergone a change of form, which has led to the present-day amusement in the calypso tents, which is unintentionally echoed in Le Roy Ladurie's description (1981: 292).

Besides the king, the chantwelle assumed an important position in the band. Sometimes he was even the leader, who preceded his followers in the confrontation with rival bands like a medieval prince. The chantwelle's songs bound the group together and the choral refrain reinforced the feeling that each member had a share in the victory. This street choir can be regarded as a precursor of the road march, the calypso genre, which nowadays too is mainly composed to be played and sung by the revellers in the masquerade parades during carnival. When the playing of African drums and stick-fighting were prohibited in 1884, the chantwelles were forced to vent their aggression through verbal channels. They could find ample precedents in the Calinda tradition.

Word as weapon

Gordon Rohlehr (1983: 76–110; 1990: 51–84), an expert in West Indian literature, refers to a number of aspects of the meaning of the word during the confused Emancipation period, when acute problems arose connected with status and identity in relation to the existing power structure. The African slaves who had recently arrived lived alongside creolized blacks with a French, English or Spanish background, as well as Indian contract labourers and a dozen other ethnic groups. It is understandable that serious language problems occurred within such a mixture, and thus that the ruler of the word, the spokesman of a group, occupied an extremely important position. The chantwelle of the Calinda bands was assigned this position. Like the stick-fighter, he was assumed to possess supernatural powers (for a characteristic example see Pearse 1956). Thus the fighting-stick was supposed to be treated with *obeah* to guarantee the fighter invincibility. Rohlehr (1983: 79–80) sums it up concisely:

> The boasting of the 'batonnier' wasn't a matter of pose, but had its roots in magic and obeah. By boasting of his power, the stick-fighter sought to gain possession of it, in order to reinforce a skill developed through hard practice. By boasting of his invincibility, he sought an immunity to his opponent's blows. His rhetoric was a serious one, a formalized verbal prelude to a game in which manhood, status, identity within the group and sometimes life itself were at stake. Language for the chantwel who reinforced the stick-fighters' boast and would himself sometimes actively participate in stick-play, was power; the word was magic, its form, incantation, its purpose, inspiration and celebration.

According to tradition, the first chantwelle was a certain Gros Jean. He was appointed *Mait' Caiso* (master of the calypso) by Pierre Begorrat. This immigrant from Martinique settled in Trinidad with the first group of French planters in 1784 and managed to secure a regal style of living, complete with retinue. He held court in a cave on his estate in the Diego Martin valley to the west of Port of Spain, where he and his friends were entertained in various ways by a group of slave singers of the *cariso* or *caiso* 'which were usually sung extemporare and were of a flattering nature, or satirical or directed against unpopular neighbours or members of the plantation community, or else they were 'Mépris', a term given to a war of insults between two or more expert singers' (Pearse 1956: 253). This account of the earliest songs indicates three important elements which are still characteristic of the calypso.

Nowadays most of the songs are composed and rehearsed before they are presented to a critical audience. The calypsonian who can sing extempore, however, is still greatly appreciated and admired; in fact, this practice is even on the increase. The satirical manner in which 'unpopular neighbours' are treated (in order to curry the favour of the audience) has become often caustic socio-political commentary, in which modern calypso singers are masters. The singers were skilled in accusing or insulting one another, which was later to turn into the so-called calypso wars. Their heyday is now a thing of the past, but they have also been making a come-back in recent years. In the nineteenth century the calypso was sung in a French patois which was the everyday language of ordinary people, or in a mixture of patois and English. The patois calypsos were the only source of news for the largely illiterate audience who had no access to information in the French or English newspapers. In this way, commentary could be made and malicious gossip spread about affairs and people from all layers of society. This use of language is exemplified in a calypso on the famous Bakewell Affair in 1870. An English official is tarred and feathered for insulting a colleague of mixed ancestry (Brereton 1979: 162):[1]

> *Bakeway, qui rive*
> *Qui moon qui fair ca*
> *Is two black men tar poppa*
> *Moen ca garde con you negre,*
> *Moen moen blanc mes enfants.*
> *Is two black men tar poppa.*

Although patois was a sort of code to the establishment, which made it difficult to censor texts which sounded displeasing, its use made this sector of the population even more suspicious and disapproving. There were regular protests in the official newspapers against the songs in patois which were performed in public during carnival. At the end of the nineteenth century patois was increasingly replaced by English, but the tendency to use it as a code which the English-speaking officials could not understand continued for a number of years. In 1927 a calypso contest took place between Lord Beginner and Atilla the Hun. The winner was Lord Beginner, but in the end the prize was awarded to Atilla because the jury objected to Beginner's use of a patois word in his calypso (Liverpool 1973: 25). Scandalous gossip and forbidden sexual innuendos also reached the ears of a willing audience by means of this dialect right up to the 1930s. During this period the government once again tried to adopt measures against unacceptable calypsos; the censors in the Colonial Secretary's office in Port of Spain underlined all patois words, certainly – not because they understood them, but because they were suspicious (Rohlehr 1983: 99).

Sans humanité

The turn of the century heralded a new period in the history of the calypso. Not only was the song first referred to by its present name in the *Port of Spain Gazette* of 20 January 1900 (Hill 1972: 64), but it also acquired a new language and reputation. With obvious relief and pleasure, the same paper reported on 7 February of that year that during the forthcoming carnival 'the singing will be patriotic tunes in English, a decided improvement on the old patois style' (Hill 1972: 60).

Education in the English language was seriously tackled at the end of the nineteenth century. Of course, this did not take place without any hitches, in view of Trinidad's long history in Spanish, French and patois. A teacher at the time claimed that the pupils in secondary school were more intrigued by the sound of words than by their meaning, so that their function as a vehicle of communication was overshadowed: 'Boys and young men spend hours poring over dictionaries, simply to try and master the meanings of words which for length may be measured by the yard' (Rohlehr 1983:

82). The transformation of the calypso with its specific rhetorical tradition into a different language led to a change of style. This is known by the name 'oratorical' or *sans humanité* (spoken in Trinidadian English as 'sandeemaneetay') calypso, which is more or less the artistic reflection of that transformation process. Fascination by the sound and length of the word can be clearly illustrated by a fragment from a duet between Atilla the Hun and Roaring Lion, entitled *Asteroid* (Quevedo 1983: 47):

> **Lion:** *On grammatical subjects I will now state*
> *Inviting lexicographers who can debate*
> *With Ramsomfousis asceticism*
> *They may try to argue but are bound to run*
> *Through the extensive alteration of anklyosis*
> *And my encyclopedic analysis*
> *Makes me a man of psychology*
> *And I can always sing grammatically.*

> **Atilla:** *I hate to tell you this but I must*
> *Your nonsensical oration fills me with disgust*
> *If there is a thing I greatly detest*
> *Is to hear the English language badly expressed*
> *You are brutalizing etymology*
> *And crucifying syntax and orthography*
> *For you are no man of psychology*
> *And you will never sing grammatically.*

This calypso style, which maintained its popularity from around 1900 to 1925, can be explained from the interplay of a number of factors. A new generation of calypsonians (now including people of mixed ancestry, as well as a few whites) wanted to use their newly acquired linguistic knowledge, often obtained through self-education, to distinguish themselves from the many chantwelles who continued the tradition of the nineteenth-century Jamet subculture with its emphasis on rude insult and sexual scandal. In his article on nineteenth-century carnival, Andrew Pearse (1971: 551) characterizes the Jamets as follows: 'skill and bravery in 'bois' or stick-fighting, sharpness or wit and repartee in conversation and in song, talent in dance and music, indifference to law and authority, and great sexual accomplishments.' He concluded: 'Thus they represented the reversal of the values of respectability and a flamboyant rejection of the norms of the superstructure.'

Intellectual singers such as Hannibal, Cedric Le Blanc, Lord Executor and George Adilla the Duke of Marlborough wanted to polish up the reputation of calypso. One reason why this was important was that the world of business in Trinidad believed that increasing profits were to be made from some kind of sponsoring or patronizing of calypso amusement. Moreover, a sympathy, previously latent among the French and Spanish Creoles, was now burgeoning; they embraced the censored carnival and its practices nostalgically as the genuine heir to Catholic Trinidad in the old days of the French. Commercial interest and cultural sentiment joined hands, because members of this middle-class group made sizeable profits during carnival (Rohlehr 1983: 60 and 74). The shaky grasp of English at the time led to (or was camouflaged by) a form of over-accentuation in an attempt to mimic the snobbish obsession of the local middle class by the use of tongue-twisters. This goes some way to explaining the exaggerated language and the partiality for long and difficult words, also called 'Rococo English' (Winer 1986: 123), but the latter can also be seen to be a continuation of the existing tradition of former Calinda songs, in which mastery of the word and a strong instinct to boast represented important values. The often aggressive verbal confrontations between two or more singers, each with his own choir, his own group of musicians, and the repeated chant of *sans humanité* at the end of every refrain, also recall the stick-fighters' songs of the notorious street gangs of the past. An example is provided by a recitative from the calypso war between Patrick Jones and Lord Executor in 1918 (Rohlehr 1990: 62). Jones tries to intimidate his opponent by attributing to himself supreme power in the course of World War I:

> *In the extension of this rebellion*
> *We hear the cries of assassination*
> *The extermination of nation by nation*
> *And the feeble expostulation*
> *When babies cling to their mother's breast*
> *The angel of heaven will confess*
> *For I'm the terror of the land and I have no compassion*
> *Sans Humanité.*

It should be noted that the vast majority of calypsonians in this period lived a life of poverty and unemployment and had virtually no say in national political decision-making. There is a striking gap between their monotonous and bleak existence, characterized by social and political incapacity, and the power to cause worldwide disasters which they assumed in their songs. These can be seen as over-compensatory attempts to neutralize their lack of power in the colony by a flight into fantasy (compare Gilmore 1987: 149–53), or, in the words of Naipaul which I have cited in another context: 'A king of the night, a slave by day.' The verbal fulfilment of ambitious desires resembles the daydreaming of Naipaul's Mr Biswas, when he applied for a job at the paper and saw himself as the commentator of 'Amazing Scenes' (Naipaul 1983: 319):

'I want to see the editor.'

... Amazing scenes were witnessed in St. Vincent Street yesterday when Mohun Biswas, 31...

'You got an appointment?'

... assaulted a receptionist ...

'No', Mr. Biswas said irritably.

... In an interview with our reporter ... Mr. Biswas said ...

Living newspaper

Another type of calypso that belongs to the oral tradition and emerges in the 1920s is the ballad, from which the most important forms of present-day calypso music have developed. The calypsonian The Roaring Lion claims direct descent from the fifteenth-century French poet François Villon. However, Errol Hill's (1972: 71–2) account of the old Bel Air song as the precursor of the Trinidadian ballad variant presupposes the existence of a few intermediate links in the island's musical history:

The music was more lyrical than the calinda.... The belair could be a song of praise or satire on an individual or a group; it could be a witty or humorous commentary on topical events; or it could record personal adventures, real or imagined, amorous or otherwise.

The elements listed here are all characteristics of the ballad and also apply to the majority of modern calypsos.

Walter (Chieftain) Douglas deserves the credit for having introduced the ballad calypso. Unlike the oratorical calypso with a preference for English vocabulary, the emphasis in the new genre is on the narrative, or on what Quevedo (1983: 27) calls 'comprehensive topicality in kaiso'. Douglas focused on the everyday life of people from the lowest strata of society, earning the nickname 'the barrackroom kaisonian' from his fellow singers. The following is an example of one of his songs (Quevedo 1983: 28–9):

> *A bacchanal, a carnival*
> *Was the Woodbrook scandal*
> *(bis)*

> *The husband went to work but with tact*
> *Caught the wife redhanded in the act*
> *And called all the neighbours around to see*
> *His loving wife's infidelity.*
>
> *Some said look scandal, others bacchanal*
> *It was a carnival*
> *And I myself went, maliciously bent*
> *To see the correspondent*
> *Like an athlete he jumped the window*
> *Down the road in sliders and merino*
> *And as he rounded the corner*
> *The people shout: Look the seducer!*

In this case we do not know whether the story is fact or fiction, but it is true that the calypso permanently established its role as living newspaper or folk archive with this ballad genre. V.S. Naipaul (1982: 75) aptly remarks: 'It is only in the calypso that the Trinidadian touches reality.... The calypso deals with local incidents, local attitudes, and it does so in a local language.' This is a compliment from this regular sharp critic with a keen eye for the weaknesses of Trinidadian society. He has realized that, behind the frivolity of most calypsos lies a realistic view of the world, in which the calypsonian presents not just his own point of view, but also the feelings and ideas of the man-in-the-street. The calypso is not just fun, a flight from reality. Despite the persistent prejudice cherished by the opponents of carnival in Trinidad, the calypso is not the product of a carnival mentality in which all kinds of matters of great importance are flippantly dismissed.

In V.S. Naipaul's earliest work, *Miguel Street*, published in 1959 (1982a: 72, 99), circumstances involving a number of eccentric figures from a fictional street in the city are interspersed with quotations from real or invented calypsos, which are deployed by the characters in the book as ready-made moral views on life or as the point of an incident. This is a good illustration of the way in which calypso latches immediately on to current affairs thanks to the singer's talent for improvisation. For instance, when the house of one the characters in the book goes up in smoke, a calypso immediately establishes a connection with a similar event in the past:

> But what a fire it was! It was the most beautiful fire in Port of Spain since 1933 when the Treasury (of all places) burnt down, and the calypsonian sang:

> *'It was a glorious and beautiful scenery*
> *Was the burning of the Treasury.'*

In another example the calypso has the function of a kind of parable. This occurs when someone wants to warn his friend about his girlfriend's cunning now that she is pregnant ('making baby'):[2]

> *Boyee began whistling the calypso:*
> *'Chinese children calling me Daddy!*
> *I black like jet*
> *My wife like tar-baby*
> *and still —*
> *Chinese children calling me Daddy!*
> *Oh God, somebody putting milk in my coffee'.*

From the street to the tent

Chieftain Douglas was a member of the last group of calypsonians who led the masquerade bands through the streets. In the weeks before carnival the masquerade bands met in the backyard tents to rehearse the calypso refrains which they wanted to perform during the street parades. The calypsonian was present to sing the verses, and the members of the band functioned as a background choir. These nocturnal meetings were viewed with suspicion by the authorities and with disdain by the bourgeoisie. It was only when English replaced patois in the lyrics that a good deal of the suspicion and hostility vanished. 'Respectable' citizens attended the rehearsals to get a preview of what the new carnival hits of the year would be like and to entertain themselves with the typically native *picong* (stinging remarks; from the French *piquant*) and *fatigue* (teasing jokes).

Quevedo (1983: 35) reports an explicit system of class distinction in the selection of the chantwells for certain calypso bands:

> Norman Le Blanc, a store walker ... was chantwell to Shamrock Syndicate, a band of whites and persons described as near-whites. The Duke of Marlborough ..., who was a senior shop assistant, was chantwell to Crescent, a band composed from the coloured middle class and persons described as near-whites, ... Kaisonians like Red Box, Lord Baden-Powell, and Conqueror could not in their wildest dreams aspire to become chantwells of such bands.

At the end of World War I the tents demanded an admission fee from people wanting to listen to the calypsos before the start of carnival. Increasing interest in this amusement led to an independent programming of the event. Rival calypsonians were invited to test their skill and talent with that of the resident singer, and young dancing girls added to the colourful spectacle.

The local singer thus avoided the obligations and responsibilities towards the masquerade band, which was to go its own way in terms of organization and artistic design. He could now dedicate himself entirely to the calypso and to the professionalization of his occupation. In the 1930s the calypso singers formed teams which presented a full-length programme. The spread of commercialization reduced the number of tents where the calypso concerts were held to one-quarter of their original number. However, this also resulted in a concentration of quality in a competitive atmosphere in which each singer tried to better his rivals and to win the favour of the audience. A singer with some reputation could play tent managers off against one another and exchange one tent for another ('tent-hopping') as long as it was in his financial advantage. This involved their bosses in financial problems on more than one occasion, for which they tried to compensate by attracting as large an audience to their theatres as possible with all kinds of novelties. From 1934 on leading calypsonians were regularly sent to New York to record their best compositions. They also performed in nightclubs and concert halls in the USA. This brought them into contact with a pampered foreign public, leading to a raising of quality and craftsmanship and the development of a commercial mentality. Furthermore, the growing international reputation which calypso acquired was of the greatest importance for the prestige of the art form and the respect of its practitioners. The chantwell underdog, still only too often associated with impropriety, indecency and bacchanals – in short, with everything that took place 'below the diameter of decency' – came home a celebrity recognized by the international world of show business. A joyful self-confidence can be heard in a song by Atilla, who celebrated triumphs in the United States and was one of the first to be on the air from coast to coast via the National Broadcasting Company. His calypso recounts the history of carnival in a nutshell (Quevedo 1983: 52):

> *From a scandal and hideous bacchanal*
> *Today we got a glorious carnival*
> *We used to sing long ago*
> *'Moen tini youn seine pour seiner yo'*
> *But today you can hear our kaiso*
> *On the American Radio.*

> *Long ago you used to see*
> *Half-naked woman call 'pissen-li'*
> *With chac-chac and vera held in the hand*
> *Twisting their body like electric fan*
> *You were not even safe in your own home*
> *With 'negre jardin' and bottle and stone*

But today you can hear our kaiso
On the American Radio.

A prophet hath no honour in his own land
The truth of the proverb I now understand
When you sing kaiso in Trinidad
You are a vagabond and everything that's bad
In your native land you are a hooligan
In New York you are an artiste and a gentleman
For instance take the Lion and me
Having dinner with Rudy Vallee.

What do those Englishmen know about calypso?

It is true that 'a prophet hath no honour in his own land': the acceptance of the calypsonian abroad was not paralleled in Trinidad itself. While the happy marriage between West Indian talent and American enterprise enabled the calypsonian to become a professional entertainer, for the British colonial administration this meant a loss of opportunities to manipulate and control rhetoric, propaganda and image; the alternative poetry hardly displayed the spirit of 'Rule Britannia' or 'Children of the Empire' (Rohlehr 1986: 45).

The need to limit the freedom of expression of the calypsonians continued unabated. The government could justify its actions with a law of 1868 which prohibited the singing of profane songs or ballads (Hill 1972: 67). In the meantime, in view of the double standard that was at issue, it was not always easy for the calypsonians to decide how far they could go with the authorities; the latter intervened whenever it was convenient, but they left the singers alone when it was in their interests, or at least did not stand in their way. Often, however, it was patently obvious how the double standard was being applied. For example, the law prohibited calypsonians from referring to people by name in the social incidents or scandals they sang about. In practice, however, the police only intervened in cases of scandal involving white people. For instance, in 1933 King Radio had distributed pamphlets announcing that he was going to sing a kaiso about the so-called Country Club scandal. Rumours spread that a high-ranking police officer had been caught *in flagrante delicto* with another man's wife at a club party. On the evening of the performance there was a conspicuously large police presence in the tent. One of them climbed onto the stage and announced that the performance of the song was not permitted. Fellow singers of King Radio appealed to Captain A.A. Cipriani, member of the Legislative and Executive Council and leader of the largest political party in the country. His voice boomed through the tent: 'Put a chair for me on the stage and sing your song. Let the police do their damnedest. I am by your side!' The calypsonian was still not completely convinced and replied: 'Captain, the police threatening to lock me up!' Now Cipriani mounted the stage himself: 'I am with you. Go ahead and sing your song.' He did, and no one was arrested (Quevedo 1983: 57).

This incident was probably one of the reasons for the promulgation of the Theatre and Dance Halls Ordinance in 1934, which was intended to muzzle singers more rigorously than ever. While the old law meant that censorship was applied to offending calypso lyrics after the event, from now on the calypsonians had to submit their compositions to a critical examination by the police beforehand. The censorship was vigorously criticized and the calypsonians stuck to their guns in passing comment on whatever they chose. It was not until 1951 that a kaisonian was given the opportunity to speak as an elected member of the Legislative Council. It was the 'Honourable' Raymond Quevedo, alias Atilla the Hun. Some proposed amendments to the law in question were under discussion. Quevedo delivered a passionate plea for the abolition of a number of legal provisions. From time to time he had the laughs on his side, especially when he made fun of corrections to calypso lyrics which the police censors had proposed. This was his reaction to the prohibition of Lion's 'Nettie Nettie', one of the first calypsos to which the new legislation was applied: 'The police heard sung the calypso: "Nettie, Nettie, gie me de ting you have in you belly". And they said they wanted the words changed to: "Nettie, Nettie, give me the article in your abdomen" ' (Quevedo 1983: 62). Quevedo wanted to know 'what those Englishmen know about calypso' and what the difference was between the alleged obscenities which could be read in books in the public library and those which occurred in the calypso songs. The examples referred to in his speech recur in stylized form in a famous calypso (Warner 1983: 60):

> To say these songs are sacrilegious, obscene or profane
> Is only a lie and a dirty shame
> If the calypso is indecent, then I must insist
> So is Shakespeare's Venus and Adonis
> Boccaccio's tales, Voltaire's Candide
> The Martyrdom of Man by Winwood Reid
> Yet over these authors they make no fuss
> But they want to take advantage of us.

The Theatre and Dance Halls Ordinance was not officially repealed, but the prior censorship of calypso lyrics was no longer applied.

Rum and Coca Cola

The outbreak of World War II and, more important still, the Anglo-American Lend-Lease Agreement of 1940 meant enormous socio-economic changes for Trinidad (Black *et al.* 1976: 71). The agreement concerned the lease (in exchange for fifty old torpedo boats) of a number of territories in the British West Indies to the Americans. They were primarily to be used as marine bases. Trinidad was strategically important, for instance, as an assembly point for convoys of oil tankers from the Caribbean sailing for North Africa and Europe, or later as the site of the final exercises (in the Gulf of Paria) before sailing through the Panama Canal for the war zones in the Pacific (Brereton 1981: 191). The peninsula in the north-west with the deep-sea harbour in the bay of Chaguaramas was to be American territory for ninety-nine years. The construction of the base and other facilities and maintenance provided work for tens of thousands. The average daily wage, which had been the equivalent of 40c before the arrival of the Americans, soon rose to $5, while skilled labour was rewarded with a top salary of $10 a day (Quevedo 1983: 72). The cost of living rose enormously and thousands of people left the sugar and cocoa plantations and the existing industries to profit from the much more favourable employment that had been created by the foreign 'guests'. The American Occupation, as this period was called, accelerated the exposure of the people of Trinidad to the outside world. The American (and the Canadian) military presence on the island created a sort of 'boom times' atmosphere (Oxaal 1968: 81), accompanied by increased prostitution, organized crime, violence and conflicts between gangs. The Trinidadians were impressed by the efficiency of American high tech, their competence, the modern staff policy and the ease with which the Americans spent their money, but their racial attitude was cruder and expressed in less veiled terms than the subtle racism of the British. This all brought about a change of mentality which heralded the approach of an imminent new era in the history of Trinidad: decolonization and reorientation to a surrounding world which was larger and different from the old mother country. Brereton (1981: 192) writes:

> The 'American occupation' demolished the myth of white superiority; Trinidadians saw white Americans perform hard manual labour, and laughed at the antics of drunken 'bad behaviour' sailors. The automatic deference to a white face became a thing of the past; as one writer put it, 'the humility of a subject people disappeared'.

The presence of the Americans was of enormous importance to the development of later trends in calypso music. This art form acquired a cosmopolitan allure now that thousands of American GIs enthusiastically visited the calypso tents. The calypso songs of this turbulent period naturally reflected the reactions to World War II, although the island of Trinidad was unaffected by its catastrophic effects. Despite the presence and activities of the Allied forces and the proximity of numerous German U-boats which popped up from time to time, the basic reaction of the Trinidadians to the war was one of indifference: 'This war with England and Germany, going to mean more starvation and misery', sang the Growling Tiger, 'but I going plant provision and fix me affairs, and the white people could fight for a thousand years' (Johnson 1987: 46). Later the mood changed as British chauvinism gained the upper hand, as can be seen in this calypso by Growler (Quevedo 1983: 67).

> *Britain will never*
> *Britain will never*
> *Surrender to Hitler*
> *We going take the whole of his head next summer*
> *A million destroyers*
> *Commanding the waters*
> *Warm [sic] them mr. Churchill*
> *Don't you venture to enter the English channel.*

Besides commenting on the universal aspects of the war, the calypsonians remained loyal to their art and reflected on the remarkable stage in Trinidadian history, especially now that many of them were personally involved. Atilla sang: 'The Yankees help us financially / But they've played hell with our morality.' The influx of young men with plenty of cash had a profound effect on sex and morality, and even love had chosen to side with 'the fellas with the most dollars' (Quevedo 1983: 72). But, as usual, there were two sides to the picture: although the calypsonians criticized the Trinidadian women for going out with American soldiers, they rarely objected to the income resulting from these escapades (Warner 1983: 61). In 1943 Lord Invader sang what was later to become a calypso hit all over the world, 'Rum and Coca Cola', which brutally sums up the complexity of the developments. More than five million records of this song have been sold, including illegal covers (Brereton 1981: 224); the most popular version is the one by the Andrew Sisters. Quevedo is right in claiming that this kaiso highlights in a few verses what it would take a sociologist pages to describe (1983: 76–7). The complete lyrics are as follows:

> *Since the Yankees came to Trinidad*
> *They have the young girls going mad*
> *The girls say they treat them nice*
> *And they give them a better price.*

Chorus:

They buy rum and coca-cola
Go down point Cumana
Both mother and daughter
Working for the Yankee dollar.

I had a little mopsy the other day
Her mother came and took her away
Then her mother and her sisters
Went in a car with some soldiers.

There are some aristos in Port-of-Spain
I know them well but I won't call names
In the day they wouldn't give you a right
But you can see them with the foreigners late at night.

A couple got married one afternoon
And was to go Mayaro on a honeymoon
The very night the wife went with a Yankee lad
And the stupid husband went staring mad.

Inspector Jory did a good job
At St James he raid a Recreation Club
They was carring on the club as a brothel
The condition he found the girls in I cannot tell.

The initial impression conveyed by this coherent summary is of a comprehensive, realistic, warts-and-all exposure of what many experienced as their own moral decline. At the same time, it contains a sharp denunciation of the Americans in Trinidad. A good many of the denigrating remarks on Trinidadian women which can be found in the modern calypso are due to the reaction of the calypsonians to the fact that the Americans were stealing their women from under their noses. Once the 'benefactors' had gone, the women (and their often light-coloured, fatherless offspring) were abandoned to the wrath and vengeance of their former lovers.

A number of years later, Mighty Sparrow's extremely popular 'Jean and Dinah' was one of the many calypsos which commented on the American presence and its consequences. Under its influence, a whole subculture of Saga Boys had developed in the ghettos of Port of Spain. These youths imitated the American way of life with their trendy lifestyle, flashy clothes and sexy manner in an attempt to pick up women, but they were no match for the GIs, who merely had to wave their dollars to get what they wanted (Brereton 1981: 224–5). Sparrow sang about the revenge of these glamour boys, who took over Port of Spain again when the war was over (Warner 1983: 61–2):

> *Well the girls in town feeling bad*
> *No more Yankees in Trinidad*
> *They going to close down the base for good*
> *Them girls have to make out how they could*
> *Is now they park up in town*
> *In for a penny, in for a pound*
> *Yes, is competition for so*
> *Trouble in town when the price drop low.*

We are the memory of man

Of course, this is not the end of the calypso story. Social and political developments in Trinidad and Tobago, as well as international problems – in so far as they affected the islands – in the postwar period continued to attract commentary. The main events in Trinidad's postwar history can be traced in the calypso songs: the electoral victory of Eric Williams' People's National Movement (PNM) in 1956; the changes in the tax system in the 1960s and the increase in civil servants' pay; the foundation and collapse of the West Indian Federation (1958–62); Independence (1962); and the Black Power riots and army mutiny in 1970 (Rohlehr 1971: 7–8, 14–18; 1985, 3–6; Warner 1983: 63–89). Moreover, the story of the calypso is not complete in that a number of characteristic aspects of the contents of the musical genre have not received much attention so far, such as the specific humour and fantasy within the calypso; the man-woman relation and the related *double entendre* approach to sex by means of a seemingly endless series of symbols and metaphors to disclose and disguise at the same time; what at times is virtually a xenophobic attitude on the part of the Trinidadians towards the 'small islanders' from other parts of the Caribbean; and the view of various ethnic groups within Trinidad itself, which is often based on prejudices. These topics will be discussed later in this book where appropriate.[3]

The trade unions and political parties which achieved maturity after World War II were the result of increasing emancipation within Trinidadian society, whereby the calypso as the mouthpiece of specific marginal groups within the power structure had to share its position with other critical information media. All the same, it is a fact that the calypsonian is not tied to a trade union or political party, which gives him more freedom than any other medium to view many events in a critical light. In the mid-1940s, the politician Albert Gomes, himself the target of calypso criticism on more than one occasion, called this art form the most effective political weapon in Trinidad: '... people go to the Calypso tents to be entertained. What politician, who must harangue from the rostrum, can boast of a better opportunity for influencing people's minds?' (Warner 1983: 61).

The *griots* of West Africa sang: 'We are word-containers, the memory of man.' That is certainly the function of the calypso in a country where political circumstances (and scandals) succeed one another and oust one another out in record tempo; there is hardly any time to check the official version of an event, so that it falls prey to gossip and hearsay from a kind of powerless cynicism. The calypso catalogues the flow of political events and places them in the context of previous events. This is of crucial importance in a society where people forget so easily, writes Rohlehr (1985: 12), and where there is little respect for history, research or archives: '... no memory, only a sort of blankness, breeding indifference to present, past and future.' In his discussion of the calypsonian between 1970 and 1984, Rohlehr regards even the political calypso as an opposition forum, a necessary alternative to the ineffectual operation of the official opposition party in the face of the PNM government which was all-powerful until 1986.[4] He calls the calypsonian a special kind of 'investigative reporter' of political events, citing the famous calypsonian Chalkdust, who declared in 1976 that 'the calypsonian had a far greater freedom to articulate protest than anyone else in the society' (Rohlehr 1985: 11). The importance that the (political) calypso has had up to the present cannot be summarized better than in the words of Rohlehr (1985: 13) with which I will close this section:

> ... the political calypsonians have been poets of a nation in search of its soul; in search of a way of moving beyond machismo towards the inclusion of a larger measure of feeling and compassion into our personal and civic consciousness.... The calypsonians have kept open a vein of desperately sane reflectiveness on the chaos of our civic life, and in the process have inched an art form rooted in conflict, celebration and the catharsis of light entertainment, towards the deeper qualities of anguish and compassion.

From street gang to steelband

The whole music world talking 'bout de steelband,
Experts cannot understand what dey hear,
Sweet, sweet music coming from out a steelpan,
Music that could make angels shed a tear.
>   (Pete Simon 1975: 99)

On 22 July 1988 the Dutch daily *De Volkskrant* ran an article on the New York rap group Stetsasonic in connection with the release of their second album, *In Full Gear*. The article reported that a number of the rappers in the group had grown up in the black neighbourhood of Brooklyn, where the keyword is survival. 'But', says one of the spokesmen, Daddy-O, 'you learn to survive in an environment like that.' Some members of Stetsasonic had belonged to the street gangs which plagued New York some ten years ago. Daddy-O explained why the street gangs in New York were so different from the ones in Los Angeles:

> We didn't wear those headbands, but denim jackets with fur collars and the name of the gang on the back, like bike clubs. And we didn't use weapons, but we did all our fighting with our fists. And do you know what put a stop to it all? ... Hip hop! Everybody was suddenly a DJ or a rapper. From then on we did all our fighting in the rap competitions and the breakdance contests!

This recent case has illustrative value because in essentials it is surprisingly close to the way in which the steelband has developed in Trinidad. Like New York, Port of Spain was terrorized by street gangs (incidentally, in Port of Spain music had played a part in them for a long time) whose confrontations gradually assumed a less violent character and were transformed into forms of artistic sports contests which acquired a certain social prestige. The newspapers report fighting between various street gangs until long after World War II as shown by these headlines from the *Trinidad Guardian (TG)*:

'Steelband clash marks last lap carnival' (20 February 1947)
'Steelband clash creates short "state of emergency"' (3 March 1949)
'Steelbands clash, Cutlasses Used. Masqueraders, Spectators Alike Flee In Terror' (21 February 1950).

Such occurrences have now become a thing of the past. Today steelbands compete with one another every year during the pre-carnival weeks within a well-organized contest framework appropriately named 'Panorama' (from 'pan music'). These are strikingly non-violent spectacles which attract thousands of spectators. On one occasion respectful mention was made of a steel orchestra, when Catelli All Stars, joined by famous soloists, gave a concert performance of Mozart's Concerto in A for clarinet and orchestra and Telemann's sonata in B minor in November 1985. Thirty years ago, it would have been inconceivable that the sounds of a steelband would accompany the mass celebrated by Pope Paul II in the national stadium of Port of Spain during his one-day visit to the island in February 1985.

The early history of the steelband which follows is shorter than that of the calypso in the earlier part of this chapter, mainly because the calypso, with its colourful musical and oral tradition, is a far more informative guide through history than the steelband can ever be and reflects the cultural period in which the latter has developed.

The drums of 'darkest Africa'

After Emancipation in 1834, the white elite street carnival passed into the hands of the blacks. This was followed by a search – which was not only necessary because of government repression and censure – for a type of music and musical instrument that would correspond the closest to the spirit of the festival. This search has taken a century, and resulted in the invention of the steelband.

Unlike European music of the time, rhythmical percussion formed the basis of what can be called native music-making. The African drum in all shapes, sizes and functions was the main musical instrument, followed by the shack-shack and the banjar. The shack-shack is a rattle, consisting of an empty gourd that has been filled with seed and fitted with a wooden handle. The banjar was a native African kind of guitar with four strings, made from half a large gourd and a wooden neck, held together by catgut or wire. The non-stop beating of the drum for religious or secular purposes was a source of irritation and probably also of alarm to the privileged classes. The edition of the *Port of Spain Gazette* for 20 February 1849 voiced the general feelings of superiority experienced by this group in society: 'Bands of music (soi-disant), including those elegant instruments, the tin kettle and salt-box, the banjee and shack-shack, have paraded the town in all parts, and at all hours of the day and night' (Wood 1986: 245). The editor of *Fair Play and Trinidad News* of 1 March 1883 gave more open vent to his aversion when he wrote: 'The state of civilization of a people whose members can be set in movement by the repetition of such barbarous sounds can easily be gauged' (Hill 1972: 44).

Dancing, drumming, singing, noisy nocturnal wakes and magical obeah practices were the manifestations of the Afro-Creole culture to which the predominantly negative criticism was addressed. The bourgeoisie felt surrounded by the rites of 'black Africa', with only a highly precarious boundary between this 'barbary' and its own 'civilization'. 'Instead of the sound of the Gospel on the Sabbath, the sound of the Banjee Drum, the drunken riots, the firing of guns, the oath, the curses, and the cutlass reign supreme', wrote a contemporary (Wood 1986: 242–3). No one could have imagined that practices which were held in such scorn would become the music of the steelband and the calypso, which are now cherished and acclaimed by friend and foe alike, especially to non-Trinidadians, as the pride of the nation.

What is the explanation for this hostility and depreciation towards African music and practices, which have continually served as the pretext for all kinds of restrictions and prohibitions into the present century? Such an attitude, claims Wood (1986: 248), forms part of a much larger complex of myth and reality, observation and presupposition, which has shaped the white view of blacks. In retrospect, it is only possible to speculate on the origins of the mixture of condescending benignity and patronage, of sympathies and antipathies, of sentimental pity, fear and a feeling of responsibility, which have combined to form the racial attitude. As Wood (1986: 248) puts it:

> Behind it lay the whole intricate experience of the Afro-European encounter since the Renaissance, the stereotypes formed by slavery, the legacy of the master and servant relationship, and, equally important, the growing dogma of the superiority of European culture and technology.

Alonso (1990: 116) argues that the claim of the whites to possess 'civilization' evokes the existence of its logical opposite, 'wildness'. By portraying the blacks as the antithesis of civilization, the whites unwittingly endowed them with the power of the opposite of culture. That, Alonso goes on to argue, is why whites find carnival so threatening. Carnival created and confirmed the natural and supernatural powers of the blacks. The world of carnival turned the hierarchy of dominance and subjection embodied in the official discourse upside down:

> ... disorder triumphs and the devil reigns. The power of disorder is the only power available to those who are, by definition, excluded from order.... The outlaw is the only hero, the devil is the only ally in a world in which both justice and God are on the enemy's side.

Rohlehr (1990: 24) writes:

> It is recorded that during the 1870's Maxwell Phillip, a mulatto Attorney General in Trinidad, objected to a stickfighting song which he believed 'stigmatized the Negro race atrociously'. The words translated from the French Creole read:
>
> > *The Devil is a Negro*
> > *But God is a White man*
> > *Bamboula, Bamboula,*
> > *Bamboula, Bamboula.*
>
> The stickfighters claimed that the words of the song acted as prayer and charm, infusing them with the satanic spirit necessary for the fight they were about to undertake.

A more direct ground for suspicion and fear prompted by African customs, and especially by their percussion instruments, was the independence of Haiti, where anarchy and despotism vied with one another for supremacy. The nocturnal drumming as menacing signals of the unknown must have stimulated imaginations intensely. Unconsciously or in traumatic awareness, the religious and cultural manifestations of the black population were experienced as the prelude to disturbances and riots; after all, it was not so long ago that planters had fled to Trinidad for this very reason. D.R. Hill (1993: 21) cites the case of a French planter who overheard slaves singing in patois about the successful slave revolt in Haiti:

> *The bread is the flesh of the white man, San Domingo [Haiti]!*
> *The wine is the blood of the white man, San Domingo!*
> *We will drink the white man's blood, San Domingo!*
> *The bread we eat is the white man's flesh*
> *The wine we drink is the white man's blood.*

Dances such as the Calinda, Bel Air and Bongo, performed to the accompaniment of drums, were regarded with particular disdain and were characterized as immoral and obscene at the end of the nineteenth century. Although sex was the main theme of these dances, physical contact between the dancers was not permitted; the Calinda and the Bongo were performed exclusively by male dancers, the Bel Air exclusively by female dancers. The exaggerated reaction of the white elite to these dances as if they were the most unimaginable sexual orgies probably says more about their own mental world than about their grasp of the actual world in which they lived. *Fair Play* for 1 March 1883 describes the dances as 'the most disgusting obscenity pure and simple, being an imitation more or less vigorous and lustful by the male and female performers of the motions of the respective sexes whilst in the act of coition' (Brereton 1979: 160–1). The last explanation for all this aversion, which Wood (1986: 248) presents in a rather laconic manner in this context, is that there were 'two different styles of sexual behaviour'. The Victorian ideal of chastity and marital fidelity was contrasted with the lifestyle of the Creoles and former African slaves. Wood concludes: 'For some whites at least there must have been a psychological ambivalence, and open condemnation masked the hidden envy.'

In 1883 the government promulgated the Music Bill, which prohibited the playing of drums, tambourines or shack-shacks between the hours of six in the morning and ten in the evening unless a police permit had been issued for the purpose. The playing of these musical instruments in the intervening hours of the night was completely outlawed. Much milder regulations were issued for European musical instruments. These measures were felt to have gone too far, even for the 'respectable members of the community'; the law too obviously discriminated between the classes, and the poor could not be deprived of the little relaxation that they had, a newspaper argued (Brereton 1979: 161). The loudest protests came from the French Creole class. 'There is more in the sound produced than the discordant noise which alone strikes the European', was how the *Port of Spain Gazette* voiced this group's views (Hill 1972: 44). The long experience of these French Creoles with black plantation workers had familiarized them with their music, and they even joined in the dancing during carnival and other festivities. The law was repealed and replaced by a regulation which placed the responsibility for preventing meetings of 'Rogues and Vagabonds' with their drums, shack-shacks and other instruments on the shoulders of the owners of sites and houses (Brereton 1979: 161). In practice, the effect was the same as that of the law which had fallen into discredit, since it made drumming virtually impossible.

The practitioners and fans of the African drum did not take the restrictions lying down. In 1891 serious riots broke out in Arouca (some thirty kilometres east of Port of Spain) when the police tried to stop a drum dance and confiscated the instruments. The participants in the dance rushed at the police and recovered their drums after a fight. When police reinforcements arrived, the whole village joined the attack with sticks and stones. The disturbances continued until the military arrived on the scene.

Stringband and tambour bamboo

The prohibition of the drum in 1883 created serious problems for the carnival bands. They had to find alternative instruments for their tent performances and masquerade processions. Two different kinds of carnival music developed, which lasted until the 1930s. The first kind concerns the introduction of stringbands or country orchestras into carnival with instruments like the guitar, the cuatro (Spanish four-string guitar resembling the African banjar), the mandolin, the banjo, and shack-shacks. This development was connected with the fact that at that time groups from the middle class were once again beginning to take part in the street masquerades, to which they brought their own musical taste. Furthermore, the increasing professionalization of the calypso called for a greater variety of musical alternatives.[5] In particular, from 1895 and especially during the jazz vogue in the 1920s, the trombone, clarinet, cornet, followed by the saxophone, were added, laying the basis for the orchestra that accompanies the calypsonians in the tents today.

The second development of carnival music was closer to the demands and taste of the working class. Deprived of their drums and scorned by the stringbands for social reasons (they did not feel at home in them either because of the lack of sufficient rhythmic power), members of the lower strata of society sought a satisfactory substitute. They found it in a new type of percussion orchestra, consisting of bamboo stems, known as the tambour-bamboo band. The length and diameter of the bamboo determined the nature and pitch of the sound. For instance, the boom or bass bamboo, some 1.5 m long and 12.5 cm in diameter, produced a booming sound when it was struck on the ground, making it suitable as the rhythmical basis of a piece of music. The foulé or buller bamboo was to provide harmony, and the cutter bamboo produced a rhythmical counterpoint. This battery of instruments was supplemented by a bottle filled with water which was struck with a spoon, and a file which was played with a piece of metal. Tambour-bamboo bands have been associated with carnival in the minds of a sizeable proportion of the population for almost fifty years. Early in the morning on Carnival Monday, the bands appeared in the streets of the city during the old mask entertainment, a residue of the Canboulay procession, and after nightfall they provided the music for the jump-up dancing. This music also met with the disapproval of the authorities and the guardians of respectability, but it was never prohibited by law.

Sweet pan

Around 1937 more than one newspaper reported a 'terrific din set up by the clanking of pieces of tin'. Four years later, a news magazine stated: 'The music in the majority of cases, was furnished by the biscuit drums and dustbin orchestras, the performers on which instruments exhibited a degree of skill and brought forth the rhythms which particularly suited the maskers' (Hill 1976: 62). It was the members of the tambour-bamboo bands who experimented in the various backyards of Port of Spain with metal objects such as dustbins, buckets, biscuit tins, tar barrels and wheel hubs to produce a sharper and more exciting sound to improve their music. The steelband was about to be born in the working-class ghettos of the city such as John John, Rose Hill, East Dry River, Gonzales, Hell Yard, and New Town. During the period leading up to World War II, the carnival bands were formed by this colourful assembly of metal objects.

The specific origin of the steelband, the question of which individual or band first managed to produce a recognizable tone with steel or tin and when, is surrounded in confusion and controversy. Whether it concerns the Mafumba band, Alexander's Ragtime Band, or the Gonzales Place Band, the story about the very first moment goes something like this (Hill 1972: 48):

> It all started in 1936 in Tanty Willie's yard about carnival time. The boys had gathered as usual to beat bamboo; one of them, Sousie Dean, picked

up a dustbin and started beating it, there was an old motor-car in de yard and Arnim began to beat the gas tank. Realizing it was sounding sweet they discarded the bamboo. Rannie Taylor got hold of a paint pan, 'Killie' found a piece of iron and my brother, 'Mussel Rat', suggested the cutting down of a cement drum to be used as a kettle and so the first steelband was formed in time for carnival day.

During the war years carnival was suspended between 1942 and 1945 for security reasons. A number of steelbands ignored the prohibition and clashed seriously with the police, who knew that they could count on the support of a large percentage of the population who were sick of the perpetual drumming wherever they turned. Like the stick-fighting warriors of the past, the panmen fought not only with the police but also with one another. Knives and firearms replaced poui and bamboo sticks, and the steelband came very close to being prohibited by law as well. 'Steelband fanaticism is a savage and bestial cult and must be completely wiped out', wrote an exasperated correspondent to the *TG* (Johnson 1987: 47).

In the meantime, within the defences of the backyards, others persevered in experimenting with metal instruments until they came up with a drum which could produce different tones. The leading figures in this innovation were Winston 'Spree' Simon from the John-John band (later Tokyo), who came from the neighbourhood of the same name, Neville Jules from the Hell Yard Band (now Catelli All Stars), and Ellie Manette from the Oval Boys (now Trintoc Invaders). They are the ones who can be credited with first having played a melody in full on the pan (Brereton 1981: 226). Characteristic of the bands of the time is the choice of warmongering names — Casablanca, Invaders, Destination Tokyo and Red Army, to name but a few. Often alluding to actual events in the Second World War, they emphasized their own belligerence. Continuous practice and rehearsing in the backyards created a tight group cohesion which provoked rivalry, often leading to violent incidents. Police action was often forceful, but the steelband members were no waterboys either. A band leader from the time recalls: 'They were difficult boys and I renamed the band "Desperadoes" ... they were famous for their "action". The steelband, which then numbered about 20, was supported by numerous strong robust dangerous men who were respected in the community' (Johnson 1987: 47). The nicknames of the calypsonians were often *noms-de-guerre*, because they fought their own calypso wars too. Names such as Atilla the Hun, Roaring Lion, Lord Kitchener, Mighty Terror, Mighty Destroyer, and Mighty Spitfire gave the singers self-confidence, expressed grandeur, and were intended to arouse fear and panic (Warner 1983: 15–16).

All this feverish experimentation led to an explosion of pan music on VE Day in 1945. In a spontaneous upsurge of popular entertainment, the bands marched through the streets with their new instruments, made from biscuit tins and sawn-off oil drums. The whole of Port of Spain was in a frenzy and the steelbands sprang up everywhere like mushrooms. The feverish enthusiasm spread to the other towns on the island. The process of perfecting the newly discovered instruments continued, carried out by illiterate men without any musical training, or as one of the band leaders once put it: 'When I played a tune and a note was missing on the pan, I remembered the note and made a new pan to put it in' (Hill 1976: 63). These pioneers developed various kinds of pan instruments which could produce a large number of tones. It was a sport to try to better one another in playing extremely complex and refined melodies.

All the same, the steelbands were viewed with hostility after the euphoria of VE Day had subsided. The panmen were uneducated labourers from the backstreets. Hill quotes the words of the chairman of an official committee of investigation on the steelband movement at the time, to the effect that they were

> normally shunned as the unwanted and undesirable and subjected to taunts and reproaches. Thus ostracized and estranged from the circumstances and the people who alone could help them, they are driven out like lepers of old into the wilderness and waste places of society.

Members of the middle class especially objected to the din of the 'pan yards', the increasingly popular name for the places where the bands regularly practised. In their eyes it was just hooliganism, and firm measures should be taken against it. They were confirmed in this view by the continual intense rivalry between the bands, frequently leading to serious acts of violence, which recalled the fighting gangs of the second half of the nineteenth century. The whole movement was regarded as a threat to society. Brereton (1981: 226) comments: 'They failed to see that the steelband movement could play a crucial role in promoting social stability, by providing an outlet for the creative energies of underprivileged, often unemployed ghetto youths.'

In 1949 the T&T Steelband Association was set up to reduce the tension between the wrangling enemy bands. At the same time, it was in the late 1940s that a few prominent Trinidadians, for example Beryl McBurnie, Albert Gomes, Canon Farquhar and Lennox Pierre, began to see the social and artistic potential of the steelband. Pan pioneers such as Bertie Marshall, Anthony Williams and Rudolph Charles unconditionally stood up for the steelband. McBurnie, who as a specialist in West Indian folk dance has made a very important contribution to the development of African traditions in song and dance, featured The Invaders steelband on the stage of her Little Carib Theatre, which was founded in 1948. That was the year when the 55-gallon oil drum was introduced in Trinidad, which gradually came to replace all other kinds of pans. There was a guaranteed plentiful supply of these discarded drums because Trinidad produced and refined a lot of oil at the time.

A drum is turned into a pan more or less as follows. First the base of the drum is heated. The metal is now carefully beaten out until an even, sunken, hollow surface has been produced. This surface is then embossed to create different sections so that different vibrational frequencies are obtained and thus a limited number of tones. At this stage the pan tuner sets to work. He hammers below and above the slightly convex sections until the desired tone has been obtained. As the oil drums are sawn off in different lengths, there is a series of tones: High-Tenor pans, Double pans, Low-Tenor pans, Cello pans, Guitar pans, Tenor-Bass pans, and Bass pans (Gonzalez 1975: 15–22).

The attitude towards the steelband movement gradually changed. The most important event in its struggle for social respectability was probably in 1951, when the Trinidad All Stars Percussion Orchestra was chosen to take part in the Festival of Britain in London, where it scored a great success. In the following year steelbands were invited to perform at the Music Festival, a major event which had only admitted European forms of music until then (Brereton 1981: 226). The conflicts between the bands decreased in the 1950s, and with them the stigma of street terrorism. Pan remained in essence the music of the Afro-Trinidadian working class, but the steelband was on its way to becoming an important element of the national culture.

The masquerade

> If the steelband get me delirious,
> I going to roar like a lion in the circus,
> With my spear in my hand, playing Wild Indian,
> And I flying like Superman.
>> Mighty Zebra (quoted in Hill 1972: 84)

A man is what he is not

A number of aspects of the earliest developments connected with masquerade have already been discussed in Chaper 1. That more general account may serve as a background to the more specific treatment of masks, costumes and public performances found in this section, and will be referred to where necessary.

As we have seen, carnival was introduced to Trinidad at the end of the eighteenth century by French immigrants; the festival remained primarily a matter for this predominantly white elite until the abolition of slavery in 1834. Determined efforts were made to isolate the sphere of activities of this group from that of the slaves as much as possible, but this did not mean that they were entirely ignorant of one another's practices. The annual state of siege provided an excellent opportunity to size one another up and to borrow from one another. This state of siege, which was a traditional feature of Christmas in the British colonies, was imposed to put restraints on the traditional, high-spirited festivities of the British (Christmas) and the Scots (New Year). However, that was not the only reason to transfer ultimate control temporarily to the military government. The slaves were also allowed considerable liberty for dance, display, parades, and traditional contests between plantation bands (Pearse 1971: 534). There were fears that the slaves might abuse their temporary freedom to plan an uprising, and as a preventive measure to stop that from happening, a state of full military alert was considered necessary (Hill 1972: 13).

As Roberto Da Matta (1977) has demonstrated in the case of Brazil, military inspections and parades legitimized the existing social order in Trinidad too, while at the same time the festivities provided scope for an inversion of this system of social roles and positions by means of costume and mask.[6] However, in the course of time the state of siege in Trinidad came to be regarded as a pretext for having fun rather than as a consequence of it. (Later on, the military parades as a popular theme were parodied by the carnival bands.) Since the negroes were allowed a certain freedom for amusement and pleasure, it was particularly during this period of the year that the two social groups encountered one another's festivities, and were in a position to influence one another in terms of form and content.

A striking aspect of the masquerade is the exchange of roles which takes place between the participant and the figure that he represents. In her study of the mask, Marjorie Halpin (1979: 46) writes: 'The essence of a mask is that a man "is" what he "is" not.' In terms of social classification, it is only natural to suppose that a reversal of social roles could be effectively achieved in the society of Trinidad at that time by the distinction between master and slave. The white planters liked to disguise themselves as plantation negroes (*negue jadin*); 'even residents of Government House mimicked their "garden niggers"' (Crowley 1956: 192). They appeared in this disguise in torchlit processions in the streets of the city and thereby mocked the horde of slaves who were herded towards the place where a plantation fire was raging (*Canboulay*). The (freed) negro slaves, for their part, created the figure of Dame Lorraine and performed a grotesque drama in which the behaviour of the elite during its refined dance parties was mocked (Hill 1972: 40–1).

The specific historical course of development of the Trinidad carnival as a (street) festivity of the planter elite which was taken over by the former slaves after Emancipation in 1834 has produced a number of interesting carnival figures or scenes, as a result of the double exchange of roles or inversion referred to earlier: white slavers imitated the behaviour of their slaves, which the latter imitated after their emancipation as the behaviour of their former masters. The Canboulay procession of the emancipated negroes probably developed to some extent from an attempt to copy the elite's parody, while it was also a dramatization of the genuinely traumatic events of the era of slavery. The aristocratic Negue Jadin costume was taken over by the *batonniers* or stick-fighters. At times the imitation was taken to extremes. Hill (1972: 24) mentions the account of Charles Day, an eye-witness of a masquerade band of 1848, which performed slave scenes of 'almost naked primitives bedaubed with black varnish'. Hill supposes that the black varnish which was applied to the black faces was a direct imitation of the make-up which the white planters used to represent the Negue Jadin. A carnival creation dating from the beginning of the twentieth century provides a variant of this mechanism of inversion. The Yankee Minstrels were derived from the minstrel shows which were popular at the turn of the century in the United States. They were probably introduced in Trinidad by travelling theatre and music companies or by Trinidadians who returned from the United States. Originally the minstrels were played by negroes, but the most popular figures were whites who wore a 'blackface' and whose behaviour conformed to stereotypes of the negro. The Trinidad version was indeed performed by a negro, but the white representation was maintained in the masque: the 'blackface', with exaggerated white 'lips' traced around the mouth, red dots on the cheeks, an Uncle Sam tailcoat, pinstripe trousers, white gloves and a felt top hat – a negro imitating a white imitating a negro (Crowley 1956: 217).

Violent, obscene and dangerous

'After the Emancipation of the slaves', writes a former police constable in the report of his investigation of the carnival revolt of 1881, 'things were materially altered, the ancient lines of demarcation between classes were obliterated and as a natural consequence the lower classes degenerated into a noisy and disorderly amusement for the lower classes' (Hill 1972: 16–17). The white elite became less and less involved in the street parades and withdrew to its comfortable houses, tasteful salons and official residences to continue its festivities there with an elaborate masked ball. The relation with traditional carnival weakened with the years and there was no impetus to breathe new life into it. The newspapers of the period referred mainly to the scandal of the increasing crudeness of the street festival, which was more and more under the influence of underworld elements, the Jamets. The *Port of Spain Gazette* referred to the masquerade as an 'orgy indulged in by the dissolute of the town' (1846), 'an annual abomination' (1857), 'a licensed exhibition of wild excesses' (1863), 'a diabolical festival' (1874), and 'a fruitful source of demoralization throughout the whole country' (1884) (Hill 1972: 17). Headlines of this kind suggest that carnival degenerated immediately after Emancipation into a riot of unfettered barbarism. By way of exception, however, we also have an account that corrects this alarming image (which, though certainly true of the later Jamet carnival, is not applicable to the festival described in the *Trinidad Standard* of 5 February 1845). The following extracts (Wood 1986: 244) provide information on characteristic elements of the masquerade at the time:

> The streets are thronged by parties and individuals in every variety of national and fanciful costume.... Now we observe the Swiss peasant, in holiday trim, accompanied by his fair Dulcima – now companies of Spanish, Italians, and Brazilians glide along in varied steps and graceful dance... But what see we now? – goblins and ghosts, fiends, beasts and frightful birds – wild men – wild Indians and wilder Africans. Pandemonium and the savage wilds of our mundane orb are pouring forth their terrific occupants. It would seem as though the folly and madness and fitful vagaries of the year had been accumulated in science and solitude to burst forth their exuberant measures and concentrated force in the fantastic revels of the Carnival.

A few traditional figures of the modern carnival can already be discerned in 1845, such as the prototype of the Red Indian Band, the Wild Man, and grotesque illustrations of what were later to belong to the categories of National Bands and Animal Bands. This sympathetic account of carnival is practically unparalleled at the time and it could not bring about much change in general public opinion. The attitude towards carnival was negative: people would have preferred it to be abolished in one fell swoop, but they were even more afraid of the possibility of a revolt arising from it. Like calypso and the steelband, the masquerade was affected by all kinds of restrictive measures as well.

Mas', mas', ah know yuh by yuh nosehole

This cry was used when a masked carnival reveller was recognized. From 1840 on attempts were made to ban the wearing of masks. They were only partly successful; the mask gradually lost popularity, but it never disappeared from the scene entirely. The anonymity which it provided the wearer enabled him or her not only greater freedom of movement in the sexual field, but also made it difficult for the authorities to identify and prosecute the troublemakers and rioters. As we have seen in the case of the steelband, the fact that the masks were often of a bizarre character may have suggested mysterious rites from 'black Africa' to the white minority, who felt themselves surrounded by them, the combination of religious and cultural manifestations of the 'naked primitives' even perhaps encouraging the fantasy of an imminent revolt. The anxious visions of this group, which were based on fear of the unknown rather than on genuine, non-romanticized knowledge of African customs and practices, are understandable if one considers the deeper significance of festival and mask more closely.

The two or three days of carnival were the only time of the year which provided a break in the bleak existence of many members of the lower classes, usually with little prospect of any improvement. The mood was one of anarchy in which people thought they could do as they liked. The preparations – devising and making a costume or mask – and the approach of the festival created what De Verteuil (1984: 137) calls (in connection with the Hosein procession of the Indian community) 'a psychological change in the "insignificant man"'. Such a psychological change is illustrated by an episode in Gogol's novella *The Cloak*. The plan of buying a new cloak gradually takes shape in the mind of Gogol's hero: 'even his character grew firmer, like that of a man who has made up his mind, and set himself a goal.' When he has bought the cloak, 'that whole day was truly a most triumphant festival for him.'

The carnival revellers were seized by such a mood of euphoria, combined with self-assurance and bravery in action, which seemed all the more legitimate because of the change of personality brought about by the mask. Crocker (1982: 80) writes in *Ceremonial Masks*:

> ... masks are more than a painless way of changing personal identity: just because they completely hide the wearers they 'transform'. By donning a mask one becomes what otherwise one could never be. Men into women, old into young, human into animal, mortals into gods, dead into living.

If mortals could imagine themselves gods – omnipotent beings – it is understandable that this behaviour alarmed those who wanted to remain in power themselves. The extent to which this mysterious change should be assigned a religious significance is considered by Crocker (1982: 78) to be less important than the fact that 'in all cultures that traditionally disguise themselves, masks are credited with supernatural powers. This is true even when masking is highly "secular", as in the masquerades which accompany Mardi Gras.'

Not only the wearing of masks was affected by government measures. Many more restrictions followed, which were intended to take the edge off carnival. In 1849 the festivities, which had lasted almost a week until then, were limited to the two days before Ash Wednesday (Wood 1986: 245). The main argument advanced was the unacceptable profanation of Sunday (Carr 1975: 58). In 1868 a law was promulgated to prevent the carrying of torches, though to no avail (De Verteuil 1984: 64). The Canboulay revolt of

1881–4, however, was the most important pretext for the government to do away once and for all with a number of features which displeased the well-to-do bourgeoisie. Torchlit procession, beating the African drum, and the stick-fight were prohibited as part of the traditional Canboulay procession (Pearse 1971: 548).

The protest of the higher and middle classes was perhaps directed even more against the obscenities of the Jamet carnival than against all these violent aspects. Groups of prostitutes roamed the streets of Port of Spain, shocking the public by displaying their breasts, making immoral gestures and singing dirty songs, while they wore traditional masks which explicitly represented all kinds of sexual themes (Brereton 1979: 171). The most notorious was the Pissenlit (literally 'bedwetter'), or stinker. Those who represented the Pissenlit were mainly masked men dressed as women. Some of them wore long, transparent nightgowns, others were practically naked except for a 'blood'-stained menstrual towel. The songs they sang were described in the *Port of Spain Gazette* of 1884 as 'obscenity of gesture and language'. The dancing was accompanied by rude fun of an unashamedly sexual nature (Crowley 1956: 196). Victorian Trinidad, with the corresponding Victorian morality, especially in public, was certainly less tolerant and more puritanical than in the days of slavery. The newspapers made a lot of the alleged corruption of young people from the lower classes, which was not confined to the few days of carnival. There was not a single word, however, about the miserable living conditions which formed the background to this 'degeneration' and 'moral corruption' in the backyards of the Port of Spain slums where these young people were forced to grow up (Brereton 1979: 171). It was not until the early years of the twentieth century that Pissenlit disappeared from the scene for good.

The description of Pissenlit above indicates that it was not just a question of a costume or mask with which the wearer made use of a limited number of movements to express something. The disguise is an essential part of a short piece of street theatre that is performed. Though not unique to the Trinidad carnival, this expanded meaning of the phenomenon 'masquerade' is important.

The relation between costume/mask and performance has remained fully intact in contemporary carnival. The result is not only a carnivalesque simplicity or fun, for essential questions and social engagement can equally be embodied in the mythical, bizarre and sometimes frightening creations. An example is the 1986 masquerade band designed by Trinidad's most famous costume designer and band leader, Peter Minshall. Three thousand band members represented human society as one big Rat Race. Divided into groups with subsidiary themes like The Bureauc-rats, Mauvais Langue Gutter-rats, The Race to Extinction, and What about the Worker-rats, the result was an interminable procession of rats with corresponding variations in the costumes and masks. It was a dazzling and frightening spectacle, in which corruption, cynicism, love of money and consumerism, discrimination and class inequality were all criticized. The costumes were carefully designed and the selected colours were in harmony so that the entire manifestation acquired a potent and unambiguous theme. The making of these often fantastic and ambitious creations demands skill in working with metal, leather, beads and other materials. It is an art to construct the complicated wire frames around which the extremely ingenious costumes are wrapped. Imagination, skill, discipline, leadership and organizational capacity are absolute requirements for the creation of the masquerade.

In this connection Daniel Crowley (1956: 192) makes a distinction between the words 'masque' and 'mask':

> The word 'masque' indicates that the band wears costumes based on a theme from history, current events, films, Carnival tradition, from the imagination, or from a combination of these. It is thus differentiated from 'mask', the covering of the face and/or head sometimes worn by the masquers.

'Masque' can thus be understood in its traditional sense as a 'spectacular entertainment which combined music and poetry with scenery and elaborate costumes' (*The Concise Oxford Guide to the Theatre 1992*). Characteristic of the intertwining of the two meanings in Trinidad is the word 'mas', which can be used for either of them, but at the same time they are experienced as separate notions by the masquer. The dramatic or theatrical element is betrayed once more in that participation in a band is called 'to play mas'. 'Mas in yuh mas' is a popular expression which illustrates the fusion of disguise and performance. *Cote ce, Cote la*, Trinidad and Tobago Dictionary (Mendes 1985) defines it as: 'an expression of delight or appreciation for a well-presented costume or band. Also used with sarcasm for poor attempts'.

The man-of-action, the man-of-words

This is the background to an understanding of a number of masquerade creations which emerged from the Jamet carnival after the government purges of the 1880s. After the disappearance of stick-fighters and Pissenlit players, the street drama had lost much of its violent and 'obscene' character, but the spirit of militancy and competition remained intact. This can be seen from the example of the Dragon or Devil Band, which was introduced in the 1910s (Procope 1956: 279. See also D.R. Hill 1993: 59–61):

> There was a reigning beast, a man so dexterous and inventive in his dancing and portrayal of the beast as to be proclaimed best. Each year

aspirants for his crown would 'challenge him to combat'. The challenge to combat occurred automatically when the two bands met for the first time. The combat took the form of the execution of the reigning beast of various dance steps which the challenger had to imitate. If he succeeded in imitating them he then executed steps of his own for the reigning beast to imitate. The beast who first failed to imitate the other's steps lost the contest.

Besides this form of competition, the man-of-action (Abrahams 1983) had exchanged his physical weapons for the power of the word, harking back to the tradition of the earlier *calinda* songs. This change was thus not confined to its reflection in the development of the calypso, resulting in the calypso wars in which the man-of-words could show his excellence, for the display of verbal mastery also became a feature of the masquerade, above all in the figures of Pierrot, Pierrot Grenade, and the Midnight Robber.

Pierrot was a transitional figure for whom verbal contests were even less important than violent combat. As traditional clowns of the French *comédie italienne*, Pierrot and his female counterpart Pierrette appeared at masked balls of the planter elite before the emancipation of the slaves (Carr 1956: 282). Forty years later he reappeared under the same name and in a costume closely resembling his original attire as the solo successor to the champion *batonnier* of the stick-fighter gangs, which had been prohibited in the meantime. He was metamorphosed from a European clown who played innocent tricks to a belligerent and fearful braggart, whose rhetorical skill was merely the preliminary to a fierce duel with sticks and whips, often assisted and spurred on by women armed with bottles and stones (Carr 1956: 282; Hill 1972: 28). Like the champion stick-fighter, Pierrot ruled over a territory, a couple of streets in the city, where he had won his victory. Every other Pierrot was kept out. If a confrontation occurred, the intruder was first made aware of the identity of his opponent: 'I am the King of Dahomey, but I also rule over many countries that I have conquered. Do you now visit my dominions to offer your subjugation, or do you come as an enemy to dispute my rule?' (Carr 1956: 283). This was followed by a verbal exchange on dangers that had been braved, rivals that had been defeated, and victories that had been won. The swelling audience clustered around the two Pierrots and waited excitedly for the moment when the tirade of misunderstandings and accusations would reach such a pitch that a violent combat could no longer be averted. The final question: 'Do you wish to battle with me?' remained unanswered, because words had already been superseded by vigorous blows (Carr 1956: 283).

The main difference between Pierrot and his Jamet predecessor lies in the tendency to display learning, as expressed in the grandiloquent speeches on the lives of famous monarchs and warriors, based on works by classical writers like Shakespeare. This rhetorical skill may well have influenced the origin and development of the oratorical or *sans humanité* calypso (Rohlehr

1983: 97). Both Pierrot and calypsonian wanted to shake off the Jamet stigma which clung to the pejorative names of stick-fighter and chantwelle. This knowledge of literature, and the mild attitude displayed by the generally hostile press, indicate that Pierrot was popular among the members of a higher social class than that to which the stick-fighters belonged (Hill 1983: 21). All the same, Pierrot and the *batonnier* both gradually disappeared from the carnival stage around 1920. A police permit was required from 1892 onwards because of the violence of his act, which removed the necessary anonymity of the Pierrot player (Hill 1972: 30, 91). The effect of numerous arrests and imprisonments was to discourage most people from assuming the disguise of one of the most colourful masquerade figures of the Trinidad carnival. The figure of Pierrot Grenade is a satire on both his richer, more 'civilized' but more violent brother Pierrot, and the inhabitants of the island of Grenada (and thus all 'small islanders') who came to Trinidad to look for work. He makes his appearance on Trinidad around 1900, coinciding with the influx of a large number of immigrants from the impoverished island of Grenada. This masquerade figure was an artistic, somewhat condescending reaction to the presence of these 'foreigners', born of a persistent insular sense of superiority towards the rest of the region which still characterizes Trinidadians to this day (see Lewis 1968: 18–19; 1983: 11–12, 325). The language spoken by the people of Grenada came especially under fire as an instance of 'bad English' — a prejudice which has hardly lost any of its force during the rest of the century. The foundation of the Federation of the West Indies (1958–62) brought about another, short-lived wave of immigration, including a fresh group of poor Grenadians attracted by the higher wages on Trinidad. The calypso singer Lord Blakie commented (Warner 1983: 71):

> *If you see how they holding the scamps and dem*
> *Friends, you bound to bawl*
> *Some o' dem could read and spell*
> *But dey can't pronounce at all*
> *The policeman telling dem say 'pig', you stupid man*
> *And as dey say 'hag' — straight inside de van.*

The language of Pierrot Grenade from around 1900 revealed the same attitude towards foreigners, but it was even more the result of the ambivalence within Trinidadian society itself towards the use of dialect (French Creole or patois) which was already on its way out, on the one hand, and the rudimentary English that had been taken over from the colonial powers, on the other. This position betwixt and between two languages led to a heightened awareness of words which sound the same but have completely different meanings in the two languages (Rohlehr 1983: 98). Pierrot Grenade was particularly skilful in playing on words which illustrate this feature of the language. His favourite ploy was to choose a complex, polysyllabic word. He would then weave a story around one of these syllables through which it was metamorphosed into an independent (key) word and linked to the following syllable as an autonomous word in a successive episode of the same story. In the end, all the syllables formed the chosen word, which was thus the 'explanation' (Carr 1956: 281–314; Hill 1972: 92). Language games of this kind are also to be found in calypso lyrics of the period. The transition from Pierrot to Pierrot Grenade marked two mutually overlapping traditions and languages: that of the literate class, and that of the semiliterate majority. The figure of Pierrot Grenade expressed above all the ambivalent feelings of the poor and illiterate in both imitating and satirizing the 'superior' tradition of Pierrot (Rohlehr 1983: 97–9).

The third man-of-words, who first appears around 1920, is the Midnight Robber. Unlike the Pierrots, who engaged in a verbal contest before coming to blows, the Midnight Robbers did not fight and only rarely engaged in debate. The costume was based on the theatre version of the American cowboy which was popular at the time, but it soon acquired a form and character of its own. Leaving a wealth of variations to one side, Hill (1972: 90–1) provides the following description:

> ... the most representative style ... is the Elizabethan doublet and breeches enriched with beading and braid, an enormously exaggerated and elaborated hat with fringed brim and a crown molded into some creature or edifice, and shoes usually in the form of an animal with moving eyes. The whole is set off with a flowing cape on which symbols of death and destruction are embroidered or painted. In his hand he carries a revolver and a wooden moneybox in the shape of a coffin. A cartridge belt and more guns adorn his waist.

The figure of the Midnight Robber could frighten the lives out of his victims, and children were panic-stricken at the sight of this terrible *mas*. He attracted the attention of bystanders as he brandished his revolver or dagger in the air and blew continually on an ear-piercing whistle. If he approached one of them, this display of bragging was accompanied by a rushing monologue characterized by bluff, grandiloquence and fool's wisdom. The only way to escape this compelling flow of words was to offer the Robber some money. Nowadays, colloquial Trinidadian still calls the uttering of idle threats and braggadocio 'robber talk'. The language closely resembles that of the *sans humanité* songs from the calypso wars. Warner (1983: 38–43) claims that the style of speech of the West African *griots*, especially their recourse to grandiloquence, reappears in the form of the Midnight Robber, who in turn served as the model for this current within the calypso tradition. Like the calypsonian Patrick Jones, who claimed to have influenced the First World War with his power, the Midnight Robber often assumed supernatural powers. Crowley (1956a: 269) provides an example:

> For the day my mother gave birth to me, the sun refuse to shine, and the
> wind ceased blowing. Many mothers that day give birth, but to deformed
> children. Plagues and pestilence pestered the cities, for atomic eruption
> raged the mountains. Philosophers, scientists, professors said the world is
> come to an end, but no, it was me, a monarch, was born. Master of all I
> survey, and my right where none could dispute.

The figure of the Midnight Robber gradually disappeared from the
streets of Port of Spain in the 1950s. In his study of this carnival figure,
published in mid-decade, Crowley believed that it still had a future. The
costume was spectacular, offering plenty of scope for extensive variation
and further development. Moreover, 'the speeches provide worthy
opportunities for the ever-glib West Indians to show their sensitivity and
skill with words and their delivery' (Crowley 1956a: 265). However,
Crowley's prophecy did not come true. The Robber underwent the same
fate as many other traditional and mythological carnival creations, such as
the Borokit (from Spanish *borriquito*, 'little donkey'), Moko Jumby and
Papa Bois (originally West African phantoms), Soucouyant (an enchantress
who turned into a fireball at night and sucked human blood), and Pierrot
Grenade. Now that their folklore and religious significance is gone, they are
no longer a vital part of modern carnival. Relegated to the status of nostalgic
relics, they are staged as visual rather than verbal attractions for a public
which is often indifferent, if not downright disapproving. Probably the
modest scale in which all these figures were individually presented was no
match for the growing demand for that audiovisual sensation and spectacle
on a much larger scale which has become the hallmark of carnival since
World War II.

Mass spectacle

As a result of the carnival events of the nineteenth century, around the turn
of the century tumult and violence had to make way for amusement of a
more peaceful kind. The growing participation of the 'respectable classes'
in the festival meant that more emphasis came to lie on bourgeois values
such as having a good time and looking good. This was a gradual process,
because it took some forty years more before the chic ventured to leave the
safety of their carriages to mix with the people celebrating carnival in the
streets. The curbing of an excessively rebellious spirit is reflected in an
important change of presentation of the masquerade bands: the anarchy of
Pissenlit had to make way for a more orderly, splendid display. The
Trinidadian writer Michael Anthony (1985: 159) has the following to say:

'Since bright and colourful costumes looked better when they appeared in numbers and were uniform, it led to a further development: people dressed the same way setting out to depict a certain idea.' A newspaper report on the carnival in 1900 stated: 'A marked feature of this year's Carnival has been the general adoption of the idea of combination into bands, each with a distinctive banner, bearing a title and motto' (Anthony 1985: 159). This marked the birth of the masquerade band in its present form.

Hill (1972: 85) provides a picture of the course of the growth and scale of the carnival masquerade. Twenty-six organized bands were registered in Port of Spain in 1900, with an average number of participants somewhere between twenty and twenty-five. There was a sharp increase in the number of bands after World War I. Official competition centres were set up in the city where the bands presented themselves before a jury. In 1946 the number of registered bands rose to 125, and an estimated one-third of the urban population took an active part in the carnival procession. In 1965 there were 171 bands, plus a number of individual *mas* players. In the late 1960s a rough estimate of 100 000 people dressed up in carnival costume during the two days of the festival.[7] It would be impossible, besides being unnecessary in the present context, to describe every facet of the development and manifestation of the masquerade. The discussion of Pierrot, Pierrot Grenade and Midnight Robber provides ample illustration of the transition from the disorderly Jamet carnival via these individual characters to the orderly masquerade bands, whose purpose was determined by a local or international theme. This is not to say that, apart from the thematic differences, the carnival procession was a smoothly operating, homogeneous entity. Inspiration was drawn from existing traditions, which were elaborated and combined with new ideas and styles to form a number of diverse categories among which the various themes could be arranged. As Crowley's study *The Traditional Masques of Carnival* (1956: 192–223) provides an extensive list of them, I shall only touch on a few points. For instance, there was the category of Fancy Bands 'to describe any band which was "pretty", dressed in colourful velvets and satins, and boasting a variety of characters carefully graded from King and Queen downwards', in contradiction to the Old Masque Bands, which featured old clothing and unrefined materials. The participants in the Congo or Shango Band, consisting of five or six men and women, fervently recited 'African' prayers to make fun of local religious practices. Crowley classifies the Military Bands, which were popular down to the 1950s, as Fancy Bands, while the Sailor Masque is formed by Bad Behaviour Sailors, Sailors Ashore, Sea Bees, Ships' companies, King Sailors and Stokers. Equally popular are the bands which have not entirely disappeared from carnival today, the Wild Indians and Fancy Indians, as well as the various demonic creations. The Jab Molasi ('Jab' comes from the French *diable*) wears a short, tattered pair of trousers with a tail at the back. Around his waist there are usually a few chains, a wooden lock and two keys, while in his hand he holds a pitchfork. He has horns on his head, a seaweed garland or a worn felt hat, and his whole body, face, ears and hair are covered with molasses, tar, grease, creosote or mud. He is accompanied by a pair of boys, who beat on cooking pans or biscuit tins with sticks or other instruments. Crowley (1956: 214) writes:

> In one case another boy carried a bucket of extra grease or mud with which to replenish the 'costume'. The Jab Molasse dances a fast version of 'winin' through the streets, threatening to touch the beautiful costumes of other masquers or the clean clothes of bystanders unless they give him money....

This diabolical figure and the accompanying scene still play virtually the same role in carnival today, especially during the Jouvert procession on Sunday night which marks the opening of the climactic two days of the festival.

Crowley provides a wealth of information on a large variety of carnival bands up to the 1950s. However, his classification of masquerade categories, types and themes is not very consistent or clear. It is questionable whether all his specific labels were recognized and used by the *mas* players of the time, or whether the will to order has entailed the imposition of a classification on manifestations which were much more spontaneous and diffuse. All the same, it is still true that the development of the masquerade after World War II tended towards larger band units with themes which can certainly be distinguished, but which are hard to arrange in terms of different categories. The bands which perform during Jouvert Morning or Jouvay (from *jour est ouvert* – Crowley 1956: 222), the nocturnal commencement of the actual masquerade, certainly deserve separate mention, but the distinction between Historical Bands and Original Bands (which Crowley did not invent himself) is rather artificial, serving only to illustrate the crumbling of boundaries which could be indicated with more conviction in the past.

Hill (1972: 85) attributes this incorporation of small bands into larger units to the high price which had to be paid for a first-rate steelband during the band parade. As a result, the diversity of the bands and with it the variety within the masquerade are diminished. In the end, Hill suggests, if this trend is not halted, we may expect a masquerade of twenty or thirty enormous bands, the only ones able to pay the astronomical sum required for a steelband. Hill's prognosis has been largely confirmed by the present-day situation of the masquerade in carnival.

In anticipation of developments which became more pronounced in the 1960s and 1970s, Crowley (1956: 220) regarded the existence of a tighter organization of certain types of bands, often brought out by semi-professionals, as characteristic of the post-war masquerade. They designed the costumes and assumed responsibility for their production, and made a contract with a band of musicians to accompany their own band. They retained control of the production in the street and on the stages of the various venues. Consequently, the average participant in a band had little choice except to select a particular role that he wanted to play and to pay the organizer for it. In 1972 Hill wrote: 'The days of personal involvement with choosing, making, and rehearsing a masquerade character are fast disappearing. The craft guild is giving way to the mass-production factory' (1972: 87). Crowley (1956: 222) also reports the common complaint that carnival had become over-commercialized; people claimed to miss the vitality and spontaneity of the pre-war festival. However, he adds:

> It is difficult to find this commercialization, unless by it they mean the relative organization of the bands' movements through the exigencies of the several competitions. Aside from the merchants who sell the cloth and the rum, only a very few organizations or individuals seem to profit directly from carnival.

This view no longer squares with the present-day massive scale and organization of the masquerade bands. Many people are involved for commercial reasons, and large sums of money are involved. 'The relatively prosperous times of Trinidad since the Second World War', Crowley concludes (1956: 219), 'have encouraged the development of historical masques with their large numbers and expensive costumes.' The situation in the 1950s, however, is nothing compared with the current scale of the masquerade bands, which sometimes number two or three thousand participants, and the extravagant and absurdly expensive costumes, which can easily cost US$6 000 or more. There is an irresistible demand for enormous costumes, which overshadow the bare necessity for the player to be able to move in them and thus to bring the creation to life. Errol Hill (1983: 35) gives expression to the indignation that many people feel at these excesses:

> I have watched with awe and concern the incredible elaboration of costuming for the kings and queens of carnival until the figure of the masquerader disappears completely within the spectacle. Hidden from view as some dumb beast of burden, he or she drags around an elaborate fancy structure on wheels.

The dominant mentality of mutual rivalry and jealousy and the hunt for prizes are in tune with the view shared by many jury members that the larger a costume is, the more chance it has of winning.

Women in the majority

In the *Sunday Guardian* of 3 March 1981 we read:

... we find that straitlaced young lady who on Ash Wednesday dresses in knee-length skirt and long sleeved blouse, stripped to the barest essentials and 'wining' oblivious to the public gaze. Or the staid banker who during the rest of the year, wears a stiff upper lip, taking the opportunity to lie full length on the pavement alongside the 'society' doctor.

The participation of the banker and the doctor drowsing by the side of the road does not go any further than alcoholic apathy. As Johnson (1983: 197) puts it in his reaction to the newspaper report: 'They are not dancing and there is no mention of any costume. We can dismiss them, for carnival has obviously become ... a festival of women.'

There is no doubt that during the last twenty-five years the masquerade bands have become increasingly dominated by women, and this phenomenon has become a topic of discussion in Trinidad. Men were over-represented in the bands until the mid-1950s, but that situation has changed drastically. In 1983 1700 of the 1900 members of Harold Saldenah's masquerade band were women, and Irwin McWilliams' presentation included only 200 men against no less than 1200 women (Rique 1983: 35). During the 1988 carnival, masquerade bands consisting mainly of women even appeared in the streets of Port of Spain, including Showcase Associates, Mas Men, Glenn Carvalho, Edmond Hart, and Penny Prescod/Richard Affong (Blood 1988: 37). Since then the annual average female composition of the bands is estimated at 80 per cent.

The increased participation of women in the masquerade is primarily attributed to their considerably improved position on the labour market, providing them with a degree of economic independence. Many women are now in a position to meet the expenses connected with celebrating carnival from their own purse. In addition, the process of emancipation which got under way in Trinidad in the 1970s and 1980s, influenced by feminist ideas from Europe and the United States, brought about a change of mentality which encouraged an autonomous enjoyment of the festival in the band of one's choice. Men now have less control over how women have fun at the festival. Costume designer Lil Hart recalls that '30 or 40 years ago it was not considered ladylike for women from good families to play mas. [Bands of ladies] had numbers of about 25, in fact that was a big band. The bands were roped, and no men were allowed to get in to play with the ladies' (John 1988: 95). 'My grandmother used to hide to play mas with a mask so that no one would recognize her', says TV personality Allyson Hennessey. 'Nowadays women don't need permission anymore to play mas, they have attained a greater self-confidence. In addition, women can afford to buy their own costumes, so naturally this independence is an important factor' (Rique 1983: 35).

The extensive participation by women can thus be accounted for in terms of various factors. All the same, these factors do not provide a satisfactory explanation for the revolutionary reversal of the sex ratio. Why is it that present-day masquerade bands have virtually become a woman's preserve? In other words, why have men pulled out on such a massive scale?

Lil Hart (John 1988: 95) claims that, before the rise of the 'fantasy mas', as she calls the contemporary masquerade, there was much more emphasis on the 'military type mas' and on historical presentations which appealed particularly to men. Men do not feel at ease in bands with themes like 'Local Sights and Delights', 'Mas Sweet Mas', or 'Splendour of Moonlight'. Rique (1983: 35–6) writes:

> Men prefer other types of entertainment at Carnival.... mas is no longer masculine enough to attract the males. The power and machoism [sic] have been removed and replaced with beauty and elegance. Men therefore can only look on....Which came first, the chicken or the egg? Have Carnival bands changed designs to accommodate the greater numbers of women, or has the very nature of mas changed to a more feminine portrayal?

At any rate, it looks as though, after large numbers of women had been admitted to the masquerade, they introduced a choreography, expression, aesthetic and choice of themes which made it less attractive for men to appear on this stage. Typical masculine carnival characters such as Dragons, Midnight Robbers, stick-fighters, JabJabs, Papa Bois, Pierrots, Sailors, Wild Indians and so on largely disappeared with them. After all, what is the point of performing a macho act if the target audience of female admirers is thronging the stage itself to become totally engrossed in its own show? There are still small or medium-sized bands with names like 'Rambo' or 'Wild Africa' which present aggressive male themes, but they are clearly in decline. Men do not seem to have a reply to the challenging women's manifestations, and they have largely withdrawn to the virile bastions of calypso and steelband – although here too the number of women is on the increase.

I propose to discuss this question in more detail in connection with the work of two scholars. First, Miller (1991; 1994) is important because he has specifically tackled the changed character of the masquerade. He believes that he has detected an aspect of the contemporary masquerade which exposes the deeper significance of the female predominance. Second, Winkler's study of the meaning of sex and gender in ancient Greece (1990), whilst it certainly involves a big jump from Trinidad to antiquity, also (in particular Winkler's analysis of Greek festivals that were exclusively for women) provides interesting points of view which throw light on the phenomenon in the Trinidadian situation.

Wining

Miller's analysis focuses on a very popular dance called 'wining', which he studied during the 1988 carnival. His research was concentrated on low-income women who had to 'jump-up' on the periphery of carnival or at carnivals in towns other than the capital, but he has no doubts that his conclusions also apply to the middle-class and upper-class women, mainly from Port of Spain (1991: 328; 1994: 116).

A lot of people indulge in wining, which provokes heavy criticisms every year from the custodians of decent morality. It involves rotating the hips and moving them up and down in an exaggerated manner which is sexually highly suggestive, and leaning further and further forwards or backwards while bending at the knees – a sort of limbo dance act. Men and women do this dance in pairs or in a row, which may sometimes number eight or ten dancers. 'Wining' is not exclusively confined to the carnival period. It can be observed the whole year round at many fêtes, parties and other festive occasions, where it is usually male and female partners who 'wine' together. However, the number of women who do the dance on their own or with one another in the masquerade bands is striking. Miller tries to explain why women predominate in wining as soloists or in combination with other women during the carnival period. In the public debate carried on in newspaper, radio and television commentaries, wining is regarded as obscene, but, Miller claims (1991: 327; 1994: 115), obscenity has been connected with the Trinidad carnival for generations. The nineteenth-century 'Pissenlit' (where the men and women were practically naked except for a 'blood'-stained menstrual towel) caused just as great a commotion in its time as the wining does today. And women played a central role in the construction of this 'Jamet Carnival' in those days as well. Wining thus belongs within a long carnival tradition, but, in Miller's words, 'the specific form it takes ... may be interpreted in relation to certain recent shifts in the wider context of sexuality and gender relations, and through this to the very possibility of sociality for a section of Trinidadian society.'

Many commentators, most of them male, link wining among women with an enormous growth in carnival of the number of 'zammees' (lesbians), women with a sexual predisposition which many regard as unnatural.

> ... a host of men can stand on the sidelines and shake their heads and tell their priests and holy men how offended they are, and can rant and rave in the papers about the growing incidence of lesbianism, and the lewd and indecent behaviour of women, and how disgusting it all is.

Pires (1988: 54) reports from the front. Miller, however, interprets this phenomenon not as lesbianism but as autosexuality. The dancing women are not interested in who or what they are wining. They can do it with a man, with one another, or on their own, because the object of wining is in the first place nothing but themselves. Miller (1991; 1994: 113–25) draws the rather curious conclusion that the dance should be understood as a rejection of sexuality as an act of exchange. Autosexuality rises above the problems of sexuality and boils down to a rejection of sociality. It entails a brief escape from the act of exchange which binds people to the world and its relations, especially those relations which women have increasingly come to regard as oppressive. He illustrates this by means of Hegel's concept of Absolute Freedom. This notion applies to the form of pure negation – whether in a philosophical movement such as Stoicism or a religious moment of transcendence – in which a cosmology or culture leaves no room for all the ties between an individual and the world.

Miller's explanation is certainly profound, but it leaves at least one important question unanswered in another kind of chicken-or-egg conundrum. According to Miller (1994: 113), the question of wining could throw light on the predominance of female participants in the masquerade over the last twenty-five years; he too notes that eight out of every ten members of masquerade bands are women. But what should this be taken to show? Does Miller mean that the numerical preponderance of women is to be explained by the fact that women's wining act excludes men so that they stay away? On the other hand, if men pull out of the masquerade for many other reasons as well or instead, we can just as easily draw the commonsense conclusion that women have to make do with other women once the men have left.

What were women laughing at?

Nevertheless, Miller notes an aspect that sets wining in a broader and more meaningful perspective, even though it is not the perspective that he envisages. As we have seen, women introduce their own choreography, expression, aesthetic and choice of themes into the masquerade, of which the wining dance as it is manifested during carnival *may* be a part. Miller (1991: 333–4) claims:

> The choreography of the act is important here: ... it consists of a gradual crescendo in the gyration, which is mostly autonomous until the last moment. The women who are jumping up more or less constantly will build up towards more systematic gyrations of the hips to lift their legs and to touch often momentarily before subsiding back into the general 'jump up' rhythm'.... It is striking that at that final point, whether of contact or autonomous climax, there is almost always a look of rapture, a smile as this moment is reached and passed.

It is this 'finale' which causes such a stir in Trinidad. It can be seen from items in the newspapers that men find wining terrifying rather than inviting, despite the fact that they are not generally immune to sexual charms and seductiveness. Miller (1991: 336) writes:

> When an article in the *[Daily] Express* (20 February 1988) says of the Carnival women that 'In fact so secure are they that they seem to spend much of the time taunting men who fail to perform', it is precisely echoing one of the most common conflicts heard in cuss-outs.

To explain the 'look of rapture', 'the smile', he adduces two circumstances which can evoke a similar expression of ecstasy in other societies. One of these concerns is the association with orgasm; in the other a link is established with ecstatic religion 'which tends to signify a moment of transcendence imbued with a sense of escape or release from the ordinary world, towards some mystical union or enlightenment.' Both associations may be relevant to wining, Miller claims (1991: 333). Perhaps this is the case in the light of his ideas on autosexuality, but I am not convinced. We shall return to this point in a moment.

In *Women in Mas* (Baptiste 1988), a carnival magazine on which Miller has drawn for some of the inspiration of this argument, Pires (1988: 51–2) also reports the striking laughing of the women:

> They wined, straight-faced, for the camera, and I saw (several times) women wining on each other — facing each other — with grim expressions on their faces, and then they spun away from the camera and each other, **laughing**.... But no one seems to have noticed the laughing. The commentators talk about the indecency of the behaviour. They claim to be morally outraged. They suggest, in some cases, state openly that they were repulsed by the **sexual** indecency of the women. I wonder, do **they** laugh when they're having sex? ... All they were doing, as far as I can tell, was 'freeing up'. (original emphasis)

Pires' observation is interesting, but he does not explain its significance, although his mention of 'freeing up' suggests an association with the concept of Absolute Freedom adduced by Miller.

This is where Winkler comes in. The main thesis of his book on sex and gender in ancient Greece is that sex is above all else a cultural instrument to help to construct and maintain social phenomena. Noteworthy is Winkler's discovery that in ancient Greece the epithet 'unnatural' is not determined by the fact that the sexual actions or behaviour are not in the service of propagation, but by the absence of implications for the social hierarchy. There is a strictly androcentric set-up: the only positions of social importance are those in which a man is involved. Relations between women are 'unnatural', not because they are 'perverse' (a point which the Trinidadian critics do not stop making), but because within the androcentric world they cannot serve as indicators of social relations, of honour, shame, superiority and inferiority. Men find this disturbing. It leaves them bewildered, empty-handed.[8]

Winkler (1990: 188) mentions Greek women who met a number of times each year without men (but not in every case outside the field of view of men)[9] to indulge in hilarious obscenity: 'Both ancient and modern male interpreters tend to feel a certain discomfort at the spectacle of women in groups laughing uproariously as they handle genital-shaped cookies and other objects of sexual significance.' 'What were women laughing at?', Winkler (1990: 206) too wonders. He establishes – and the difference from Miller's view emerges clearly here – that the women in the festivals portray the Greek male as a rather desperate actor burdened with a role which is more than he can handle.[10] His everyday macho performances are parried by a laughing or cheering, winking or whistling female audience during the festivities. Miller too (1994: 123) observes: 'While dancing they continually parodied the manner in which males respond to their assumed sexual indiscretions. For example, one might roughly pull a friend from her wining partner with feigned anger.' In this sense there is a connection between women and men in the Greek women's festivals and during the Trinidad carnival. Male behaviour is ridiculed through parody. *Pace* Miller, I do not consider that this should be seen as a 'rejection of sexuality' or as a 'brief escape from the act of exchange'. A man is tolerated during the wining act, but only like a ball of wool which a cat plays with for a while if it happens to cross her path. Women do not want to copy the macho showing-off of men; they want to provoke, to poke fun. It is a direct mockery of the phallus: phallocracy is a risky business and, in terms of sex, of short duration; 'phallic men are peripheral and their pretensions amusing', says Winkler (1990: 206). That is the object of the women's commitment at women's festivals. We shall note here that since time immemorial it has been customary at official performances by steelbands for flagwomen to hold high the band's banner. The flagwoman does a sensual dance around the band all the time. From time to time she lets herself go in a vigorously performed wining act, during which she rubs against the flagpole in a highly suggestive sexual fashion, to which the audience responses with loud cheers. During the last few years the poles (without the flag) have increasingly been assigned the same phallic function by the wining women in the masquerade. It is a pity that Winkler fails to refer to striking parallels in modern Greek women's festivals, in which once a year very prim and proper ladies shriek with laughter as they play with enormous sausages, leaving not a shadow of doubt as to their significance (NRC 29 December 1990). All of these festivals can be interpreted as brief rites of reversal, like the inversion in carnival, traditionally followed by a return to 'normal' sexual relations: the reversal emphasizes the correct relations. However paradoxical it may seem, women create order from chaos. DaMatta (1984: 235) writes:

... the Brazilian world of carnival gives enormous emphasis to women and makes the world feminine during Carnaval. Here, also, the reversal is perfect, since if men are responsible for mediating between the home and the street in the everyday world, at Carnaval it is women who are permitted to create a utopia of abundance and pleasure. Thus, the social world becomes feminine because it is through the woman that all the contradictions can be reconciled in the framework of values of this society.

(The significance of the home/street opposition as one of the metaphors by which, just as in Brazil, a dominant value dichotomy can be illustrated in Caribbean society will be discussed in more detail in Chapter Five. It is important for present purposes that DaMatta refers to the richer and more comprehensive idiom available to women to express the social reality of both women and men.)

Winkler's brilliant analysis of the work of the Greek poetess Sappho brings this into perfect focus. He writes: 'From the point of view of *consciousness* (rather than physical space) we must diagram the circle of women's literature as a larger one which includes men's literature as one phase or compartment of women's cultural knowledge' (Winkler 1990: 174). In her sometimes unmistakably lesbian poetry, Sappho betrays a deep insight into the ambiguity of the woman, sandwiched between her own consciousness and the dominant androcentric ideology. The heroism of the epic male is disclosed as a purely erotic love of his own masculine ideal. Winkler (1990: 176–7) cites from a poem by Sappho: 'Some assert that a troup of horsemen, some of foot-soldiers, some that a fleet of ships is the most beautiful thing on the dark earth; but I assert that it is whatever anyone desires.'

Winkler's analysis also makes clear the difference in the repertoire of disguises of men and women in the Trinidad masquerade which I have already discussed:

Against the panoply of men's opinions on beauty (all of which focus on military organizations, regimented masses of anonymous fighters), Sappho sets herself – 'but I' – and a very abstract proposition about desire. The stanza first opposes one woman to a mass of men and then transcends that opposition when Sappho announces that 'the most beautiful' is 'whatever you or I or anyone may long for.'... According to Sappho, what men mean when they claim that a troup of cavalrymen is very beautiful is that they intensely desire such a troup. Sappho speaks as a woman opponent entering the lists with men, but her proposition is not that men value military forces whereas she values desire, but rather that all valuation is an act of desire. Men are perhaps unwilling to see their values as erotic in nature, their ambitions for victory and strength as a kind of choice. But it is clear enough to Sappho that men are in love with masculinity and that epic poets are in love with military prowess.

Winkler concludes (1990: 174–5):

> Insofar as men's public culture is truly public, displayed as the governing norm of social interaction 'in the streets', it is accessible to women as well as to men. Because men define and exhibit their language and manners as *the* culture and segregate women's language and manners as a subculture, inaccessible to and protected from extra-familial men, women are in the position of knowing two cultures where men know only one.... Women in a male-prominent society are thus like a linguistic minority in a culture whose public actions are all conducted in the majority language. To participate even passively in the public arena the minority must be bilingual; the majority feels no such need to learn the minority's language.

In short, women have 'an enclosing vision, rather than an imprisoned one' (Winkler 1990: 209).

Why do women laugh at the crowning moment of the wining act in the Trinidad masquerade and during women's festivals in ancient Greece like the Stenia, Thesmophoria, Haloa or Adonia? Winkler's reply is twofold: recognition of the fundamental feminine contribution to life; and a simultaneous putting into perspective of the role of the male. To quote the last sentence of his book: 'Behind the facade of public docility women had lives of their own and, arguably, a more comprehensive understanding of men than men had of women.'

The notion that women have a better understanding of men than the latter have of women, and thus a more comprehensive picture of social reality – is this perhaps the triumph that rings through the carnival hit 'Woman is Boss', composed by Len 'Boogsie' Sharpe/Reynold Howard, and performed by the 1988 Calypso Queen, Denyse Plummer? Here is a fragment:

> *The woman's role we know is a miracle maker*
> *wife, mother, teacher, etc.*
> *with the ability to combine all of these roles*
> *well you must agree, it's a woman's work*
>
> *Cause we women have changed the course*
> *without remorse woman is boss*
> *when it comes to caring,*
> *sharing and achieving,*
>
> *... when it comes to substance,*
> *advantage, performance,*
> *... when it comes to quality,*
> *production and dignity*
> *woman is boss.*

As soon as this song was played in the calypso tents, a sort of small-scale revolt broke out among the women in the audience. They promptly entered a state of euphoria, performed wining acts on one another, jumped up on the chairs and joined in the chorus at full volume, combined with undisguised sexual gestures, gestures of superiority, teasing mockery, and scorn in the direction of the men. The men sat there timidly and cowering, not knowing how to react.

Notes

1   Brereton (1979: 232) offers the following incomplete translation: 'Bakewell what happened/ who did this to you/ I look like a Negro/ But I am white my children.'

2   Actually sung by The Mighty Terror (Hill 1976: 76). For a more detailed treatment of the calypso in Trinidadian literature, see Warner, 1983: 123–38.

3   For detailed accounts of calypso and society in colonial Trinidad the reader is referred to Rohlehr's 1990 study entitled *Calypso and Society in Pre-independence Trinidad* and D.R. Hill's 1993 study *Calypso Calaloo; Early carnival music in Trinidad;* also Cowley 1996.

4   The elections held on 15 December 1986 reduced the party, which had held an absolute majority for thirty years, from 36 – the maximum – to two seats in parliament: a political landslide!

5   In 1988 a band of this kind, consisting of four old men of French-Creole origin, accompanied the participants in an extempore calypso competition in Queen's Hall, the main theatre in Port of Spain. It played a repetitive traditional melody to which the competitors could adapt their improvised text, ending each time with the familiar *sans humanité*. After the jury had chosen the winner, the participants gave a short demonstration of a calypso war as it used to be in the past. Both the band and the contest form part of a more general recent revival of traditional carnival phenomena. The term 'revival' should be used with caution, however, as the phenomena do not generally have the character of popular spontaneity from which they originated, but are directed by the official (state) carnival organizations to promote a sense of national history, or are the products of artists who want to breathe new life into traditions which they regard as valuable.

6   Da Matta (1977: 247) connects the Portuguese word *parada* (parade) with the verb *parar*, 'to stop', and concludes: '... the military procession ... appears as nothing short of a freezing or 'stopping' [*parada*] of the social structure.'

7   In 1970 Port of Spain (excluding the suburbs) had 67 867 residents; the total population of Trinidad and Tobago at the time was 945 210 (Black *et al.* 1976: 17).

8   In summarizing Winkler's argument I have also drawn on the extended review by Versnel (*NRC-Handelsblad*, 29 December 1990). (This periodical is cited in later chapters by the shortened form *NRC*.)

9   For instance, Winkler (1990: 190–1) writes on the Adonia women's festival: 'Note that the display seems to involve only women but that the goings on are not secret. They are visible and audible ...'.

10 Pat Bishop, pan music arranger and composer, made no attempt to disguise the mockery in her voice in her response to my presentation of this image of the male: 'How men are playing mas is how they are living life.'

3

The social and political significance of the Creole middle class and its increasing intervention in the 'black bacchanal'

A nation, like an individual, can have only one Mother. The only Mother we recognize is Mother Trinidad and Tobago, and Mother cannot discriminate between her children. All must be equal in her eyes. (Eric Williams 1982: 279)

In the discussion of the development of calypso, steelband and masquerade as the main components of carnival, we saw how the diverse and in many cases spontaneous manifestations of the nineteenth-century festival combined to form a more organized dramatic unity. This is not an independent process, but one which is closely connected with the fact that, under the pressure of social and cultural circumstances, the festival of the black lower class has gradually divested itself of violent and moral aspects which the establishment regarded as shocking and repulsive.

However, it was not just the survival of carnival that was assured by the disappearance of these aspects; it opened up the possibility of participation by social groups, especially the Creole middle class, who had associated the festival until recently with the black masses which were held in such low esteem. Carnival acquired a stronger and broader social basis, which eventually led to its current national status.

In focusing on this process, I begin with an account of the origin and development of the Creole middle class from a perspective which illuminates its increasing receptivity to carnival. In the pursuit of its own identity, whose roots can be referred to by the terms Creole culture or Creole society, the carnival festival was gradually incorporated in what the middle class came to regard as its own cultural heritage.

The festival played a by-no-means insignificant role in the social and cultural emancipation of this class. After World War II, typical middle-class virtues such as a concern for respectability and order and the imitation of West European, but above all North American, show elements, were added to carnival, both in the organization and the content. They can be considered as an expression of growing socio-political dominance and an awakening national consciousness on the part of the middle class, resulting in the independence of Trinidad and Tobago in 1962.

This national consciousness was Creole, because the large Indian sector of the population was almost entirely excluded from this process, in which racial and national struggles for identity overlapped in an inextricable fashion. This exclusion came partly from the isolation chosen voluntarily by the Indian population, and partly from the socio-economic position assigned to it by the colonial system. It is necessary to describe the Indian group in this connection in order to obtain a comprehensive picture of Trinidad society, in which carnival as a national festival occupies a relative but still striking place. The post-war political consolidation of a bloc dominated by Indians and a separate Creole bloc, and their continuation in the 1980s, reveal the existence of a society organized and in many respects divided, or even determined, by 'race' and class.

The predominantly Creole People's National Movement (PNM) held power for thirty years until 1986. This fact determines to a large extent the national profile of Trinidad and Tobago. As the celebrations came more and more under the control and patronage of the authorities, carnival became the popular symbol of this national profile.

Jamet culture acquires middle-class respectability

After Emancipation in 1834, only certain elements of the carnival of the white elite, which was doomed to die out, acquired a place in the boisterous street festival of the emancipated slaves. At the turn of the century, on the other hand, existing festivities were adapted so that not only the lower class but also groups from other classes, and from the middle class in particular, could take part. Participation by both classes did not yet mean that they merged fraternally during the festival. The groups maintained a distance from one another by situating their activities within the defences of the backyard or club, and difference in social and cultural origin led to a difference in the appreciation of and participation in the various events of carnival. The masquerade at this time was indeed a cheerful and colourful free-for-all, and both men and women from the middle class joined in wholeheartedly, but the women wore masks more often than today to ensure that their identity remained secret, and they preferred to jump-up in the nocturnal street festivities and band parades when darkness reduced the chance of being recognized to a minimum. Parents were not generally prepared to abandon their daughters to the tumult of the street festivity, afraid that lower-class revellers in particular might 'violate' them – a somewhat exaggerated term for what in the carnival setting was often no more than touching or pinching the more prominent parts of the female anatomy. Together with musicians and a few middle-class men, the dancing and singing girls were placed on lorries which drove a few times around Queen's Park Savannah (Powrie 1956: 228), still the site of the most important part of the carnival festivities.

There was thus no complete merging of the black lower class and coloured middle class during the festival. What is more remarkable, however, is that the latter group felt at ease with the cultural heritage of a group with which there was little willingness to be identified socially. History contains more moments at which this class (whose composition at that time was somewhat different), displayed a measure of sympathy for black culture, particularly the black carnival, from its own problematic intermediate position. Government endeavours to impose restrictions on the festival were sometimes interpreted by the middle class as over-enthusiastic attempts to anglicize the colony, which drove them even more in the direction of the lower-class camp. The essence of the Trinidad carnival was unchanged for everyone: it was indivisibly determined by calypso and steelband as the cultural and artistic products of members of the lower class. They left the most important mark on the development of these carnival achievements and it was their ranks which produced the largest numbers and the most prominent of the calypsonians and panmen. The middle class has not contributed much to the essence of the festival. Lewis (1968: 28) writes on popular amusement that: 'if there is a common "West Indian culture" it has been created, first and foremost, by the social classes at the bottom of the West Indian social compost, "the view from the dunghill".' After World War II, middle-class groups annexed the festival, above all at the level of organization, for political and nationalistic reasons.

Who forms the middle class in Trinidad? How did this class arise, and what position does it occupy? What made it so receptive to the 'black bacchanal', and why did it join in taking it over? What has been the influence of this social class on carnival during the past decades? What significance does it attach to the festival, and what is its relation to it? These questions call for a detailed response. Without a clear characterization of the middle class which has appropriated the festival, it is impossible to understand the social and cultural implications of the modern carnival, its position within society as a national festival, and the direction in which it is moving.

Social stratification

In his book on the social stratification of Trinidad, first published in 1953, Braithwaite (1975: 41) stresses the problems that it presents to analysis because:

> ... together with the ranking of the communities we have also to consider the ranking of the various ethnic groups in the island. The existence of a large variety of ethnic groups has led, not to the development of an eclectic cosmopolitanism, but to a certain separateness of the groups and a ranking of them in terms of superiority and inferiority, as groups.

Braithwaite attributes the main reason for this to the fact that the various ethnic groups acquired a place within a society which was already organized along racial lines. What is more, 'the biological division of skin colour played an important part in the differentiation of social class, even within the broad bounds determined by race' (Braithwaite 1975: 41). The writer compares the social stratification in the nineteenth century after Emancipation with that of the system in force in Trinidad in the early 1950s (see figure 1).

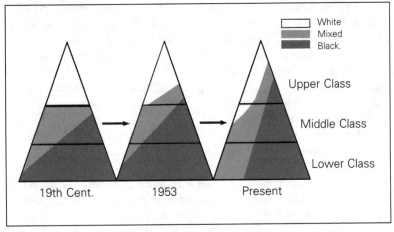

Figure 1   Social stratification in Trinidad.
Source: Braithwaite (1975), supplemented by Glazier (1983).

In the nineteenth-century situation, the upper class consisted exclusively of whites. It was virtually impossible for people of mixed ancestry or coloureds from the middle class to penetrate the ranks of the upper class, which was thus more like a caste than a class. The middle class consisted mainly of coloureds, – 'light-skinned' and 'brown-skinned' people – while the lower class consisted predominantly of blacks. The social order was based on particularistic and ascribed values. There was a positive appreciation of the white group and a negative one of the black group. The intermediate groups did their best to distance themselves from the blacks, while the usual goal – acceptance by the whites – remained unattainable (Braithwaite 1975: 41–4). This rigid division of society persisted into the twentieth century. It has gradually been replaced by a more open class system with opportunities for social and economic mobility, association between the members of the three groups, and miscegenation, though on a limited scale. Groups of immigrants – Portuguese, Chinese, Syrians and Indians – who came to Trinidad in the nineteenth century, do not feature in Braithwaite's diagram. The largest of these groups was that of the Indians, who were employed as contract labourers on the island from 1845. In 1871 they accounted for 25.1 per cent of the total population; 143 939 people arrived from India during the period 1845–1917 (Brereton 1981: 103–5). It was not only their late arrival and a number of legal restrictions which kept them to a large extent out of the existing social system; they isolated themselves from the rest of society by emphasizing their own cultural, religious and 'racial' values. This group was aware, according to Braithwaite (1975: 44), that the social order was based on ascribed values. Ethnic affiliation and purity were the values on which the system of social stratification was founded. This encouraged the new groups to cling to their ethnic identity as tightly as they could.

The immigrants were ranked on the lowest rung of the social ladder by the rest of society. Portuguese were treated alike as dirty shopkeepers who spoke 'rash-potash' instead of English. The Indians were disparagingly referred to as coolies, meaning slavish labourers or imbeciles. The Syrians tended to work as door-to-door vendors of manufactures and were prepared to make loans in return for small monthly payments. Their exorbitant prices, their type of contact with ordinary people, and the modest nature of their commercial activities, associated with their foreign culture, were sufficient to exclude them almost entirely from the social system.

None of these groups took part in what was referred to at the time as Creole society or Creole culture, consisting of a majority of blacks, a small white elite which wielded political, economic and social power, and the children born from the contacts between these two groups – called 'coloured' or 'mixed' – as a separate, intermediate class whose primary goal in terms of culture and social mobility was the white-dominated society (Black *et al.* 1976: 77). 'European institutions adapted to new local circumstances by provincials were soon being used by Africans and their Creole children, who gave them a content never found in Europe', Crowley (1973: 277) wrote. He defined Creole culture as a local variant of Western culture, though with considerable retention of non-Western forms, attitudes and values (see also Klass 1973: 291).

A more detailed historical description of the origin and development of the middle class will also help to flesh out the notions of Creole society or

Creole culture, within the framework which accounts for the significance of the growth towards national awareness and the role of carnival in that process.

The middle class

Following Brereton (1981: 116–30), the powerful white elite of the years after Emancipation in 1838 can be broken down into two main groups – the British administrators, civil servants, English and Scottish merchants, planters and other professionals resident on the island; and the so-called white Creoles born in Trinidad, who were descended from French, Spanish, English, Italian or German immigrants. The largest group within the white Creole sector consisted of the French Creoles, mainly descendants of French colonists, though they also included people of English, Irish, Spanish, Italian or German origin in so far as they were born on the island and were traditionally Roman Catholics, the strongest link between them. Those who had been born in Europe but who had already been on the island for some time and were connected with this group by marriage were also known as French Creoles. The most important values for this group were 'racial purity' and an aristocratic tradition; status was determined less by education than by the ownership of land.

Another, smaller but influential, group within the conglomerate of white Creoles was formed by the English Creoles. They too were natives of the island, but they were predominantly Protestant. The distinction between French Creoles and English Creoles was determined by religion rather than by country of origin. The white Creoles resented the presence of British administrators and civil servants. In the eyes of the old Creole families, the English were mere parvenus who were bent on taking over from the 'native' aristocracy. During the first decades after Emancipation, the white elite as a whole was internally most divided by the question of the anglicization of the island. A powerful English Protestant group attempted to organize Trinidad society on the basis of English institutions and values, while Creoles without any English origin (the French Creole sector) resisted this move because it might entail a depreciation of their position. Legislation, language, the relation between church and state, the position of the Catholic and Anglican churches and education were all at stake. It was only from the 1870s onwards that the divisions between the white English and French 'parties' began to diminish. The relations of the French Creoles to France were of a sentimental rather than a historical kind. They still cherished their aristocratic origin and their 'ancestral blood', but in practice they increasingly came to form a single power bloc with the English Creoles, which in political, social and economic terms was only second to the British Empire.

However, the position of the white elite as the actual dominant class in the colony was gradually undermined by the rise of an emergent middle class of blacks and coloureds, who eventually claimed the right to political leadership. The educational system that had been introduced to Trinidad after 1838 played a major role in promoting this development. For many blacks and coloureds it provided an opportunity, despite its limitations, to escape from the subhuman existence of the uneducated labourer. The middle class, however, did not consist only of these self-made blacks and coloureds, even though they soon formed the majority after the abolition of slavery. There was also a small group of free coloureds dating from pre-Emancipation society, mainly the offspring of liaisons between masters and female slaves (Braithwaite 1975: 87) and of the descendants of French free coloured planters. Catholic, French-speaking until the turn of the century, evidently aware of their descent from these planters and slavers who had settled on the island from around 1780, the latter resembled the white upper-class French Creoles in their belief that they formed the aristocracy within the non-white middle class. The present-day middle class is barely aware of this entire historical background any longer. A large proportion of them originate from other islands in the region and maintain extensive contacts with relatives on those islands. Braithwaite (1975: 97) notes that people did not like to be reminded of the accursed days of slavery and preferred to look forward to what the future had in store: 'Even where the middle-class individual could trace historical continuity back for a few generations on a "middle class" basis it would reveal them in the humiliating position of the free people of colour.'

The expansive social progress of the middle class after Emancipation was however largely due to blacks and coloureds who through their own efforts or through education managed to climb up the social ladder. The colonial government felt some measure of responsibility to provide education for the former slaves and their children, and were urged to do so by the spirited exertions of a few of the island's governors. The development of education was also significantly affected by the rivalry between the religious denominations, especially between Catholics and Anglicans, who regarded school management as an effective way of winning souls. As a reaction to the low level of education and organization in these schools, the government set up district schools with predominantly secular curricula. The tug-of-war between state and church came to an end in 1870 when a system was established which gave equal status to denominational and secular district schools by the allocation of a state subsidy to the former.

A large percentage of Trinidad children attended primary schools by the beginning of the twentieth century. This offered members of the lower class an opportunity to rise to a sort of lower middle-class status as craftsmen, petty retailers, lower-ranking civil servants and shop assistants. Children from the Indian population still tended to stay away from school. Secondary education was primarily intended for the middle and upper class. Teacher training colleges, in particular, provided blacks and coloureds with an opportunity to climb socially as primary school teachers. It is this group which forms the core of an emergent middle class in the nineteenth century, and which gradually acquires stronger contours through a variety of white collar jobs such as those in the civil service, journalism, and the lower echelons of the world of commerce and law. Finally, every year a contest was held between the two major secondary schools in Trinidad – St Mary's and Queen's Royal College – for the state scholarship which enabled two talented students to study at a British university for three years. It was usually upper-class boys who were eligible, but occasionally a bright spark from the middle class managed to win the scholarship. Graduation in law or medicine was a guarantee of relative wealth and a higher social position (Brereton 1981: 126).

Mimic men

Brereton (1981: 128–30) describes the development of a meritocracy which enabled members of the middle class to act as (political) leaders of the non-white population. Despite the limitations of the educational system introduced by the British colonial government, it did facilitate the emergence of an educated middle class and thereby initiated the growth of a political awareness which was eventually to lead to resistance to the government of the Crown Colony. According to Brereton, historians have generally assumed that blacks and coloureds from the middle class strove to assume white values and betrayed or denied their own African heritage, their slave past and their race. She claims that this is not entirely true. While many members of this group undoubtedly tried to deny their racial origin, there was nevertheless a significant number of persons in Trinidad who were not ashamed of it and openly admitted it. They did not want to deprecate their black identity as a group. Not everyone is appreciative of the crop of political leaders and fighters for emancipation produced by the middle class in the years 1838–1938. Unfortunately Brereton's list of individuals from the middle class who are supposed to be outstanding for their political courage and consciousness of racial emancipation is not particularly impressive, and displays a lack of genuinely important historical figures. A.A. Cipriani, for example, who is generally regarded as the father of the anti-imperialist, democratic movement in Trinidad after World War I, was a white. Uriah Butler, the most important labour leader between the two world wars, was a lower-class black. The famous Trinidadian non-conformist writer and champion of racial and class equality, C.L.R. James (1973: 82), does not mince his words when discussing the middle class:

> They have no trace of political tradition.... On rare occasions they would make a protest and, the ultimate pitch of rebellion, go to the Colonial Office. They did not do any more because all they aimed at was being admitted to the ruling circle of expatriates and local whites.... For generations their sole aim in life was to be admitted to the positions to which their talents and education entitled them, and from which they were unjustly excluded.

Characteristic of this class, James continues, was its lack of access to the main sectors of economic life, inability to draw on political experience, and absence of political tradition. Political activity consisted mainly of using 'safe' positions in the civil service to provide direct or indirect assistance to the existing governmental apparatus, or of securing a position within circles which were not lacking in sympathy towards the colonial government. The policy of these politicians contained the weakness which was so typical of their own class, he claimed (1973: 81).

It was the revolt of the labour movement in 1937–8 (scarcely led by the members of the middle class), which provided the impulse for a genuine process of democratization and West Indianization. This development forced the British government over a period of time to take on more West Indian civil servants, recruited from the ranks of the middle class. The Colonial Office carefully trained them to take over administrative functions, and by extension the creation of formal political parties could be controlled by the same middle class. The call for independence did not come from this group; its members were more or less contented with the life that they led, and this was expressed in their political position. 'Everyone spoke of nation and nationalism but no one was willing to surrender the privileges or even the separateness of his group', is how V.S. Naipaul described it in *The Middle Passage*, published in 1962 (1982: 254). James (1973: 83) vigorously claimed that in 1959 there was only one person who advocated independence with genuine conviction: Dr Eric Williams. The support by other politicians consisted merely of the parroting of a few popular political slogans. Still, the policy of Williams' People's National Movement, which was in power from 1956 without a break for thirty years, was characterized by a typically middle-class attitude, determined by what a Trinidadian writer has called the historically rooted psychological dialectic which has put this class in a paradoxical position: it wants to exercise political power over whites, but at the same time it has a compulsive need to earn the respect and admiration of this very same group (Singh 1985: 56). Finally, James (1973: 84) has characterized the middle class as follows:

Their own struggle for posts and pay, their ceaseless promising of jobs, their sole idea of a national development as one where everybody can aim at getting something more, the gross and vulgar materialism, the absence of any ideas or elementary originality of thought; the tiresome repetition of commonplaces aimed chiefly at impressing the British, this is the outstanding characteristic of the West Indian middle class. The politicians they produce only reproduce politically the thin substance of the class.

It was James (1973: 88) – in agreement with a respectable company of historians, sociologists and writers – who located the source of all this in a complex of social and cultural values which leave little of Brereton's attempt to provide a balanced picture intact. The problem of the middle class is its half-hearted position between the economic rulers of the country and the black masses. James did not consider it a conventional middle class, in which strong personal ties with the elite guarantee a certain measure of social mobility. On the contrary, it was totally cut off from the elite. Though probably difficult for outsiders to understand, James claimed, it is a commonplace in the West Indies that the middle class has embraced for centuries the unshakeable conviction that it is clearly distinguished from the lower classes by status, education, manners and morality (James 1973: 88). The self-complacency of this attitude, which is also revealed in a variety of guises each year in certain carnival practices, was illustrated by Rohlehr (1969) – whose view of the middle class as 'an historical sick joke' is equally uncomplimentary – with the following anecdote. When Archbishop Pantin of Port of Spain suggested that the content of a number of calypsos encouraged immoral behaviour, Mighty Sparrow replied that 'it is not a question of too low morals in the calypsonian, but one of too high morals in some other people.' James (1973: 91) concluded his philippic with the words: 'The West Indian middle classes have a high standard of formal education. They are uneducated and will have to educate themselves in the stern realities of West Indian economic and social life.'

The other half of the cultural heritage

Middle-class coloureds and blacks avoided social contact with members of the black working class as far as possible, especially before World War II. At the same time, they were denied admittance to the society of the white elite in the country. They embraced the values of the white elite, attached top priority to education, and were indignant at the fact that they were excluded from the leading positions in society. Nevertheless, this resentment did not lead them to assume any form of solidarity with the lower class, which was ruled out by a deep-rooted scorn for the blacks. To some extent they were responsible for their own isolation, to some extent it was enforced.

Combined with the general aspiration of being treated as a white, this resulted in a tightly meshed internal solidarity, characterized by a specific morality. Powrie (1956: 225) referred to a dualistic cultural heritage – the openly rejected and condemned black culture, and the colonial white culture – which turned middle-class coloureds into split personalities:

> It is this duality which gives rise to so much inner conflict and outward lack of positive quality or personality.... Generations preoccupied with the cultivation of negative personal character have produced the curious lack of character which today typifies the coloured middle class.

Social life is organized in a way that guarantees a minimum of individuality and a high level of conformity. In his summary of some psychological characteristics of the middle class, Braithwaite (1975: 109–10) claims that this ambivalent situation has produced an authoritarian personality, which is excessively submissive towards superiors and despotic towards subordinates. Johnson (1983: 178) claims that the position of the middle class created a prudish and obsessional form of respectability which was oppressive and neurotic in character, and typifies this complex with the words of the Trinidadian writer Alfred Mendes: 'Smiling when you wanted to frown and frowning when you wanted to smile.'

Respectability – in other words the set of norms of the white upper class – was the guiding principle, expressed most clearly in (Christian) marriage. Powrie (1956) provides an outline of middle-class marriage and morality which applies particularly to the period before World War II. Despite the present, more liberal views of these questions, the middle class is still the group in society which observes a strong conventional morality (Braithwaite 1975: 106). The prevailing form of common law or consensual union without ratification by church or state that was practised by the lower class was thus condemned as immoral by the church and the white dominant class (Powrie 1956: 224, 226–7). Sensitive to the cogency of this point of view, the middle class attached great importance to the ceremony of marriage as a precondition for the establishment of a family. Church and social convention prescribed a strict code of sexual behaviour on which the morality observed by the middle class was entirely based. Devoted, naïve chastity was the highest ideal which young, marriageable girls were expected to follow; those who failed to do so ran the risk of social exclusion. In (covert) practice, the impossibility of coming up to this lofty ideal produced a complex of guilt and anxiety among many young women. This stood in sharp contrast to the open display of blameless moral behaviour, expressed above all in regular churchgoing. The situation of married women was not much better. They were expected to devote themselves wholly to the business of procreation and domestic matters, leaving little time for partying. They were more or less house-bound and were expected to display complete sexual fidelity. Besides weddings and funerals, regular church attendance also provided an opportunity to leave the home. Churchgoing had more of a social function than a religious one, enabling married women to meet other people and to exchange the latest gossip.

The position of middle-class men was of a completely different kind. They expected their future wives to be virgins who would remain ever faithful after marriage. On the other hand, they could indulge in affairs as long as they took place discreetly and were kept from the knowledge of their wives. The womenfolk were expected to show a degree of tolerance towards these outside affairs provided they did not threaten family life, although protest was regarded as fully legitimate. In this connection Braithwaite (1975: 106) notes the presence of a 'puritanical-obscene' attitude towards women on the part of middle-class males. This attitude was encouraged by the social system, in which the choice of a marriage partner was determined to a large extent by status. It is therefore only natural, Braithwaite claims, that this situation regularly produced emotional tension among the men, for which they tried to compensate with lower-class women who generally had freer morals. This was common practice. Johnson (1983: 180) attributes this complex to the Victorian morality of the middle class, which was taken even more seriously than by the white elite from which it was copied. The extreme prudery, which converted women into elevated goddesses, left little scope for sexual pleasures and liberties, which were almost immediately associated with lewdness, corruption and fallen women. The 'vulgarity' of the black majority which was held in such low esteem was at the same time the object of envy for its spontaneity, enticing middle-class men to the forbidden pleasures of the dark underworld of the jamets (Quevedo 1983: 23). The Jacketmen mentioned in Chapter 1, members of the middle class who acted as patrons of kaisonians and stick-fighters in the second half of the nineteenth century, could easily take advantage of this situation to engage in liaisons with women from the backyards of Port of Spain (Quevedo 1983: 23). In the words of a newspaper of the day (cited in Johnson 1983: 179):

> ... there is less danger to the morals of the females of the lower order ... from the people of their own class than from the men above them in social rank, some of whom, joining the parties and using masks, take advantage of the Carnival and avail themselves of the facility it affords, to lead into vice and immorality the weaker sex.

A calypso from the same period (Quevedo 1983: 23) expresses an aspect of lower-class female morality that was apparently ignored by the 'bourgeois' comments in the press:

> *Point pour point*
> *Moen si mieux point youn jacketman*
> *Jacketman pas ka ba moen bois en la rue-la*

> *Point for point*
> *I prefer a jacketman*
> *Jacketman don't beat me with stick in the street.*

There is no need to prove here that the carnival festival provided the ideal opportunity to indulge these pleasures and passions. Powrie (1956: 226) sums it up with the following, rather obvious explanation:

> ... the confines of life are narrow in all spheres, [this] together with the tension created by the highly competitive 'sparring' for the few positions at the social and economic peak, necessitates some kind of periodic safety valve. This then is the value of Carnival for the coloured middle class.

Despite its lack of originality and tautological nature, it is hard to avoid the safety-valve theory as an explanation for a significant aspect of carnival in general, which justifies a brief excursus on its importance. The historian Peter Burke (1978: 179–204) notes that this idea of the function of carnival was already expressed in fifteenth-century Europe, albeit by means of simpler technological metaphors. The French clergy defended the carnivalesque Feast of Fools (held on Holy Innocents' Day, 28 December) as follows (Burke 1978: 202):

> We do these things in jest and not in earnest, as the ancient custom is, so that once a year the foolishness innate in us can come out and evaporate. Don't wine skins and barrels burst very often if the air-hole (spiraculum) is not opened from time to time? We too are old barrels...

Burke stresses the aspect of control during the escape of what is causing excessive pressure. The expressions of sexual and aggressive impulses are stereotyped and thus channelled. The wealth of symbolism, the double meanings of the songs, the aggression sublimated as ritual – these are all expressions by which the revellers, who are aware of their transgressive behaviour, throw a veil over the limits of what is allowed. However, there is also control in a more immediate sense. The Roman *sbirri* (police) kept a close watch to ensure that the revellers did not go too far. The same is true of Port of Spain, both today and in the past. In many parts of Europe, Carnival was personified as a burlesque figure, for example a fat, pot-bellied man decked with comestibles such as sausages, poultry or rabbits. At the end of the celebration, this figure was given a mock trial, sentenced to death and buried. Burke regards this literal execution of Carnival as a demonstration to the public that the period of ecstasy and licentiousness is over, and that the time has come for a sober return to the realities of everyday life.

The final stage of the festival in Trinidad, Las Lap, does not feature an explicit ritual of this kind, but the rigorous way in which the traces of carnival are eradicated from city and society in an unexpectedly short time may be seen to produce the same effect. The revellers shuffle and dance through the streets until the stroke of midnight marks the passage from Carnival Tuesday to Ash Wednesday. The festival comes to an abrupt end and hundreds of people are employed in the night to clean up all the mess that has been left in the streets and squares of Port of Spain. A drive in the early morning of Ash Wednesday is an anachronistic experience. The hectic strains of the calypso have been abruptly replaced by American light music on the car radio, and it is difficult to discern any traces of carnival. Dressed in the uniform disguise of anonymous business activity, people rush off to their offices or other places of work. Every shred of evidence has been carefully removed, as if normal life can only be resumed by a collective disavowal of the previous day's chaos. In twentieth-century guise, this long-standing tradition seems to go back to the era of slavery, as can be seen from the analogous description of Christmas ('Black Saturnalia')[1] on the British West Indian plantations (Dirks 1987: x):

> But for all its high-spirited energy and drama, this startling transformation ended as abruptly as it began. After two or three days, the planter was once more in command, issuing his orders to slaves who for the most part slipped back into their accustomed roles. The saturnalia over, a traveller might pass by the fields without a hint that anything extraordinary had happened or that the people at work had ever experienced any but the most drudging existence.

To return to Powrie's conclusion, it should be noted that carnival did not really gain significance for larger groups of the middle class until it had been purged of the worst excesses of aggressiveness and obscenity. Middle-class women did not begin to take part until the 1930s, and when they did so they were heavily chaperoned and placed on lorries to keep them out of reach of the people in the street. Nevertheless, it is undeniable that men took an interest in certain aspects of the popular festival at a much earlier stage. Carnival gave them the opportunity 'to prowl for low flying birds from the lower class', as Johnson puts it (1983: 179).

To a certain extent, then, lower-class culture was accepted during carnival. All the same, down to the 1950s the way in which the festival manifested itself was clear evidence of the existence of two separate, distinct cultural patterns of expression, which did not just symbolize the differences between the classes (the lower class versus the rest of society), but also helped to accentuate them. Popular carnival was rooted in a historical fusion of African and Creole elements and had still retained much of its crude and potentially violent character. The upper-class revival of carnival was characterized by splendid ostentation and a rather rigid decorum as a local expression of European culture in the dignified aristocratic tradition of Schumann's *Karneval*, as Lewis (1968: 33) formulates it. Between these two poles, the middle-class carnival developed as a context in which its cultural ambiguity took shape, but also as an important intermediary capable of reconciling the divergent cultural expressions of the classes.

Middle-class intervention

Powrie (1956: 230–1) mentions several post-war developments in the carnival festivities which indicate the participation and influence of the middle class. The increase in the number of middle-class masquerade bands is striking. This is partly due to the disappearance of the resistance to appearing in public in the revels, and partly to the tendency to the formation of social cliques within its ranks as an expression of group solidarity. The competing bands – a single band could consist of a couple of hundred members at this time – are subdivided into sections to illustrate variations on a central historical or legendary theme. A good deal of time is spent on detailed research in order to illustrate the desired characteristic precisely in a costume. The growth in women's emancipation, under the influence of the American presence on the island during the war, is another factor which contributed to the formation of middle-class bands. Women enjoyed increased social freedom and had less need to be concerned of being accused of promiscuous behaviour if they were seen in the company of men or took part in entertainment which had been a male privilege until then. Braithwaite (1975: 105) points out that the changes in attitudes to sex and the new life-style tended to make the distinction between the middle and lower classes less clear-cut. A similar change in morality made it easier for the middle class to claim the festival as a part of its own cultural heritage.

Another consequence of the post-war middle-class interference in the festival was the rise of the well-organized contests. A serious children's carnival was set up, which was held on the Saturday afternoon before the official carnival began. Individually and in groups, children competed for prizes in various categories (age, theme, etc.). This junior version of the band competitions held by adults on Carnival Monday and Tuesday has expanded to become a spectacle that matches them in splendour and grandeur.

Beautiful, but not perfect

The most typical contribution by the middle class to the festival, which caused quite a sensation in the 1950s, is the Carnival Queen Contest, organized by a local newspaper with full commercial sponsorship. Powrie (1956: 230) writes that the worth and desirability of these Miss Contests as part of the Dimanche Gras show were the object of a heated debate among the ranks of the middle class itself. Many considered that an event of this kind did not belong in carnival and bore no relation at all to the tradition of the festival.

Creole culture, particularly that of the 1950s, attributed great value to everything that is regarded as European or North American; correspondingly, it held everything with an (alleged) African origin in low esteem. This preference emerges clearly in views about physical attractiveness and the relation between physical appearance and social stratification, which are not to be conceived as a simple continuum with 'pure' European at one extreme and 'pure' African at the other. Hoetink (1967: 120) regards the term 'race' as insufficient to describe and explain this phenomenon, since it has racist overtones which are out of place in any scientific discussion. Moreover, the concept refers to a biological source, which presupposes a 'purity' of genetic features which is never to be found in reality. Even worse, its foundations are far too physiological, in that it concentrates on a number of characteristics which are only transferred or changed by means of biological processes, a view which will be discussed further in the next paragraph. Hoetink therefore proposes to replace 'race' by the socio-psychological term 'somatic norm image', which he defines as follows:

> the complex of physical (somatic) characteristics which are accepted by a group as its norm and ideal. Norm, because it is used to measure aesthetic appreciation; ideal, because usually no individual ever in fact embodies the somatic norm image of his group.

This is on a socio-historical level in line with the social constructionist view, which is embraced by Handler (1988) and Segal (1994) in their research on nationalism in Quebec and Trinidad and Tobago respectively (see Introduction, page 2), and is also considered useful by Segal in his treatment of 'race' and 'colour' in pre-independence Trinidad. Segal (1993: 81–2, 107) notes that 'racial categories and identities have increasingly been analysed as socially constructed, or historically invented, phenomenon' (sic). Most accounts of Caribbean societies describe the interaction of transhistorical, 'collective selves', whose existence is taken for granted. For instance, in Trinidad 'whites', 'East Indians', and 'Afro-Trinidadians' are regarded as 'collective individuals, composed of numerically definite populations, which occupy particular social strata and compete for political power and economic resources.' Examples can be found throughout history, however, of individuals who do not fit the definitions of these groupings in terms of all kinds of criteria. Segal considers that

> approaches which take races to be transhistorical actors reproduce, rather than work through, the most fundamental premise of post-Columbian racism – specifically, that races have a reality independent of human invention! By contrast, the social constructionist approach takes the existence of racial groupings as something to be explained and interrogated.

After World War II, probably as a result of the American presence during the war, which brought about a change in the image of the white, the function of white Europeans as symbols of physical attractiveness was gradually superseded by the light brown skin of the native West Indian Creole (Klass 1973: 289) – 'the somatic type of the colored with light brown skin and Caucasoid traits' (Hoetink 1973: 99). According to Braithwaite, the idealization of a light-brown skin, particularly among middle-class coloureds, coincided with the tendency among at least some white Creoles to value this type positively. Braithwaite (1975: 157) is vague when it comes to explaining this phenomenon, suggesting that it is connected with the 'intimate personal relationship with domestics on the part of the white creole group', 'the attraction of the stranger', and the 'bias against the inner group'. Be that as it may, the increasing influence on carnival of the lightly coloured middle class which was marked by many characteristics of the upper class led to the incorporation of a 'light-brown skin' as the ideal of beauty, and thereby to a greater appreciation on the part of society as a whole for the 'brown-skin girl'. In practice, this meant that the winner of the Carnival Queen Contest was always a coloured girl.

It is more interesting, however, to examine the objections that were raised against the choice of virtually every candidate for the role of Carnival Queen, revealing as they are of the feelings of the middle class towards itself. There was general agreement that the winner must be representative of Trinidad. The middle class interpreted this to mean that she must represent its own ideals. However, it was never possible to arrive at complete satisfaction with the result because of some 'defect' by which the girl was supposed to be handicapped. She was too dark-skinned, too light-skinned, insufficiently intellectually developed, untalented, spoke with too heavy a Trinidadian accent, or had dubious family origins. These objections, according to Powrie (1956: 231), concern middle-class mentality at its core. An outsider might suppose that a contest of this kind would encourage middle-class coloureds to appreciate feminine beauty in relation to a form of local reality, rather than following a norm dictated by the idealized images associated with Europe or Hollywood. However, the ideal of a white skin is so deeply rooted that the only reaction to the choice of each candidate was one of distrust and disapproval. Only too often, the candidates themselves claimed to have a lighter pigment and more European features than was in fact the case. Powrie concludes that the choice of a girl who typified 'coloured beauty' also focused attention on the social distinction between whites and coloureds, which was still experienced as painfully as ever.

The prize for the winning candidate was a trip abroad with a number of events in which she appeared as a sort of informal ambassador of Trinidad. The middle class had its doubts about this as well. The Carnival Queen must not be allowed to make any mistakes in her behaviour or manners, for a single slip would betray a lack of education and culture, bringing the Queen (and Trinidad with her) down from her throne in disgrace to the mocking amusement of the outside world.

In spite of all this, the Carnival Queen Contest came to be a major event in the carnival programme. The spectacle in the Grand Stand of Queens Park Savannah was mainly attended by a middle-class audience, with the presence of whites and rich coloureds in the expensive seats conferring an extra air of respectability on the proceedings. All the same, the Carnival Queen Contest was short-lived. The parade of women in evening dress jarred too much with the traditionally highly adaptive festival. It was probably a brief expression of the euphoric mood which had gained control of the middle class as a result of its newly-won liberties, channelled into the excitement of what was new and the attractiveness of carnival.

Even though the spirit of a middle-class Queen Contest has been (more or less) expelled from carnival, it still lives on in a real cult of beauty queen competitions which still function today 'to alleviate the intense boredom' of the wealthy bourgeoisie of the island, as a famous Trinidadian carnival costume designer described it to me. The year is packed with competitions between rivals for the title of Miss Republic, Miss Photogenic, Miss David's Film Vue, Miss Colgate Palmolive Best Complexion, or Miss Caribbean. At any rate, no holds are barred in their attempts to gain the prize title. For example, the candidate emerges from a swimming pool, wearing only a bikini slip and a T-shirt, to face a battery of photographers as she shows off her profile at its best in the few seconds that it is dripping wet, to compete for the title of Miss Wet T-shirt. The press profiles of these girls correspond to the middle-class way of life. 'Miss Central Trinidad', for instance, 'loves meeting people and "partying". One day she hopes to become an accountant and her favourite pets are rabbits' (*Daily Express* – hereafter *DE* – 26 February 1988). There is also a brief reference to intellectual capacities: 'She believes that there is too much war in the world and wishes that she lived in a world with more love' (*DE*, 3 April 1987). The intellectual background is not passed over either in another type of typical modern middle-class entertainment: the female mud wrestlers The Chicago Knockers from the USA all hold a university degree (*TG*, 7 May 1986).

In a country 'which denies itself heroes' (V.S. Naipaul), very high scores are still attained in the beauty-queen sector. In 1977 Janelly 'Penny' Commissiong was chosen Miss Universe (a DC-9 belonging to the Trinidad air company British West Indian Airlines is named after her), and in 1986 Giselle La Ronde won the hotly contested title of Miss World. Although the press referred to 'the first black Miss Universe' ('... neither pushy nor self-effacing, neither hoity-toity nor determinedly "creole", but apparently, unalterably, herself') and the candidate said of herself 'I was really a role model for blacks, for Third World people' (*People Magazine*: June 1986), she and the other successful contestants all corresponded to the light-brown ideal of beauty embraced by the Creole middle class. Little has changed since the calypsonian Atila the Hun sang in 1953 (words quoted in Rodman 1971: 207):

> *One thing in this world will never be seen*
> *Is a dark skinned girl as Carnival Queen.*

In 1953 the Calypso King competition, which had been held elsewhere until then, was added to the Queen Show and immediately won the status of the most popular item in the programme. In 1958 the government-funded Carnival Development Committee took over the commercial Dimanche Gras show and replaced the Carnival Queen Contest – which had fallen into disrepute by this time – with the Queen of the Masquerade Bands competition, which fitted in perfectly with the rest of the festival. In the present-day carnival the Calypso Monarch of the Year and the Masquerade King and Queen contests are the major items in the Dimanche Gras show, in which the Creole middle class is preponderant (Hill 1972: 105).

All these middle-class activities have given carnival a greater veneer of respectability. Later on, it will be demonstrated that not every component of the festival has become the preserve of this class, and that 'counter-forces' have ensured that the original rebel spirit of carnival has survived, even though its vitality is no longer what it was. Carnival has not (yet) degenerated to the status of a slick American-style show, a cultural attraction domesticated and desired by the respectable bourgeoisie.

The role played by the middle class in carnival in the post-war years is important in another respect as well. Powrie concludes (1956: 231): 'The middle class are at last inclined to take pride in something which is Trinidadian. In doing so they are developing a sense of nationality, or rather, expressing the emergence of this sense.' This 'sense of nationality' only concerns the Creole population of Trinidad. The sizeable Indian population hardly plays an active role in it, though this should not be taken to mean that it has not affected developments. Besides, a historical description of a society does not offer a realistic picture if almost half of the population is left out. The following account of the East Indians will also show the low degree of affinity that this group has with carnival, 'the Creole bacchanal'.

The Indians do not count

As late as the 1860s, the Indians still did not regard themselves as permanent members of society. In the eyes of those who had imported them – and of others too – they were temporary migrants, whose only importance was as a labour force within the plantation economy. This situation changed from around 1870, when the government offered former contract labourers the opportunity to acquire a few acres of Crown territory in lieu of a free passage back to India. The land they were offered was of inferior quality, barely supplying enough to keep them alive. Moreover, it was situated in the immediate vicinity of a sugar plantation. This compounding of the system of contract labour with a form of colonization thus had the sole objective of providing the planters with a permanent supply of cheap labour.

The majority of the original labourers on these plantations, the negroes, had left sugar cultivation towards the end of the nineteenth century and started afresh either in cacao production or, more especially, in the cities. Although the work they found as shop assistants, craftsmen or domestic servants – or in education and the humble ranks of the civil service, for the better educated – was poorly paid, it nevertheless conferred on them a degree of respectability which the sugar cane workers lacked.

Agricultural work was generally held in very low esteem. The conditions under which the Indians entered society degraded them to the lowest status in the eyes of the other social groups. Their unskilled labour and contractual bond to the plantation made them half-slaves, a position from which the black population had emerged not so long before and which they heartily despised. In general, the Indians were regarded as inferior human beings who could live in conditions which would be rejected by other 'races'. That this view was widely held in society can be seen from the reaction to the Indian revolt against working conditions on the sugar plantations in 1884–5. The general condemnation of this action was even shared by critics of the contract labour system. They considered that the Indians had no reason to complain and that they were well treated in accordance with the regulations. This reaction seems to indicate that having been stereotyped as an inferior human race which should therefore acquiesce in an inhuman existence, the Indians were expected to conform to this stereotype. This can be seen from a remark in the *Mirror* of July 1901 that agricultural work in Trinidad is not attractive for people 'who have got beyond the stage of civilization that is satisfied with a loin cloth and a pot of rice.' Another paper, the *San Fernando Gazette* (10 February 1894), called the Indians 'the scum of the effete civilization of India', and culturally inferior to other groups in society (Singh 1985: 36–7). The *Port of Spain Gazette* described the Indians in 1884 as a people 'whose every thought and habit are antagonistic to our system of civilization ... a permanent source of danger hanging over our heads' (Samaroo 1985: 80).

The strong Eurocentric view of civilization which was particularly shared by the middle class and the elite ruled out respect for or acceptance of other cultural and social values. Christianity as the major exponent of true civilization put Hinduism and Islam entirely in the shade; they were merely pagan ceremonies. Similarly deprecatory remarks were passed on Hindi and Urdu, Indian history, dress, traditional art forms and music, as 'melancholy, lugubrious and depressing in character' (Singh 1985: 37).

A powerful provincial bias among the 'developed' middle class and elite was responsible for the enormous lack of interest in the Indian community and in the way in which it adjusted to its new, foreign surroundings. From the time of Sir Warren Hastings on, many European scholars and British administrators in India displayed considerable interest in Indian civilization, but there were no traces of such a curiosity to be found in Trinidad (Wood 1986: 138–9). In *The Middle Passage*, Naipaul (1982: 42–91) explains that 'white civilization' in Trinidad was no more than a form of behaviour of whites who seized the opportunity to make their fortune in the West Indies in a way which was closed to them in England.

Superficial observations from the second half of the nineteenth century led only to stubborn prejudices which are still rife today. For instance, the Indians were assumed to be perjurious. This assumption was based on a misapprehension. The moral force of an oath before a Western court of law was subordinate to loyalty to a caste and had little value in the vendetta-like relations between the members of the same community (Wood 1986: 153). At the same time, people spoke of the 'well-known litigiousness of the race', as a black lawyer put it in 1902 (Singh 1985: 38). Few people seemed to understand that the nature of the contract labour system, in which the plantation authorities had so much power and the labourers could merely appeal to the Protector of Immigrants, encouraged such a litigiousness. The lack of rights of the 'free' Indians, which meant that questions of inheritance, for instance, were not clearly settled, frequently forced them to engage in expensive law suits, the more so as the Indian village council (*panchayat*) did not have any legal powers in Trinidad (Lewis 1983: 244; Singh 1985: 38).

Indians were also ascribed a high degree of violence and *crimes passionels* and the large number of murders of women was indeed striking. Here too, judgements were made without taking the background fully into account. Tension arose because there were far too few women on the plantations – a mere 9 280 of the 28 030 adults who came to Trinidad between 1845 and 1870. This lack of balance made it virtually impossible to maintain the rigid Indian rules of marriage, which were also diametrically opposed to the concubine tradition of the colonial plantation culture. The lives of wives or mistresses were regularly threatened, and what was dismissed within a Creole marriage as a relatively innocent escapade was a motive for murder among the Indians (Wood 1986: 154).

Their fondness of saving – a Victorian virtue whose alleged lack among the blacks earned them the scorn of the middle class and the elite – was interpreted negatively as miserliness. According to a newspaper of the day which championed the rights of the black population, it could be claimed without exaggeration that by the criteria of dress, diet and personal hygiene, the 'coolies' belonged to the wildest kind of human race: 'they generally go almost naked and show no disposition to abandon this habit' (Wood 1986: 156, see also Singh 1988: 4).[2]

As a result of the deteriorating working and living conditions on the plantations, small groups of Indians left for Port of Spain, and to a lesser extent for San Fernando, at the end of the nineteenth century. Their new living conditions were even worse, and as unskilled agricultural labourers they had to be content with work which the other lower-class groups refused to touch. A few of them managed to make a living as small businessmen or moneylenders. The favourable employment situation created by the presence of American bases during World War II also spelled an economic breakthrough for a number of them. These Indians carried out pioneering work in setting up transport services in the rural areas and the taxi network in the cities. As a small minority they achieved a reasonable level of prosperity, only surpassed by the Indians who arrived in Trinidad after the contract labour system had come to a close in 1917 and continued the commercial activities on the island which they had set up with varying degrees of success in India. Their penchant for business and ownership is proverbial in Trinidad, and is brilliantly portrayed in Naipaul's *A House for Mr Biswas* (1983).

Inter-racial solidarity – appearance and reality

The effort to retain their own culture and at the same time the need to take part in the culture of society at large, dominated as it was by Western and Christian values, constituted a major dilemma for the Indians and other non-Creole groups. Individuals who grow up in the West Indies, according to Braithwaite (1974: 5–6), are aware of themselves less as West Indians, as Trinidadians or Jamaicans, than as members of a racial group. As a result of the diversity of racial and cultural origins, people feel a strong need for racial identification.

The social groups in which individuals are involved in the West Indies are racial groups at the same time. It is therefore out of the question for any attempt to tackle the racial problem to disguise itself behind some doctrine of equality. Braithwaite goes on to formulate the ideal and reality of more than one hundred years of Trinidad history:

> We should face up to the fact that there is a high degree of consciousness and sensitivity about race in the West Indies, and should seek to achieve a form of integration which allows people to assert their racial identity as well as their nationality.

The force linking (the maintenance of) 'racial' identity and (the striving for) national identity in Trinidad is formed by Creole culture, regarded as the local variant of Western culture, the shared heritage of whites, blacks, and the coloureds born from the two groups. The large number of Creoles, the relative permissiveness of their culture, and the long period of their cultural domination are the factors which have exerted a strong influence on the assimilation of non-Creole groups by their wider cultural setting (Crowley 1957: 819). Opinions vary on the amount of influence of this force on the relation between racial and national identity and on inter-ethnic relations in general. Some writers, many Creole politicians, and a sizeable proportion of the middle and upper class, cultivate the image of a racially egalitarian society, a cosmopolitan melting-pot, in which ethnic tensions evaporate and the best elements of the various groups are combined to form a West Indian and Trinidadian 'culture-trait pool' which everyone shares (Klass 1973: 292). They point out the existence of a positive form of 'cultural pluralism', in which everyday interaction between the groups indicates acceptance of and respect for cultural differences. This view was also expressed in the 1950s by the anthropologist Crowley (1957: 819–23). He regarded Trinidad as a conglomerate of ethnic mixtures in which every group had more or less internalized the lifestyle of other groups, or at least had learned to appreciate them. This point of view, with its emphasis on creolization (the assimilation of non-Creole groups by Creole culture), cultural merging and the development of a cosmopolitan syncretism of various groups, called 'plural acculturation' by Crowley, is also a major element in the ideology of the Creole middle class. Crowley illustrated his perspective as follows:

> While attending a Catholic school run by an Irish priest, the child fills and lights the oil lamps (diya) at his grandmother's Hindu Diwali festival, hears African folktales and witchcraft stories from the 'small island' servants, secretly attends Shango and Shouter church services with his age peers, and eats such radically different cuisines as corned pork, pelau, chow mein, and roti with fork, chopsticks, or fingers as required.... Thus in

the very process of learning the way of life of his own group, he is also acculturated to other ways of life in their various aspects and to degrees varying by group and individual.

This idealized picture of the development of inter-ethnic relations increasingly fell out of favour with the writers of the 1960s and 1970s. There are even a few politicians who, despite the fact that the idea of peaceful integration and a growth toward national unity are often just what they need, reluctantly admit that the facts of life are somewhat less rosy. In the words of C.L.R. James: 'Everybody in public life pretends that ethnic differences do not exist ... they talk about them only to one another and in whispers' (cited in Black *et al.* 1976: 89).

Despite the dislocations mentioned earlier, the existing culture of the tightly meshed and considerable Indian community in Trinidad proves that reality is different. This community is distinguished from the Creoles in terms of religious tradition, family structure, material culture and system of values. The prominent American sociologist David Lowenthal (Black *et al.* 1976: 85) adds a number of other elements. The Indians are characterized by group endogamy, a stereotypical (and mutual) animosity towards and avoidance of the negroes,[3] and a self-conscious pride in their cultural heritage. Although they do not occupy the social foreground as a community, their potential power and influence in political and business circles should not be underestimated. As a united subculture in Trinidad society which is now well represented in the middle and upper class, the Indians are increasingly serious rivals of the Creoles in the attainment of national power and status (Black *et al.* 1976: 85).

In dealing with the 'East-West Indian' complex in the 1960s, Klass (1973: 298) wondered whether the successful resistance of the Indians to creolization meant that they had developed as an ethnic group from a cultural enclave to a genuinely parallel socio-cultural system within Trinidad society as a whole. What will happen, he asked, if the Indians become the largest ethnic group on the island within the next twenty years or so without any change in their desire for a separate but equal position within society, or in the West Indian (that is, Creole) desire for complete integration? Almost thirty years on, when the latest census (1980, published in 1986 by the Trinidad Central Statistical Office) indicated that 40.8 per cent of the population is of African descent and 40.7 per cent of East Indian descent, the answer is less spectacular than Klass' prognoses would lead one to expect. The conclusion reached by Crowley (1957: 824) in the late 1950s is more appropriate to the present situation. Every individual and every group has undergone a process of creolization to a greater or lesser extent and with regard to some or other aspect of his or her culture, while at the same time certain features and complexes of his or her original culture have been retained:

Without losing identity, groups exchange and share members, so that even relatively unacculturated individuals (e.g. rural Hindus) have a good deal of knowledge of and experience with members of groups other than their own. This differential acculturation and the existence of aspects of the Creole culture as 'common denominators' between groups are the means by which this complex plural society has preserved desirable segments of each cultural entity without fragmenting the society to the point of dissolution.

It is knowledge and experience rather than adoption or adaptation which have won the day. The people of Trinidad have learned to tolerate existing differences and in doing so have developed what has been called 'negative indifference' (Black *et al.* 1976: 90), which more or less means 'tolerance without positive acceptance of the intrinsic validity of the beliefs and life-style of the other group'.

Political development towards independence

Lewis (1968: 207–12) regards the period from 1938 to 1956 as a nadir in the (political) life of Trinidad. The politicians were in fact no more than street agitators without a coherent programme, which was inevitable at the stage at which the development of a national movement found itself. They had no idea how to set up a strategy for bringing the mass movement to power. In retrospect, they can be credited with two merits. First, they hastened the introduction of trade unions, which were to develop into independent forces. Second, these politicians from the very beginning assured access for the working class to colonial politics. However, Lewis argues, they did not have a theoretical framework from which these gains could be seen as the result of deliberate action with a specific objective in mind.

The inadequacies of political co-operation and organization were conspicuously revealed during the first general elections in 1946 and 1950, which were contested by individuals rather than parties. Opportunism was concealed behind some kind of political slogan, but in fact it was the racial factors and the cunning skill of the campaign leaders which succeeded in manipulating the voters. Bossism and 'bobol' (a term for corruption which has spread all over the British Caribbean) were widespread, while integrity, idealism and unity were hard to find (Black *et al.* 1976: 72–3). In 1950 141 candidates contested eighteen seats. Ninety of them had no party, and the rest often had no more than a vague connection with one or other political party (Brereton 1981: 198). It was the heyday of the independent politicians without party discipline or programme, who promised a largely uneducated electorate the moon – from higher pensions to more scholarships, from cleaner water to an 'improved' carnival – according to the Trinidadian writer Johnson (1987: 48). One candidate solemnly pledged to abolish dog licences, while another promised to strive to 'demobilize unemployment'. These 'rum-and-roti' politicians exploited every conceivable division by race, class and culture in order to win votes: Butler and Rojas relied on the black unions; Bryan on the farmers in the east of the country; the Sinnanan brothers tried to win over the Indians; Bhadase Maraj manipulated 'his' Maha Sabha (an orthodox Hindu association); Norman Tang championed no one in the hope of winning everyone's favour; and the 'politician' Ajodhasingh made a name for himself as a mystic masseur. Some candidates did not shrink from using obeah to further their cause (Johnson 1987: 48). Many events connected with this political collection of curiosities were recorded by the journalist Seepersad Naipaul, father of the author Vidiadhar Naipaul; drawing on recollections of his youth, the latter has written two brilliant satirical novels on these elections. *The Mystic Masseur* describes this style of politics with the case of an Indian pundit who gains power by exploiting the naïve faith that the rural Indians place in those who pride themselves on their learning. *The Suffrage of Elvira* is the story of the high price which a village community which has been corrupted by blackmail, bribery, racial prejudice and isolation has to pay for its lack of familiarity with the true nature of democracy. In a certain sense, Lewis (1968: 210) claims, this was all the political expression of a social reality, a truth perhaps only hidden from view by the fact that Trinidadians have the tendency to project their atonement in the figure of the politician, to the same extent as they use their calypsonians to indulge in revelling. Political individualism reflected social individualism. The political charlatan was simply the social 'streber' in Trinidadian 'picaroon society', who had chosen politics as his field of activity. This national character was notorious for its naked egocentrism, a reputation which extended to the other islands in the British Caribbean, which themselves were hardly a model of social honesty. Lewis (1968: 210–11) writes:

> The typical Trinidadian was the 'homme moyen sensuel', living 'now for now', ... the gay troubadour of the West Indies, for whom rum, fashionable clothes, a quatro, the races, the thrill of illicit amorous liaisons, the rhythm of dancing and a precarious modicum of lightly earned dollars, would constitute the perfect existence.

Such a moral condemnation is out of place unless it is combined with an account of the extent to which the characteristics in question are the result of various forces which have influenced the creation of Trinidad society. Lewis proceeds to list a few of them.

1   The colonial system traditionally permitted an autonomous and limited form of government by nomination, so that able political leaders outside the system could never reach the highest echelons of the governmental

apparatus. The historian and politician Eric Williams (1982: 281) writes in his *History of the People of Trinidad and Tobago*:

> In this climate ... social climbing has become the major industry of Trinidad and Tobago – invitations to cocktail parties, and appearing in the photographs and social columns of the newspapers. Legal slavery and political slavery implicit in the nominated system have led to a capacity for individual ingratiation with the political powers or the social arbiters.... The pronounced materialism and disastrous individualism have spread to all parts of the fabric of the society ... The political parties are riddled with individualism. The trade unions are riddled with individualism. The professions are riddled with individualism.

2   According to Lewis, the situation on Trinidad is one of cultural and ethnic heterogeneity, very different from the relative cultural homogeneity of Barbados or Jamaica. Historically speaking, the country has not had much time to convert this mosaic of cultures and peoples into a dominant, jointly experienced shared identity.

3   Lewis's third point is the dangerous mistrust between the city and the countryside, expressed in the dominance of Port of Spain over the rest of the country, although he does not explain the connection between this factor and his character sketch of the Trinidadian. However, we can gain some insight into this aspect from Lieber (1981: 6–7), who claims that the plantation system in Trinidad, unlike the situation on many of the other Caribbean islands, was never on a large scale or of great importance. This is connected, among other things, with the problems of opening up the rugged territory of Trinidad, which is partly covered by rainforest, as well as with the chronic shortage of labour in the eighteenth century caused by the low population figure. The most important cause isolated by Lieber, however, is the relatively late British colonization of the island (the end of the eighteenth century), by which time the sugar economy had already passed its zenith. The exploitation of the oilfields reduced the importance of agriculture even further. The move away from agriculture, to a larger extent than elsewhere in the Caribbean, had important consequences for the formation of the island society. There was a rapid development of an (urban) proletarian segment, political consciousness and cosmopolitanism, a sceptical attitude towards work and economic 'improvements', and what Lieber cryptically refers to as 'inventiveness in the fluid arrangements of residential styles'. Trade unions emerged as a result of the concentration on industry and the rise of a proletariat, which caused considerable social unrest in the oilfields in southern and central Trinidad in the 1930s in particular. In Lieber's words (1981: 8),

Trinidad 'shook with violent turmoil as strikes and states of emergency sent the colony into a paroxysm of political crisis.'

4   The last point mentioned by Lewis is the disastrous effects of the American presence in the colony during World War II. Many of the modern Trinidadian types, such as the sophisticated prostitute, the saga boy and the gang leader ('the king of the Port of Spain underworld, Chicago-style') are direct products of American influence, of 'working for the Yankee dollar'. Lewis (1968: 212) refers to the natural anarchism of the colonial society, only exacerbated by the disruptive Americanization. The result is a present-day Trinidad characterized by a 'roughly-hewn combination of British snobbery and American vulgarity'.

Political hegemony of the Creole middle class

A drastic change took place in this political situation in the years 1955–6 with the advent of a new kind of political leader – Eric Williams – and a new kind of political party – the People's National Movement (PNM), a product of the Political Education Group and the Teachers Economic and Cultural Association. The core of the new movement was thus formed by developed and educated blacks and coloureds (Black *et al.* 1976: 74). This time the election was contested by only thirty-nine independent politicians and seven parties with virtually identical programmes, though they differed in their style of operations and targeted different social groups. The PNM emphasized moral principles, discipline, mutual understanding, nationalism and modernity, but it profiled itself above all as the black people's party versus the rest. The main opponent to the PNM was the People's Democratic Party (PDP), led by Bhadase Maraj. The rural Indians attributed the same charismatic qualities to him as were attributed to Williams – a man who managed to elevate an entire ethnic group (see LaGuerre 1991). Familiar with engaging in racial politics, Maraj supposed that PNM stood for Pure Negro Men (Johnson 1987: 51). Williams stressed the importance of multi-ethnic nationalism and solidarity with the Third World, but did not miss an opportunity to accuse the PDP of being nothing more than the mouthpiece of communal Hindu interests. The great leader was no stranger to racial thinking either. In the wake of the general climate of racial oppositions which cropped up in society time and again, he, whom Oxaal (1968: 100) called the 'racial messiah', labelled the Indian community in a 1958 speech as 'a hostile and recalcitrant minority' (Samaroo 1985: 91). Borne on the waves of black nationalism, it was not just the Indians who were a PNM target, but the trade unions, the independent politicians, the French Creoles, the newspapers, and the Roman Catholic Church as well. As one journalist put it, the party had decided 'to eat the whole hog, or be violently anti-pork' (Johnson 1987: 51).

Despite the moralizing of the PNM, little changed in the social attitude of many Trinidadians; they continued 'to play the fool rather than play the game' (Lewis 1968: 224), mainly because of the persistent lack of a generally accepted code of ethical behaviour. Racist feelings proved stronger than the PNM dogma of inter-racial solidarity and even led to a revival of closed-community thinking among a number of members of the Indian political camp. Within the PNM itself, Williams repeatedly had to take action against undisciplined behaviour and the recurrence of all kinds of intriguing and personal careerism. Williams regarded egoistic individualism as the biggest problem in new Trinidad. Lewis (1968: 225) queries Williams's analysis, where the cause is one-sidedly situated in colonialism, but he concurs with the claim that this problem was not diminished after Independence either as a result of the specific class character of the social structure.

The September 1956 elections brought the PNM into the Legislative Council with a majority (thirteen out of the twenty-four seats). The party won 39 per cent of the votes. The PDP gained five seats, the Trinidad Labour Party two. Between 1956 and 1962 the PNM consolidated its position, and the opposition, consisting of a variety of groups including the PDP, united in the Democratic Labour Party with a clear Indian preponderance. While the introduction of a two-party system may have put an end to the anarchy of independent politicians, the ethnic demarcation between the blocs was an ominous sign for the future (Black *et al.* 1976: 75). 'The black intellectuals came to power', in the words of Johnson (1987: 52). The calypsonian Mighty Sparrow was inspired to compose the following verse:

> *Well the way how things shaping up.*
> *All this nigger business go stop.*
> *I tell you, soon in the West Indies*
> *It's please, Mister Nigger, please.*

This joyful announcement of a rapid victory over the oppressive colonial system is silent about other ethnic groups, particularly the large Indian community; the singer is expressing the feelings of the Creole middle class. Singh (1985: 59) explains this attitude by referring to the dominant ideology held by some of the black and coloured intellectuals. According to this 'racial paramountcy', people in the Caribbean with a negroid background have a moral right to political leadership on the basis of their numerical preponderance and of the fact that they have suffered more than the other races in the history of the region. Black Stalin's award-winning calypso

'Caribbean Unity', popularly known as 'Caribbean Man', provoked a lively controversy on this question in 1979. The refrain of this song (Warner 1983: 83–4), which appeals in general to the feelings of the black masses, is as follows:

> *Dem is one race — De Caribbean Man*
> *From the same place — De Caribbean Man*
> *Dat make the same trip — De Caribbean Man*
> *On de same ship — De Caribbean Man*
> *So we must push one common intention*
> *Is for a better life in de region*
> *For we woman and we children*
> *Dat must be de ambition of de Caribbean Man.*

The social psychologist Ramesh Deosaran (of Indian origin) claimed that the calypso was racist because it openly expressed the opinion that only people with an African background are entitled to share in Caribbean unity. In a rather cryptic commentary, the *Express* reacted by stating that people of African descent form the largest ethnic group in the Caribbean. While it was not ideologically correct in the context of Trinidad and Tobago to limit his (sc. Stalin's) vision to the descendants of slaves, the paper continued in extenuation, within the context of the region as a whole it is clear that Stalin's intention was to break through the 'big island – small island' complex (Warner 1983: 84). Selwyn Ryan ('of African descent'), a columnist for the *Express*,[4] wrote: 'One of the reasons why Blacks believe that they are more integrally Caribbean than any other group is that they alone have completely severed primordial ties with their "Motherland" (Warner 1983: 85). Deosaran (1987: 81) aptly summarizes the controversy as follows:

The emotional impact and widespread interest generated by the controversy is evidenced by the fact that it occupied a total of 660 column inches and involved six of the seven national newspapers across the country. (..) As far as responses to the newspapers were concerned, the public debate lasted for two and a half months – 28 February, 1979 to 12 May, 1979. It provided an exciting snap-shot of the social psychology of race relations in the country.

To return to Singh's 'racial paramountcy', his oversimplistic approach to a complex problem cannot be denied some foundation in truth, but in view of the special position of the Indian community, the conclusion of Vera Rubin's comparative study of Creole and Indian young people in Trinidad comes over more convincingly: 'The East Indian tends to think in terms of the community because it is an East Indian community, the Negro in terms of the nation because he conceives of it as a Negro nation' (Rubin 1962: 454; Rubin & Zavalloni 1969: 163). All the same, the Indians were no longer indifferent to the dominance of the Negro nation with its Creole culture. The lip-service paid to patriotism for the benefit of outsiders is evidence of the strong ideological influence exercised by the official nationalist credo. I regularly hear my Indian conversation partner praise carnival and he displays evident pleasure when I indicate wholehearted agreement with his pride – but when I ask whether he and his family take part in carnival, the answer is usually negative. He prefers to spend the carnival period on the beach with his family: 'All that jumping up, wining and obscenity. It's a negro ting, you know.' Nevertheless, Indian participation in carnival is gradually growing. During the Mardi Gras masquerade band parade, I saw an Indian mother and her two teenage daughters watching with interest from the side of the road. The mother was uneasy, but the girls in modern disco outfit were energetically dancing to the rhythm of the deafening calypso music. 'Do you play in a band?' I asked. 'Maybe..., next year,' they shouted back.

The politicization of carnival and the attempt to achieve national identity

For thirty years (until 1986), Creole political leadership was in office without a break. This dominance was largely based on the tactical manipulation of the traditional racial and social rivalries between blacks and Indians, accentuated by the fact that the opposition remained predominantly Indian in composition. At the same time there was an attempt to develop a national culture that could command respect, emerging from the multifarious assortment of traditional and modern elements of African, European, American and Asiatic origin. The main cohesive factor in this cultural amalgamation is the old Creole legacy or Creole culture; and nowhere is this complex model so clearly expressed in Trinidad as in the carnival (Stewart 1986: 296).

Crowley (1957: 821–3) wrote that socio-religious festivals on Trinidad, which had arisen on the basis of a variety of traditions, provided an opportunity for friendship and mutual participation by the groups. The people of Trinidad themselves regard this as an important factor of cohesion in their society. Members of the Shango and Rada Movements (Herskovits 1947: 321ff. and Carr 1953: 35ff. respectively, which originated in Africa, nevertheless take part in the Catholic rituals as a part of their religious obligations. Christian Indians continue to observe Hindu festivals such as Diwali and Phagwa, and they carry out more or less secret healing and thanksgiving ceremonies (pujas) indoors. *Vice versa*, orthodox Hindus follow the French Catholic custom of placing lighted candles on their family tombs on All Saint's Day (Toussaint). I have already mentioned the fact that Hindus take part in the annual pilgrimage to the black statue of Mary, La Divina Pastora, in the Roman Catholic Church of Siparia, and that the festival of Hosein is an originally Muslim festival in which Hindus and black 'unbelievers' enthusiastically participate as drummers and dancers. 'As a pantheistic people, Hindus had little difficulty in identifying with other people's religious beliefs and practices without abandoning their own', Singh (1988: 6, 7) notes. 'It was probable, too', he continues, 'that the Negroes found tassa drumming not very different from their own ancestral drumming and were naturally drawn to it. The stick-wielding "combats" of the Muharram celebrants were not very dissimilar from that of the "jamet" bands that had come to dominate the creole carnival.' Creoles, Hindus and Christian Indians also helped to make the paper and bamboo miniature temples (tazias) which were carried in the Hosein procession. Ramleela, a ten-day dramatization of the Ramayana, features Creole boys and men as performers. They may only assume the role of the enemies of Lord Rama, and the (different) colour of their skin is attributed to their having been exposed to the fire of the ape Hanuman, Rama's lieutenant, with which he destroyed the enemy Lanka (Ceylon). After adducing far more illustrative material than I have done here, Crowley (1957: 823) concludes: 'the "fete" itself, and the drive for self expression and for prestige have obscured the original religious purpose of the activity.'

Crowley regards carnival as the most important of all these intra-group festivals. Since the 1940s there has been a growth of participation in the dances and masquerade processions in the streets of Port of Spain and San Fernando on the part of urban Indians as well as coloureds and whites from the middle and upper classes. Trinidadians are proud of the fact, and they regularly state that all class and racial consciousness is forgotten during carnival. In fact, as Crowley rightly points out, the structure of the masquerade groups is a faithful reflection of both vertical (racial and national) and horizontal (class) divisions within the community, on the understanding that every group is penetrated by the basically Creole traditions to a greater or lesser extent. This is still true of carnival in the 1980s. The various classes meet in carnival, without its either becoming a homogeneous festival or splitting into two separate carnivals, as Johnson (1983: 189) remarks. He continues: 'Instead, the modern carnival contains the different elements united to form a differentiated whole, with each of its constituent elements in symbiosis or conflict with the other.'

The influence of Americanism and Creole nationalism on carnival

Post-war carnival has undergone two important changes. First, as a consequence of the general social changes described earlier, the structure and theme of the carnival-calypso complex underwent a process of increasing Americanization. The American military presence during the war and the post-war influence of the extravagant Hollywood spectacle movie introduced the very expensive and over-organized grand production to carnival. The Dimanche Gras show from the 1950s is a good example of this trend. The producer, like his Hollywood counterpart, and his assistants felt called upon to organize pompous royal and statuesque mass scenes, sacrificing movement to posed freezing. Pretentiousness was confused with grandeur, and the idea had taken root that art inevitably flowed from a full purse. Choreographers such as Bailey, Wallace or Bobby Ammon spent sums of $30 000 or $40 000 just to prepare their large-scale scenarios, which took a year to produce. The original dazzling splendour of carnival, in which satirical, grotesque and clownish elements held an important place, was degraded to the display of historical tableaux vivants, with themes drawn from classical antiquity or from the contemporary world of any country except Trinidad itself. 'Research is right', a local critic remarked, 'but not into the decline and fall of the Siamese dynasties or the authentic choreography of American Indians in a war dance or, worse yet, the artistic canons in the proper stage production of stills' (quoted in Lewis 1968: 33–4).

The second important post-war change, the formal and aesthetic appeal to carnival as an expression of elevated Creole nationalism, appears hard to reconcile with the attraction which the materialistic American-style world of showbiz held for the festival. We shall see more clearly in Chapter 8 how these two changes are intimately connected when we consider carnival as a manifestation of the inner contradiction which is characteristic of so many aspects of Trinidad society.

As pointed out earlier, the nationalization of carnival began to make its presence felt in the 1930s, when the festival was extended more and more openly to the domain of middle-class entertainment. The period of World War II witnessed an acceleration of this process. The rise of female economic emancipation, more liberal attitudes towards sexual freedom and nationalism itself, and the breaking of other taboos helped the coloured middle class to adopt a more positive view of the Creole bacchanal. The new respectability of the event, combined with the morally censured calypsos, and the official recognition of carnival as the national cultural legacy by the PNM government in 1956, all contributed to a further disintegration of the pre-war image of the jump-up as a black working-class activity worthy of the scorn, though in some respects also the jealousy, of the middle class (Lewis 1968: 33).

The acceptance of steelband and calypso in the 1950s was facilitated by local support by members of the elite and professional musicians, as well as by the recognition of both forms of music in England and the USA as unique expressions of a cultural genius that was the property of the whole of society.

Love at arm's length

Carnival presented a 'native' alternative to the colonial culture. It formed the centre of a cultural movement or climate as the embodiment of the political goal of national independence (Stewart 1986: 305). The calypsonian Mighty Sparrow, Calypso King of the Year in 1956, and the politician Eric Williams, who led the PNM to an electoral victory in the same year, were individual personifications of this nationalist spirit. They were both immensely popular, Sparrow for his creativity, Williams for his tremendous charisma. The elements of which the PNM programme was composed – national pride, party discipline, moral government and civil service – were not so shocking in themselves, and they were also to be found in other colonial nationalist movements. Williams's uniqueness lay in his ability to achieve an extraordinary marriage between the Creole intellectuals and the colonial masses, based on his conviction that politics and culture must be combined in colonial societies which are searching for a new identity, and that the inspiration of the political leader must stimulate the young, 'native' culture (Lewis 1968: 213). He put his principles into practice by giving lessons in political and national issues to the crowd in the popular Woodford Square in the centre of Port of Spain. Both Eric Williams and his party were idolized for a long time.

Borne along by the euphoria connected with independence, the calypsonian underwent a temporary metamorphosis from the jester of society, tolerated by the well-to-do citizenry with dismay and condescension during the period of Mardi Gras, to national hero. He became the living symbol of an independent, local culture, and with it the conductor of national feelings. In the words of a Guyanese poem dedicated to him: 'While you stand singing your merry mood. You're singing us all into nationhood' (in Lewis 1968: 223). In the period from 1956 to 1963, most calypsonians celebrated the party in office and cultivated the image of the leader, which Williams had created himself, as father, founder and teacher of the nation. 'When you ask the people what party they voting, they shouting out P.N.M.', cheered a calypsonian (Warner 1983: 64). Mighty Sparrow – the ever loyal PNM supporter (although later on he adopted a more critical attitude towards the policy of Williams as Premier) – sang (ibid.):

> *Praise little Eric, rejoice and be glad*
> *We have a better future here in Trinidad*
> *P.N.M., it ain't got nobody like them*
> *For they have a champion leader*
> *William the Conqueror.*

Sparrow identified strongly with Williams's political campaign. In more than one of his calypso songs he compares his own artistic revolution to Williams's efforts to create something 'from the wilderness of the Crown Colony' (Rohlehr 1971: 8). Nevertheless, in the eyes of many, his calypsos of the period were not always up to standard. 'Model Nation', his ode to independence, for example, was an embarrassing example of simplistic nationalism and chauvinism, telling foreign visitors 'to spread the word anywhere you pass – tell the world here's is a model nation at last' (Warner 1983: 74–5):

> *The whole population of our nation*
> *Is not a lot*
> *But oh what a mixture of races and culture*
> *That's what we've got*
> *Still no major indifference*
> *Of race, colour, religion or finance*
> *It's amazing to you I'm sure*
> *We didn't get independence before.*

Rohlehr (1971: 7) notes a genuine outburst of narrow-minded, uncritical and naïve 'anthem-and-flag patriotism', reviving once again the persistent illusion of the Trinidadians that they live in a perfect society with a surplus of oil, racial harmony, stability, a mystic Pitch Lake, the most intelligent leader in the world, steel band music, calypso, and carnival as the world's greatest festival. Even a dedicated fan like C.L.R. James (1973a: 372–81), who regarded the immigrant from Grenada (Sparrow) as the greatest political commentator ever produced by the West Indies, felt unable to subscribe to the sentiments expressed in the song mentioned above. He and many other leading figures abandoned the 'model nation' soon after its birth. James and his writing desk emigrated to London; Gomes and his large family left for England too; Sir Learie Constantine 'went home' to London as Trinidad's High Commissioner (Oxaal 1968: 175). In his *The Mimic Men*, published in 1967, Naipaul (1977: 8), who had left Trinidad for good in 1950 at the age of eighteen, puts the following words into the mouth of Ralph Singh, the Minister of a fictitious West Indian island who has fallen from favour and made his escape to London:

Our transitional or makeshift societies do not cushion us. There are no universities or City houses to refresh us and absorb us after the heat of battle. For those who lose, and nearly everyone in the end loses, there is only one course: flight. Flight to the greater disorder, the final emptiness: London and the home counties.

As late as 1986 the complacent sector of the nation was shocked by a statement in the same vein by President Ellis Clarke, that he would immediately leave Trinidad after his resignation from office to settle permanently in London. Feelings ran high when he mentioned some of the motives for his departure in an interview (interviewer: '... especially as I knew how much he loved Trinidad' – the *Express*, 15 May 1986):

> ... I walk in the parks in London ... as an absolute nobody. I am completely anonymous.... London is a city that has special appeal for me. It is a city in which I might say I matured.... I derive full intellectual and social satisfaction in London.

The myth of cultural unity

According to Johnson (1983: 193), among the socio-cultural aspects of nationalism in Trinidad were the fact that the middle class came to power, and that the myth of cultural unity, with carnival as Leit-Motiv, was created or further reinforced. Trinidadians, Lewis writes (1968: 223), realized that they could enjoy themselves in spendthrift pageantry in a way which was closed to the 'cold' English or the 'materialistic' Americans. This gave them a feeling of distinction, of being different from the rest, which is the essence of nationalism. Many of the frequently heard complacent remarks like: 'Trinidadians real good for themselves, oui!'; 'Trinidad sweet too baad ...'; 'Where else could people fête like this?', deny the existence of social barriers (Stewart 1986: 311). In the festive atmosphere the opinion is often expressed, especially in the presence of a foreigner like myself, that Trinidad is a free society without problems, without racial conflict, without religious intolerance, and without clashes between ethnic groups.

Johnson (1983: 194) claims that the mythic component lies in the word 'Trinidadian' without distinction between black, Indian or white. Johnson illustrates the myth with a line from the Trinidadian national anthem, that 'every creed and race find an equal place' in carnival, while the wasteful ostentation of carnival was by no means accessible to all lower-class blacks, only a small percentage of Indians took part in it, and a large majority looked down on the 'national' festival. Back in 1965 Hindu leaders successfully protested against an alleged Indian 'motif' in one of the masquerade bands; and in 1988 the Indian female singer Drupatee faced strong protests from the orthodox Hindu community against her competing in the calypso contest with the song 'Roll up the Tassa, Bissessar' ('And is she to be cried down for doing what Indians are always calling for – Indian culture to be part of our national culture, and introducing tassa in calypso?' asked the *Sunday Express*, 7 February 1988).

In 1957 the government set up the Carnival Development Committee (CDC). This gave the festival the status of an official national culture, recognized and encouraged by the State. The CDC (renamed in the late 1980s the National Carnival Commission, NCC) still organizes competitions for calypsonians, steelbands and masquerade bands. However, according to Johnson (1983: 195) the founding of this organization has a deeper significance: 'This was the triumph of the middle class conception of carnival: pretty mas, brass music and gay abandon; consumption and hedonism'.

The British sociologist Ivar Oxaal (1968: 17–18) refines this picture. The core of the so-called Creole way of life certainly did consist of 'dance, drink and be merry – play your mas – have your fête and spree, that good, old-fashioned Creole bacchanal', but the more sober-minded leaders of the Trinidadian middle class viewed this lifestyle with mixed feelings. The traditional colonial view that social stability could be maintained as long as the government came up with the bread, while the Creole lower class could keep itself occupied with circuses, had not yet lost its attractiveness in their eyes. The foundation of the CDC was a sign of solidarity with the Creole culture, but a few PNM leaders continued to harbour doubts about the stability of the support from the black lower class. A member of Williams' circle of advisors stated: 'Dr. Williams captured the imagination and faith of the lower class. The steelband movement and the calypsonians have been important sources of support. But if something should happen, if we let them down or they lose their faith in the Doctor, they may turn on us overnight' (Oxaal 1968: 17). Shortly before Independence in 1962, Williams launched the sober slogan 'Discipline, Production and Tolerance', and suppressed plans to celebrate Independence in the traditional spirit of carnival. If these measures were not taken, it was argued in private in some circles, it was not out of the question that what they interpreted as the social chaos which had ensued after the emancipation of the slaves would be repeated. Belief in the fickle nature of the black mass is widespread in Trinidad, according to Oxaal (1968: 18).

Be that as it may, the success of the centralized Carnival Development Committee has undoubtedly had an important effect on carnival as a vehicle in the struggle for national identity. The national allure which carnival has acquired, however, does not guarantee that the organization and content of the festival coincide entirely with what this committee has in mind. The very fact that the government's attitude to carnival with regard to its own nation-building and national planning ambitions is not unambiguously positive is an indication that the actual celebration of the festival is not entirely in line with its political and ideological aims.

Notes

1   On the relationship between Carnival and Christmas, see Miller 1994: 126–33. He writes (page 131): 'In the earlier sources it seems clear that almost all the elements which are today associated with Carnival arose originally in Trinidad, and indeed in the Caribbean more generally, under the auspices of Christmas'. (See also D.R. Hill 1993: 20–1.)

2   In *The Middle Passage* Naipaul (1982: 86) writes: 'In money matters generally there is almost a superstition among both Indians and Negroes about the unreliability of their own race; there is scarcely a Trinidadian who has not at one time felt or said, 'I don't have any luck with my race'. I came across the most extreme example of this form of self-deprecation with a taxi driver. His reaction to the dangerous driving of a black colleague was a theatrical flood of words to convince me of the inferiority of the black race. His point of view was in no way modified by my cautious remark that he was a member of the same 'race' too.

3   The mutual antipathy between Indians and blacks was expressed by Naipaul (1982: 86–7) as follows:

> The Negro has a deep contempt ... for all that is not white; his values are the values of white imperialism at its most bigoted. The Indian despises the Negro for not being an Indian; he has, in addition, taken over all the white prejudices against the Negro and with the convert's zeal regards as Negro everyone who has any tincture of Negro blood. 'The two races', Froude observed in 1887, 'are more absolutely apart than the white and the black.'

4   The *Express* became the *Daily Express* (*DE*) in 1987.

4 | Contemporary Trinidad, stage of the greatest show on earth

The populations in the West Indies have no native civilization at all. People dance Bongo and Shango and all this is very artistic and very good. But these have no serious effects upon their general attitude toward the world. These populations are essentially Westernised and they have been Westernised for centuries.

(C.L.R. James, cited in Oxaal 1982: 1)

The foregoing chapters placed the significance of carnival within a historical perspective as its successive relations with diverse ethnic and social groups were investigated in the light of an emergent national sense of identity. The intervention in the festival by the Creole middle class has meant that carnival has definitively left the social and cultural sphere of influence of a specific social group. Modern carnival has become a shared national symbol and it sparks off reactions to all kinds of issues from every stratum of the population. At present the festival offers the people of Trinidad an unprecedented opportunity to celebrate, criticize or theorize their own society. Not only participants, but also spectators in the widest sense of the word take part in this 'national debate'. Since the festival and society constantly reflect one another, it is evident that the views and opinions of initiates and outsiders, participants and observers, supporters and opponents of carnival can only be portrayed properly against the background of a characterization of present-day society. The presentation of an economic, socio-geographical, political and mental setting in this chapter is intended to provide a portrait of Trinidad. The oil boom of the 1970s; Port of Spain as an uncontrollable capital; the charismatic and revolutionary practices of several politicians, the product of a people of creative copycats; together constitute the theatre for carnival and its revellers.

The economic setting

American glamour

Aspects of slavery, the colonial system, cultural and ethnic heterogeneity, the disproportion between city and countryside, and the effects of the American presence during and in the aftermath of World War II, have for various reasons prompted writers and scholars analysing culture and personality to make statements which combine to produce a pessimistic image of the people and society of Trinidad, especially of its middle class. As we have seen, Rohlehr (1969) calls the Creole middle class a historical 'sick joke', Powrie has them mangled between black and white culture (1956: 225), and James (1973: 82) fails to find any trace of a political tradition among this group of the population. Braithwaite (1975: 108–9), following Maslow, attributes an authoritarian character to middle-class men and women, while Johnson (1983: 178) claims that their behaviour also betrays 'a prudish and obsessive "respectability" which was psychologically oppressive and neurotic.' In the context of post-war politics, Lewis (1968: 210–11) typifies the Trinidadian as a cheerful but egocentric troubadour.

A salient feature of this historically constituted image is largely determined after World War II by the overwhelming physical and socio-economic American presence on the island, which has already been discussed in connection with the development of the calypso in Chapter 2. A gradual Americanization of the economy of Trinidad took place. The oil industry was rapidly dominated by American and multinational corporations like Texaco and Shell. Industrial and commercial growth on the island is predominantly due to the establishment of local branches of American and Canadian companies. The Trinidad economy has gradually become an appendage of American industrial investment abroad, just as it was once a by-product of European economic plans and intervention (Lieber 1981: 9). In the cultural arena, British style and form were replaced by those of the USA. Feature films were enormously popular and formed the most important medium for the transfer of the glamorous image of the American way of life to the Trinidadians. In the words of Naipaul (1982: 48, 64–8), America is what the cheap Hollywood formula displays. Anything that is not included in that formula, even if it comes from the USA, fails to make an impact.

Trinidad's self-image, and the image entertained by the neighbouring West Indian areas, is that of a modern nation. It has nightclubs, restaurants, air-conditioned bars, drive-in cinemas, drive-in snackbars and drive-in banks. But Trinidad's modernity is more than this (Naipaul 1982: 65). The concept implies a constant alertness and readiness to change, a receptivity towards everything that is presented as American by (usually second-rate) films, magazines, advertising and comic strips. Being modern also implies looking down on local products and displaying a preference for foreign consumer goods, which are commended in large numbers in a typically American middle-class setting by white and (nowadays) slightly coloured models in television commercials and in the advertisements in papers and magazines. The local media are virtually a serving hatch for the imported American cultural and material products. The homes of many middle-class Trinidadians, their furnishings, the way they spend their time, and a significant proportion of their diet and eating habits are direct imitations of the images generated by this Hollywood B-world. For most Trinidadians, however, these images are no more than vehicles for ideas about a desirable but unattainable lifestyle.

In short, business affairs and patterns of consumption are often associated with the American way of life, which people then obstinately try to imitate or in which they inevitably become entangled, despite the expressions of criticism and rejection which are occasionally heard in society. In particular, the calypsonians register a protest against American cultural imperialism from time to time (see Rohlehr 1985: 9). Chalkdust's 'Uncle Sam Own We' of 1978 is about the almost voluntary sacrifice of Caribbean identity to the hegemony of American commerce. The Caribbean has become a refuse tip for American cultural rubbish. Lancelot Layne's 'Get Off The Radio', of 1982, makes the same point in connection with the role of the media.

The consequences of this development, as is to be expected, are not all rosy; they threaten to damage the independence and peculiar character of Trinidad even further. To a large extent, according to Naipaul (1982: 79), this complex history has 'recreated the attitudes of the Spanish picaroon world', in which the 'picaroon delight of trickery persists.' The formulation of such a view may be attributed to the writer's licence, but such a serious scholar and West Indian expert as Gordon Lewis (1968: 225) is no less scathing when he refers to an 'acquisitive society based on the private profit motive ... a pervasive social climate of predatory individualism; which then adds new fuel to the Trinidadian legacy of Byzantine hedonism.' Lewis wrote these words on the eve of an unprecedented and abrupt economic expansion for the island nation of Trinidad and Tobago, in which the 'Byzantine hedonism' was able to flourish once again.

Oil boom

For decades the centre of gravity of the Trinidadian economy has been the oil industry. Trinidad is the only commercial oil producer and exporter in the Caribbean, and has had a large refinery for twenty-five years. When oil prices reached astronomical levels in 1974 as a result of the pressure of the OPEC oil exporting cartel, an 'economic miracle' took place in Trinidad. Whereas the balance of trade in 1973 was marked by a deficit of TT$188 638 (US$1 = TT$2.40), by the following year it displayed a surplus of TT$387 872, and in the record year of 1980 this surplus amounted to TT$2 158 368. More than 90 per cent of it came from oil exports (Johnson 1987: 61). The national budget revealed a positive surplus almost every year between 1974 and 1980, and in 1981 the total oil industry accounted for 58 per cent of state revenue, which rose from US$33 million in 1972 to US$1 580 million in 1980 (MacDonald 1986: 195). In 1982 the country had TT$7 600 million in foreign currency reserves, while the foreign debt was a mere TT$1 200 million (*Neue Zürcher Zeitung*, 30 December 1982). The government invested lavishly in all kinds of expensive and ambitious projects. Wages rose between 1977 and 1982 by an average of 20 per cent per annum (*Financial Times*, 8 July 1985). Unemployment gradually fell to 8.8 per cent in 1980, inflation increased dramatically by 10 per cent in 1978 and 16.1 per cent in 1979 (MacDonald 1986: 194). There was an equally feverish increase in spending in the public and private sectors, as well as in the import of luxury Western goods. The GNP per capita increased from US$970 in 1973 to US$3 010 in 1978 (Hope 1986: 33; for a comparison with other Caribbean countries see Table 4). Other signs of the economic upswing are the remarkable expansion in terms of productivity and employment of the processing industries, the building trade, and the governmental apparatus. The republic was literally flooded with money. Premier Williams's catchword 'Money is no problem' became the slogan of this boom period (MacDonald 1986: 191). Oil revenue was the lubricant for an unrestrained economy, which produced dozens of millionaires overnight.

Table 4.1   GNP per capita, 1970–80 (US dollars)

Year	Barbados	Guyana	Jamaica	Trinidad/Tobago
1970	720	360	590	776
1972	800	400	810	970
1973	1000	410	990	970
1974	1200	500	1190	1700
1975	1470	540	1200	1950
1976	1620	570	1150	2190
1977	1760	560	1150	2380
1978	2080	560	1190	3010
1979	2680	640	1110	3910
1980	3270	690	1090	5010

Source: Hope 1986: 33

'Money today change up so much life, calculators take the place of wife', sang the calypsonian Black Stalin in 1980 (Rohlehr 1985: 7). The economic miracle was accompanied by a collective consumer neurosis, an unlimited demand for non-durables, which David Renwick, former editor of the *Express* described as follows (MacDonald 1986: 193):

> An apparent non-stop consumer boom has put a car in at least one home in every two, electronic equipment in almost every house, refrigerators and stoves in most kitchens and vacation travel to North America within reach of increasing numbers.

The import of such commodities rose from US$860 million in 1977 to almost US$1 749 million in 1980. The consumption of electricity per kilowatt-hour per capita rose by 196 per cent between 1970 and 1979 (as compared to 164 per cent in Venezuela, 144 per cent in Canada, and 133 per cent in the United States). By the end of the 1970s, the society of Trinidad was saturated by American consumer culture, as could be seen from the construction of shopping malls on the edge of Port of Spain and San Fernando (MacDonald 1986: 193). In 1986, when the population of Trinidad and Tobago stood at 1 220 000 (Paxton 1990: 1191), it consumed fast food totalling TT$300 million. There was a chicken and chips store in every street, a video in every home, a traffic jam on every road (according to *The Times* of 4 October 1978, Trinidad and Tobago, the country with the longest traffic jams in the world, occupied fifth place in the world rankings for per capita car ownership), and every big shot had a second home in Miami, which soon became the symbol of the fervently desired, though only partially understood, American way of life. 'Check out their houses, and look', laments the writer and poet Derek Walcott, 'you bust your brain before you find a book.'

Around 1980, other social critics were also complaining from the security of their TT$500 000 homes that the oil boom was the worst thing that could have hit the country (Johnson 1987: 61). Prosperity and the wave of consumerism, according to MacDonald (1986: 190–215), went hand in hand with the expansion of the Creole middle class and the rapid growth of an Indian middle segment which felt closer ties with its Afro-Creole counterpart through their shared ideology of democratic capitalism than with the Indian lower class. The traditional middle class of small-town doctors, lawyers and tradespeople had by now been replaced by a new middle class of what Lewis (1985: 235) calls:

> the motorized salariat of both government service and private firms, high-fee lawyers and doctors, and new technocrats, who are anxiously on their way up, materialistic, full of social fear of those beneath them, often trying to hide their own recent lowly social origins.

A modern sector had also emerged within the ranks of the working class. These workers enjoyed better working conditions and on average a better level of education and organization than before, and they were more politically active. This group soon acquired bourgeois characteristics and became increasingly associated with the capitalist-oriented social consensus in exchange for material advantages – consumer goods – and limited opportunities for upward mobility. MacDonald (1986: 190–1) speaks of a 'middle classization' of the higher echelons of the working class, a process that affected society as a whole during the boom period. It was a general trend: Lewis (1985: 236) calls it a process of 'embourgeoisement', the assumption of a middle-class attitude and outlook, which seemed to justify the purchase of desired (luxury) consumer goods and a shopping spree in Miami even when this was incompatible with the actual financial economic position of those involved. 'Capitalism gone mad' was how Mighty Sparrow typified the situation in the title of a 1983 calypso. 'It is almost as if every social echelon were trying desperately to catch up with the affluent U.S. way of life, which they see all the time in their mass media' (Lewis 1985: 236). This mentality was directly connected with the way the middle class interpreted the term 'development'. A high-ranking official in the Ministry of Finance summed up the period of the oil euphoria as follows (*Financial Times*, 8 July 1985):

> The government ... found itself on a wave of affluence and embarked on a number of very large capital-intensive projects. They lost sight of the fact that if anything went wrong with the revenue stream there would be problems.

After the dream

International recession, resulting in a drop in the demand for oil on the world market, put an end to the economic boom in the early 1980s and necessitated a violent change in the basic consumer attitude. Oil revenues fell from TT$4 200 million in 1981 to TT$2 600 million in 1984 (*Financial Times*, 8 July 1985). The days were over when TT$40 million were spent on imported whisky (1982) and TT$100 million on imported cars (1984). Spending on foreign travel to the tune of TT$26 million a month also came to a halt. The balance of trade in 1981 still showed a surplus of TT$680 million (MacDonald 1986: 206), but two years later the most prosperous economy in the Caribbean was faced with a deficit of TT$2 160 million, three times as high as the 1982 deficit (*Guardian*, 1 November 1985). The foreign currency reserves, which stood at TT$7 600 million in 1982, had fallen to TT$2 800 million by the end of 1984 (*Financial Times*, 8 July 1985); by 1987 they were a mere TT$291 million (World Bank 1988). The

TT$ underwent a 50 per cent devaluation in 1985, and after a second devaluation in 1988 the exchange rate stood at US$1 to TT$4.5. The GNP fell by 3.8 per cent in 1982, 10.8 per cent in 1984, 6.4 per cent in 1986, and 2.3 per cent in 1987 (World Bank 1988). Unemployment rose from 9.9 per cent in 1982 to 16.6 per cent in June 1986 (Annual Economic Survey 1986) and 21 per cent in 1988 (*Financial Times,* 3 October 1988). Prices rose. A politician who repeated Eric Williams' triumphant 1977 catch-phrase 'Money is no problem' added 'the problem is no money'. In 1983 Prime Minister Chambers stated that citizens 'have an inescapable responsibility to adjust our style of living since Trinidad and Tobago could not continue to insulate itself from the reality of the harsh economic conditions in the world at large' (MacDonald 1986: 215). As a foreign newspaper concluded in the same year, 'The carnival is over for Trinidad and Tobago.' A fall in productivity, neglect of agriculture, inefficiency and corruption are the undeniable reverse side of the oil boom period, whose consequences and mentality, 'an obscene and philistine materialism' (Johnson 1987: 61), still leave their mark on the current situation of economic malaise. The sharp drop in oil revenue revealed the structural weakness of the economy. The oil boom had meant a strong growth in social services and commercial activities, but high wages and land prices, as well as the psychological predilection for foreign products as a result of the 'middle-classization' of society, had seriously damaged the competitive position of local food production. The minor contribution to the economy of what had once been a flourishing agriculture is expressed in the fact that 70 per cent of the country's food was imported in 1988 (this figure even reached 90 per cent during the heyday of the oil boom), despite the abundance of fertile land on the two islands. The sugar industry is faced with high costs of production, over-production on the world market, and a gradual loss of export quotas to the European and North American markets (*Financial Times*, 3 October 1988).

As a result of the relatively comfortable economic position which the Republic of Trinidad and Tobago was able to assume after Independence because of the oil revenue, the development of a tourist industry was long regarded as of minor importance. The situation among the neighbouring islands in the Caribbean was very different: the tourist industry in Barbados contributed around 19 per cent to the GNP in the 1970s (Hope 1986: 46), while the corresponding figure for Trinidad in 1970 was a mere 4 per cent (Black *et al.* 1976: 24), which had fallen even further, to 3 per cent of the GNP by 1983 (*Financial Times*, 8 July 1985). Tables 4.2 and 4.3 on pages 135–6 illustrate the minor importance – little growth or even stagnation – of tourism in Trinidad in the period 1977–87 in comparison to a number of other Caribbean islands. The lack of the economic necessity to attract tourists made room for an anti-tourist nationalism which thrived until the 1980s and had an influence on government policy. The government development plan for 1983–6, 'The Imperatives of Adjustment', still reflects the political sympathy for the views of those who opposed the growth of tourism. In short, they regard tourism as a violation of the natural heritage and as a continuation of a form of servility which is not in keeping with the post-colonial era.

Historically, the majority of the population of Trinidad and Tobago have not had much experience of tourism; their generally negative attitude emanates from a psychological complex whose main architect was the former Prime Minister, Eric Williams. Pandering to nationalist sentiments which were rife immediately after Independence, he caustically rejected tourism by focusing exclusively on the industry's excesses: casinos, gambling, foreign (non-local) mafia, and reprehensible servility. Williams was not entirely wrong in arguing that tourism would lead to alienation from the local culture, corruption of moral values, social tensions and frustrations among the populace – an erosion of their own dignity – through the confrontation with the lifestyle of tourists: reason enough to keep tourism out of Trinidad. 'For a long time', ran an editorial in the *Express* (8 April 1986), 'Trinidad and Tobago's official posture towards the tourist industry was one of disdain, if not open hostility. The tourist was not regarded so much as a visitor or a welcome guest but as something akin to a nuisance.' Today it is still fashionable to accompany expressions of genuine patriotism with anti-tourist remarks. In connection with a survey carried out by the Tourist Board in 1984 (Tourism Surveys 1986), sixty-two respondents were asked: 'Would tourism affect social morality?' Sixty individuals (96.8 per cent) answered in the affirmative. Some of them considered that tourism introduces promiscuity and other 'lower activities' to the country. Others pinpointed one of its negative effects in the encouragement of North American and European values and habits in society. The two respondents who replied negatively raised the possibility that the country would suffer from the same 'social diseases' without tourism. The recommendation of the Trinidad Tourist Board was that the public should be educated by means of a Tourism Awareness Programme.

Nevertheless, a change has become visible in the government attitude towards this branch of industry during the last few years, coinciding with the steady drop in oil revenue. In 1978 the new government plans for the promotion of tourism still stressed that they primarily concerned recreational facilities for the Trinidadians themselves (*The Times*, 4 October 1978). In 1985, the director of the national airline, BWIA, stated that tourism was already accepted in economic and intellectual terms, but that 'the struggle now is over the emotional response' (*Financial Times*, 8 July 1985). The government development plan for 1983–6 emphasizes that 'any future policy which makes tourism an important pillar of the economy must entail, as its inevitable corollary, the promotion of national receptiveness to the industry.' In the seven-year plan that it published in 1988 (*Financial Times*, 3 October 1988), the government writes that 'tourism is a potentially important source of employment as well as net foreign exchange earner.' Without any further scruples, it refers to the tourist attractions of Tobago with its beaches, coral reefs and opportunities for water sports, and to the cultural diversity, flora and fauna of Trinidad, 'its festivals, famed steelbands and calypso'.

It is important to indicate the relatively limited significance of tourism for Trinidad and Tobago if we are to situate carnival correctly within society. As we shall see, present-day critics and scholars only too easily assume that the modern carnival is at the service of and is shaped by the taste of (mass) tourism. The matter is more complicated – carnival has undergone a more original and autonomous development than elsewhere in the Caribbean, as is evident from my previous historical account. This claim will be substantiated in the following chapters as well in the discussion of the relationship to tourism.

Table 4.2   *Income from tourism (in US$m) 1977–87*

Year	Antigua	Barbados	Jamaica	Dominican Republic	Grenada	Trinidad
1977	24.7	111.5	105.6	92.3	8.0	91.2
1978	29.5	138.6	146.8	92.3	14.6	109.2
1979	38.7	207.8	195.4	123.9	19.5	119.7
1980	38.6	253.7	240.5	172.5	20.1	151.1
1981	44.9	264.1	284.3	206.3	15.1	63.3
1982	73.2	254.8	337.8	266.1	14.0	197.0
1983	98.1	255.0	399.2	320.5	14.6	87.0
1984	129.6	287.7	406.6	388.2	17.8	98.5
1985	147.8	312.6	406.8	450.0	24.4	99.2
1986	166.3	338.5	516.0	506.4	26.7	83.3
1987[1]	186.0	354.0	595.0	568.1	27.6	111.2

1   The statistics for 1987 are provisional.
Source: World Bank 1988.

Table 4.3   Numbers of tourists (in thousands) 1977–87

Year	Antigua	Barbados	Jamaica	Dominican Republic	Grenada	Trinidad
1977	104.1	373.1	386.5	442.0	137.0	202.0
1978	128.8	442.9	532.9	460.0	148.7	208.4
1979	169.8	481.0	593.7	537.9	170.9	170.8
1980	205.0	526.4	543.0	566.4	175.0	205.9
1981	209.1	488.3	552.0	613.4	110.6	215.5
1982	173.9	414.5	670.2	602.2	93.3	198.3
1983	174.8	430.8	782.9	598.6	82.7	207.3
1984	216.1	466.8	842.8	680.6	73.8	198.1
1985	260.6	481.4	846.9	816.7	142.7	187.0
1986	293.2	515.1	954.6	—	171.2	192.0
1987[1]	333.6	588.6	1037.6	—	242.4	202.0

1   The statistics for 1987 are provisional.
Source: World Bank 1988.

Our bonanza came too easy

'Walesa and Mazowiecki sell you in Europe as white negroes, as slaves.' Thus the Peruvian-Polish millionaire and businessman Stanislaw Tyminsky during a meeting of thousands of dissatisfied Poles who acclaimed him as a messiah (*NRC*, 6 December 1990). 'I have only one wish', he continued, 'I want you to be as rich as I am. It's possible, within a month.' The major challenger to Lech Walesa in the decisive round of the Polish presidential elections 'brings the cargo cult to Poland', the report continued.

> ... the illusion that wealth falls from the sky and that working is a matter of minor importance. According to his supporters, there is an urgent need for more cash desks, banks and joint ventures. Then the money will come pouring in by itself.

The demagogic claims made by the Polish politician on the eve of drastic political and economic changes in his bid for control of his country simply fell into the lap of Prime Minister Eric Williams: an economic miracle which made Trinidad rich overnight. In anthropology the term 'cargo cult' means more than is intended here, but the logic (or illogic) of establishing causal connections between factors which have little or nothing to do with one another is certainly an important part of the concept. The recently won independence of Trinidad and Tobago and the sudden influx of money with Williams as the benefactor were the fascinating factors which were considered to be connected with one another. Now that the colonial yoke has been shaken off, the period of good fortune and plenty is coming our way under the leadership of the *pater patriae*! The ensuing hangover, as well as the dominant mood during the years of plenty, are aptly summed up by the *TG* (24 December 1985): 'Our bonanza came too easy. We didn't have to work for it. We didn't create it. We didn't labour and sweat over its advent. Fate thrust it on us, and, like classical prodigals, we blew it.'

'We sometimes regret that everything happened so quickly', wrote a Trinidadian economist in *The Times* (4 October 1978). 'It might have been better if our good fortune had come gradually, so that we could have planned our direction under less pressure'. There is hardly any need to demonstrate that this combination of abrupt (financial) abundance and inadequate mechanisms of supervision and direction formed an ideal breeding ground for corruption. The medical centre Mount Hope is an example of this political and administrative incapacity. As a result of numerous machinations by financiers, contractors and government, what started in 1974 as a plan to build a maternity home for an estimated TT$11.9 million had become a colossal TT$500 million medical complex by 1986. The high running expenses meant that only a small part of it could be used, and then mainly for the benefit of the elite (*DE*, 3 February 1987). Another notorious monument of corruption is the Coroni Racing Complex. Under pressure of growing social protest against this prestigious project, with the slogan 'houses before horses', the PNM Prime Minister of the day, Chambers, was forced to stop building after an investment of TT$110 million. Besides, it transpired that, in order to secure the contract, an American construction company had paid TT$3.6 million to the flamboyant Johnny O'Halloran, chairman of the Trinidad and Tobago Racing Authority, who had disappeared in the meantime, leaving a trail of corruption behind him. The only mistake he had made in his life, he stated from Canada, was 'to fight cocks and love women' (*DE*, 5 February 1987). Statements of this kind go down well in Trinidad, indicating the picaresque heroic atmosphere with which corruption is associated. There has always been admiration for the sharp character who, in the words of Naipaul (1982: 78), 'like the sixteenth-century picaroon of Spanish literature, survives and triumphs by his wits in a place where it is felt that all eminence is arrived at by crookedness.' He tells the story of the Trinidad impresario Valmond 'Fatman' Jones, a notorious carnival reveller, who announced a tour of Trinidad by the American singer Sam Cooke. Hundreds of tickets were sold, but the singer did not turn up and

Jones fled with the takings to Martinique. Naipaul (1982: 82) records a discussion of the affair between a couple of youths who are hanging around a coconut bar near the Savannah:

> The Indian said, 'I don't see how anybody could vex with the man. That is brains.'
> 'Is what my aunt say' one of the Negro boys said, 'She ain't feel she get rob. She feel she pay two dollars for the intelligence.'

Naipaul uses this dialogue to reveal in one stroke the cynicism, but especially the tolerance which has arisen from the 'picaroon society'. It is a tolerance of every human activity or affection, every demonstration of wits and flair. There are no conventional ways in which things have to be done in Trinidad. Everybody can live as they please. It is in this sense, and not in the sense of the travel brochure, that the people of Trinidad can be called cosmopolitan. Naipaul's portrait of the Trinidadian continues (Naipaul 1982: 82–3):

> He is adaptable; he is cynical; having no rigid social conventions of his own, he is amused by the conventions of others. He is a natural anarchist, who has never been able to take the eminent at their own valuation. He is a natural eccentric, if by eccentricity is meant the expression of one's own personality, unhampered by fear of ridicule or the discipline of a class.

This harsh verdict has to be modified to some extent, for there are factors which could explain the relation between such a personality and the nature of corruption and politics in Trinidad. Stewart (1989: 102–3) bases his explanation on historical factors. Colonial Trinidad was a plantation economy, in the hands of absentee metropolitan interest groups and inhabited by an imported labour force. A social structure developed which tended towards a rigid, caste-like hierarchy and a cultural system in which all local forms and expressions were subordinated to those of the British rulers. There is still a hierarchical class system today, based on colour, origin, ethnic characteristics and profession, but the distinctions are less rigid and the social enclaves are less isolated than they were during the colonial period. The modern national elite, whose core consists of the Trinidad whites or French Creoles, is still in control of a significant part of the domestic economy, but has withdrawn from the official public sector. In so far as categorical subordination can no longer be enforced, Stewart claims, this failed system produces a belligerent social climate in which independent behaviour and personal expressions of dignity and indignation are the usual techniques for negotiating social space and legitimating the existing cultural ambiguity. Personal inviolability and open scorn of and resistance to the generally applicable rules are the guarantees of social success. These conditions impede a rapid development of broad social and cultural solidarity. They are also the factors on which the general weakness which so strongly characterizes the total system is based.

Oxaal (1982: 7) typifies Trinidad as a 'city-state; a tropical ruropolis enclosed by the sea.... [It] has its own authentic "genius loci", its own customs and sense of intimate social and spatial relationships.' With the attention that he pays to the character of the urban culture – a high level of urbanization and a quasi-suburbanism which grips the majority of the population and expands in all directions – he makes it possible to embed Naipaul's caricatural sketch in an actual social setting. Oxaal (1982: 24, 32–3) points out that industrialization and urbanization in Trinidad have not led to the significant level of atomization and depersonalization of social relations which some sociologists regard as the most salient features of a technologically advanced mass culture. With its population of 1.2 million, most of whom have a clearly-defined position within the interlocking social networks of family, race, religion, recreation, neighbourhood and profession, one's lifestyle is still to a large extent characterized by its individuality; people are always likely to bump into acquaintances, even in the centre of Port of Spain. Although Trinidadians often present themselves as slick city folk with a cosmopolitan view, very little of their private life is concealed from sight; Port of Spain lacks the typical anonymity which can usually be associated with city life. According to Oxaal, this facilitates the continuation of the insular agrarian code of inter-personal obligations and mutual assistance, and of dependence on friends, acquaintances and superiors for help in personal difficulties. These powerful remnants of folk community, the product of slavery and contract labour, are among the most important social virtues of Trinidad. The educated elite, however, often regards these 'virtues' as obstacles to the modernization of the country. These problems are expressed, for example, in the omnipresent tendency to detect personal motives behind every political decision; in the assumption that personal contacts are necessary if one is to achieve anything in dealings with official society, and in the conviction that conspiracy and machination are the main operational rules applying to what are formal and impersonal transactions only in appearance.

It is only natural to suppose that what applies in general also applies to politics. If the Caribbean can be regarded as a *sui generis* civilization, Lewis (1985: 229) argues, this can be demonstrated best by the political style of the region. Politics is the national leisure activity everywhere, but in the small-scale Caribbean societies where there is not much else going on, sex scandals and racy political gossip are often the only entertainment that the city has to offer. Politics is an endless 'year-long bacchanal', and Trinidad beats them all in this respect, according to Stevenson Sarjeant, mayor of Port of Spain, because 'it is the only place in the Caribbean and probably in the whole world, where irresponsibility is romanticised' (*Financial Times*, 8 July 1985). But the mayor himself joins in the revels too. The *Express* published a striking photograph of him in November 1985. He is standing in his office, which has just been cleared on the instructions of the bailiff, leafing through what looks like a diary, beside a rickety table with two telephones; this and the stock of soft and alcoholic drinks on the floor are all that remain. A firm of consulting engineers which had drawn up a drainage plan for the city, commissioned by the council in 1982, felt that it had been waiting long enough for the $5.2 million to which it was entitled. If the confiscation of goods proved insufficient, the firm's legal spokesman stated, the town hall would be sold at a public auction. It is not clear whether the mayor is being victimized or whether he is responsible for this 'romantic' irresponsible policy.

Before looking more closely at two other political events – the apotheosis of Senator Myers and the failed coup of Abu Bakr – it is first necessary to describe the local setting of Port of Spain in more vivid colours.

The socio-geographical setting

Port of Spain, the unruly capital

In the words of a travel guide, 'Port of Spain is an exceptionally fine city.' In the words of the poet Derek Walcott:

> *All Port of Spain is a twelve-thirty show....*
> *All Frederick Street stinking like a closed drain.*
> *Hell is a city much like Port of Spain.*

My own stay in Trinidad has resulted in a love-hate relationship with the city which oscillates between these two extremes, but my contradictory feelings are both expressed in Leigh Fermor's (1984: 151, 169) characterization: 'Port of Spain possesses a forcefulness and a vulgarity that are almost pleasing. It is a large and startlingly cosmopolitan town.... In the English-speaking Negro world of the Americas, Harlem is Rome, St Louis might be Athens or Alexandria, and Port of Spain is Byzantium: Jazz; Blues; Calypso.'

Mighty Sparrow wrote a calypso proudly claiming 'pound for pound we'll beat New York City.' It seems a grotesque assertion, but Port of Spain has much of the flair and internal complexity of a metropolis. North Americans on the island tend to call it Little New York, but they also emphasize the difference: Port of Spain is more untidy, lively, intimate and boisterous. The city is a hubbub of noise. Compared with the din produced in Port of Spain, such cities as Paramaribo, Georgetown or Bridgetown are like meditation centres. Nooteboom (1993: 18) writes:

It might be concluded that the city really does exist, but that is a downright mistake. They are decors and walk-ons for some impossible large-scale spectacle or other, abandoned at the moment when shooting was to begin... and because no one had the money to go home (to China, India, Africa, Syria, or Portugal), they just stay there and inhabit their decors with a casual and somewhat insipid grace, speak in calypsos, throw the innocent traveller into confusion....

The production of noise reaches a climax during the carnival period with the numerous *fêtes* which take place all over the city at night, accompanied by steelbands, but even more by the electronic pop and calypso music presented by excited DJs. Those who complain that they cannot sleep are grumblers and weirdos. Street corners and squares are packed with enormous loudspeakers, especially in the inner city; sometimes facing one another, they blast out different calypso melodies at the same time at top volume. There are signs of self-criticism in a report from the *Express* (13 January 1986):

I have often wondered how many people in our country feel the way I do about others being allowed to play their 'noise' as loud as they wish, 24 hours a day, with absolutely no consideration for their neighbours. It is typical of the selfish Trinidadian attitude.... The base [sic] beats in my head like pounding drums, especially while I am trying to sleep. All around me every weekend, and during the week, there are fêtes, fêtes, fêtes. The speaker boxes are getting bigger and bigger as if everyone is trying to outdo the other.

Yet noise is second nature to Port of Spain during the rest of the year as well. Just take a ride through the city by public transport. There is a disproportionately large place reserved for the hi-fi in the usually overcrowded maxi-taxi, the minibus the size of a van which is used to run a semi-organized transport system. The heavy, repetitive beat of the bass tones, which is confined in the small air-conditioned area, finds a way of escape in your wildly vibrating chest, as it threatens to disturb the pulsating rhythm of your heart and brings it up to the same level as that of your fellow passengers. Any form of verbal communication is ruled out; all you can do is, like cattle on the way to the abattoir, stare out from the box on wheels at the world outside as it passes by like a silent film, accompanied 'out of sync' by a serious level of over-modulation.

'Port of Spain is the noisiest city in the world. Yet it is forbidden to talk,' writes Naipaul (1982: 58–9). He continues:

'Let the talkies do the talking,' the signs used to say in the old London Theatre of my childhood. And now the radios and the rediffusion sets do the talking, the singing, the jingling; the steel bands do the booming and the banging; and the bands, live or tape-recorded, and the gramophones and record-players. In restaurants the bands are there to free the people of the need to talk. Stunned, temples throbbing, you champ and chew, concentrating on the working of your jaw muscles. In a private home as soon as anyone starts to talk the radio is turned on. It must be loud, loud. If there are more than three, dancing will begin. Sweat-sweat-dance-dance-sweat. Loud, loud, louder. If the radio isn't powerful enough, a passing steel band will be invited in. Jump-jump-sweat-sweat-jump. In every house a radio or rediffusion set is on.

Port of Spain extends eastward from the Gulf of Paria, which separates Trinidad from Venezuela, to the deepest valleys of the steeply rising northern mountain chain, covered with tropical forest, which implacably marks the border. Most of the city is on the level, but towards the east, north and north-west it becomes more hilly. These slopes accommodate the illegal colonists, some of them migrants from the other islands, in slums. In the rainy season the hills which partly enclose the city are bathed in a beautiful emerald green, regularly and exuberantly interrupted by the bright red of the Flamboyant and Immortelle and the yellow-gold of the Poui. In the dry season the relentless sun turns Port of Spain into a dusty, grey-brown oven, as the radiated heat from corrugated iron roofs and concrete buildings postpones the cool of the night to the early morning. The smouldering forest fires which suddenly flare up on the slopes of the hills deposit smoke ash on the city from time to time; at night this fiery encirclement creates an oppressive atmosphere, with the sound of exploding bamboo carrying far in the distance. This is the setting for Naipaul's drama *Guerrillas* (1975), based on the true story of Michael X or Abdul Malik, which makes it clear how far a revolutionary spirit can degenerate into romantic demagogy. Fortunately, the rainy season is longer than the dry season. A couple of heavy showers are enough to transform the many parks, squares and gardens of the city in record time into green oases with a wealth of tropical greenery.

Half of the people of Trinidad live in Port of Spain or the outskirts in the so-called East-West corridor. This extends from the foothills of the northern mountain range for about 35 km from Chaguaramas in the west to Arima in the east. A large percentage of this half lives in the city itself or in the outlying townships of Diego Martin, Morvant, Barataria or San Juan. With the development of the inner city area into a centre for commerce, government and entertainment, the residents have moved out to suburbs such as Laventille, Belmont, Woodbrook, Newtown, St Claire, St James, Cascade, St Ann's and Ellerslie Park. The centre of the city is a mass of shops, offices, modern boutiques, oriental bazaars, cinemas, night clubs, brothels and Indian, Creole and Chinese restaurants, interrupted here and there by slum housing and demolition areas, which are often used as car parks for Trinidad's enormous volume of vehicles. The heavy traffic can hardly move through a labyrinth of semi-illegal street stalls, where ghetto-blasters set among the wares compete with one another with deafening calypso and pop music. The vendors of fake brand watches, T-shirts and sunglasses, peanuts, coconut milk, chicken and chips, and Indian roti are generally young saga boys, their Rasta dreadlocks tucked away under brightly coloured woollen caps. In some parts of the city boxwood shopping centres have arisen without any permit or facilities – the most famous is the People's Mall in Frederick Street – where the same kind of vendors try to peddle all kinds of bric-à-brac in the stifling atmosphere of incense combined with a high decibel level. Behind these formal and informal street façades, hidden from the view of the unsuspecting tourist or outsider, are the impoverished backyards, the haunts of the poorest people in the city – though they are probably better off than the growing numbers of homeless who live on the pavement. As a result of the absence of urban ghettoes, these urban nomads have spread over the inner city streets with their heavy traffic and street lighting. All of these people, who live in miserable circumstances and whose behaviour and (often mutilated) physical appearance offend the cityfolk, are labelled as vagrants. The public debate on the problem ignores the social background and differentiation of the phenomenon, which includes not only drifters, homeless and evicted people, but also a large number of mentally ill from the St Ann's psychiatric clinic, which is forced to be an open institution from lack of space and funds. It is tempting to shift the responsibility outside society by calling upon the police and the government to remove these people 'with hate and malice in their eyes' from the streets of Port of Spain, 'not just because they can obstruct the plans of the Tourist Board to develop tourism by frightening away visitors, but because they are a genuine threat to public safety' (the *Express*, 11 February 1985). The purely cynical annoyance which the phenomenon usually provokes can be seen from a photographic series in the *Evening News*, not a representative of the gutter press. For months this newspaper printed a photo of a vagrant every day. For instance, on 5 February 1985 it published a photo of a half-naked negro, lying on the pavement and staring rather woodenly into the lens, under the caption: 'Horror no. 185'.

The inner area of Port of Spain displays the typical characteristics of a city centre: shoppers, clerical workers and a lot of traffic in the daytime, but not many people at night; a gradual but steady migration to the suburbs (although this is compensated to some extent by newcomers and transmigrants); a continuing deterioration of the housing sector; and rapid change in the types of buildings and their uses, combined with a concentration of newly constructed buildings (see Lieber 1981: 23).

The grid-like arrangement of the streets devised by the Spanish gives the untidy city a structure which is easy to grasp and functions as a system of co-ordinates which confer some semblance of order on the ratatouille of architectural styles and forms. Old-fashioned Caribbean gingerbread houses, modern offices, Gothic cathedrals, Hindu temples and Muslim mosques are juxtaposed with rickety stalls and run-down chipboard shop fronts which tell the story of Trinidad's past, independence and amazing though short-lived prosperity. Many of the architectural motifs of Port of Spain betray French influence, especially the metal filigree work with which the balconies are ornamented. The English influence can be seen in the serene parks and gardens and their sense of pompous dignity in the style of the public buildings. The commercial heart of the city is American in style. Its literal and metaphorical peak at present is formed by the Financial Complex, a pair of skyscrapers, Twintowers, which cost TT$400 million and which house the Ministry of Finance and the Central Bank of Trinidad and Tobago. The best way to gain an impression of this urban mosaic is to take a trip in one of the hundreds of route taxis. On my daily drive back from the city centre to the Hillcrest Haven Guesthouse where I was staying, I passed the largest and most famous park in the city, Queen's Park Savannah, which is surrounded by the most striking buildings. The architecture varies from a Scottish castle to a Moorish house and offers a fascinating cross-section of the cultural influences and dominant fashions from the beginning of the century in particular. To the west of the Savannah, Maraval Road is flanked by the Magnificent Seven or The Queens of the Bands. These seven pseudo-castles with romantic names such as Killarney, Roomor and Mille Fleurs display a bizarre combination of Baroque, Rococo, Gothic, Romanesque and Venetian styles. Six of them were built in 1904 by wealthy plantation owners (cocoa was very profitable at the time) as an expression of their stylish way of life, resulting in what was probably unintended extravagance. The largest of the seven monuments, Queen's Royal College, a building in German renaissance style dating from 1857, is the prestigious boys' secondary school whose past pupils include Eric Williams and Vidia S. Naipaul.

There is another reason for taking a route taxi. These are luxurious American and Japanese cars which maintain irregular services all over the city (as well as outside it) for a fixed rate (TT$2 in 1988). Unlike the maxi-taxi, this mode of transport has not yet fallen victim to the culture of noise. Though accompanied by the inevitable background sounds of a radio or cassette recorder, a ride in a route taxi provides an excellent opportunity to keep abreast of the latest gossip. It often happens that a brief political debate arises, which may take surprising turns in the course of the relay of passengers who get in and out during the ride. The route taxi (and the driver as my most important informant) is the microcosmic embodiment of Port of Spain life, in which 'all the strands of Trinidad and Tobago's multicolored fabric are tangled in a knot ..., providing constant interest, confusion and conflicting images' (Mills 1987: 123).

The character of the districts or neighbourhoods of Port of Spain, which do not form administrative units, is determined by a combination of classes and ethnic groups, with some components ranking above others in importance. Belmont, the densely populated neighbourhood to the east of the Savannah, is dominated by blacks from the 'respectable' working class and lower middle class. In the late nineteenth century (from about 1870) this part of the city was the home of African Rada, Ibo, Congo and Mandingo groups, and there is still an active Rada religious community there today. St Anns, situated in a deep valley between the foothills of the northern mountain range, contains a variety of classes and ethnic segments. Cascade forms a middle-class community within the neighbourhood, while the steep slopes have been taken over by semi-rural occupiers, and the economic elite of the country have built their residences on a big hill to the west of the valley. Woodbrook and Newtown to the west and north-west of the centre are enclaves of the lower middle class, where the homes of those who are reasonably well off contrast with those of the poor. The neighbourhood also contains large numbers of Portuguese, Chinese and above all 'Syrians' (as all migrants from the Middle East are called). St Claire and Ellerslie Park are the home of the *crème de la crème* of the Trinidad elite. St James, with a reputation for crime and violence among outsiders, especially blacks, is largely populated by Indians, who live on friendly terms with blacks in the neighbourhood 'in almost complete "inter-racial harmony"', according to Oxaal (1968: 21). This is where the Hosay Festival is held each year; though originally an Islamic festival, it now includes blacks among the participants. East Dry River, on the south-east border of the centre, is the district of the large Afro-American lower class, and can in many respects be regarded as the political and cultural centre of black Trinidad. After Independence it was the ideological base of the People's National Movement, but today it is more of a bulwark of bitter opposition to this party and its policies. Further to the east is Laventille, a very poor neighbourhood with a high concentration of unemployed and thousands of immigrants, many of them illegal, from the nearby islands. East Dry River, but especially Laventille, is regarded as the birthplace of the steelband, and in the 1950s it was the base for the street gangs associated with famous bands like the Desperadoes or Renegades, which were frequently involved in territorial battles. This entire area is now usually referred to as 'behind the bridge' (over St Ann's River, which is dry most of the year and has been channelled through a concrete river bed) – which means more or less 'the wrong side of the tracks' (Oxaal 1968: 19).

Lieber's study (1981: 14–32) of Afro-American culture in urban Trinidad indicates that, although the districts and suburbs of Port of Spain are characterized by a particular social category, this has not led to the formation of class ghettoes or racial and ethnic segregation. He quotes the example of Diego Martin, a rapidly developing residential area to the west of the city with dispersed housing estates for the upwardly mobile middle class alternating with places where squatters live. He calls this one of the juxtapositions of modern Trinidad (1981: 28):

> Squeezed in among what otherwise would be a uniformly bourgeois preserve, live (much to the dismay of the city's respectable escapees) clusters of squatters who grow their crops on tiny tracts of unpopulated land, usually a few miles from where they reside – modern and traditional Trinidad living cheek by jowl.

At first sight, he continues, East Dry River and Laventille seem to be no more than depressing slum neighbourhoods, but in fact they are also the homes of middle-class blacks who are insensitive to the bourgeois exodus to the better neighbourhoods. The same goes for the squatter districts of Shantytown and LaBasse to the south-east of the city beside the swampy banks of the Gulf of Paria, where for the most part blacks live together with impoverished Indian migrants.

Lieber (1981: 29) considers it typical of Port of Spain that people live cheek by jowl; as a result of the concentration and social fluidity of a polyethnic population in a limited area, the city residents regularly encounter one another, enabling them to study the behaviour and style of other ethnic groups than their own at close quarters.

Sociological analysis of the position of the various groups in society and of their level of integration is largely focused on two views, especially in the case of the complex situation in the Caribbean. Braithwaite (1954, 1960, 1975) and R.T. Smith (1956) for example, follow the consensual approach or the structural-functional theory of the stratification school, which assumes that internal cultural differences are subordinate to the national institutions, which exert a widespread influence on society. Society has a heterogeneous but not necessarily plural character, in the sense of consisting of essentially separate sections. M.G. Smith (1965, 1967, 1971, 1974, 1984, 1991) and LaGuerre (1975, 1982, 1988, 1991) represent the pluralist approach or the plural society school, in which society is viewed as an entity consisting of essentially separate cultural systems, with national government set above them. The level of integration is low. Pluralists emphasize institutional and organizational differences, conflicts and rivalry between groups and classes, and coercion from above. Yelvington (1993: 15) mentions a third approach to explain Caribbean society, namely the plantation society school. Theorists of this view (e.g. Mintz, 1959; Rubin, 1960; Williams, 1960; Best, 1968) 'emphasise that the society's social relations were shaped by the plantation economy and argue that those relations have not really changed since the days of slavery and indenture.'

In terms of the opposition between plural and consensual society,

Lieber (1981: 31) claims that there is no question of a symbiotic or compatible relation or fusion between the two main groups or cultures in Port of Spain – that is between the blacks and the Indians. Instead, he refers to the 'Negrofication' of the Indians, as well as the Americanization of both groups. In other words, a Creole style develops with virtually complete exclusion of Indian elements. 'The visibility of a wide variety of "different" behavior and display', Lieber concludes (1981: 30), 'is a key ingredient of the culture of the city.' Following Lynch (1960: 9), he considers that Port of Spain is characterized by a 'crisply legible imageability'. He continues with a somewhat cryptic explanation (Lieber 1981: 18–19) which the Lieberian manner of expression renders difficult to paraphrase:

> The composites of the cityscape are organized so that the mind easily transforms the physical design of the city into coherent images which facilitate recognition of the city's topographical features and structures, and allow for fluid and knowledgeable movement within its confines.... Such facilities make it possible to regard the city as an arena which residents can explore and apprehend, rather than one which engulfs them in an unpredictable formlessness. Port-of-Spain, as such a setting, is marked by an abundance of visually stimulating nodes – parks, squares, buildings, intersections – as well as more generalized structural features. ... These features make the city a place which is relatively easy to 'feel' structurally and to move around in knowingly.

What Lieber means precisely here has perhaps already been put into words in my sketch of Port of Spain. To throw more light on his typification, I shall conclude my outline of Port of Spain by focusing on the two most important public spaces and pre-eminently 'visually stimulating nodes' in the city: Queen's Park Savannah and Woodford Square.

QUEEN'S PARK SAVANNAH

A large part of the city area, eighty-one hectares, is occupied by the Savannah, which extends in the north to the Botanical Gardens and the Emperor Valley Zoo. The Savannah has been called the 'world's biggest roundabout' because all the traffic races around it in a single direction without encountering many obstacles. In many respects this park is the centre of the city, with a Trinidad Turf Club racing course (horse-racing is the most popular form of gambling in Trinidad) and numerous sports fields for cricket and football. A wide variety of public activities take place on the edge. At sunset during the week, numerous joggers can be seen pitting themselves against the size of the park. Sunday is traditionally the day for residents of Port of Spain to saunter through the Savannah and treat children to an ice-cream, or to hang around in groups and enjoy a good view of the medley of activities and situations from a strategic position. Musicians meet here to practise or perform, and children play all over the place. One of their favourite sports is flying kites, and in the dry season the sky is studded with Madbull Kites (for aerial battles), birds, fish and other fantastic creations. Dozens of stalls are set up along the gravelled paths on the perimeter of the park, selling all kinds of Indian and Creole delicacies. At night these stalls are also meeting places for couples out for romance and for prostitutes, who keep a distance until they hook their bait and disappear into the park with it. The edge of the park is illuminated by the traffic and the vendors' stalls, but inside it is pitch dark and the bustle of the city soon dies down. It is a pleasure ground for paid and unpaid sex, but it is also the stamping ground of thieves and rapists; crossing the Savannah at night almost inevitably involves some embarrassing or violent confrontation with somebody or other.

Queen's Park Savannah is the setting where all the important carnival events eventually come together. The finals of the various competitions are held on a huge, long and narrow platform (4 300 sq m) between the stands of the equestrian sports club, the Grand Stand and the North Stand, during the last week of the carnival period.

WOODFORD SQUARE

Woodford Square is for the ideologically, politically and religiously deliberating part of the nation what the Savannah is for sporting, recreating and carnival-celebrating Trinidad: Trinidad's version of London's Hyde Park Corner. Named after a nineteenth-century British governor, Woodford Square is situated in the heart of the inner city. Surrounded by official repositories of religious and secular authority – the Anglican Trinity Cathedral, the Red House (the parliament building), the Hall of Justice, the Public Library, and the City Hall – and shaded by trees against the tropical sun, Woodford Square is the traditional centre of political agitation, action and ideological expression. In 1903 it was the scene of a large-scale protest against the increased water rates which turned into a riot; parliament went up in flames and seventeen people were killed (Mills 1987: 133; D.R. Hill 1993: 52–5). In 1970 it was the political focus of Black Power protest, climaxing in a massive funeral ceremony in memory of a member of the movement who had been shot by police.[1] It had also been the scene of previous mass demonstrations of the People's National Movement; it was at these demonstrations that the leader of the party, Dr Eric Williams – professor of history, brilliant speaker and political strategist – gave his famous lectures on Trinidadian history and developed his plans for the future of the country. In 1955 Williams named the square University of

Woodford Square because of its traditional role as a forum for many leading politicians. It was in the context of this development, according to Lieber (1981: 18), that he consolidated his role as national symbol and political wizard: 'He brought a politically attuned sophistication to Port of Spain's proletariat, whose prior exposure to education had amounted to little more than an assortment of trivial British homilies.' However, the promises of the University proved to be in vain, the seed Williams had sown turned out to yield different fruits from those he had expected, and in the 1960s and 1970s the square increasingly became an arena for anti-government and anti-PNM demonstrations.

Serving as a large meeting place for all kinds of political opposition groups is not the only function of the square. As the product of a wide range of fragmentary and diverse social conventions which coincide in Port of Spain, Woodford Square is a meeting place or assembly point for everything the city has to offer in the way of deviants and eccentrics whose only relation to one another lies precisely in the lack of an unequivocal social convention – Naipaul's idea of Trinidadians as cosmopolitans (see page 138). At almost every hour of the day the square accommodates a colourful assortment of lay preachers, self-made political commentators, prophets of doom, cabbalists, scribes, Rasta and Black Power renegades, oracle-mongers and Spiritual Baptists, each of whom usually manage to attract a predominantly male audience of a couple of dozen. Speakers on social and political themes challenge bystanders to denounce and counter their arguments, and heated exchanges are treated with roaring laughs of approval or lead to separate discussions on the fringe of the group. These verbal battles are almost invariably accompanied by the picong style of sparkling repartee which attracts admiration for its brilliance and cannot be regarded as insulting. Speakers know that they must be on their mettle if they are not to be made to pay by the biting humour of the audience's comments (Oxaal 1968: 21). As Lewis says (1985: 229–30):

> Grand oratory flourishes, for West Indian politics are nothing but oral ... these are the West Indian 'men of words' responding to the unlettered West Indian crowd eager to appreciate any display of 'learning' that the orator can show, all the better if accompanied with a few Latin tags or bookish allusions.

The following reminiscence may serve as an illustration. One of the many incidents I recall which took place in the square, which I visited almost every day, was the appearance of Aldwin Primus, former leader of the Black Panther movement in Trinidad and one of the protagonists in the 1970 Black Power revolt. On 4 March 1970 he addressed a crowd of ten thousand which was preparing for a large protest march from Woodford Square to Shanty Town. He told the demonstrators that what was happening that afternoon was much more than 'just a confrontation with the white man'. It was, he stated, an indication of the black struggle which had broken out all over the world (Oxaal 1982: 224). When I saw him in Woodford Square, he was explaining to a dozen bystanders by means of cabbalistic figures and diagrams drawn on the asphalt that Williams and his successor Chambers were false prophets and that the white civilization had emerged from the powerful Egyptian empire, populated exclusively by blacks. The audience was very impressed by this display of knowledge and scholarship, but after a while an old man standing next to me began to raise objections, holding a tattered book without a cover in the air as he did so. The strength of his argument was derived, not from the content of the book, but from the fact that it had belonged to his great-grandfather. At some point somebody asked to examine the book. After a cursory inspection he called out that it was a publication from 1976, and added mockingly: 'How old is your great-grandpa, old man?' The polite respect for the confused account of the old man turned immediately into hilarity and a general discussion ensued, whereupon Primus, seeing he had nothing to gain from staying, slipped quietly away.

All the same, it is wrong to suppose that Woodford Square, People's Parliament during the 1970 Black Power revolt, is no more than a platform for marginal politicians whose ambitions are greater than their capacities. Elected members of parliament, who generally observe the rules of the official parliamentary system which confers on them their respectability, sometimes find it necessary to leave the assembly room of the Red House and to walk over to the 'neighbours' in the square for a populist face-lift. This brings us back to the theme of Trinidadian politics, for an understanding of whose dimensions and setting we have had to take this excursion through Port of Spain.

The political setting

The social comedies I write about can be fully appreciated only by someone who knows the region I write about. Without that knowledge it is easy for my books to be dismissed as farces and my characters as eccentric

(Naipaul 1958, in Hamner 1977: xxii)

Myers, Abu Bakr and Robinson: theatrical rivals in doing penance

The cool, rational, Westminster model borrowed from the British ('cool', because my impression of the British parliament is of a calculated theatre rather than a setting for genuine emotions) is not suited to the typical Trinidad political ethos, which was going through a particularly climactic period in the years preceding Independence. Its most salient characteristic, according to Lewis (1985: 229), is a Caribbean *personalismo*: the intimate association linking the charismatic leader with his fanatical supporters in a form of political messianism. In *Black and White*, a bleak but entertaining investigation of the underlying causes of the collective suicide of the members of the People's Temple and their leader Jim Jones in Jonestown (Guyana), Shiva Naipaul writes (1985: 15):

> I still remember my sense of shock when, in 1955 or 1956, I saw a group of black women parading with placards that proclaimed Dr. Eric Williams – our future Prime Minister – as the Messiah appointed to lead his people out of bondage. It was my introduction to the idea that the language of religion could be transformed into the language of politics.... Becoming part of the Third World is, to some degree, a psychological process; a quasi-religious conversion. It is, at bottom, a mode of being, a state of mind. That state of mind spreads like an infection and begins, after a while, to create its own political, social and personal realities, stimulated by the vocabulary of resentment and racial self-assertion.

A similar state of mind lies at the root of the racial clichés and fantasies which have created the figure of Michael X, alias Abdul Malik, as reported in Vidia Naipaul's *The Killings in Trinidad* (1981a), a detailed study of the actual events and psychology behind the murders in a Trinidad commune. I would not venture to suggest that the ultimate consequences of the history of the 'canonization' of Senator Lincoln Myers (my example, below) might result in a fatal denouement of that kind; nevertheless, it certainly does attest to a confusion of political and religious spheres which creates a socio-psychological climate in which racial self-assertion and all kinds of resentment can proliferate.

SENATOR MYERS' SACRIFICE

I have already cited Lewis's claim that the Trinidadians tend to project their penance onto the figure of the politician to the same degree that they use their calypsonians to party. The case of Senator Myers presents us with an instance of double projection. As chairman of the Public Accounts Enterprises Committee and as a member of the opposition in parliament, he protested against the impotence of this supervisory organ, as well as against corruption in the higher echelons of society in general, by fasting for forty days on the steps of the Hall of Justice, looking out on Woodford Square. In this way he managed to arouse a state of mind among a growing number of supporters and interested parties which gradually assumed the form of a collective act of atonement. Furthermore, he organized his action (28 December 1985 to

5 February 1986) to coincide with Trinidad's most ritually laden period of the year, bringing it to a close as a perfect temporal inversion just before the main days of carnival (10 and 11 February). Every day from six in the morning to six in the evening he squatted there in the burning sun. Within a few weeks, this worldly politician had been transformed into a sort of oriental martyr or saint. The metamorphosis was reflected in his clothes too: at first he wore a T-shirt, but later he appeared in the orange-yellow robes of a sannyasi or Hindu mendicant. 'I am not claiming to be a saint', he stated later in an interview, 'but I wanted the people to focus on purity ... That's what the clothes were about' (*People Magazine*, 6 April 1986). His immediate surroundings were transformed along with him. Political sympathizers, including members of the government party, who joined him in fasting for a while, gradually had to make way for leading representatives of the numerous religious communities and sects in which Trinidad abounds. Myers was increasingly claimed by Brahmins and gurus, imams and mullahs, Anglican and Catholic priests, Rastafarians and ministers of the Divine Life Society, and the Shango and Spiritual Baptist communities, who surrounded him with a sweet aroma of incense, sacred writings and paraphernalia, turning the steps and landing of the Hall of Justice into one massive syncretic altar. In this religious merry-go-round, everyone wanted a piece of the fasting senator for his own cause. Myers was astute enough to state in newspaper interviews that he did not adhere to any particular religious persuasion, but that he did believe in one God.

Every day was marked by the bustle of prominent social figures who came to pay Myers their respects. The world of carnival was not left out either, certain as it was of getting its photo in the paper. The popular eleven-year old calypso star Machel Montano came to shake him by the hand. So did the leading costume designer Peter Minshall, who symbolically joined in Myers' protest by putting on a huge black plastic rat mask. This mask was part of a costume from his masquerade band for that year, illustrating the theme of society as a rat race. School pupils and their teachers also came to take a look. Teacher: 'What is the senator doing, children?' 'Fasting!', was the sing-song reply. 'Why is he fasting?' 'For corruption!' the children shouted. Teacher (mildly annoyed): 'No, against corruption'. The square became the scene of debates between supporters and opponents of Myers as to whether his fasting had any point. One remarked that the senator only took honey and water. Another claimed that too much honey is bad for your system, and a third added that too much of anything is always bad for you. After a good deal more profundities about honey had been uttered, some people came to the conclusion that this was fake fasting. It is hardly surprising that this was also the conclusion of Minister Ronnie Williams of State Enterprises, one of Myers' main targets: 'What is the essence of this martyrdom? I mean, if he was going on a hunger strike, then I could say, well, the man has pure motives. But to go from six to six? Most days I don't eat from six to six .... I do harder work, not eating, harder work' (the *Express*, 27 January 1986).

However, all these criticisms were overshadowed by the massive popular success of Myers's action, culminating in the apotheosis of 5 February. After concluding his fortieth day of fasting, on the stroke of six, the visibly exhausted senator was helped to his feet and supported by his mother and a woman from the Divine Life Society to the ovational applause of the public. The painful expression on the senator's face and his outstretched arms, supported by many hands, suggested that he had just been taken down from the cross. He clasped three burning candles and then addressed the crowd (estimated at 2 000): 'Say with me, God is eternal... in all of us. We are divided, there is need for unity here. We must burn those rats in the society and go on to a new Jerusalem.' Crowned with laurel garlands, the senator concluded his speech. The crowd remained still for a minute as Anthony Woods of Mount D'Or played the national anthem on a steel pan. Myers and his supporters went on a silent procession around the Hall of Justice, which was followed by an hour-long ecumenical religious service in Woodford Square, observed by Myers from the bandstand. Many people could no longer master their emotions when it came to singing 'I once was lost but now am found' and 'Rejoice in Jesus' name'. A man wiped away his tears and shouted: 'That man made me cry... He took the rap for the whole of Trinidad and Tobago.' A Baptist woman cried in her excitement: 'That man has belly... that man is man!' Soon afterwards the opposition leader Basdeo Panday and the leader of the National Alliance for Reconstruction (NAR), A.N.R. Robinson, arrived on the scene and embraced the senator warmly before the watching crowd.

'I deal with symbols', Myers later confessed in an interview (*People Magazine*, 6 April 1986). 'Because in my view the traditional means of protest or of making statements have exhausted their usefulness.... I mean, I am in Parliament and it's ineffective.' This statement was made, however, at a time when his predilection for symbols was clearly becoming increasingly important to his aspirations in the arena of formal politics. His fast, bathed in a sacral atmosphere, far removed from the parliamentary bickering and, so it seemed, free from any form of corruption, turned out to be the start of a more politically coloured campaign connected with the national elections to be held on 16 December 1986. Religion gave way to the steelband as a source of symbolism, and Myers had both feet firmly on the ground, ready to engage in combat in the worldly arena of deceit and corruption which he held in such scorn. Dressed without fail in impeccable white, he visited poor Creole families in Laventille, the political and cultural centre of black working-class Trinidad. His inseparable attribute was now the hammer, the symbol of the inner strength which lies in the neighbourhood, as he explained it (the *Express*, 24 March 1986). Despite Myers's feigned innocence, however, everyone knew that he was appealing to the heavily charged symbolism that the hammer had acquired during the previous year. Cultural life in Laventille is largely focused on the steelband The Desperadoes, headed by the living legend Rudolph Charles until his death in 1985, when hundreds of mourners had accompanied his 'shariot', a coffin made of steel drums, to the crematorium. During his lifetime, Charles had done a daily round of the hilly neighbourhood, always dressed in military outfit and high boots and with a hammer in his hand. The hammer was not only to tune his steel drums, but also to teach unruly Laventillians and badjohns a lesson. The reigning Calypso King of 1986, David Rudder, immortalized Charles with his award-winning song 'The Hammer' ('Where has the man with the hammer gone?'), which was also nominated Carnival Road March, the most popular song among the parading masquerade bands. This stormy carnival history and Rudder's success had turned the hammer into a national symbol which Myers cleverly adapted to his own political ends.

At first sight what S. Naipaul calls 'racial self-assertion' does not appear to play any part in Myers's activities, but closer inspection reveals that appearances can be deceptive. At the beginning of April he caused a scandal by consistently and solely connecting his objections to a proposed amendment by the Minister of Finance, Anthony Jacelon, to the lot of 'black people'. The proposed amendment would not change the 'suffering of black people' or the fact that 'black people have to feel the brunt of the economic crisis and not the likes of the Minister in the Ministry of Finance.' Government policy had resulted in 'black emasculation' (the *Express*, 2 April 1986). Jacelon responded by walking out of parliament in anger with the words: 'When a Member of Parliament get racial, I done with that.' Senator Myers defended his action in the newspaper (2 April 1986) by explaining that 'black' was a sociological term connected with how people experience society, how they see the world, and how they relate to other people. It is not so much a question of the colour of their skin. There are whites who are black, Myers claims, and there are blacks in decision-making positions who are white.

A few days later he revealed in the interview in *People Magazine* cited above (6 April 1986) that he had not fasted for political reasons alone:

> The 40 days was never in question, for two reasons... It is symbolically Christian and there was also this statement I wanted to make – you see there are people in this country who do not believe that anyone black has any stamina... that we are a weak people not given to any kind of sustained effort, and to me it was important to be able to say, to young people particularly, that we have to get used to the idea that we are a very strong people capable of making sacrifices ... there can be no resurrection without the crucifixion.

The interviewer goes on to ask Myers for his favourite recollection of the fast:

> Well, there are quite a few but I remember Abu Bakr showing up on the evening of the first day of my fast at about five minutes to six bringing with him the loveliest pawpaw I ever saw. People have all kind of conflicting views about Bakr but it was a gesture of love which I will always remember.

It is doubtful whether Myers would later have wanted to be reminded of this. After a crushing electoral victory on 16 December 1986 (33 of the 36 seats), the National Alliance for Reconstruction (NAR) took over from the People's National Movement (PNM) after thirty years in government. Robinson became premier and Myers was appointed Minister for Agriculture and the Environment. It is this government which was taken hostage by the same Bakr during a coup four years later.

ABU BAKR'S COUP

'Despite Cuba, Grenada and Suriname, the region remains remarkably stable, in political terms' is Lewis's verdict in 1985 (227). 'Even in Haiti, the peasant majority, which has never known democracy in the Western sense, continues to accept the oppressive Duvalier regime with stoic equanimity.' During a lecture in Port of Spain in April 1986, the Jamaican historian Sir Philip Sherlock claims that, despite differences in origin, language, customs, political views and party connections, West Indians can count on a remarkable reputation for good governments 'by the people, for the people'. Progress has been made in the attempts to bring all these differences into harmony and to dissolve them in a national unity. Both claims have been proven untrue by recent events, as can be seen from the more realistic picture provided by Knight and Palmer (1989: 18). They argue that violence has assumed endemic forms throughout the region. There is a high level of criminal violence, not only violence against persons and property, but also politically inspired violence aimed at the destruction of the existing political system. The main cases of open political violence, they claim, have taken place in Haiti, Jamaica, Puerto Rico, Guadeloupe, Trinidad, Guyana, Grenada and Suriname. According to the sociologist Maharaj (1990), in Trinidad 'dependence on cocaine has penetrated all levels of society, combined with large-scale crime and violence. Modern Trinidad is an unsafe and neurotic society.'

Reflecting on his younger years, S. Naipaul writes (1985: 15):

> In Venezuela there were coups, revolutions, dictators. We certainly had no solid conceptions of these phenomena. It would never have seriously occurred to any of us that one day we too might have our coups, our revolutions and our would-be dictators. Such things simply did not happen

in Trinidad. The result was a happy innocence: we laughed at the whooping, barbarically painted Africans in Tarzan films; we loved cowboys. Those days have gone. Consciously, brutally, we have set about remaking ourselves in the Third World image.

In 1970 Naipaul returned to Trinidad, just in time to witness the student unrest. He saw the 'riff-raff' of Port of Spain marching through the streets with their fists clenched, chanting 'Power! Power!' The protest turned into riots, with broken shop windows and arson. Later on an army unit rebelled, led by an officer who did his best to look like Fidel Castro. The rebels tried to march on the city, but their plans were thwarted in the nick of time by the coastguard. 'Farce and revolution: both walked hand in hand, confused beyond separation', Naipaul writes (1985: 16). A state of emergency was declared and a curfew was imposed. Jeeps full of loyal troops in combat gear patrolled the empty city streets. 'It could have been an elaborate carnival tableau. Only the city's silence warned that this was no masquerade; that this, however obscurely, however fantastically, was for real', he concludes.

On Friday 27 July 1990 a group of black Muslims under the name Jamaat Al Muslimeen took the island government hostage and – somewhat prematurely – announced its downfall. The rebels, numbering about 250, set fire to the central police station and occupied the state broadcasting company. At least three people were killed, one of them in parliament when armed young men burst into the Red House during a government sitting and opened fire. The leader of the group of rebels, the former policeman Imam Yasin Abu Bakr, read a statement on television in which he said that God had 'removed' Premier Robinson (*De Volkskrant*: 31 July 1990) and that his ministers were under arrest. According to Abu Bakr, the coup had been staged because of government corruption and the 'continuing poverty' among a large sector of the population (*NRC*, 28 July 1990). Two ministers, Clive Pantin and Lincoln Myers (!), who were not in the government building at the moment of the coup, used a different broadcasting company to announce that the government had the situation under control. Large-scale plundering took place in Port of Spain during the weekend following the coup. Many shops were ransacked and set on fire. Hospital spokesmen reported at least three hundred wounded and thirty dead. The Deputy President of the Republic, Emmanuel Carter (President Noor Hassanali was on holiday in England) declared a state of emergency, imposed a curfew, and kept the armed forces (numbering 5 000) and police (numbering 1 500) on the alert. The government building, which the hostages were believed to have laden with explosives, was surrounded by troops and police, who showed no signs of wanting to join the coup. The situation in Trinidad aroused great concern in the neighbouring Caribbean countries. Barbados and Jamaica also put their troops on the alert and the United States announced its readiness to provide military assistance if the government of Trinidad and Tobago requested it. However, the Foreign Minister Eden Shand, who was released by the rebels on Saturday, stated that foreign intervention was not necessary (*NRC*, 30 July 1990). As a result of negotiations, partly thanks to the mediation of church dignitaries such as the Roman Catholic Bishop Anthony Pantin, the rebels released Premier Robinson on Tuesday 31 July and the rest of the hostages on the next day. Abu Bakr and a number of his associates surrendered unconditionally to the army.

Persistent rumours in Trinidad had it that Abu Bakr had spent some time training in Libya and that the Jamaat Al Muslimeen was funded by the Libyan leader Qadaffi. Bakr confirmed that he had spent some time in Libya in a speech delivered in Woodford Square on 17 April 1986. Paying scant heed to historical accuracy, he declared: 'Colonel Qadaffi liberated people of Libya from colonialism from the Italians. No one should forget that. Qadaffi freed all Libyans, and I am happy to know that Qadaffi is a man who promotes freedom, not terrorism.' His insecure grasp of history was also revealed when he stated in the same speech that 'his organization will fight Reagan until he surrenders Waller Field and Tucker Valley' – the Americans had already given back these military bases in 1967 at the time of Premier Eric Williams's populist government. Had the imam lost his head? wondered the *Express* of 21 April 1986.

The events leading up to the coup were characterized by a mixture of personal frustrations, poor communication and ideological commitment. In 1968 the government gave the Islamic Missionaries Guild permission to settle on a plot of land in Mucurapo, to the west of Port of Spain. The fact that this permission was never recorded in any official contract or lease agreement was the cause of years of confusion and growing frustration. In 1972 the Jamaat took over the land from the Guild, which had by now been weakened by internal rivalry, but without acquiring any title deeds which would enable the government's permission to continue to apply to the new organization. In the meantime, after a stay in Canada to study engineering, during which he was converted to Islam, Lennox Phillips returned to Trinidad in 1984 as Abu Bakr. Under his guidance, the plot of swamp land was prepared for the realization of an ambitious project, comprising a mosque, school, medical clinic, offices, shops, housing units and a small textile factory. However, the required government permits were not issued. In 1983 the Jamaat was ordered by law to demolish the mosque which had been constructed in the meantime. The organization turned a deaf ear and continued its building activities undeterred. The ensuing period was one of political and legal wrangles, in the course of which the repeated police raids on the Jamaat commune exacerbated the relationship between Abu Bakr and the authorities. As a result of these police actions, the imam issued threats to some ministers and the police during his public speech in Woodford Square on 17 April 1986. He and his henchmen would manage to track down the ministers responsible, and if they continued to intervene, the Jamaat would avenge itself on them. They did not intend to engage in open combat with the police, but to surprise the officers in their sleep.

Press opinions at the time are divided. Prophetically, the *TG* (22 April 1986) warns that Bakr is an 'agent of lawlessness' and a serious threat to society, but Owen Baptiste, writing in the *Express* (21 April 1986), takes Abu Bakr's menaces with a pinch of salt: 'In societies like ours – societies in which corruption is a way of life, where political leadership is absent, and where there is a vast moral chasm between what is preached and what is practiced – demagogues are born every day.' The imam is not the only one to have made a fool of himself in Woodford Square, Baptiste writes, for his predecessors include George Weekes (president of the Oil Workers' Trade Union), Makandal Daaga and Aldwyn Primus. Addressing an audience in Woodford Square, Makandal Daaga from the radical left-wing National Joint Action Congress had sworn that the NJAC would be in power within two years 'or we are intent on making blood flow in the country'. After Bakr's coup, the Trinidadian sociologist Niala Maharaj stated (*NRC*, 30 July 1990):

> The international media have labelled Abu Bakr and his followers as Muslim extremists, the local authorities refer to them as 'madmen'. For those familiar with the characters in the work of Trinidad's novelists – Naipaul, Selvon, and Lovelace – they are above all Trinidadians. The only atypical thing about them is the fact that they are armed and dangerous'.

It is not difficult, writes Holder (1990: 18), to reduce Abdul Malik as the leader of the Muslim commune in Naipaul's report (1981: 29) to 'a character, a carnival figure, a dummy Judas to be beaten through the streets.' But the recent events were not 'Carnival in July' because 'the game was no longer a game ... If in the "Killings in Trinidad" art copies life then in Port of Spain today life in its turn may well be mimicking art.'

No one paid any attention to the battalion of soldiers and police that took up position on the site on the Mucurapo Road on 21 April 1990, during the Feast of Ramadan, the sacred month of the Muslims. All eyes were on a group of elderly revolutionaries who had assembled on the campus of the University of St Augustine to commemorate the fact that a sector of the army had wanted to join the Black Power movement precisely twenty years before. Parallels were drawn during this meeting between the social conditions which had led to the Black Power revolt in 1970 and their modern equivalent. Many speakers warned of the imminent threat of social turmoil, but no one pointed towards Abu Bakr or the Jamaat Al Muslimeen. No one was to see the movement of troops in Mucurapo Road as anything more than a tactical manoeuvre in a 22-year long land dispute between the State and the group of Muslims. Nevertheless, according to the *Trinidad and Tobago Review* (September 1990):

> all the gore, all the fervour, all the bizarre that would erupt with the Muslim sect three months later was, for those willing to see, very much evident in the sordid tale of the battle for 8 acres of swamp land which on July 27 would erupt into a battle for control of the state.

The occupation of the Mucurapo site by army and police was the spark which ignited the gunpowder, or as Abu Bakr himself put it in an interview: 'That mosque is the trigger, if they pull it, boom!' (Holder 1990: 18).

ROBINSON'S TRIALS AND TRIBULATIONS

The succeeding events leading up to the coup and the coup itself expose the complexity of Trinidad's political machinery, in which what Lloyd Best (1990: d) calls leaders 'who favour ballots' and leaders 'who favour bullets' are driven by the same intention and motives and thus resemble one another to a remarkable extent. Political life is acted out in a socially belligerent atmosphere in which personal expressions of indignation are the usual techniques, and politicians transform their personal motives and moments of crisis into a public crusade against poverty, drug abuse, injustice, corruption, incest and pornography. The message that Myers was conveying on the steps of the Hall of Justice, in an attempt to secure his political career just before the elections, is the same as the message of Abu Bakr, for whom the ideals of founding a Muslim commune were in danger of being obstructed. However, Premier Robinson also had his personal crisis, and he sublimated the trauma that it left behind into a general campaign against corruption and injustice. For twenty years he had cultivated and propagated an image of himself as someone who was prepared to risk his own life, when as the crown prince to Eric Williams's monarch he left the PNM in 1970 because of the rampant corruption in the party. Or was the real reason for his resignation the fact that the PNM was not very likely to win the elections at the time and Robinson wanted to detach a part of the fraction from the PNM camp and set himself up as the leader of a new party, as Samad (1990: 2) suggests?

While Bakr was hatching plans to overthrow the government, Robinson became more and more deeply enmeshed in the Tesoro bribery scandal. The NAR government had thwarted an investigation by an arbitration board into malpractices by the former Tesoro oil company by making an extra-legal agreement by which the company's debt to the government was drastically reduced. According to an arbitration of 1985, a sum of TT$97 million was involved, but the government agreed to accept repayment of only

TT$12 million. The Minister for National Security, Selwyn Richardson, called the deal 'a victory for the people of T+T in its struggle for corruption' (*Trinidad and Tobago Review*, September 1990), but in the meantime evidence piled up to suggest that the government had intervened in order to prevent painful revelations on its dubious involvement in the case. The more awkward the situation of the Premier himself became, the more frequently he had cause to refer back to his 1970 action in his statements: 'When I did so [sc. left the PNM], I knew that not only my reputation but my life was on the line.... There is nobody in this country who has placed his life, his career, and everything that he has stood for on the line more than I did' (*Trinidad and Tobago Review*, September 1990). Indeed, as Samad claims (1990: 2), Arthur Robinson and Abu Bakr have a lot in common: not the battle against corruption, but the tendency to cultivate the myth of martyrdom. We can easily add Lincoln Myers to this list.

It was probably in an attempt to divert public opinion and to buy off his alleged complicity in the recent corruption scandal that Robinson made half a million dollars of the Tesoro sum available for the setting up of a monument to commemorate Gene Miles, a former civil servant, who died in suspicious circumstances in 1973 after she had exposed the large-scale corruption of the previous government. In a speech on television, Abu Bakr referred to the plans to set up the monument as the immediate motivation for his coup. He regarded it as an incredible deed of corruption to waste half a million dollars while there were people without enough money to buy food and a serious shortage of medical supplies in the hospitals. Without scruples, the NAR connected the death of Gene Miles with a pitiless PNM persecution. 'To victimize those who are righteous, those who seek to see things go right, ... was standard behaviour during thirty years of PNM rule', a fellow party member of the Premier declared (*Trinidad and Tobago Review*, September 1990). The more embarrassed the 'empty-headed political coalition' became and the more vociferous social criticisms became of 'the clique of arrogant, unruly and insensitive powers in the cabinet', the more grotesque were the attempts to put the blame on the former government party, the PNM (Maharaj 1990).

During a parliamentary session on Monday 23 July, Premier Robinson declared that he had documentary evidence that prominent PNM politicians who were also well-respected outside the party, including ex-Premiers Williams and Chambers and the last but one President of the Republic, Sir Ellis Clarke, maintained 'highly treacherous relations' with Tesoro. This shocking revelation brought him 'to his knees at 2 a.m. in the morning in prayer for the country' (*Trinidad and Tobago Review*, September 1990). On Friday 27 July Robinson summoned parliament again, apparently with the sole aim of continuing the anti-PNM campaign. His ministers and fellow party members each made their own contribution. Margaret Hector bore witness to her loyalty to the Premier and claimed that the corrupt PNM government 'has sold our sovereignty for the proverbial thirty pieces of silver'. Minister Jennifer Johnson read out Robinson's 1970 letter of resignation again and concluded: 'He was destined to assume the leadership, but he abandoned the PNM once and for all'. Eden Shand called the PNM party symbol, the 'balisier' (a local species of flower) a symbol of corruption, and declared that everyone who owns a party tie should burn it. Another speaker compared Robinson and his departure from the PNM with Moses when he left the Pharaoh's court. Samad (1990: 2) describes the atmosphere in parliament on the day in question:

> In all of his machinations he was aided and abetted by his brainwashed lieutenants of the NAR who all gleefully joined in the macabre ritualistic 'murder' of the PNM, in of all places the nation's Parliament. Is it not ironic that Joseph Toney was speaking of the use and abuse of Parliamentary privilege when proceedings were brought to an abrupt ending?

It is one minute to five. Joseph Toney is still speaking. 'The issue', he is saying, 'The issue...', when he and all the other members of parliament are violently silenced by the irruption of the Jamaat Al Muslimeen (*Trinidad and Tobago Review*, September 1990).

The mental setting

Get it now, no pay later

To speak of charisma in connection with the imam and his Muslim rebels is meaningless nonsense in the opinion of Lloyd Best (1990: d), the leading light of the left-wing political heritage sympathetic towards Black Power in Trinidad. The Jamaat movement could not count on popular support, certainly not from the 6 per cent (mainly Indian) Muslims, with which it had no real connection. Abu Bakr's action did not meet with the support of any social organization apart from his own army of 250. Naipaul's (1981: 59–60) characterization of Michael X as 'a prime minister of himself and his little group' applies to Bakr as well. In other words, according to Best, the imam is a complete charlatan in the best political tradition of Trinidad – Trinidad, not Tobago, he adds, although, ironically enough, the ultimate charlatan does come from Tobago (Robinson's place of birth). The failed coup has revealed the naked truth that after all the years of independence and freedom, politics in Trinidad is still no more than 'declaration and agitation'. Politicians increasingly refuse to adopt genuine political involvement. 'In 1970 Mr Geddes Granger [leader of the Black Power revolt] repeated himself; in 1986 Mr Robinson repeated Mr Granger; and now in 1990 the Imam has contrived to repeat Mr. Robinson, only such a short memory ahead of events' (Best 1990: d). The events of July 1990 force us to admit, Best concludes, that political charlatanism is dominant in Trinidad and Tobago. 'We are still depending on demonstrations, placards and the ballot box to get people out of office', sang calypsonian Black Stalin some time ago, as long as 'Robinson had not reached the stage of being called a Papa Doc or a Gairy' (Holder 1990: 18).

One of Bennett's (1989: 141) conclusions in his analysis of the Black Power revolt in February 1970 is that the poor, particularly the urban blacks, were sympathetic towards the aims of the movement as long as it promised material improvements. This attitude is typical of their limited interest and in the long run it was responsible for the infiltration of reformism and the eventual disintegration of the Black Power movement. However, if the 1970 Black Power revolt could still be characterized as a rejection of what Oxaal (1971: 66) calls 'the neo-colonial consumer culture', Abu Bakr's revolutionary escapades in political no-man's-land are a powerful confirmation of its continued existence. The only direct effect of his action was unrestrained looting in Port of Spain. This had nothing to do with Bakr's ideological message, but was simply the result of the collapse of the supervision of public order by police and army during the ensuing confusion. Bakr's coup achieved on a large scale what a warehouse fire did in 1985: it acted as the signal to take advantage of the consternation that arose in order to engage in an orgy of plundering and stealing. From Diego Martin in the north to Arima in the east, eye-witness reports claimed (*Daily Gleaner*, 30 July 1990), gangs of plunderers looted warehouses, shopping centres and even private homes. No one appeared to pay any heed to the curfew, even though there were strong sanctions on contravention and the police had been instructed to shoot plunderers with live ammunition. The looting soon assumed an organized form. The Anglican bishop Abdullah referred in a broadcast to convoys of vehicles which drove from shop to shop to pick up refrigerators, videos and similar items. His opinion is curious. He would not condemn a plundering expedition for food by hungry people, but he would not approve of the illegal acquisition of consignments of luxury goods (*Daily Gleaner*, 30 July 1990).

It was not hunger which motivated the plunderers (hunger barely exists on the island, if at all), but the suppressed desire for material possessions. The coup was an opportunity for the have-nots finally to gain possession of all the objects they coveted, which had been surrounding them for years from behind barred shop windows, and with which they were nevertheless confronted in a never ending stream of aggressive advertisements and TV commercials. The outburst seems to be anticipated by Lewis (1985: 233) when he writes that the bars on the windows of the homes of the urban middle-class areas were originally intended as decoration, but now function as a protection against crime, 'which in a sense represents the revenge of the poor against the well-to-do.' The plundering was the result of a process which had been going on for years: what MacDonald has called 'middle-classization', that is, the supposed right to own more than what one's income allows, the no-man's-land between economic reality and consumer ideals which are constantly urging people to satisfy their needs immediately. Maharaj (*NRC*, 30 July 1990) regards this short-term thinking, in which things have to be accessible or to happen as if by magic, as typical of the Trinidadians.

> We [Maharaj comes from Trinidad] are by definition eccentric and short-sighted. We spend all our savings on a single carnival costume and throw it away the day after. It is a national habit not to look further than today. For the people of Trinidad it is therefore not surprising that Abu Bakr believes that his bombastic action offers a solution to the problems of the economic misgovernment and lack of political direction of the country. He acted [like Myers] in the spirit of the carnival tradition. Unfortunately, it is part of our national charm, which leads us to tempt ourselves to impotence.

In another interview (*De Volkskrant*, 17 November 1990) she says: 'It is carnival 365 days a year in Trinidad. The two days before Ash Wednesday are merely the apotheosis.'

Carnival mentality

The phenomenon put into words here by Maharaj is referred to in Trinidad as 'carnival mentality', a popular expression for an alleged state of mind – connected with the more theoretical notion of 'middle-classization' – in which the national festival provides the idiom to stereotype it. Carnival mentality refers to an undisciplined character, not predisposed to serious or sensible activities, crazy about parties and partying, unwilling to face up to problems, and at the same time bragging and puffing oneself up (Johnson 1983: 201–2). The term usually carries negative connotations. When the oil revenues slumped, Premier Chambers called the nation to sobriety with the slogan 'fête over, back to work'. Since then the words have become proverbial for spurring workers on to increased productivity. However, by no means everybody shares the view of carnival as one big unproductive festival, the opposite of purposeful work, as many remarks in the press indicate. 'If all workers in the community ... were to adopt the "carnival mentality", the level of production in both the public and private sectors would surpass even Mr Chambers' wildest fantasies', wrote an *Express* reader (Johnson 1983: 202). 'So now, don't get rid of the "carnival mentality", put it to work and you would see the wonders it can do', writes another in the *TG* (26 February 1988). During the last few hours of the 1963 carnival, Premier

Eric Williams and some members of his party ran into a bunch of revellers who were performing 'a serenade for the servants of the law' in front of police headquarters. Williams immediately asked the Planning Unit to see how the inventiveness and energy which Trinidadians put into carnival could be used in the interests of national development (Oxaal 1968: 18).

It is unrealistic to suppose that the terrific motivation to party can also be channelled to get people to engage in productive work. A different question is whether the alleged carnival mentality hinders or slows down economic activities and market-oriented labour, which are the characteristics of modern development. As far as I know, no research has been carried out on this. With regard to basketball, another passion of the people of Trinidad and Tobago, Mandle and Mandle (1988: 71–2) pose a similar question. In the first place, they establish that a large number of basketball players are badly paid, work part-time, or are unemployed. They then consider whether people involved in basketball opt for unemployment (training and competition take up a lot of time) in order to be able to practise the sport, or whether they turn to sport because they do not have any work. Their research indicates that the latter is true in almost all cases. The ambivalent attitude usually adopted towards carnival mentality, the negative and positive values attached to it, are connected with two opposing value sets which are operative in black Trinidadian society and which are usually referred to by the Trinidadians themselves as 'respectability' and 'reputation'. Discipline and obedience contrast with the urge for individual idiosyncrasy, making a social career at odds with the egalitarian practice of the rumshop, sobriety the opposite of hedonistic pleasure, and so on. In the following chapter I shall show that the respectability/reputation value dichotomy covers much more than this, and that it is closely implicated in and characteristic of Trinidadian social structure. At this point, it is sufficient to point out that most Trinidadians regard a set of happy-go-lucky attitudes as their shared culture, irrespective of whether they approve of it or not. At the same time, they are aware that they live in a prestige-orientated capitalist society whose values of social mobility and individual success they also uphold. To illustrate this ambivalence they often point to the readiness with which corruption – though it is experienced as painful – is not punished in society, as proof of its 'open' nature and 'sweetness' (Stewart 1986: 298). Eriksen (1990: 36–8) remarks in this connection that the contradiction between the value systems, and especially the fact that it is easier to sell reputation values than respectability values, is often experienced as problematic in relation to nation-building and national planning.

This ambivalence is shared by members of the middle class and the lower class. Eriksen cites the case of Eric Williams. During his famous lectures in Woodford Square, where he was enthusiastically received as a great calypsonian by a predominantly urban proletarian audience, he placed special emphasis on the desire of Trinidadians to be seen to be respectable, and to be regarded as cultural and intellectual equals by the rest of the world. Williams attacked the morality of reputation by propagating serious political organization and intellectual ambition. The reputation morality, according to Eriksen, contains a powerful element of resentment against the colonial morality of duty and service. Williams urged his audience at the University of Woodford Square to turn their resentment into a positive, productive force, to transform it into an 'authentically Trinidadian' value system, which can be used to their own advantage and to which respectability should be subservient. However, at European conferences Williams invited his colleagues to come to Trinidad 'to learn how to enjoy the good life' (Eriksen 1990: 37; Oxaal 1968: 18). In other words, Williams himself was caught in the contradiction between two systems of morality.

The flamboyant, elegant, carefree man-of-words or man-of-style is a favourite prototype for Trinidadians from all classes, Eriksen writes (1990: 37–8). He continues: 'On the one hand it expresses a rejection of hierarchy and formal organisation.... On the other hand, it also expresses an affirmative national identity. But like every modern nationstate, the Trinidadian state demands obedience to values of respectability.' That practice does not always proceed as theory dictates can be seen from the common complaint that 'it is difficult to get anything done around here, because nobody cares to make long-term plans.'

Creative copycats

Oh fantasy, who sometimes so ravishes us from ourselves that we are unaware of anything, even though a thousand trumpets sound around us. Who makes you, if the senses fail to present you with something?

(Dante, *The Divine Comedy*, cited in Cox 1970: 73)

According to Hodge (1987: 81), it is justified to accuse the 'Trinis' of not being serious if you consider their determination to carry on enjoying life in times of recession, oppression and calamity. When the authorities imposed curfew during the period of the Black Power riot in 1970, Trinidadians went indoors at the last moment to hold nocturnal 'curfew fêtes'. And when the economy collapsed as a result of the sudden, drastic drop in oil prices, accompanied by far-reaching austerity measures, unemployment, inflation, shortages and poverty, posters all over the country characteristically invited people to attend recession fêtes. 'Come hell or high water, Trinidad and Tobago go down fêting', Hodge writes. After the heavy devaluation of the TT dollar in 1985, the Stag national brewery disguised necessity as a virtue with an aggressive advertising campaign under the slogan 'Stag, the recession fighter'. In the months after the dramatic events of the attempted coup, the 'Trinis' indulged in calypso dance parties and drinking bouts as if it were carnival. The national comedian Tommy Joseph played to packed halls with his shows full of caustic and hilarious sketches and comments on the attempted coup, the plunderers, hostages and police. It was a novelty to fête in the daytime because of the curfew from 21:00 to 05:00 hours, which in this case only a few dared to ignore. While the Jamaat Al Muslimeen appealed in court to the validity of a written amnesty agreement with the government which had been made during the coup, this was overshadowed in the public debate by the general indignation at the plans of the authorities to maintain the curfew during the two days of carnival as well. After continued protest the government gave in and abandoned its unpopular plan. It then suggested extending the climax of the carnival to five days instead of the traditional two, a proposal which the islanders regarded as equally absurd (*Caribbean Week*, November 1990; *De Volkskrant*, 17 November 1990).

In an article in which she tries to explain the stereotype view of her fellow Trinidadians and to account for its origin, Hodge herself (1987: 82) gives the following stereotype: 'The experience of growing up in a multicultural setting, and the continuous exposure to international currents, make the Trinidadian an eminently flexible person, able to adapt to a variety of situations, able to continually absorb new experiences and learn new roles.' She continues:

> 'Trinis' sometimes are referred to as 'Trickidadians' by other Caribbean people, for what may be perceived as chameleon behavior. Their adaptive nature also reveals itself in a great capacity for imitation.... Trinis adopt and master every new dance form that comes out of Black America, performing the pop songs of the world as though Trinis had composed them, wearing avant-garde fashions from international salons with more aplomb than the models who first launched them. An important aspect of what Carnival is about is the temporary borrowing of another persona.

Seen in this light, the distinction between everyday behaviour and behaviour during the festival blurs: carnival as the celebration of mimesis itself – a mimicry of mimicry. 'It may be said', Hodge claims in the same section, 'that Trinidadians are entirely too eager to mimic, and that they are a nation of copycats.' Naipaul would agree. He refers to 'mimic men'; 'a society which produced nothing'; 'with no standards of its own'; 'the picaroon delight in trickery persists'; 'Trinidadians ... remaking themselves in the image of the Hollywood B-man'; 'living in a borrowed culture'; 'in the absence of a history'. Hodge, however, adds to her generalization: 'Amazingly though, their flair for imitation does not rob them of their originality or creativity. It is almost as though the process of continually borrowing and discarding stimulates creative energies and serves in some way to affirm individuality.' Both the motivation to assimilate by cultural borrowing and dependence as the motivation behind creativity and independence remain as powerful as ever. Lieber (1981: 10) refers to this striking combination of imitation and creativity: 'Not only does the American mainstream have its effects on the development of a Trinidadian mainstream, but "counter-mainstream" American styles are often adopted and fused with counter-mainstream Trinidadian styles.' This applies to political and ideological views, fashion, music, and so on. The counter-streams, as Trinidadian variations on the original American ones, offer a native alternative to the mainstream and express its inadequacies and contradictions for Trinidadian society. This borrowing and internalization is often a result of migration to the United States and subsequent return to the island (see for example Kasinitz 1992). In a broader Caribbean sense, Lieber (1981: 10) cites the example of the Jamaican Marcus Garvey, whose influence and personality have combined and merged Caribbean and American consciousness. Naipaul is unable to understand the original and creative cultural and social achievements at all. For instance, he hates steelband music (1982: 43). In a newspaper interview in *NRC*, on 11 January 1991 he says: 'You see? The noise never stops. It's torture to me, but they like it here. They don't work with the mind.' He comments on society after the oil boom: 'Material wealth is now measured in terms of how many times a week you can get drunk and by the volume produced by your hi-fi.' His negative attitude has attracted a lot of criticism. His writings are almost all about the theme of the failure and defeat of colonial society and the inability of the intellectual born and bred in the colony to fit in anywhere. This is the view of Angrosino (1989: 117, 122), who cites MacDonald's claim that Naipaul's vision of colonial society is marked by nothing but 'taint and despair'. Márquez (1989: 329) speaks of Naipaul's 'perception of islands and colonies as crushingly insular enclosures incapable of supporting large events.'

However, the fact that Naipaul calls the West Indians a people without history (for example in *The Middle Passage*, page 29: 'History is built around achievement and creation; and nothing was created in the West Indies') is in line with the existential philosophical theme of Caribbean intellectuals and writers, as presented by Angrosino (1989) and Márquez (1989), on the question of national identity. The colonial past with its traumatic experience of slavery and contract labour has happened to involuntary migrants who have filled those areas in the Caribbean depopulated largely by the extermination of the original inhabitants. This hardly offers a frame of reference for a positive and coherent sense of history from which a common identity or national pride might be derived. It is of great importance for West Indians to gain a proper understanding of the nature of the influence of slavery on their history, claims the historian Elsa Goveia (cited in Rohlehr 1974: 81), but they will only be in a position to do so when they regard the white colonists, the coloured and the negro slaves as related participants in a human situation which has shaped the lives of all of them.[2] Instead of this problematic history, Márquez (1989: 325) speaks of 'creative imagination' as a source of inspiration for Caribbean self-realization or, according to Lloyd Brown (1984: 9), 'that creative sense of self-affirmation, which salvages a cultural identity from the past.' This is a quality which Naipaul, with his denigratory comments on Caribbean culture, denies the West Indians. This idea has been expressed best by Derek Walcott (cited in *DE*, 10 February 1988):

> History, taught as morality, is religion. History, taught as action, is art. Those are the only uses to which we, mocked as a people without history, can put it. Because if we have no choice but to view history as fiction, or as religion, then our use of it will be idiosyncratic, personal, and therefore, creative. All of this is beyond the sociological, even beyond the 'civilised' assessment of our endeavour, beyond mimicry. The stripped and naked man, however abused, however disabused of old beliefs, instinctually, even desperately, begins again as a craftsman ....
>
> In the Caribbean history is irrelevant [sic], not because it is not being created, or because it was sordid; but because it has never mattered, what has mattered is the loss of history, the amnesia of the races, what has become necessary is imagination, imagination as necessity, as invention.

In the Caribbean, with its colonial past and its recently acquired political autonomy, there is a strong desire for a distinctive national identity. It is in the art forms of a culture – certainly for the uprooted West Indians in search of a meaningful link with their past and their origins – that this feeling can be expressed most clearly. The best example of this is undoubtedly the Trinidad carnival. What is regarded as carnival on other Caribbean islands, such as St Thomas, Aruba, St Lucia and Antigua, is usually 'tourist gimmickry', according to Lewis (1968: 30). Though he overstates his case somewhat, Lewis is right in asserting that the 'Trinidad event, by comparison, is a tremendous bacchanalian folk-fiesta drawing its vitality from at once a long historical background and the living processes of contemporary West Indian experience.'

The material prosperity and corruption, the readiness of the politicians to make sacrifices, and the cheerful looting and curfew fêting described in this chapter may be reminiscent of an operetta or carnival at times. However, this does not alter the sense of reality of the Trinidadians, for it is precisely in carnival – the annual event *par excellence* in which artistic skills and imagination are combined for a single large-scale creative and reflective display of social and cultural values – that the society recognizes itself and wishes to take itself seriously. A first step towards an explanation of the origin of this state of mind is provided by Naipaul in *Finding the Centre* (1985: 136–7) with his metaphorical account (cited in Chapter 1) of the position of the African slaves on the former plantations as 'a king of the night, a slave by day'. Fifteen years earlier he had already linked these ideas with carnival in an article (1970) entitled 'Power to the Caribbean People'. His argument boils down to the idea that Trinidadians take carnival seriously, but regard the Black Power revolt as a carnival. This chapter can be summarized figuratively by a citation from his article:

> The slave in Trinidad worked by day and lived at night. Then the world of the white plantations fell away; and in its place was a securer, secret world of fantasy, of Negro 'kingdoms', 'regiments', bands. The people who were slaves by day saw themselves then as kings, queens, dauphins, princesses. There were pretty uniforms, flags and painted wooden swords. Everyone who joined a regiment got a title. At night the Negroes played at being people, mimicking the rites of the upper world. The kings visited and entertained. At gatherings a 'secretary' might sit scribbling away.
>
> Once, in December, 1805, this fantasy of the night overflowed into the working day. There was serious talk then of cutting off the heads of some plantation owners, of drinking holy water afterward and eating pork and dancing. The plot was found out; and swiftly, before Christmas, in the main Port of Spain square there were hangings, decapitations, brandings, and whippings.
>
> That was Trinidad's first and last slave 'revolt'. The Negro kingdoms of the night were broken up. But the fantasies remained. They had to, because without that touch of lunacy the Negro would have utterly despaired and might have killed himself slowly by eating dirt; many in Trinidad did. The Carnival the tourist goes to see is a version of the lunacy that kept the slave alive. It is the original dream of black power, style and prettiness; and it always feeds on a private vision of the real world.

The picture presented in this chapter shows how the oil boom enabled a level of prosperity which only enhanced the sensitivity of the citizen of Trinidad to foreign values, especially those with a North American flavour. The capricious architectural and infrastructural physiognomy of Port of Spain – a spectrum of deviations and eccentricities simply juxtaposed – reflects decades of colonial rule which have left that mark on the complex mosaic of a society divided by 'race' and class. The section on the political setting was intended to expose the contours of power and power games by characterizing a few prominent figures in this arena who combined Naipaul's 'mystic masseur' and 'mimic man'. Finally, the discussion of Trinidadians as creative copycats was intended to illustrate the dilemma between creativity and mimesis to which the society is condemned by its 'lack of history'. The conclusion that emerges from these aspects is that Trinidad society is dominated by conflicting values and orientations, partly the heritage of its colonial past, partly still sustained by its present-day cultural and socio-economic position *vis-à-vis* the world that surrounds it.

Notes

1   The revolts and demonstrations in the early months of 1970 were the result of a combination of circumstances which included widespread labour unrest, disillusionment with government policy, economic stagnation, a power struggle within the army, and the prosecution of Trinidadian students by the Canadian government for a few incidents with a racial undertone in the Sir George Williams University in Montreal. Both the government and the trader elite in the country were confronted with a black coalition of the disenchanted, known as the Black Power Movement. This movement, a mixture of radical students, academic Marxists, left-wing unions, black nationalist groups and a rapidly growing following of lower-class black workers and unemployed, adopted an extremely militant stance. Protest demonstrations in Port of Spain and elsewhere degenerated into riots, arson and large-scale looting. The government proclaimed the state of emergency on 21 April and arrested the most important leaders of the movement. A division of the army mutinied during the ensuing consternation. A convoy of rebels heading for Port of Spain was intercepted by the coast guard, leading to the arrest of the two leaders of the mutiny and 85 men. This marked the end of what is sometimes called the February Revolution (Johnson 1987: 55–6; Lieber 1981: 11–12; M.G. Smith 1984: 96).

2   Lewis (1983: 11–12) points out that the influence of the slave system was not the same everywhere, resulting in differences in social intercourse and lifestyle on the various Caribbean islands. Barbados, for example, had a sugar economy based on slave labour for 250 years, while the period of slavery on Trinidad was a mere fifty years. There are historians, Lewis claims, who consider that this contrast is due to the phlegmatic and socially respectable behaviour of the Barbadian, 'bereft of the capacity for "fiesta" by his Cromwellian-Puritan background' (Lewis 1968: 30), and the striking Byzantine anti-social individualism of the Trinidadian. Leigh Fermor (1984: 153 and 166–8) comes to a similar conclusion in his comparison of the two islands.

5 | Reputation versus respectability

I who am poisoned with the blood of both [Africa and Europe]
Where shall I turn, divided to the vein?

(Walcott, cited in Márquez 1989: 316)

Peter Wilson (1969, 1970/71, 1973) has developed a model of value conflict for the English-speaking Caribbean based on the emic opposition between reputation and respectability. This provides a theoretical underpinning for the conclusion outlined at the end of the previous chapter. As a useful way of organizing the values which can be connected with the social structure and organization of the island societies in this region, the model offers insight into the complex ambiguity and internal dynamics of the Trinidad carnival.

By way of introduction, I bring Naipaul back onto the stage. The writer as a relative outsider, '... an exiled member (a seeming contradiction) of the diaspora' as López de Villegas puts it (1980: 229), and the resistance which the views of such a writer provoke, can serve as a model for the ideological interaction of points of view which similarly exists among the various kinds of insiders and outsiders within the existential labyrinth of Caribbean society. My characterization of the writer Naipaul and discussion of his work here are naturally confined to his attitude towards and concern with the Caribbean, especially Trinidad. According to a report in *NRC* of 11 January 1991, Naipaul was then back in the Caribbean to 'cast a new glance at the landscape of his first travelogue *The Middle Passage* (1982). He will write about it, but does not yet know how'; *A Way in the World*, published in 1994, is his most recent statement of any length on the region. The following account is intended to indicate the general socio-cultural framework within which both the two sets of values play an important role, and the formation and expression of opinions take place on the island.

The historical process of image creation

The *Trinidad Guardian* of 2 February 1987 carried an article with the heading 'Ignore V.S. Naipaul says Wole Soyinka', in which this Nigerian winner of the 1986 Nobel Prize for literature was confronted with Naipaul's statement that 'once "black (American) literature" has made its profitable protests, the writers had nothing left to say.' The award-winning writer, who received his education at the University of Leeds and was a member of the British Royal Academy of Arts and Letters, had no qualms about labelling Naipaul as an 'unfortunate creation of the British literary establishment' and accusing him of many dubious statements about the black race. He did not want to waste any more ink on the matter and considered that Naipaul was a concern of his Caribbean colleagues. Time and again Naipaul is taken to task for citations from his work that are superficially quoted and wrenched from their context. This is usually as far as interest in his work goes in Trinidad. The article in question, put together from fragments of an interview in the December 1986 issue of the magazine *West Africa*, did not contain anything newsworthy, and the statement to which the Nobel Prize winner was reacting is taken from Naipaul's early *The Middle Passage* (published in 1962). The whole incident only acquires a veneer of topicality because Naipaul is the national scapegoat, who has to be sacrificed now and then so that the discussion may appear to have been concluded again in a satisfactory manner.

The fact that an African authority has spoken, no matter how insignificant his remarks may be, confers the force of an oracle on his judgement for at least a small sector of the black population of Trinidad. It would have been possible to examine the context from which the citation had been taken, but that would probably have meant that the indignation would have reached an even higher level of satisfaction, because Naipaul claims there that the involvement of the Negro with the white world is one of the limitations of West Indian writing as it entails the destruction of American Negro writing. The theme of black American writers is the fact that they are black. This cannot be the basis for serious literature, and as is still the case – and this is where the extract is to be found in its original form – 'once the American Negro has made his statement, his profitable protest, he has nothing to say' (Naipaul 1982: 75). Apart from two or three exceptions, Naipaul claims, West Indian writers have so far managed to avoid the type of protest-writing indulged in by the American Negro, but their goals are equally propagandist: to gain acceptance for their own group. It is not surprising that V.S. Naipaul is the scapegoat, a kind of small-scale Salman Rushdie for Trinidad (fortunately, the thirst for vengeance retains human proportions here), if one reads his harsh judgement in *The Middle Passage*.

In this travelogue he regards the West Indies as a 'derelict land' (Hamner 1977: xvii). Tourism as a new form of slavery is a continuation of the humiliation of the people and it leaves the materialist and superficial 'immigrant society' fully intact. Naipaul's journalistic image complements the image that he portrays in his fiction, and neither of them is favourable to the West Indies.

A few years later Naipaul brought four centuries of West Indian history to life in his description of two episodic events in *The Loss of El Dorado* (1981). His language has lost none of its barbed, muscular quality, but in this book the writer tries to distance himself more and he has learnt to allow the irony of fate to speak for itself more. All the same, it was predictable that a controversial writer such as Naipaul, who devoted so much energy to attacking individual and social weaknesses, would both meet with bitter criticism, and also receive the highest praise. In his discussion of Naipaul's writings on the West Indians, Singh (1969: 85) considers that the writer is regarded as a despicable lackey of neo-colonialism and imperialism because of his distortions of history, culture and politics. Nazareth (1977: 147) writes that Naipaul only focuses on the weak spots in West Indian society because of his inability to see anything positive in the West Indians. This positive element to which Naipaul is allegedly blind is simply the fact that life in all its banality, even though it has little to offer to the aesthete, is still life. An anonymous critic hits upon the essential aspect of this deficiency on the sleeve of a record by Mighty Sparrow: 'But where Naipaul can observe, from afar, without getting a speck of dust on his impeccable person, Sparrow, more tactile, sees life as one long boisterous contact sport.' On the other hand, Wyndham (1971: 462) calls Naipaul the greatest living writer in the English language.

Naipaul's critical reflections (1982: 73) derive from his fundamental objection: in depicting their society, West Indian writers usually adopt an uncritical attitude towards group values and racial values. 'The guilt feelings of the whites have not done much for the blacks', he remarked in an interview (Joris 1992: 94). He would have preferred it if the whites had done more to encourage their black friends to analyse their own society instead of proffering excuses for what went wrong. Naipaul goes on:

> But the whites turned the black man into an eternal victim. He was never the man who put a bad government in office, who stole money, or who took part in race riots, as happened here in the Caribbean.... No one has written about the attempted coup in Trinidad. Black writers do not write about the mess this region is in. They still go on about the colonial oppression of the past.

Naipaul writes elsewhere (1982: 75) that, instead of analysing the disease of their society, the writers themselves become part of the problem.

This criticism may be justified in itself, but if we try to understand it in a wider sense than Naipaul would like, he can be included in the diagnosis as a writer who is at least seropositive. Lewis (1983: 24–5) makes it clear that until recently the generally accepted view among writers on the West Indies was that there was no valuable intellectual heritage in the region. This attitude, which has been connected with the Indian community in Trinidad (which Lewis' work largely ignores), is no doubt rooted in the history of the region itself. The liberal European distaste for both the poor white and the rich planter was translated into a feeling of disdain for the region as a whole ('I am a second-rater' were the words of a successful American businessman to an Englishman who told the story to Naipaul (1982: 52) 'but this is a third-rate place and I am doing well. Why should I leave?'). What London thought of Jamaica was only compared with what Paris thought about Saint Domingue and what Madrid thought about Cuba. Even when Marx spends a few words on slavery, he has the American South in mind and pays hardly any attention to the Caribbean.

This generally held attitude was in turn sustained by feelings of colonial disinterest, self-deprecation and dependence – the familiar colonial mentality – in the West Indies. In his article 'Identity and Escape in Caribbean Literature', Angrosino (1989: 115) writes that from a historical point of view West Indians have often experienced their place of residence as something temporary. The Jamaican Rastas, for instance, regard the West Indies as Babylon and its inhabitants as a nomadic people in exile. Cultural identity is like something from a distant, vague past. Even though the mother country or the metropolis is the source of oppression, it is also the source of the only directly identifiable and coherent cultural standards. It is difficult for a sense of nationality to take root because the West Indians have learned to despise their 'little island in the sun' as a worthless place of exile.

In the case of Trinidad, Vidia Naipaul cultivates the feeling of colonial self-deprecation when he explains with metropolitan scorn in *The Middle Passage* that the West Indies has never produced anything. Seen in this light, the writer also contributed to the historical process of the formation of images, and is as such a typical representative of the West Indian writers' tradition. In their differences and similarities, these writers are connected, according to Márquez (1989: 294), by the consequences and vicissitudes of a shared colonial history, of imperial rivalry, inter-territorial isolation, and ethno-class confrontation. 'They are all equally the product of the combined force of these not yet fully reconciled contradictions. They are simultaneously provoked, constrained, and challenged by a vivid appreciation of the enduring significance of their "origins".' The search for richer possibilities for identity has often led Caribbean writers to escape from their place of exile, literally or symbolically. Caribbean literature, according to Agrosino (1989: 116), has created idealized images of cultural identity which gave more satisfaction than the 'little island' *anomie* of the West Indies 'as it really is'. This explains the evocation of the image of *négritude*, the universal black soul; or the obsessional attractiveness of a romanticized and glorified past; or the endless fascination with the innocence of childhood. These three symbolic domains of escape have dominated Caribbean literature to a large extent. This literature forms one great symbolic theatre, in which the intellectuals and the 'common people' exchange ideas about identity (Angrosino 1989: 130).

Middle passage of ideologies

In a more positive spirit, Lewis (1983: 26–7) refers to two historical processes which became interlocked and which eventually led to 'creole culture' or 'creole society'. The first of these concerns the influence of the European metropolitan set of ideas and the way in which they gained acceptance among the gradually emergent literary elites in the urban centres of the Caribbean. The second implies creolization, in which absorption and assimilation of this way of thinking have taken place within the unique, historically developed conditions of Caribbean society. Both processes have led to the birth of a native set of ideas and values which can be labelled, according to Lewis, as Caribbean *sui generis*. Elsewhere (1985: 226) he calls this configuration 'a syndrome of "ideological pluralism" ', shaped by Europe, Africa, and – in the twentieth century – the United States. 'Ideologies flourish like the green bay tree', is his almost lyrical summing up: American-style social liberalism in Puerto Rico; the tremendous intellectual influence which has been exercised by the Cuban revolution of 1959; Eurocommunist and socialist ideas in the French Antilles; the Christian socialism of the Caribbean Conference of Churches, which includes both Protestant and Catholic denominations; ideologies of emergent black Afro-American pride, extending from the *négritude* movement of the 1920s to the contemporary Black Power movement, a product of the American civil rights movement, and the *africanía* of the Jamaican musical reggae revolution.

Lewis sees all this as the uniqueness of the Caribbean. It is difficult to compare it with the situation in the older, industrialized societies. In the United States, for example, a socialist was regarded as an eccentric or dangerously subversive element. Much of American radicalism takes capitalist society for granted in its struggle for a limited target or ideal: Black Power, gay rights, the pro-abortion and anti-abortion movements, the defence of Israel, the women's movement. 'The Caribbean intellectual ferment' (Lewis 1985: 227), on the other hand, regards society as an entity and attempts to change it fundamentally. The Caribbean is on a completely different intellectual wave-length. Lewis has manoeuvred himself into an awkward position in his attempt to champion the intellectual status quo in the Caribbean. After all, assigning a special character to the Caribbean intellectual heritage is no guarantee of originality, consistency or logical coherence. On the contrary, the middle passage of transported African slaves was accompanied by a middle passage of ideologies, as Lewis himself concludes (1983: 27). It should be added that the uprooting, dispersion, heterogeneity and confusion which characterized the former were the foundations of the latter.

Naipaul is unparalleled in his exposure of this Caribbean complex in his travelogues, his journalism and his literary work. It is understandable that this has provoked violent reactions and indignation. Incidentally, the 'exile' of Naipaul (or of George Lamming, or Derek Walcott) does not make him and his fellow writers any less 'Caribbean': this exile keeps on coming back, and in his work he remains extremely close to 'his' society. It is this distance and involvement which, given his talent, enable him to make observations and characterizations which many of those who remained are unable to make, or which they cannot allow themselves to make. This is why his work is a welcome source, even though, like any other source, it cannot be accepted uncritically as the truth. Nevertheless, as the reader will have realized, I would not like to miss him as a witness (often for the prosecution). His work reflects the extremely problematic relation between class, 'race' and colour, and the corresponding diversity of social conventions, references and orientations which provide a whimsical palette of what are often idealistic or mythically coloured versions of the past and the present. How do people define their identity in this world of conflicting or even alien value systems? This is the central theme around which culture in post-colonial society is organized, according to Angrosino (1989: 113). Views and points of view are not usually assessed for their merits, but weighed up in terms of the estimated position occupied by the person who expresses them within the socio-racial constellation. That person is often faced irrevocably with the dilemma of an ideological dualism determined by 'race' and class; if he or she emphasizes one of them at the expense of the other, he or she runs up against incomprehension or runs the risk of being accused of inaccuracy.

A model of value conflict in the Caribbean

It is important to decide whether the image that looms up from the past and the present can be used to construct a comprehensive value dichotomy for analytical and descriptive purposes. Peter Wilson provides such a concept, which will be discussed in detail – where relevant – because it offers a particular view of society which can be used as a background towards explaining the importance of certain aspects and themes of modern carnival.

In order to arrive at a picture of society which takes the position of both men and women into account, Wilson (1969: 71) sets out to explore 'the principles of social relations which might serve to structure the moral and social system of a community.' He does so by drawing on his own research on Providencia, an English-speaking Colombian island east of Nicaragua, and by extrapolating data from the existing ethnographic record on the English-speaking Caribbean.

Writing in the late 1960s, Wilson considers that it is no exaggeration to say that ethnographical work in the Caribbean has virtually equated social with domestic organization. Little attention is paid to the importance of the formation of informal groups which are lacking in any form of institutional expression. The existing studies also almost all report the existence of a double sexual morality. Men are admired for their virility as a constellation of qualities (understood in a wider sense than just sexual potency) by means of which they assume a place in the world, and are given a freedom which they are expected to exploit to the full. Women's sexual activities, on the other hand, are restricted both before and during marriage, and they are expected to display the appropriate behaviour (submissiveness and obedience) to these limitations. These double sexual standards, in connection with the importance attached to the structure of the household or the family, implies a marginal position for men and a central one for women. However, although the role of men may be marginal in relation to the home and family, this does not imply marginality in relation to the broader society. It is therefore naturally that there must be a male social life, associated with institutions, practices, values and activities, which complements female existence and the principles on which it is based. This organization of social life on the basis of a division between the sexes can be translated into the broader West Indian distinction between reputation and respectability according to which Wilson developed his theoretical concept. Reputation is connected with male values orientated towards friendship, in which the rumshop and other public places play an important role (see for example Brana-Shute 1979); this implies contact with friends and situating your affections and conditions of existence there instead of in contact with your family. There is a low level of organization or institutionalization because the emphasis lies on the importance of social relations which at most lead to limited social group formation, usually with an *ad hoc* character. Reputation is associated with masculine behaviour: playing the guitar or being good at singing, drinking, playing cards, and adeptness in a kind of verbal wrangling, an exchange of insults, in which verbal skill is highly valued. The calypso war and the carnival figures of Pierrot, Pierrot Grenade and Midnight Robber are good, stylized examples.

Respectability, on the other hand, entails 'proper, irreproachable behaviour', a striving for status, order, decorum and decency. It is the general, open value system of a society with a large degree of organization or institutionalization (church, marriage, school, political party) which everyone claims to support and which is used as the point of reference for definitions of what is decent and proper. Women are constantly involved with norms and expectations which arise from their activities within a network of kin, a factor which is connected with the close bond between mothers and children. A similar involvement of women in the institutions of the family and the home corresponds to the values of the legitimate society, and thus with respectability.

Native and foreign values

Drawing his inspiration from his description and analysis of informal group formation in particular, Wilson raises the West Indian distinction between reputation and respectability to a higher theoretical level by applying it to the field of institutions and broader ideological conceptions. In that case, reputation stands for the values which are experienced as native and authentic, while respectability is an expression of foreign, alien, colonial or quasi-colonial values. This more ideologically coloured distinction is highly relevant to our purposes, because it brings out very well the betwixt-and-between position of carnival. Later in this chapter I shall discuss to what extent this connection is compatible with the relation of the value complex to the male and female domains (in that case, is feminine behaviour purely the product of imported values?), but before doing so I shall present Wilson's argument without too many (critical) interruptions.

Two opposite sets of binary oppositions play an important social role in societies which have been dominated politically by outsiders for a considerable length of time. Virtually every Caribbean island society is in a colonial or quasi-colonial situation. This implies that the formal structure of institutions, with their corresponding ideology of norms and values, is imposed on society more forcefully than elsewhere. Its origin and legitimacy are primarily located in Europe and the United States, and as a whole it is only echoed by a part of the Creole middle class and elite, appropriately labelled the 'mimic men' by V.S. Naipaul. The structure may have been taken over by society, but has not been incorporated in society.

Wilson associates values of respectability structurally with the colonial experience. A person who behaves respectably assumes, consciously or unconsciously, a role which corresponds to a large extent to colonial ethics and etiquette. Respectability emphasizes continuity, decorum, social position, irreproachable behaviour and correct use of language, which appear in forms which are almost inevitably exaggerations of British models (since we are here dealing with the English-speaking Caribbean). Both style and class structure are inherited from the colonial experience.

Reputation, on the other hand, can be conceived as something native in terms of the colonial or quasi-colonial constellation, and it is both an authentically structuring principle and an anti-principle. The values represented by the concept are Creole in style and can best be illustrated by the phenomenon of the male peer group or crew to which Wilson devotes so much attention (1969: 80). The members of such groups may live or work together, but the domestic family does not function as the axis. They carry the social structure in which they operate with them, since peer groups can always arise at any point where peers meet. They are social units by means of which individuals acquire authority in society, independently of the more formal roles and positions which derive their validity and potency from the social system and political circumstances which are experienced as 'alien' and 'foreign' in relation to the social structure of everyday life. Wilson (1970/71: 30–1) writes:

> Each member protects the other, performs complementary roles and, if necessary, supports the fictions of life. In the absence of any ritualized form of conferral of adulthood onto males, in the absence of any traditional cultural ways of recognizing differential status through prowess, in the presence only of an alien, external and economically determined system of social rewards, it is at least not surprising that there should be some means whereby a man can count for something without necessarily becoming something he can never really be – a white man.

Formally speaking, Wilson argues (1973: 148–9), one would expect male social life to be realized to the full at the structurally institutionalized level of politics, economics or administration. However, in Caribbean societies with a colonial or quasi-colonial status – to put it in black and white without taking into account the possibility of gradual changes – ultimate power, authority, norms and conditions are derived from outside society, and they cannot confer any existential meaning on life in the way that genuine structuring principles can. For example, a mayor occupies an office which is at odds with the norms of society when it is exercised because it only corresponds to an 'alien' frame of reference. A position of political power of this kind does not automatically command respect or obedience, and it fails to provide personal recognition and satisfaction. The person in question is only fully accepted when he manages to act in accordance with the standards of his own society. Reputation is the ethos that the means provide for that purpose. It is the complex of values that reflects correspondence between how people see themselves and how they want to be seen by others. This is achieved by mutual attributions of value to one another by people who feel related on the basis of commonly experienced values and norms. It forms an integrated and harmonious whole with the autonomous social life, deviating from, if not opposed to, the imposed alien culture. The values enshrined in the concept are universally recognized and are the foundation of a 'communion of equal individuals' (Turner 1969: 96), while at the same time forming a basis for differentiation.

In a general critique of Wilson's work, Abrahams (1979: 448) rejects the idea of the existence of an 'egalitarian value system'. He claims that Wilson bases his account of a peer group or crew on this assumption. However, this attack is only possible because it neglects Wilson's own qualifications. Wilson (1969: 79) claimed that the members of a group of this kind present themselves as equals to the outside world, but there are certainly status differences between them. Reputation tends to emphasize the equality of human inequality, while respectability tries to arrange it in classes (Wilson 1973: 223–4).

Crab antics

On the basis of his analysis, Wilson concludes that Caribbean society is characterized by a precarious, flexible structure of relations within antithetical systems. There is the imposed, alien structure of dominance, based on inequality and stratification; seen in that light, the native structure – both subordinated to and reacting against it – is based on equality and differentiation. Both structures are interdependent. Wilson stresses the most important conclusion that 'what is uniquely the Caribbean social system is the dynamic dialectic between them' (1973: 219). The relation between respectability and reputation is expressed in an ongoing dialectic, called 'crab antics' in Providencia, of action and reaction, imposition and evasion, boasting and gossip, climbing up (like crabs in a bucket) and being pulled back down again. This fragile balance between the two value complexes is disturbed by the political independence of some of the Caribbean societies. The withdrawal of the white metropolitan power has drastically diminished the support for respectability, and as Wilson correctly points out (1973: 9, 229), that depreciation is dependent on the degree to which the colonial set of values is taken over and integrated in the social system of the former colony. Probably under the influence of his left-wing, anti-colonial sympathies, Wilson (1973: 224) gets lost in a kind of utopian wishful thinking when he speculates on the increasing domination of reputation over respectability – in the end the crab will prove able to climb over the edge of the bucket. If such domination becomes a fact, it will likewise acquire political power and authority and undoubtedly change its form. Wilson prudently refrains from telling us how we are to imagine that. Will reputation as a dominant system of values still be able to stand for equality and differentiation instead of inequality (virtually inevitably connected with power) and stratification as the main characteristics of respectability? Or will the only gain turn out to be a native socialist or capitalist system instead of a foreign one, a kind of capitalism or socialism with a human face? At this point Wilson's ideas are a long way away from his empirical material. Elsewhere (1973: 229), however, he states that nowhere in the Caribbean is reputation dominant. It is an alternative culture, which exists by virtue of a colonial or quasi-colonial situation in which respectability occupies pride of place.

Back to the native origin of the model?

Abrahams (1979: 448) has the following to say on Wilson's concept:

> Wilson is primarily concerned in his works with how this value dichotomy articulates social structure, and in what ways status hierarchies are put into action and commented upon by the ways in which people group and judge themselves and each other.... Though he finds that he must describe these groupings primarily in stylistic terms, such factors are given theoretical short shrift because of the epiphenomenal position of expressive factors in carrying out analyses of the structuring of society.

Precisely because of this methodology, reinforced by his anti-colonial views, Wilson sometimes lapses into statements and exaggerations which are not substantiated by his empirical material. As a general point of criticism of Wilson's dichotomy of values, Abrahams (1979: 448–9) regards its translation into socio-structural terms of institutions and colonial or quasi-colonial concepts as the main flaw in the analysis. He considers that this does violence to the original native model, which is expressed precisely in the personal and expressive side of life. Although I recognize the methodological problem, I do not agree with Abrahams' criticism. I do not see why a good interpretation of the concept which goes beyond the level mentioned above should be objectionable; 'wary reasoning from analogy', as Geertz (1983: 24) quotes from Locke, 'leads us often into discovery of truth and useful productions, which would otherwise lie concealed.' In abstracting the value complex from its original or native meaning, Wilson joins a discussion which has been going on since the later 1940s on the comparison of the socio-racial structure and cultural pluriformity among the various Caribbean regions, from which the concept of the segmented or plural society has arisen (see Hoetink 1967, 1973). This discussion constantly focuses on the idea of a number of sets of (often contesting) values which play a prominent role in Caribbean society. It was given particular shape in Parson's action theory, which claims that a society has to have a common value system, as against Furnivall's concept of the plural society in which a number of value systems are operational. I have already referred in a different context to the issue of whether society should be conceived as plural (for example M.G. Smith; LaGuerre) or consensual (Braithwaite; R.T. Smith). Against this background, Wilson's treatment of the native dichotomy of values is no less legitimate than that of Abrahams himself (1979: 449), who translates the concept into symbolic and metaphorical terms in order to understand social life better. In his study of the West Indian community in Richland Park on the island of St Vincent, he distinguishes between 'house-land and yard' as the social space where law and order hold sway and where respectability is a target, at least ideally, on the one hand, and the 'bush', symbol of potential natural chaos, and the 'crossroads world' where rough, male, reputation-orientated behaviour dominates and the threat of chaos finds social expression, on the other.

In his article on Christmas and carnival on St Vincent (1983), Abrahams notes that there are competing values between the norms of respectability, based on the home and family and associated with women and social maturity, on the one hand, and the more covert 'crossroads' or street reputation values. West Indian ceremonies reflect this distinction and embody the values and ideal behaviour of one of these two competing systems. Christmas performances are held in the yard, while carnival is predominantly a street festival: 'Whereas Christmas underlines the aesthetic potential of decorum and community solidarity, Carnival explores the realms of aesthetic transport involved in sudden freedom from restraints' (1983: 103).[1] Note that Abrahams' approach is not based on the idea that the two sets of values may be embodied in a single ceremony, which is how I see the Trinidad carnival.

Da Matta (1984a) also considers that the fundamental opposition between home and street can serve as an important instrument in the analysis of the Brazilian social world, especially of how it is ritualized. The category 'home' connotes harmony, warmth and calm, where everything is in its appropriate place. Social behaviour is determined and shaped by kinship and relations of blood. The category 'street' stands for unpredictable events, actions and passions. It is a Hobbesian universe where everyone is engaged in some competition or other with everyone, until some kind of hierarchy is established which imposes an order on it all. The street means the hard reality of life, where robberies take place, where you have to be on your guard, and where you have to be alert to react. Da Matta (1984a: 211) also regards the categories 'bush' (*mato*) or 'forest' (*floresta*) of the rural world or 'nature' of the tribal world as the equivalents of 'street'. The ritual atmosphere of carnival processes these two social domains or worlds in an attempt to transcend them. Carnival evokes a society which is capable of creating a social space where home and street meet one another.

Another criticism of Wilson's work, although Abrahams does not mention it, is that he is vague about or fails to bring out fully the importance of social differentiation in relation to the values of respectability and reputation, even though, as we have already seen, values are tied to a certain extent to social groups or classes. The linking of Wilson's dichotomy to both male and female worlds, as well as to foreign and native, colonial and 'authentic' dominant values and countervalues, creates confusion in this respect. Nevertheless, Wilson's study does contain hints, implicit rather than explicit, that reputation values acquire the most pronounced form among the black lower class, while respectability values acquire their most pronounced form among the middle and upper classes. Thus Wilson writes (1973: 223) that 'the backing for respectability has been drastically reduced with the removal of the white metropolitan power', and a little later: 'The origin of reputation ... is in a sense a reaction to respectability.' When he refers to 'the economics of reputation' (1969: 76), he clearly has the black lower class in mind. His conclusion to the treatment of this aspect is: 'The way money is spent ... is related to the basic complex of values dominating the lives and social relations of "lower class" Caribbean society.'

In another passage, however, Wilson (1969: 78) takes respectability to cover 'the values of the legal society', that is, the general, open system of values in society which serves as a point of reference for determining what is good and proper. However, when Rodman (1971: 195) calls these values the 'general values of the society', Wilson (1973: 220) reacts by denying this flatly. Values of respectability are 'the values of a mainland or metropolitan society espoused locally by a middle and upper class whose ambitions and pretensions are directed away from their own society and culture to that of the metropolis.' The conclusion that may be drawn from this is that, although values of respectability are the express values of the middle and upper class, they also apply as general or dominant values to the black lower class. Recognition of these values by this class, Wilson argues (1973), is just as much a part of the tension between the two systems as their more frequent rejection.

Others are clearer on the relation between the two value complexes and social classes. Powrie (1956: 224) calls respectability the loftiest goal of the coloured middle class. Braithwaite (1975: 138–9) says that this value complex is of importance for the acquisition of legitimate status and is typical of the middle class as a whole. He connects reputation with the striving for higher status within the lower class, for example through gang warfare, stick-fighting, competition in aggression, and calypso-singing. The reason why social differentiation is somewhat disguised by Wilson is that he emphatically wants to make it clear that both value systems are manifested in every social stratum. This view is most clearly expressed in his general linking of respectability to female social life and reputation to male social life. Wilson appears to regard it as less important to distinguish both women and men in terms of social groups and classes, which would have done more justice to the degree to which they observe or strive for the respective values. In this connection, the values of reputation are less problematical than the values of respectability. This can be seen from Wilson's statement (1969: 77) that 'male values' are expressed, though in varying degrees, in actual behaviour, while 'female values' are ideals which people strive to attain, but which can hardly be observed, if at all, in practice. Seen in this light, respectability is a more relative concept. For lower-class women it may be possible to strive for it, though it will always remain unattainable because of the lack of socio-economic resources. Middle-class women, on the other hand, have the greatest difficulty in maintaining the appearance of respectability. In Wilson's words, 'respectability is a degree of *approximation* to standards of the external, legal society', and with reference to the 'feminine values' he remarks 'these are the expectancies of a woman and the things she values, and they *coincide* with the values of the legal society, with "respectability" ' (1969: 78; emphasis added). Once again, however, when he gives an example of the lack of correspondence between the expectation and reality of female chastity and modesty, Wilson ignores social differentiation, which could have revealed the specific and essential difference between the position of lower-class women and that of women from the higher classes. This incongruity is illustrated by the form of cohabitation that is frequently found in the Caribbean – common-law marriage. The view that a man bolsters his reputation by marrying a virgin who will remain faithful to him as his wife, in contrast to his own behaviour, is often affirmed in this common form of union without civil or religious ratification, which acts as a bridge for the paradoxical relation between the male and female worlds. He has not openly invested his reputation or honour in her as long as she can be called a concubine, sweetheart, friend or common-law wife (Wilson 1969: 77), so that she retains a relative freedom in relationships with other men without this entailing any loss of reputation for her 'keeper'. However, Wilson fails to mention that this form of marriage is found predominantly among the lower class, where the discrepancy between reality (reputation) and ideal (respectability) is the greatest (see Braithwaite 1975: 103, 120, 121; Hodge 1987: 72; Black *et al.* 1976: 97; Powrie 1956: 224; Rodman 1971: 43–74, 124–34, 190–200).[2]

Wilson's analysis of the English-speaking Caribbean societies, based on the two value complexes, proves to be fruitful and convincing. To sum up the above discussion, I would like to emphasize a few elements which fit the model better to an analysis of the role of carnival in Trinidad society.

The values of reputation are specifically expressed, though in varying degrees, in male social life, while both men and women share an ideal image of female social life that displays correspondences to, or coincides with, respectability as the value complex of legitimate society. Within the spectrum of social strata, the different values interact to a greater or lesser extent, in such a way that the activities of the lower class are largely governed by values of reputation, while those of the middle class and the elite are under the sway of values of respectability.

Wilson's model and the specific Trinidadian situation

In the process of social change which has been under way in Trinidad since Independence, the values of respectability, which have lost none of their force, are not so much embodied by the group of native whites on the island, even though their presence may work as a role model. The Trinidad Whites or French Creoles, with surnames such as DeVerteuil, Rostant and DeGannes De La Bastide, still enjoy great prestige because of their somatic characteristics, which particularly help to determine social status and mobility in the Caribbean; but they no longer play a role of any importance in the official public sector. As a result of political developments, they have pulled out of that sector and now form separate, closed communities in society in which they pursue social activities, leisure activities and education based on a mixture of (alleged and genuine) values and norms of their mother country and the North American continent. What applied to these groups in the past still applies to a large extent today (Hoetink 1967: 110):

> these old dominant segments in 'colonial or similar' segmented societies entertained the psychic need to regard their society as the extension of the mother-country society – as a homogeneous society, in which the other segments were foreign bodies, outsiders, even aliens, however economically necessary or desirable.

With the exception of a number of impoverished branches of the family, the French Creoles in Trinidad occupy high positions in industry, commerce, manufacturing, hotels and banks, and are thus able to maintain a lifestyle which is associated with their prestige. Some of them are involved in education for light-skinned upper-class children who attend the new private schools or the old prestige schools of the religious denominations. Lewis (1985: 235) states that 147 members of this group – mostly descendants of the earliest French and Portuguese-Creole immigrants – are the actual decision-makers within the private sector in Trinidad.

Besides not usually engaging in political or governmental functions, the French Creoles also refrain from intervening in socio-ideological debate or the shaping of public opinion in the newspapers, on the radio or on television. In no way do they determine the traditional image of Port of Spain. Like the higher echelons of the Creole middle class, they avoid the old shopping centre that fans out from Frederickstreet ('all these vagrants around you!' seems to be always on their lips), and prefer to do their shopping in the sterile, American-style malls which are situated in the same suburbs as their expensive, high-security villas. Young French Creoles look for entertainment in exclusive bars and dance halls, while the older generation frequents expensive and exclusive clubs where blacks and coloureds are not welcome, although it is difficult to turn away the director of the national Medical Centre or the Prime Minister. Their self-chosen splendid isolation has found literal expression in the Calypso Beach Resort on Gasparee Island, a tiny island just off the north-west coast of Trinidad. In this resort, which was recently reopened after having succumbed to corruption, the 'whities' enjoy themselves, especially at weekends, with swimming, boat races, windsurfing, cocktail and dinner parties. This miniature Miami-on-the-cheap comes up to the superficial (television) stereotype of the American way of life. However, it is members of this same social group who maintain the European artistic traditions of ballet and opera within Trinidad society and who take part to a certain extent in carnival activities – though in many cases within the relative exclusiveness of clubs, *fêtes* or upper-middle-class masquerade bands. In Trinidad society the values of respectability of the white elite have found a staunch ally in the Creole middle class, which guarantees a genuine continuation of the alternative value orientations, albeit in a modified and adjusted form. Lewis (1985: 237) writes that it is possible to be black in physiognomy but white in social terms. Littlewood (1984: 712) claims that, if the West Indian opposition between respectability and reputation is translated into the opposition between white and black values (see also Wilson 1973: 222), the member of the black middle class is in a certain sense white.

To return to Wilson's dichotomy, it is useful to add a few comments. He realizes (1969: 70) that his study is based on little original material and that he therefore has to resort to a selection of anthropological research on the Caribbean. He calls it 'disregard of the functionalist shibboleth: "everything in its matrix"', but justifies his approach by referring to the intentional comparative character of his thesis, where a striking correspondence can be observed between the moral values under discussion and their role in social organization. His thesis is thus taken to apply to the classic picture of Caribbean society: a small group of (Creole) whites who enjoy the highest social prestige, and a large group of blacks at the bottom, with an intermediate middle class of coloureds. As we have seen, the presence of a large group of Indians in Trinidad society yields a more complex picture, which at first sight invalidates Wilson's analysis to a certain extent. However, historical and social conditions have set the Indians outside the dominant socio-cultural complex of values and countervalues of what I have called Creole society. It is this Creole social constellation which more or less resembles what Wilson has in mind, and a number of his views can be applied to it as a unit of analysis.

Another, more interesting difference between Trinidad (Creole) society and Wilson's Caribbean prototype emerges if we consider an important criterium of the masculine reputation complex – that is, the lack of native institutions as an integrated part of everyday life through which the members achieve recognition in society as a whole. Wilson's profile (1973: 166) of crews hanging around the rumshop as the only regular meeting place (no clubs or men's houses, no initiation ceremonies or organized competitions) – is a good illustration of how native values acquire form. However, while it may be a comprehensive depiction of the economically insignificant island of Providencia, with a population of a couple of thousand, this certainly does not apply to the complex urban society of Port of Spain. The crew, whose members are known as *limeys* in Trinidad, and the rumshop are to be found here too with the significance which Wilson gives them, but native social life is played out in a great many other areas as well. The word 'limey' originally referred to a British Marine (limejuicer), and was associated with the traditional use of lime on board ship to prevent scurvy. Both American and British marines were stationed on Trinidad during World War II. The presence of the former, with plenty of money in their pockets, meant a boom in the amusement industry (theatres, cinemas, dance halls and bars). The modest pay of the British marine barred him from taking part in this expensive entertainment. While his American counterpart threw himself into the joys of dancing and the calypso tent, he and his mates were left bitterly in the street, as close as possible to the noise of the fun so that they could at least pick up something of the seductive musical rhythms. 'Liming', 'to take a lime', 'we're just liming', became expressions for just hanging around. Where groups of young black males are concerned, this corresponds to the broader significance which Wilson attaches to the crew. The phenomenon has been intensively studied in Port of Spain by Lieber (1976, 1981; see too Eriksen 1990: 23–43). He regards liming as a form of work, 'with eyes and ears keenly tuned to the flow of action and the recognition of advantage' (1976: 326). The appropriation of the term by the Creole middle class has turned liming into a national occupation, transforming innocent activities like a beach picnic, an ice-cream or a roti in Queens Park Savannah into unique Trinidadian experiences which are by definition incomprehensible to outsiders.

Referring to the work of the Herskovits (1947), Wilson (1973: 207–8) picks out as one of the main differences between Providencia and Trinidad the excessive number of native religious communities, including the Shango cult (Simpson 1962; 1964), Spiritual Baptists (Glazier 1983), and secular clubs on Trinidad. These organizations provide an outlet and opportunity for quasi-political activities, which under certain circumstances may lead to actual (counter-) politics as an alternative to, for example, the formal institutions of the police and the judicial apparatus.

Wilson does not offer any further explanation of precisely what he means here. He ignores the Trinidad carnival in his comparison of the two islands, while this unique Caribbean festival has a rich tradition going back more than 150 years and is deeply rooted in a mixture of native social and cultural values. Many elements of Wilson's reputation complex have here been materialized in institution-like organizational forms. Manning (1983: 14) writes on the Rio carnival that the festival simply seems to take place as an annually recurring miracle wrought by a *deus ludens*. In fact, there is a complex organization. The samba schools and masquerade groups observe a high degree of discipline and a rigid hierarchy. They are bureaucratic institutions loaded with protocols. 'It takes a great amount of order to produce "a sweet disorder", a great deal of structuring to create a sacred play-space and time for antistructure', Turner (1983: 118) writes in connection with the Rio de Janeiro carnival. Da Matta (1984a: 228) speaks of an organizational inversion in which the groups are arranged in order to 'play'. These carnival groups are among the most authentic and spontaneous forms of association, Da Matta claims; they are not copied from any external model, deriving from frequently imitated countries like France, England or the United States.

Some of the activities connected with the festival in Trinidad likewise extend beyond the few days or weeks of preparations. They take up six or nine months and thus require durable and solid forms of co-operation. The mas camps, the workshops where the carnival costumes are made, and the pan yards call for a level of organization way beyond the loose, informal character of the crews. They imply networks of people whose positions in relation to one another are more or less clearly defined and definitive, and which interact with relative frequency and efficiency. Every masquerade band which appears in the city streets and on stage in the Savannah on Mardi Gras has a mas camp as its base. This is where the band leader and designer, relatives, friends and acquaintances meet in the weeks preceding carnival in longer and longer sessions to get the band into shape, exchange ideas and make plans for the following year. Interested parties can choose a costume from design drawings. Ordering and purchasing a costume imply taking part in the band. Weller (1966: 68–77), who carried out research on the social structure of steelbands (too early to be acquainted with Wilson's ideas, but apparently familiar with and drawing on the anthropological discussion on the definition of non-groups and quasi-groups which was going on at the time – see for example Boissevain 1968), arrives at the conclusion that the non-musical aspects of these groups can be regarded as the characteristics of formal clubs and organizations. Steelbands and the social units mentioned earlier are at any rate organization and group forms produced by a countervalue culture – of which carnival is in many respects the main expression – which often found the formal institutions of the respectable dominant culture to be obstacles to its development. We may be optimistic about the future of carnival if we follow Da Matta (1984a: 228): 'Everything that is defined as being neither serious nor bourgeois remains. The rest, subject to the waves of enthusiasm and the ideological ecstasy of the elites and the well-born, always changes and disappears.' To allow ourselves to be carried away by Wilson's speculations for a moment, might the significantly higher level of institutionalization of the reputation culture, implying a greater recognition of it by society as a whole, mean that in Trinidad the attempts of the crab to climb out of the bucket are more successful than elsewhere in the Caribbean?

To sum up, West Indian life is based on oppositions and on the dialogue in which they are dramatized but seldom resolved. Wilson's model of a conflict of values offers deeper insight into the nature, meaning and inter-relations of these oppositions, which can be illustrated diagrammatically (see Table 5.1). This is not intended to be more than a list of the most salient main and secondary dichotomies which have cropped up in the course of the discussion of the model. Note that the final opposition in the table, taken from Abrahams (1983: 3–4), does not occur literally in the text. The sweet talker uses a local version of standard English which is appropriate to structured meetings (wedding, wake, traditional performances in the context of carnival or Christmas), while the broad man-of-words speaks a stylized Creole which can be associated with crossroads behaviour in a discussion where reputation is at stake (rumshop, market stall, bus and taxi). Abrahams categorizes both forms of speech as non-Western; they are only superficially affected by European culture.

The picture of values and countervalues outlined in Table 5.1 can be regarded as the socio-cultural context which best illuminates the function and meaning of the Trinidad carnival. The account of a few important aspects of the carnival in relation to its social context that follows in the next two chapters contains many elements which refer directly or indirectly to the characteristics of West Indian society – in this case Trinidad – as delineated by Wilson. In this perspective, while remaining loyal to the spirit of Wilson's conflict model, I single out two theses which typify society at the level of culture and ideology:

Table 5.1 *Wilson's model of value conflict; main and secondary dichotomies*

REPUTATION	RESPECTABILITY
Main dichotomy	
Male world	Female world
Informal group formation	Formal structure/institutions
Native values	Foreign values/colonial/ quasi-colonial
Secondary dichotomy	
Crew (men)	(Home) family (women)
Rumshop	Church
Concubinate	Marriage
Sexual freedom	Sexual continence
Black/lower class	White/Creole middle class
Differentiation	Stratification
Egalitarian	Hierarchical
Personally achieved status, based on interaction of mutual attributions of value	Legal status Values based on legal society
Crossroads/bush	Home, yard and land
Action-orientated	Orientated towards maintenance of order
Talking broad	Talking sweet

1   Trinidad society develops within the force field of two conflicting socio-cultural orientations. On the one hand, there is the need to retain what diverse social groups each experience and regard as the expressions and products of their own culture; on the other hand, there is a strong cultural influence from abroad, particularly from the North American continent.

2   There is no single social convention or common cultural heritage or identity in Trinidad society; it is divided by 'race', colour, shade, class and divergent historical origin.[3]

NOTES

1   In the main Miller's (1994: 82–134) interpretation of Christmas and carnival follows along similar lines. On pages 82–3 he writes:

> At the heart of the distinction between the festivals lies [sic] two forms of temporal consciousness. Carnival will be seen to objectify the very idea of an event and the sense by which transience expresses an ideal of freedom. Christmas, on the other hand, acts to transcend the vicissitudes of the present for an image of an unchanging line of descent.

2   This is not the place to go into the cultural and historical background, particularly the period of slavery, which could explain this relation between men and women. There is an extensive literature on the subject. By way of illustration of more profound causes, I cite Merle Hodge (1974: 115):

> ... the whole humiliation of slavery meant an utter devaluation of the manhood of the race; the male was powerless to carry out his traditional role of protector of the tribe, he was unable to defend either himself or his women and children from capture and transportation, from daily mishandling. His manhood was reduced to his brawn for the labor he could do for his master and to his reproductive function.... The black man had no authority over his children, but the woman did. The children's mothers, or female child-rearers, were responsible for the upbringing of the race. Women became mother and father to the race.

3   By distinguishing 'race', colour and shade, I want to emphasize once again that the society is divided not only by social class, but also by 'race'. In the words of Lewis (1985: 236):

> Race is added to class. Historically, that goes back to the fact that from the very beginnings the twin processes of ethnic admixture and cultural assimilation resulted in the typical Caribbean multilayered pigmentocracy: white, black, brown, yellow, and red, with every gradation in between. So today, the society is a fantastic rainbow, in terms of both color and culture.

A little later he writes (1985: 237) that the system of classification in Caribbean societies is essentially based on the concept of shade. The shade of skin, complexion, not the possession of 'negro blood', is the criterium for social acceptability. Naipaul (1982) writes: '... the West Indian accepted his blackness as his guilt, and divided people into white, fusty, musty, dusty, tea, coffee, cacao, light black, dark black. He never seriously doubted the validity of the prejudices of the culture to which he aspired.'

6 | The dynamic interplay of conflicting orientations: between Miami and Africa

Drawing on a number of incidents that took place during the four periods of field work, this chapter provides an account of conflicting beliefs, opinions and points of view, a *potpourri* of widely discussed events, connected with the notion of culture as it is given shape by the various social classes and groups in Trinidad. These themes recur every year in a different guise, and in their range of variations and gradations they are all associated with the main theme that dominates social discussion: the search for national identity. Some themes prove to be directly linked to carnival, others are only marginally so, if at all. Nevertheless, the connecting link between the various themes is that carnival is not just a (symbolic) form of expression, but that it also (ideologically) provokes the formation of opinion on all kinds of issues. The festival creates a climate which generates a broad social discussion of issues which extend beyond the organization and content of carnival itself. It incites society to think about questions of morality, ethics, 'race', class and historical origin. It is the festival of the ticklish affairs. In this sense, the carnival period and the festival itself are the setting for a dramatization of values and countervalues which alternate turbulently and chaotically.

We are the most beautiful people of the world

Tourist Board and National Carnival Commission are the mouthpiece of the middle-class-dominated government which advocates a moderate, middle-of-the-road kind of nationalism. Although Mintz finds it useful to distinguish between political nationalism and national identity, there is a mutual relation between them – an excess of political nationalism is often a sign of a weakly developed sense of national identity ('The more portraits of the leader, the less popular he is', I heard an exiled Syrian writer say on television.) This is a logical correlation, according to Hoetink (1973: 148), because if it is only possible to speak of a national identity when the historical experience of a country is understood and transmitted as a common experience, it is evident that expressions of political nationalism both in the past and the present serve to reinforce this notion of communality; and the latter goes on all the time in Trinidad in every shape and form, including statements of self-overestimation, self-adoration and self-love. Walcott typifies it as follows (cited by Wayne Brown in the *Daily Express* (*DE*), 18 February 1988):

> ... the Creole mentality ... is the shrillest kind of hedonism, asserting with almost hysterical self-assurance that Trinidad is a paradise ... a particular boastfulness, passing for panache or a sense of the good life ... and it is a miserable failure because it passes so easily for racial pride, for communality.

An extreme form of mass narcissism was revealed by the slip of the tongue made by the Minister of Culture, Donawa McDavidson, when she opened the national song festival in the Hilton Hotel in April 1986: 'The people of Trinidad and Tobago', she declared in front of a packed auditorium and the television cameras, 'are the most creative and beautiful people of Trinidad and Tobago'. The audience chuckled. 'Shall I say it again?' she asked, undeterred. This time she got it right: Trinidadians are the most creative and beautiful people of the *world*, of course. Hardly a day goes by without a statement like the following in the papers:

> Trinidadians are unique. Physically we are the most beautiful people of the world. We are different, we are the luckiest, all because the mixture of races that make us Trinidadians happens no where else on the globe – we are blessed and lucky. Talent flows from the veins of our people that other nations grasp (*Express*, 13 February 1986).

> Trinidad and Tobago are two beautiful islands with a rich mixture of people living harmoniously together with a unique and exotic cultural background, admired by many (*TG*, 26 February 1985).
> Our style is magnificent (*TG*, 1 March 1987).

> We could play an important part ... in rebuilding humankind if the Russian-American conflict does explode. With the self-destruction of Europe and North America our creative arts would then be internationally relevant. It would be our task to start a new civilization (*TG*, 21 January 1987).
> Our island-paradise ..., a fairytale land (*TG*, 12 March 1987).

This self-adulation is supplemented with similar outpourings by foreigners, packaged in headlines such as:

> *I love you Trinidad, you are the nicest people of the world*
> *Thank you Trinidadians for a wonderful carnival*
> *German wants more of our carnival*
> *American professor loves our calypso*
> *T&T gets good rating from Washington Post*
> *Foreign journalist lauds our carnival.*

The same effulgent vocabulary is used in the propaganda and information material produced by the Tourist Board and the NCC. It is the middle-class point of view, on which Naipaul (1982: 76) remarks: 'Just as they take pleasure in their American modernity, so they take pleasure in living up to the ideals of the tourist brochure.' The process of Americanization and the oil boom period have taken the development of an aesthetic and lifestyle a stage further, particularly among middle-class Trinidadians, which correspond and appeal to the type of tourist that Trinidad would like to attract at the moment. That is why the Tourist Board and NCC campaigns to promote tourism are not just designed for the purpose of appealing to the taste and needs of the predominantly North American tourists (who still do not come in large enough numbers), but they are also reflections of the 'more original' world of the (middle-class) Trinidadians with their traditional receptivity to the foreign colonial or quasi-colonial complex of values. This ambiguity is surprisingly prominent in an editorial in the *Trinidad Guardian* (5 February 1987). The writer begins with the apt remark: 'It is we who become the assassins of our culture when we stop being ourselves, and when we present an image we think the tourist would appreciate.' He goes on to make a proposal that is perfectly in keeping with the image that he is rejecting: '... we must develop a cultural policy to make us what we are – a society whose harmony is a model for the world.' The 'dominant somatic norm image' (Hoetink 1967; 1973) and the related development of the capacity for mimesis have caused the ideal image which Trinidadians have of themselves and their surroundings to be largely 'read off' from the image of the world of the white foreigner, recreated and internalized in their own minds. Just as the Dutch might make themselves believe that they spend their life on clogs in theme park surroundings with windmills and flowering tulip fields, so the Trinidadians din into themselves by constantly trumpeting their own praises that they belong to the 'most beautiful people of the world' and live in a carefree and cheerful 'tropical paradise of sand, sea and sun'. Subsequently, the process of middle-classization or embourgeoisement (Lewis 1985: 236) has ensured that the ideal self-image has not been limited to that socio-economic group where it developed. To a greater or lesser extent, middle-class attitude, taste and morality have become the common property of every group in Trinidad society.

American trash

However, the discussion in the press on the range of programmes provided by the nationalized Trinidad broadcasting company reveals the ambiguity. The fact that the majority of television productions have come from abroad for years, especially from the United States, is still a topic for debate as to whether this is a case of cultural imperialism which threatens the native culture. The emergence of American satellite television in the mid-1980s increased the topicality of the issue. 'African and East Indian are equally treated like bastards in this country', wrote the *TG* (13 February 1988), 'and today the new colonizer is the satellite dish.' The personal view of a spokesperson for the American embassy in Barbados was that a second invasion took place after the landing of American troops in Grenada, namely the invasion by American satellite television. This has an even greater influence on the island states than Reagan's military action of October 1983 (*Express*, 17 November 1985). The Caribbean Media Workers' Association, a body set up in 1985 which was itself naturally affected by the phenomenon, expressed its deep concern at the 'concentrated cultural penetration of our region through satellite technology and the invasion of our airwaves' (ibid.). William Demas, president of the Caribbean Development Bank, complained that regional television is used for 'pure junk' from the USA, which is against the interest of the struggle for cultural identity and nation-building. The plethora of commercials and shows is absolutely no reflection of the average American citizen, he claimed, and it encourages viewers to adopt a pattern of spending and consumption which the Caribbean countries cannot permit themselves. What Demas objects to is the fact that people become obsessed by material needs which correspond to a very high level of economic activity (*Express*, 19 April 1986). 'We must change', he remarks somewhat cryptically elsewhere, 'our perception of ourselves before others will change our opinion of us.... Soap operas are an insult to our intelligence, waste of our time and drain our valuable foreign exchange' (*DE*, 20 January 1987). 'Countries in the Caribbean region should be encouraged to view and market shows based on their own culture and styles and shun pre-packaged foreign productions', concluded the Caricom Committee of Telecommunications Administrations during its first meeting in Port of Spain. 'We have to defend our own cultures, and at the same time try to counterattack certain types of material which have become a steady diet for people in the region', were the words of the Minister of Transport from St Lucia at that meeting (*TG*, 5 June 1986).

As long as there was no danger that this tough language would be turned into action, it hardly provoked any reactions from the Trinidadian public. Everyone viewed it as regional nationalistic propaganda. However, the situation changed rapidly when two ministers of the recently elected NAR government used the same language to outline their policy proposals. It was probably under the influence of the new course which the NAR government announced with much song and dance that it intended to follow – a sort of moral rearmament after what it called 'thirty years of corruption' under the PNM government – that the Minister of Culture, Jennifer Johnson, stated during her first appearance in parliament that 'shows like Dallas, Dynasty and Falcon Crest are trash, American trash' (*TG*, 31 March 1987). Soon afterwards, Brinsley Samaroo, Minister in the Office of the Prime Minister, added a patriotic note by pointing out the danger of the foreign (especially American) management and control of television amusement and information for a developing country such as Trinidad and Tobago. More attention should be devoted to local programmes with an emphasis on the rich Caribbean culture which gives people a sense of their own worth. Samaroo is quoted in *TG* (29 March 1987):

A sense, well, if I have come from Africa, I have not come from a backward and decadent civilization or a backward and decadent uncivilization, a place where you only have cannibals and so on, which is what we have been portrayed as by the Europeans. But one would like to see the African coming from a highly civilised society (from which indeed he came) ... creating in the first instance, the Caribbean out of the forest and jungle he found.

The views of these two government spokespeople unleashed a discussion:

It is ridiculous to say that seeing their TV programmes endanger our culture or our minds.

TG, 17 January 1987

The almost obscene obsession with the programme planners of our sole television station to flush us down the tank of American, Australian, Canadian or British life.

DE, 2 February 1987

Talking about American trash is a revelation of double-standards. We are thriving on Americanism for our very existence.

I can watch an American programme without being unpatriotic to my country.

Criticise American programmes and you will have a population of frustrated, bored and starved [sic] for entertainment.

TG, 28 February 1987

Some people in the country have a paranoia about American shows. But considering the way we dress and our geographical position and climate and the fact that we are more closely linked with the North American life style than that of any other country, why the fuss? ... Our children have ... to pay a very heavy price with the new culture shock imposed on them by foreign shows that are meaningless and of little moral value. That is the deculturisation process we have been subjected to.

TG, 3 March 1987

The emotional, sloppy, putrifying fed [sic] to the population is more dangerous than drugs.

TG, 18 March 1987

I cannot help but applaud Dr. Samaroo. The controversy he has succeeded in stirring, the debate he has initiated, the concerns he has caused, are 25 years overdue.

TG, 22 March 1987

I am sure that the Minister of Culture forgot in her statement to condemn the other kind of trash — the behaviour that we display on television throughout the Carnival season.

TG, 31 March 1987

What is striking in the debate that went on is that shows and soap operas of the Dallas type stand for all that American culture has to offer; the question is never raised as to whether the purchase of television productions of a different kind would provide an image to remove the objections put forward. Such a question would first of all throw light on a problem facing Trinidad, in company with so many other developing countries. A journalist from the New York magazine *The Village Voice*, who wanted to write on this topic and was visiting Trinidad as part of his project, told me that the television corporations in the USA distribute their productions in prearranged packages, drawn from the most popular and least controversial programmes, which are offered very cheaply to Third World television stations with limited financial resources. In this sense there is a large-scale dumping of American trash going on which can be called cultural imperialism. If people want something different, they will have to pay for it. This retail policy also has consequences for the production of local programmes. The Cosby Show costs the Trinidad and Tobago Television Company (TTT) US$165, while ten times that sum has to be paid for its own half-hour popular satirical programme Gayelle (*TG*, 20 March 1987). Besides, there is a strong tendency to prefer what is at any rate a technically high-quality product to a native programme produced on a low budget which barely rises above amateur level.

However, these questions are to all intents never raised in the debate, and the equation of American culture with Dallas is symptomatic of the gap between image and reality. A letter to the *DE* (15 March 1987) puts the point succinctly: 'We go on countless vacations in America – to Disneyland, Orlando and Epcot Centre ... the end result is that Trinidad and Tobago is hooked on Americanism'. In other words, America as one big consumer paradise and amusement park. It is not so much the multifaceted American culture that is being criticized as the limited Trinidadian perception of it – which has the same ideological origins as the propaganda image churned out by the Tourist Board and the National Carnival Commission. It is clear that the government also exerts an influence on the programming policy of (state-owned) TTT, even if it speaks of 'responsible distance' and 'responsible division' (*TG*, 29 March 1987). Minister Samaroo accuses the government of doing nothing to stop the growth of satellite saucers in Trinidad and Tobago. What are they for? he wonders: 'Do we want to open our society to everything that comes from any part of the world without any discrimination?' (ibid.).

The victory of Samaroo's NAR at the end of 1986 brought about a political landslide, but not the kind of radical change in the way people or the government think which could earn the approval of the new Minister's patriotism. Samaroo however attributed such a revolutionary spirit to the change: in his eyes, 'reconstruction is a state of mind' (*TG*, 22 March 1987). That the rise to power of the NAR did not change much in this state of mind can be seen from the fact that less than a week after Samaroo's statements, Prime Minister Robinson took the information portfolio out of his hands.

Yours cordially in culture

In an interview with the general manager of TTT (*TG*, 20 March 1987), the interviewer claimed that local programmes may be divided into two main categories: endless live recordings of all kinds of carnival events; and heavy, indigestible discussions. 'Cannot there be a greater variety and especially humour?' he asked. 'We do our best to cover all aspects of Trinidad's culture – drama, music, etc.', the manager replied. 'The quality is very mixed and much that is offered is hopelessly unsuitable in the form as received.'

An editorial in the same newspaper (*TG*, 6 March 1987) noted that Trinidad has no local film industry worthy of note, no national music school, no training facility for steelband music or institute for Indian culture, no school of journalism, and no national theatre. 'We can't exist solely on steelband and calypso', is the complaint of the TTT manager when he is asked to devote more attention to local culture – which implicitly reveals what is meant by the blanket term 'culture'. It is one of the many indispensable ideological non-starters, expressed with quasi-sacred respect, but seldom explained any further, or if so, only by making direct reference to masquerade, calypso and steelband. In the eyes of many, culture *is* carnival. When the chairperson of the NCC announces the 'Old Time Carnival in its true and authentic sense' in the foreword to a carnival paper as a new item in the official carnival show, he signs with 'Yours Cordially in Culture'. Naipaul (1982: 76) puts it like this:

> Culture is spoken of as something quite separate from day-to-day existence, separate from advertisements, films and comic strips. It is like a special native dish, something like a callaloo [a native soup]. Culture is a dance – not a dance that people do when more than three of them get together – but the one put on in native costume on a stage. Culture is music – not the music played by wellknown bands ... – but the steelband. Culture is song – not the commercial jingle which, as much as the calypso, has become the folksong of Trinidad, nor the popular American songs which are heard from morning till night – not these, but the calypso.

In an article in *TG* (13 February 1988) headed 'What is wrong with a callaloo culture?', Ronald John sums up a number of complaints voiced by spokespeople from the Indian camp against this view of culture. Indian culture must not be considered as the bastard of Trinidad and Tobago; some ethnic groups (people of African origin, according to the writer of the article) believe that, on the basis of ancestral rights which are superior to those of the Indians, they are entitled to call themselves the natural successors to the British administrators; and finally, a 'Callaloo culture' is imposed on the Indians, based on calypso, steelband and carnival.

John presents the latter complaint as a denigration of the most original art form that the Caribbean has produced. He detects in it an undertone of aversion to any idea of a marriage between African and Indian culture. To demonstrate that such a marriage has already been consummated, he cites a list of famous calypsonians, steelband arrangers and costume designers from various ethnic origins with an emphasis on Indian participation. It appears to be difficult for prominent Indians to accept that the rise of the 'callaloo culture' – with steelband, calypso and carnival in the vanguard as unique creations with a predominantly African backing – should be *the* element of cohesion to bring them together. 'A lot of individualists have refused to accept this as the true reason why all racial groups have responded to it', John writes.

Culture as a thing

Awareness of a Trinidadian culture is mainly connected with carnival and has hardly any ideological anchoring in a history whose cultural manifestations or products operate in a much wider field. As a result, culture is conceived as an independent thing, 'cultural objectification' Handler (1988) would say[1] — and things can be taken away from you. This may explain the fear which is regularly expressed that foreigners, or other outsiders will pose a threat to local culture or take over the masquerade, steelband or calypso. Thus the Minister of Culture stated that Trinidad and Tobago, together with Barbados, must join forces to prevent 'foreign cultural penetration' (*DE*, 18 January 1988). Henry Antoine, president of the North American and England International Carnival Association, was eager to assure his audience at a media conference in Port of Spain in 1988 that it was not the purpose of his delegation to take away the cultural riches of Trinidad; a sample was all that was required to make it clear to people abroad where they could find the rest. The report that crops up now and again in the press that the calypso originated in Grenada, St Lucia or somewhere else immediately sets many pens to work to emphasize once again that Trinidad is its crucible.

The most striking expression of the relation between carnival and culture during the last few years is the attention that has been paid to the alleged threat to the position of pan as a musical instrument, or of the steelband as a whole. 'Pan in Danger', sang the calypsonian Merchant; 'They can't take pan away from us' was the incantatory headline above a large newspaper article (*Express*, 17 November 1985). The Premier George Chambers must have been terribly shocked, claims columnist Rhona Baptiste (*Express*, 21 January 1986), when he was welcomed on a visit to Japan by a group of young Japanese who played the national anthem on the pan. He was told that the 'world's best known imitators' needed only one week to discover how to knock a musical scale out of the steel. 'If we don't watch out', Baptist cites a despondent secondary school teacher, 'foreigners from both the USA and Canada will soon be teaching us pan.'

The cause of the panic must be sought in the decreasing importance of the pan or steelband within the complex of carnival activities. Of course, the steelband still comes completely into its own during the lively competition with its spectacular conclusion in the final (Panorama) in Queen's Park Savannah, but many see the very fact that this musical form is being more and more confined to this part of carnival as proof of its decline. '[It] transformed the steelband music from an essentially street music to a stage music', Cohen (1993: 97–8) writes. He refers to Roger Taylor's (1978) study entitled *Art, an Enemy of the People*, in which the latter argues that when popular cultural movements are made to imitate high culture they are thereby destroyed as people's culture. During Jouvert Morning room is still made for the steelband among the masquerade groups in the street, but when the mas bands move from the inner city to Queen's Park Savannah on Mardi Gras, the sound of sweet pan – which does not carry very far – is drowned by the electronic violence pouring out of the enormous lorries which escort the procession. The steelband is no longer a match for the musical taste of the younger generation of carnival revellers in particular, with their unlimited hunger for the maximum number of decibels. For example, in 1987 the traditional children's procession on carnival Saturday was a fiasco because the carnival commission had decided to exclude all music except that of the steelbands, 'not only to give the steelband its rightful place in the culture and history of our country', according to the chairperson of the committee, 'but also to introduce to mas-playing children of this country the rich heritage of jumping and chipping to the steelband on the road' (*TG*, 25 February 1987). However, the volume of the steelband is no longer adequate for the contemporary masquerade groups of a hundred or so participants, so that many children just jostled around without any musical accompaniment; one could no longer speak of a cohesive group of dancers whose costume and theme came across. Thus the attempts by carnival aficionados to restore the steelband to its original place in the carnival end up as rather contrived manifestations which have the character of invented traditions (Hobsbawm and Ranger 1983).

An example of the discussion of this question is provided by the debate organized by the University of the West Indies in the City Hall auditorium of Port of Spain in November 1985. One of the topics discussed was whether the steelband should perform classical music. A number of speakers considered that the melodic arrangements of classical music were 'anti-progressive' for the steelband. Standardization of the pan and learning to read and play European music would amputate its native roots, it was claimed. After all, panmen were already less and less involved in the carnival festivities. Lennox Pierre, Trinidad's historian of the steelband *par excellence* (one minister called him 'a living national treasure'), warned against this kind of cultural isolationism. He argued that the history of the steelband had produced a new family of musical instruments. The steelband was a new kind of orchestra, which was eminently suitable for European symphonic music. He thought it ridiculous to suppose that this would mean a severing of its native roots: 'Suppose that it was only allowed to play music from the country of origin on the piano!' Imprisoning the steelband within the confines of carnival hampers its further development towards a mature position among all the other musical instruments of the world. The mayor of Port of Spain, Stevenson Sarjeant, referred to the general ambivalence of the people of Trinidad with regard to the diffusion of their culture – they want international recognition of the pan, but at the same time they want to keep the instrument entirely for themselves: 'When the outside world recognises it, we become afraid that they would take it from us, that we would lose it'.

Pan has acquired a definitive place in the international music world, and the series of concerts under the name 'Pan is beautiful' which is held every year in September has developed into a renowned and curious festival of classical works performed by steel bands. All the same, the fear still remains that 'the only new musical instrument created over the past hundred years throughout the entire world!' (*Express*, 21 January 1986) is in serious danger of extinction. It is as if pan's marginalization from carnival entails its marginalization from Trinidadian culture. The phenomenon ends up in a sort of cultural no-man's-land where, shorn of all defence, it is prey to any outsider who greedily reaches out for it.

The African connection

The resoluteness with which people treat carnival as the be all and end all of culture is matched by the uncertainty or lack of clarity on the historical or ideological legitimation of that claim. Once (national) culture demands a wider perspective and a broader cultural basis, the discussion rapidly runs into a twilight zone in which terms like Yoruba, Shango, Rada, Rasta, Black Power, and Black Muslim combine as the amalgam of what is regarded as the African heritage. Representatives of this kind of eclecticism are usually to be found among the ranks of self-taught intellectuals and artists who cultivate a West African image in their style of dress and behaviour and who try to emphasize their psychical rebirth by changing their name. S. Naipaul (1985: 15–16) connects this phenomenon with the period which followed colonial domination: 'As imperial ties and restraints dissolved, one reality, one self, was lost. Something snapped. Wild dreams rushed in to fill the vacuum.' He cites the case of a prominent lawyer in Port of Spain who changed his name overnight to Atta Khufu Obafemi Kujifi. 'You see', the latter explained to an interviewer from a Trinidad newspaper, 'once you start thinking African then a name like Arthur Fleming Lawrence is a plain embarrassment.' The Trinidad-born BBC television producer Darcus Howe changed his name to Owonsu, and the poet and head of the West Indian Reference Library Pearl Springer – 'with a degree in information science', according to a newspaper article on her – adopted the name Eintou after she had assumed a rasta lifestyle. 'It should be no surprise though', the article continues, 'that Pearl Eintou Springer, red beret conspicuously planted atop the flowing locks which is part of the lady's fixed personality, is culturally obsessed' (*TG*, 29 March 1987). The popular calypsonian David Rudder told music reviewer Dave Elcock (*DE*, 21 February 1988) that he called his son Khafra after what he claimed was the first in a series of black pharaohs of Egypt:

> He was the first one with African features, African complexion, y'know? And he was one of tst influential Pharaohs also, and I believe the Sphinx is one of the manifestations of Khafra. I took him (my son) back to the source of creation, like.

Rudder's explanatory remarks demonstrate the tendency among people who are orientated towards Africa constantly to sublimate and idolize an African heritage put together from a mixture of mythical and historical elements. In that case, S. Naipaul (1985: 16) remarks, Africa would have given the world jurisprudence, philosophy, medicine, religion, astronomy, music, magic and natural science; it was Africa that brought civilization to Europe, not vice versa, despite the misleading claims of the white world. This entails the daunting task of Africanizing the entire history of the world. An article in the *Sunday Express* (31 January 1988) with the headline 'African blood in all peoples' veins' offers a good selection of this style of historiography: the first Hindus were black, curly-haired Ethiopians who had settled in the valley of the Indus; African rule in India lasted thousands of years; African tribes conquered Greece, Persia, China and other territories; the Veda mentions Krishna as the black leader; the powerful Indian emperor of black origin, Shah Jahan, had an African architect build the Taj Mahal for his beloved wife, Muntaz Mahal; there was an African empress on the throne of China from 373 to 397 and many Chinese emperors had African wives; King George III of England was married to Charlotte Sophia, a descendant of Cardinal Medici and an Ethiopian woman; five hundred years before Columbus African merchants from the Nile delta and Sidon were already trading in the New World; Columbus's helmsman was an African who had made the journey before. Schopenhauer had already argued that the white race was a pale version of the Grimaldis, an African people that lived all over Europe for seventy thousand years.

The Africanization of carnival

Because Africa is the key concept when it comes to referring to the wider context of culture or tying it down to a genuine history, these members of Trinidad society have a great need, more than is already evident, to derive carnival as the cultural event *par excellence* from Africa or to Africanize as many elements of the festival as possible. David Rudder is an exponent of the latter tendency. He explains his personal relation with Africa as follows: 'I am seeking to be African, as in the sense of, er, y'know, a man will say you're a black man... you supposed to deal with Africa. I am a black man, so... Africa deals with me' (*DE*, 6 March 1988). He gives his calypsos a pan-African allure by adding musical elements from jazz, samba, soul, reggae and other genres ('the music have Africa in it, y'know?' – *DE*, 21 February 1988). He has an equally strong urge to give his compositions a mystically coloured Afro-religious significance. Discussing 'The Hammer', his famous ode to panman Rudolph Charles, he claims that the song is also a eulogy of the pan as a glorious substitute for the African drum which was prohibited by the whites, but he goes further:

> Because of that tearing away through Middle Passage experience, you get tearing away of the culture. The drum just take on a different face and the drum come back. But it come back, and the warrior come back again, and the tribe come back again because Laventille is a tribe. The tribe regroup again and even the sense of – if you check Yoruba, the old African tradition, iron, metal is always a strong symbolic force; and 'The Hammer' was more than just a hammer that pound pan. Pan was metal too, but the Hammer was like a source of strength. The Hammer was like the image of victory and survival.... Europe come and create all this confusion, and we now have to kind of regroup and recreate something out of the confusion now. And carnival was one of the areas that we regrouped.

It is also noteworthy that Rudder's compositions combine rhythmical and vocal elements which are directly derived from the moments of trance experience in the Trinidadian version of the Shango ritual. It has happened on more than one occasion that dancers went into a trance during Rudder's performance. Under the headline 'Rudder's Orisa chant invokes spirits; 2 women possessed at discotheque', *DE* (9 March 1987) carried a report of the change of mood which took place in a disco during Rudder's song 'Calypso Music'. When he repeated the chant 'Orisa, this music is trouble, Orisa, on and on, it makes you shake like a Shango, calypso, why you shaking you don't know, calypso' above the melody, the public in the disco clapped to accentuate the stirring rhythm and gradually formed a large circle around two women dressed in white who, jerking wildly, their eyes closed, their faces sweating profusely, seemed to be unaware of what they were doing and where they were (see too Nunley 1988: 115–16). Rudolph Eastman, a *soi disant* 'cultural researcher and founding member of the Orisa religion in Trinidad and Tobago', commented:

> The conditions were right and Rudder's chant was an invitation to an Orisa deity.... That is what this religion and the chants do to people. It affects the mind, body and soul and takes you out of yourself. These women had an unconscious manifestation.

Eastman is in fact as keen as Rudder to regard carnival entirely as a manifestation of African culture. In 1988 he was invited by Eintou Springer to give a lecture for primary school children in her library on the relation between religion and carnival. Without any reservations, he included carnival figures like Pierrot Grenade, Dame Lorraine, Burrokeet, Dragon, Papa Bois and Midnight Robber in the African heritage. The main line of his argument was that the festival was a continuation of West African ritual practices. It was therefore unwise for mas players frivolously to represent things which he considered to belong to the sacred and esoteric preserve of the African religions. It was necessary to make libations and food offerings to the supernatural powers which lay behind these masquerades before one could don their appearance with safety. Otherwise, the participants soon found themselves guilty of blasphemy and could incur all kinds of curses and misery. Organizations which had not been blessed were bound to fail. This explained why masquerade bands such as George Bailay's Relics of Egypt (1959), Stephen Lee Heung's Paradise Lost (1976) and Peter Minshall's Danse Macabre (1980) often met with catastrophe, because their alleged religious or mythical content had simply been put on show on the secular carnival stage.

Eastman was here voicing an opinion which is also shared by a number of the masquerade band designers. Various of them confided to me that they dared not tackle certain themes, because these are shrouded in a veil of supernatural mystery. The successful costume designer Wayne Berkeley, for example, told me that he had to abandon a project on the pharaohs of Egypt because fire kept breaking out in his studio. Minshall, apparently insensitive to these threats, came up with a band called 'Jumbie' in 1988. Eastman and his followers protested because 'Jumbie', which means 'spirit', should not be used like that for worldly pleasure. Action against a ten-year-old Indian singer who wanted to perform a composition entitled 'Is ah Jumbie' in the semi-final of the NCC Junior Calypso Competition had already been successful when the young girl promptly withdrew with the following precocious explanation: 'The culture and traditions of all our people must be treated with respect so that they may enrich our lives, make us strong and increase our sense of pride' (*DE*, 3 February 1988). Minshall refused to pay any heed to the protest, but Eastman claimed that he had reason to regret his action, for when a thirteen-year-old boy was killed under one of the music trailers in Minshall's procession, Eastman interpreted the accident as an act of divine vengeance. Eastman also saw the divine hand at work in the death of the brother of Minshall's King of the Band a few days before carnival. The famous masquerader, who was due to appear as Moko Jumbie (a spirit on stilts), burnt the costume on Carnival Sunday to fulfil his pledge: 'I told Norris that if he should die, the Moko Jumbie would never cross the stage. It was a promise I kept' (*Express*, 24 February 1985).

Eastman tends to see carnival as a ritual for initiates. They can only attain the holy state of mas player by observing a number of prescripts

(Eintou Springer kept interrupting him during this lecture in the library with remarks such as 'When a man play mas for a certain number of years, if he don't continue he dead'). The colonial notion of 'carnival' should be replaced by 'masquerade', which would better bring out the connection with the African mask rituals. During his lecture, Eastman showed photographs of masks from African magazines, which he considered to resemble the masks worn during carnival. Incidentally, this view is diametrically opposed to that of Jacob Elder, another famous Trinidadian Africanist. In his study *African Survivals in Trinidad and Tobago* (1988), Elder calls upon all blacks to join ranks in a world which has so far refused to recognize African achievements in the field of physics, art, literature, politics and government. To this end, Elder (1988: 71) claims, 'Black studies programmes which emphasize cultural and social differences rather than similarities among peoples of African ancestry are negative and wasteful.' Be that as it may, his view of carnival is worlds apart from that of his fellow Africanist Eastman. As the following extract shows (Elder 1988: 51), a lot of research will be required before the similarities emerge clearly:

> ... masks are absolutely absent from the carnival although the players are called 'masqueraders'.... Costumes worn are not related as in Africa to spiritual beings – they are perfectly secular in function and imitate historical or ethnic period dress, regalia or make-up. Reality is approached through authenticity in design and construction of all paraphernalia, except masks.

The uneasy camaraderie between Shaka Zulu and Bill Cosby

The Afro-centric view of Trinidadian culture can be thrown into greater relief if we focus on the controversy which arose in connection with the ten-episode film serial 'Shaka Zulu' which Trinidad television began broadcasting in 1987. The broadcast of the series ran smoothly and there were few criticisms or objections, until an article was published on 20 April 1987 under the headline 'Jamaica bans "Shaka Zulu"; Made in South Africa'. The Jamaican national television corporation had decided to suspend broadcasting at the instigation of the Jamaica Council for Human Rights. This organization had sent a letter to the Minister of Foreign Affairs stating that the series was funded by South African television and had been filmed on location in the country of apartheid. Broadcasting was in conflict with a 1985 UN resolution, to which Jamaica was a signatory, calling for a cultural boycott of South Africa. Once this became known in Trinidad, a similar protest followed and, to the disappointment of many viewers, as their reactions showed, the broadcasting of the series was stopped almost immediately, although there were only three more episodes to go.[2] In the discussion which followed, the content of the series soon replaced the formal reason to ban it from the screen (the UN resolution). Particularly among the cultural champions on whom I am focusing, the simple fact that the series was a South African product was taken to justify the conclusion that the content was bound to be of inferior quality. The film was a deliberate attempt to discredit a great African tribal leader, over-emphasizing tribal rivalry, fighting and bloodshed (*DE*, 22 April 1987).

It is true that the film does deal with an episode in African history which must have been confusing for those who tended to idealize this history, because it disturbed the romantic image of the mother country that they wanted to cherish. The renowned historian of Africa Basil Davidson (1984) describes Shaka Zulu as a military genius who united the tribes who lived on the borders of the white territories into a single kingdom with unparalleled skill and ruthlessness. Shaka was a tough warrior who drastically changed the weapons, discipline and tactics of waging war. His regiments (*impis* in Zulu) wrought destructive slaughter on all those who stood in their way; the many wars of conquest that he undertook were known as wars of extermination, in which one people after another was defeated, driven from its territory, or completely subjected. In terms of this account, my view of the film is that it presented a convincing historical picture of Shaka Zulu as a warrior. It was acclaimed by a number of commentators in Trinidad, who also referred to Davidson's work. One of them, writing under the name of Ngosi Zulu Mzilizaki, who claimed to have carried out in-depth research on the Zulu tribe of the province of Natal, was hardly able to detect any distortions or errors in the screen adaptation. The actors were real Zulus, and the customs and rituals in the film are depicted accurately (*DE*, 11 April 1987). The singer and poet Lancelot Layne, another popular guest speaker at Eintou Springer's cultural information meetings for school pupils, was of a different opinion (*DE*, 23 April 1987):

> When the series on Shaka, King of the Zulus, started, I somehow expected that with its coming from an imperialist propagandist perspective we would have had misconceptions and a certain degree of deliberate lies perpetrated on us, but nothing as the serious misrepresentation of a great warrior and people of South Africa as we have had in this series. With Archbishop Tutu paying a visit to our country in just a few weeks the television censors should have been more sensitive and checked out the authenticity or even the origin of the history of the people we see so subliminally maligned.
>
> It is well known among those who know something of the past of our people in that part of Africa that because of the military humiliation experienced by the European forces which clashed with Shaka in battle[3] they have for the past eight decades or so set out on a racial vendetta

programme in an effort that, while it seeks to psychologically debilitate the African there, ostensible justifies its own atrocious deeds against the people.

It is a shame that we just sit by and mouth protestations within the comfort of our living rooms and do not come out and make our national television station explain why it would allow itself to be the tool of racist propaganda and historical falsehood.

In reaction, the *TG* (29 April 1987) wrote that those who had always supposed that the wars in Africa had been between blacks and whites could not accept the sight of their ancestors engaged in man-to-man fighting with one another. 'I get the distinct feeling sometimes', the commentator continues, 'that even if it was made in another country by whites, and was authentic and factually honest in its depiction, there would still be a loud noise.'

Layne's words, however, suggest something else as well. His protest is not just against the falsification of history as a part of racist propaganda, but is equally an expression of displeasure at the disruption of an experience of Africa which has more in common with the imaginative world of those he attacks than can be admitted. Getting reality into focus involves surrender to an image of Africa which in its exaggeration, romanticization or poeticization unintentionally inverts, and may even be related to, the distorted view of Africa within the Christian-Hellenic colonial view of civilization which has been imposed on the Caribbean for centuries. In *The Middle Passage* (1982: 70–1), V.S. Naipaul writes that until recently the Negroes in the New World were reticent about confronting their past. They found it only natural to live in the West Indies, to speak French, English or Dutch, to wear European-style clothing and to share the same religion and eating habits as the Europeans. Writers of travel accounts who knew no better labelled them 'inlanders' who could assent to what Harry Belafonte sang: 'This is my island in the sun, where my people have toiled since time begun.' During the period of slavery, Naipaul writes, the Negroes were imprinted with a deep feeling of self-deprecation. The ideals of white civilization were held up to them, and they learned to despise all other forms of civilization. As a slave without Christianity, education and family, the Negro had to appropriate these things after Emancipation; 'and every step on the road to whiteness', Naipaul writes, 'deepened the anomaly of his position and increased his vulnerability.' Later in the same work (1982: 90) he writes:

> ... the Negro problem lies not simply in the attitude of others to the Negro, but in the Negro's attitude to himself. It is as yet confused, for the Negro, while rejecting the guilt imposed on him by the white man, is not able to shake off the prejudices he has inherited from the white man ....

'Our people are portrayed as a bunch of primitive savages', was the reaction of Eastman during his lecture on the Shaka Zulu controversy. He went on:

> It is even claimed that after the death of his mother, Shaka forbade his people to plant fields and to milk cows for a year, and that anyone who did not display enough grief had to pay for it with his life. Nonsense! And all that nudity ...

In 1962 Naipaul (1982: 72) wrote: 'Until the other day African tribesmen on the screen excited derisive West Indian laughter; the darkie comic (whose values were the values of the Christian-Hellenic tradition) was more admired'. In the meantime a lot has changed in Trinidad. Seriousness has taken the place of derisive laughter when African 'fellow tribesmen' appear on the screen, but the fact that the Cosby show (featuring mainly middle-class blacks) has been broadcast with enormous success for years without provoking a single word of criticism, while 'Shaka Zulu' was treated to a torrent of ridicule and abuse, would seem to show that Naipaul's observation has lost none of its topicality.

The boundaries of paradise

The people of Trinidad and Tobago are the most beautiful people in the world and they live in a tropical paradise of sand, sea and sun. This illusory self-image is an attempt to drown out the troublesome and confusing socio-ethnic ambivalence which is manifested in the real world and which is expressed in a feeble rejection or an acceptance of external influences on the one hand, and in a constant emphasis on and, at the same time, uncertainty about its own cultural specificity on the other. Self-deception and a sense of reality go hand in hand, just as carnival is presented nationalistically as a festival of harmony and unity while in practice it is an arena of conflicting socio-cultural values and opinions. Such a universe of interpretations of the world people live in, partly constituted by ideas which are imagined to correspond to reality or which people would like to see put into practice, is very sensitive to divergent images from 'outside' (which is not necessary the same as 'abroad') and is wary of any criticism which exposes the fragility of its own image of self. People try to maintain the monopoly of a particular way of looking at things and to reject vigorously anything which contravenes it. Tourism is to be encouraged, the steelband and the calypso are to be promoted internationally, the masquerade costumes are to be sold to foreign museums, the carnival festival as a whole is to be extended worldwide and exported by satellite television, and Trinidad is to be profiled as the tropical paradise on earth. The ideal image of self is both a source of inspiration and an obstacle with respect to all of these goals because of the high level of ambivalence, which boils down to the need to propagate and protect Trinidad culture at the same time – telling the world what is so unique about Trinidad society, while at the same time living in fear of what it will reply; trying to win the admiration of outsiders, while expressing great indignation at their praises, which are taken to be a form of criticism.

I shall try to illustrate this remarkable mental complex with some examples. During my second field trip to Trinidad in 1986, I had also been asked by the Rotterdam Ethnological Museum to collect costumes and other carnival objects for an exhibition on different festivals of the world. As I was also expected to supply a series of slides, I decided to try to obtain a place in the press area just in front of the stage in the stadium in Savannah, where the large-scale competitions and spectacles take place. For this I needed a permit from the NCC. To get the permit, I had to go through the customary rigmarole of bureaucratic red tape and networking. The result – as unintentional as it was fruitless – was that I ended up with a subcommittee specially convened to handle my request, consisting of a few of the senior officers of the NCC. First of all, they made it clear that there was no getting around the sum of US$900 that I would have to pay for the permit, but even then they were still reluctant to grant me permission. The main objection of the committee was that I might aim my camera at individuals or events which, as they put it, 'are not representative of Trinidad society'. As they pointed out, how would I like it to see the image of my country defined in illustrated books by photographs of Amsterdam slums and beggars?

One of the members of the committee put their anxieties into words most clearly. During his period of study in London, he and his Trinidadian companions used to go to the pictures. Before the main feature started, there was usually a short film about hunger, poverty and other distress in some Third World country or other. A collection was then taken and the group of friends dipped into their purses. On one occasion, when they were about to do the same again after seeing some emotional footage, they suddenly realized that this time the film was about Trinidad. Enraged at the violence being done to the actual situation, they left the cinema before the film was over. How could the committee be sure that I did not have the same intentions as the people who had made that terribly misleading film? I solemnly promised not to descend to that level. The committee was still not satisfied with my assurance and remained inflexible. In the end, I got my permit through another channel, free of charge.

A year later, in 1987, the Ministry of Youth, Sport, Culture and the Arts organized a seminar on carnival in the auditorium of the Central Bank (Twin Tower complex). The invitations to the public were extended on the air and in the paper. The Minister chaired two days of discussion of the most varied topics or varying importance by calypsonians, panmen, costume designers, band leaders, representatives of the Tourist Board and the NCC, and anyone else who wanted to join in. For instance, an architect presented plans for a new carnival stadium, and a band leader argued for a drastic review of the masquerade routes through the city, but the discussion was equally lively on the need to replace crowd barriers and on the frequency with which television cameras zoomed in on the buttocks of dancing women.

As it was a public occasion, I supposed that I could make sound recordings without any objections being made. There were no problems during the first day, but on the second day, half an hour after the opening of the session, the NCC secretary came up to me to announce that the permanent secretary of the Ministry wanted a word with me. He was sitting towards the front of the hall and whispered to me to join him for a few minutes in the foyer, where he told me that I was not allowed to make sound recordings without the explicit permission of the Ministry. There had been complaints because people felt unable to speak freely. Moreover, he objected to the fact that the material could find its way abroad, because 'this is our intellectual property, sir'. I told him that I did not understand how I could be taking away that property (unless he meant it in the sense in which Dr J.D. Elder, Secretary for Culture in the Tobago House of Assembly, had used it when he said: 'all intellectual property has good money value' – *DE*, 26 January 1987 – in which case he would certainly have been right in his supposition). The high-ranking civil servant would not budge, and in the end I was allowed to resume my seat in the hall after I had promised to stop recording. Soon afterwards I felt another tap on my shoulder. Someone urgently had to speak to me. This time it was an official from the Ministry of National Security who stood waiting for me in the foyer. We joined three of his colleagues who were dealing with another foreigner who had been removed from the hall as well. The security official curtly refused to allow us to attend the seminar. It was a government affair and did not concern 'strangers' like us. Topics were discussed which were not meant for our ears. I told him that the newspaper had announced the seminar as a public meeting to which everyone was warmly invited. This was confirmed by the composition of the audience, with many ordinary Trinidadians in the hall as well as those with a direct interest. Why were we singled out for special treatment? The man was not prepared to listen to any arguments and threatened to expel us from the country if we did not observe the rules. When asked what the rules were, he replied: 'Your freedom is limited to the Hilton and the beaches!'

We stood there crestfallen for a moment, until the permanent secretary of the Ministry of Culture came up to us with a big smile. We had no idea of what had been going on behind the scenes, but he was gushingly friendly. 'Be my guest'; we could resume our seats in the hall. When I asked him whether that would make us liable to be arrested, he replied that he could guarantee our safety.

During the rest of the day I was able to follow the discussions without any further disturbance, including the question of what role carnival could play in attracting tourists (which sounded a bit strange in my ears after these incidents). A high-ranking member of the Tourist Board suggested putting a stop to selling drink in bottles during the shows to allay the fears of tourists. This would put an end to the spontaneous bottle-and-spoon bands in the notorious North Stand (the cheap seats) so that they would no longer disturb the official programme. This met with a strong protest from those who considered that this would be to sacrifice the spirit of carnival to the tourist industry. Et cetera....

Ideal reality

The shock endured by the NCC member as a student in London, when he saw his cherished country as others presented it, is repeated time and again among the public of Trinidad whenever the island is successful in attracting the attention of outsiders. It is above all television documentaries on a particular facet of the country, in the first instance intended for a foreign public, which cause a commotion among a broad sector of the population. The criticisms reveal once again the high level of sensitivity to the way in which Trinidad is presented to the world. At first sight the objections seem to be directed at specific fragments in the documentaries which contain inaccuracies or do violence to the actual situation in some other way. Closer investigation, however, gives the impression that this is only a front to conceal a more serious motive: Trinidad must look like a picture postcard. No presentation to the outside world can stand up to criticism if it is not in accord with the stubbornly upheld image presented in the tourist folders. And even if the picture corresponds almost entirely to that image, it can still arouse hostility, as we shall see. It is as if the image that people want to present of Trinidad is always different from the version of reality that is recorded on the sensitive film. This tendency to reject almost every presentation or interpretation of the actual situation of Trinidad is translated into feelings of bitter indignation and offence which are always directed against the documentary makers. If the television programmes were only intended for domestic consumption they would hardly have caused a stir. It is simply the exposure to the risk of criticism by outsiders that gives relatively innocent themes an importance which can assume grotesque proportions.

On 14 February 1987 the British Channel Four broadcast a fifteen-minute documentary entitled 'The Gathering Storm', in which four prominent Trinidadians – an ex-minister, the director of the power company, the chairperson of the Export Development Corporation, and a hotel manager) gave their opinion on the political and economic situation of the country after the elections of December 1986. The interviews alternated with shots of striking workers, protesting civil servants and a couple of hundred unemployed crowding together for the mere six jobs available. The sharp criticism from Trinidadians in England which erupted soon after the broadcast rapidly spread to the mother country, where it commanded general assent even though no one had seen the programme. With headlines such as 'What that documentary projected to the world' and 'A damaging and dangerous film', the press protest was aimed at what one newspaper called 'the programme's blatantly anti-NAR stance and one that was clearly designed to show Trinidad and Tobago as a place about to revolt against the new government' (*TG*, 22 February 1987).

The point which particularly annoyed people was that one of the interviewees was supposed to have said that the government would have three months to clear up the mess. Otherwise, problems would ensue, including revolts (*TG*, 1 March 1987). Strangely enough, this statement was not to be found in the text of the programme, of which the *Daily Express* published large sections on 8 March 1987, nor was there anything else of a shocking nature that could justify the emotional uproar. The images in themselves, and the fact that a couple of Trinidadians gave vent to a not particularly optimistic view of their country, were apparently sufficient to arouse anger and indignation. 'Such ugly scenes televised abroad will do irreparable harm to the prospect of attracting investment, or tourists, to Trinidad and Tobago', were the words of a letter from London in the *TG* (1 March 1987), but, the writer continued hopefully, as a people we have an enormous potential, and as a small country we have produced big names: V.S. Naipaul, Penny Commissiong (Miss Universe), Giselle La Ronde (Miss World) and 'men of exceptional achievement in the academic field, men who have been key advisors to leaders of nations in Africa, China and India'. In another issue of the *TG* (10 March 1987), a programme assistant attempted to dam the criticism by pointing out that it is not the responsibility of British television to attract or repel investors in any economy at all, 'not even that controlled by Her Majesty's Government under Mrs Thatcher.'

The producer of the programme, Darcus Howe (Owonsu), a Trinidadian who has been living in England for twenty-five years, also came in for abuse. He is constantly referred to in the reactions as the former 'Black Power agitator' involved in the 1970 revolt. The *TG* of 10 March 1987 described him as someone who makes a song and dance about defending his 'black brothers', but flees to the 'white man's country' when the going gets rough. It continues: 'Perhaps the fellow is no political opportunist, schemer or Trinidad smartman, but simply a believer in the old adage that he who fights and runs away, lives to fight another day'. What gives him the right to pass judgement on Trinidad? The hurt feelings of many are summed up in the following comments:

> The so-called documentary has upset quite a number of intelligent Trinidadians who have perceived it as a perverse, mischievous, clandestine and possibly unpatriotic bit of left-wing propaganda and unprofessional journalism designed to smear the national image and sabotage our efforts to attract much needed foreign investment.   *TG*, 10 March 1987

> What angered Trinidad and Tobago citizens was the total absence of any representative of the government which would have given some balance to the negative picture that was presented.   *TG*, 22 February 1987

> There were threats of the poor plundering the rich and threats of violence from a big man wearing a lot of jewelry. What is going on in Trinidad and Tobago?   *TG*, 1 March 1987

> The programme conveyed an undercurrent of social menace and violence and Trinidad and Tobago was seen as a place on the brink of volcanic eruption. There was a very 'Grenadian' aspect about it.   *TG*, 1 March 1987

How could we tolerate this sensational and unethical journalism, to what extent have Trinidadians themselves been involved in making it, and who is responsible for the final version? asks the *TG* (23 March 1987) in an editorial. In the future we must be more careful in allowing so-called professional film and television teams in, and Minister Panday (Foreign Affairs) must investigate the matter thoroughly, the paper concludes.

In the meantime the Minister had already requested the British television station to send him a copy of the controversial programme. He was concerned at the damage which had been done to the image of the country and regretted the fact that just when the government and the people were trying to build the country up in economic and other ways, people inside and outside Trinidad were sabotaging these endeavours (*TG*, 22 February 1987). Later the Minister of Information, Samaroo, announced that he had seen two fragments of the programme. Predictably, he called the interview with Minister Panday of Foreign Affairs – which no one had mentioned so far – a balanced interview. The rest 'was not as balanced as it should have been', was how he dismissed the affair (*DE*, 8 March 1987).

Not everyone took part in the national indignation. Wayne Brown wondered whether the government had nothing better to do than to waste time on insignificant television programmes (*DE*, 12 March 1987). Another columnist in the *DE* (1 March 1987) spoke of a 'storm in a tiny teacup' and feared that government interference might endanger the freedom of the press; all that worked-up nationalism might suggest to customs officials, who were implacable enough as it was, that it might be patriotic to make life even more difficult for foreign television crews than it already usually was.

And local personalities would think twice before they say anything in front of the television cameras if it is likely to end up as nothing short of an accusation of treason.

I conclude this drama with the only comment I could find by a Trinidadian who had not emigrated to England and had seen the film by chance. It is a sort of urge to self-investigation:

> I have just returned from a three-day visit to Britain ... and I was given the privileged opportunity to view the 'anti-patriotic Gathering Storm'. At the end of the film I wondered where is the 'maliciousness'.... So I simply ask the NAR government to release the film via TTT [Trinidad and Tobago Television] for public viewing and to let the population judge and comment. And we will then see who is malicious and paranoid.

A fresh commotion arose six weeks later with the broadcast of a film on the steelband, 'Fire and Steel', on Trinidad television. It was one of the series 'National Explorers' under the auspices of National Geographic, in which the makers tried to portray this musical phenomenon within the framework of the history of its genesis. It was therefore naturally filmed on typical locations, such as Laventille, the Afro-American lower-class neighbourhood where the major developments have taken place and with which the present-day steelband culture is still intimately connected.

The criticism of the film concerns the choice of steelbands featured and the fact that the voice-over consistently replaces 'pan' with 'pon', but these are minor blemishes compared with the irritation aroused by the local colour. The NCC subcommittee had been afraid that a foreigner such as I would want to photograph beggars and slums; this film team confirmed the worst of their suspicions. 'The true way in which foreigners see our beautiful and richly endowed twin-isle republic', according to the *Sun* (6 April 1987), is as follows:

> There was footage of half-naked people, no doubt labourers from our neighbouring islands, off-loading bananas and green figs on the Caricom Jetty; vivid shots from some of the slums on the city's periphery; shiftless, wide eyed 'natives', aimlessly shuffling along some back roads, and barefooted coconut vendors selling to barefooted customers.

Various critics express their amazement that there was no footage of the hypermodern Twin Tower complex (housing the Central Bank and the Ministry of Finance), Riverside Plaza (a shopping centre), the oil platforms off the coast of Galeota, the artistic carnival performances, or the Caroni bird reserve. Even the beautiful girls, the pride of the nation, are omitted. Of course the producers did not intended to make a sort of tourist travel account, remarks a well-known commentator in the *Sun* (6 April 1987), but he still thinks that the programme is inadmissible. Somebody, whether the

Tourist Board, the Ministry of Culture, or the Ministry of Foreign Affairs, should be given the task of checking the final material of all these foreign anthropologists, film companies and writers before it is released internationally.[4]

The authorities concerned appear not to have taken this recommendation seriously, because a year later a new commotion arose, more serious and on a larger scale than the previous ones, in connection with another television programme. This time it was a BBC production about carnival in New Orleans, Rio de Janeiro and Trinidad. The film was broadcast live by satellite to various countries. For a proper understanding of the typically Trinidadian criticism, we have to begin by considering the form and contest of the programme in question.

It is virtually impossible for a few live recordings of carnival within a relatively short time-span (there were about thirty-five minutes on Trinidad) to convey a general impression in a satisfactory manner. The festival lasts for days, or even weeks, contains a large number of characteristic aspects, and is held simultaneously on various locations. The producers therefore decided that the best way to get the three carnivals across was by alternating live recordings with archive footage and reports which had been made beforehand. The Trinidad contribution consisted of a balanced combination of direct recordings of revellers in costume parading on the stage in the Savannah in front of the audience, and canned impressions in which the focus was on calypso and steelband. The controversial Darcus Howe provided the commentary on the live shots. Unfortunately, the recordings were made at the moment that Edmund Hart's 3 000-strong masquerade band filled the stage. It takes an hour to present a band of this size, so that the characteristic rich variation in bands did not emerge. This shortcoming was more than compensated, however, by fragments from the performance of the Calypso Monarch of the Year, Cro-Cro, and from the King and Queen of the Band finale, where the most fantastic costumes are displayed. There was also coverage of the three 'classic' calypsonians Roaring Lion, Lord Kitchener and Mighty Sparrow. They made clear the importance of this art for Trinidad, supported by brief archive shots, and sang fragments of lyrics in a good-humoured, comradely spirit. A particularly impressive part of the film was the report in which the popular calypso singer David Rudder visited The Hill in Laventille, where the traditional panyard of the steelband Desperadoes is situated. Shots of the steelband rehearsing one of Rudder's hits were fitted smoothly into recordings of the singer's own performance. There were shots of the funeral of the famous band leader Rudolph Charles, 'the man with the hammer'. Fragments from Rudder's composition 'The Hammer', an ode to this panman, were an original way of making clear the historical relation between calypso and steelband. The voice-over indicates passion, respect and pride in this musical form:

If you want to say Trinidad you say pan. Not even calypso, because you can find the traditions of calypso up the islands and so on. But pan is totally ours and is the only source of Trinidadianism. We created that, it came out of us.... When the Desperadoes come down off The Hill, the whole of Laventille is coming down, you know. The Desperadoes are the representatives of Laventille. In a sense everytime we make a trip to The Hill... it is like you are making a pilgrimage to the music... to where Rudolph Charles and the hammer might be. The hammer is the key of the music. That's why we are seeking the hammer, because if you lose the hammer you lose the key to the music.... The bands in this area come from a more downtrodden setting... they have more to go for, they have a deeper hunger. You can see striving all around The Hill, but at the same time it's a journey towards something so beautiful you know.

I have seen a videotape of the three carnivals a number of times and can only agree with the conclusion drawn by a reviewer from the British paper *The Independent*: 'The Trinidad broadcast offered the most accomplished and informative sequences of the night.' The Trinidad headlines tell a very different story: 'BBC show a disappointment', '30 minutes of agony', 'A poor projection of T&T carnival', 'Outrage over satellite coverage of carnival', 'T&T citizens embarrassed', 'Total distortion of the truth', 'The travesty of the century'. As soon as the programme was over, the telephones in the newspaper offices and in Trinidad television began ringing as angry viewers and Trinidadians abroad gave vent to their displeasure. The main objections were the manner of presentation, the way the producers interpreted the word 'live', and the 'primitive' and distorted image of carnival that they portrayed. According to one editorial, Howe does not know what a live programme means, and he presented a dreadful caricature of our carnival (*TG*, 18 February 1988). 'While world viewers probably saw the grandeur of the Rio samba dancers and the ornate floats of New Orleans in the carnival hookup, they were treated to a woman toting water past poverty stricken shanties in Trinidad' was the newspaper's comment on a fragment from the Laventille report lasting less than three seconds. 'Are we telling the world that we are a nation of slums, and ghetto life? Are we telling the world that our announcers are "drunk" and totally unprofessional?', was the burden of a letter to the editor of the *DE* (26 February 1988). The average tourist does not want to know how a pan is made, the letter writer continued; American and European tourists are only interested in finding a paradise to escape to, a country with friendly people where partying is a non-stop activity. The steelband umbrella organization, Pan Trinbago, also considered that the programme had tarnished the image of carnival; it would discourage tourists from coming to Trinidad and taking part in the annual festival. What the British showed of the world of carnival was more in line with the Brazilian version: 'Emphasis was placed on the masqueraders in a Brazilian or New Orleans setting' was the curious verdict of this organization. People were extremely surprised to hear David Rudder, 'whom we do not recognize as a panman' (*DE*, 18 February 1988), talking about the history and development of the steelband.

Once again the question was raised from various sides of who in the government, Tourist Board or NCC can be held responsible for the fact that a harmful product of this kind was allowed to pass without any restrictions: 'Too much democracy can hurt the state and its citizens', were the firm words of one angry letter-writer (*DE*, 6 March 1988). A letter from England urged: 'Make decisions and take steps that will not further put our country's image in jeopardy'. In the meantime, the writer would attempt to save that image by making it clear to her acquaintances that it was all the fault of a bad presenter and that what they had seen was not carnival as it really is (*DE*, 21 February 1988).

Howe reacted by stating that he is not in the employ of tourism or the Ministry of Information. He is a television producer, not a propagandist. He calls those who attack the programme arrogant and asks what gives them the right to tell him or anyone else how Trinidad should be projected to people thousands of miles away. He considers this arrogance remarkable for a small island, and concludes: 'There is a tendency to project Trinidad and Tobago as sun, sand, sea and calypso. Whites don't want that. It's complexity that they are sympathetic towards' (*TG*, 3 June 1988).

Tourism without tourists

One of the few commentators who opposed the collective lamentation was Geoffrey Frankson, columnist of the *Daily Express*. In his discussion of 'The Gathering Storm' and the BBC carnival production (4 March 1988), he begins by stating that he has not noticed any unmistakable blunders, inaccuracies or factual misinterpretations, and that there is absolutely no question of a wilful attempt to discredit the country or carnival. He is surprised at what he calls the 'hysterical' reactions to the two films. Why the flow of panic-stricken letters to the editor and the hasty general consent by what are usually intelligent column writers? Why do seven seconds of Rudolph Charles' funeral and a fragment with a resident of Laventille carrying a bucket of water cause such consternation? And why do people make such a fuss about the sombre views of four businessmen and the interviews with a trade union leader and a few strikers? Frankson's answer to these questions is that public opinion is determined more and more by the middle class. The man in the street hardly gets a look in. It is the well-to-do bourgeoisie that complain about 'crime', 'foreign currency' and 'import restrictions' from behind its burglar-bars. It makes a fuss about 'negative images' and the effect they have on the tourist industry, which suddenly assumes such importance. Trinidad has to look like a tourist resort, and that is why its image is the major concern of the Nice Upper Middle-class Person (NUMP) and all those who belong to that category. Even the weeklies, whose *raison d'être* is traditionally derived from anti-NUMP points of view, seem to have jumped onto the band-wagon and vociferously join in to undermine local culture in what Frankson calls an 'orgy of self-degradation'.

The remark that the tourist industry has suddenly become so important for the middle class is interesting. As we have seen, tourism's economic role was of little importance for a long time. In fact, it was even 'the done thing' to express negative views on the development of tourism. Although people are aware of the need for this development since the oil industry's decline as the main pillar of the economy, this negative attitude is still an important obstacle to an effective approach to tourism. Tourism still occupies a position of minor importance among the total range of economic activities, and this is an expression of its actual importance to the middle class. Incidentally, by no means all of those who complain that images of Trinidad could damage tourism are representative of this sector of society. Frankson's comments on the role of the weeklies suggest that NUMP values are equally expressed by other people besides NUMPs. This can also be seen from the comments of the steelband organization Pan Trinbago, which is dominated by the lower class.

If all this is taken into consideration, it would appear that the process of middle-classization which has taken place in Trinidad is the reason for the hypersensitive reactions from all layers of the population to a variety of presentations of Trinidad in the media. The traditional receptivity to foreign values, combined with the Americanization of society and the oil-boom period of consumerism, have imposed an inflated self-image on the people of Trinidad which regularly conflicts with certain aspects of the contemporary situation. The offence caused by practically every visualization of Trinidad apart from the one which the Trinidadians see through their own heavily rose-tinted spectacles (whatever that may look like) is inevitable. The harsh criticism is justified by resorting to the tourism argument (Frankson writes: 'The ostensible reason is the need to earn the almighty tourist dollar'), but it is by no means just economic interest groups which fall back on it. In general, people are not so keen on tourists and they are not in favour of a sanitized image of Trinidad for tourists; rather, they project their own threatened perceptions, feelings, wishes and ideas onto the imaginary phenomenon of tourism.

Be nice, it's nice

This curious relation to reality is betrayed in a striking way in the attempts of the Tourist Board (clearly an interested party) to sell the country, and in particular carnival. In 1988 a large-scale campaign (the Get Ready Campaign) was launched to promote tourism. It was not aimed at the target group itself, but at the people of Trinidad, calling upon them to be prepared to behave as on the picture postcards, moulding their behaviour to what the imaginary tourist expected of them. The campaign had the character of a collective re-education programme. Its main message was that Trinidadians should be nicer to other people and to one another. In particular, the staff of customs offices, the police, government bodies, taxi firms, shops and catering establishments were asked to be more friendly towards customers, on the assumption that a change of mentality of this kind would automatically promote tourism. Overseas visitors, particularly Trinidadians, were urged to take a Carnival Champion Kit home with them to induce their relatives and friends to spend a holiday in Trinidad. This policy was the practical implementation of the conclusion of the small-scale inquiry conducted by the Tourist Board in 1984, which had recommended that the public should be educated through a Tourism Awareness Programme. The slogan 'Be Nice, it's Nice', which accompanied the campaign in full-page advertisements for weeks, also bears witness to the wishful hope that the actual situation could be turned into the desired ideal image by magic.

Part of the text of the advertisement (*TG*, 7 February 1988) runs:

> Most people will smile when they read this headline. That's because we are, by nature, really very nice people. True, it's sometimes hard to be nice when you have to deal with people who give you bad service, bad manners and bad vibes. But that's already changing. Lots of people have started E.S.P.. E.S.P. stands for Extra Special Person.... Naturally, you, too, must be part of the E.S.P. awareness programme. You are an extra special person and it will help if you would make a special effort to be nice to the next person with whom you come into contact; and every other person after that. Make everyone else feel extra special, and let the whole world know that as far as you are concerned, we in Trinidad and Tobago are all extra special people. So, let's all say together: Me E.S.P. You E.S.P. We're E.S.P. We're nice!

This kind of address to the people of Trinidad caused far less commotion than Darcus Howe's attempts to visualize the country, although some people disliked the patronizing tone of the Tourist Board. A columnist in the *DE* (26 February 1988) wrote: 'It is directed, not to tourists, but to nationals. It is a slap on the hand of the little ones who, sadly, don't know better, and have to be trained. It is an insult to the people of this country; it talks down to them.'

This irritation is understandable, for the Tourist Board's appeal is certainly not devoid of paternalism. After all, the tourist organization is only an extension of the government, which had been promoting a sort of anti-tourism policy for decades. That very government cashed in on the existing resentment of colonialism and propagated the development of a native culture, free of foreign taint. This encouraged a mentality which equated providing service with servility, resulting in a disdain for anything connected with tourism. There are numerous complaints about the rude, almost hostile treatment to which tourists are subjected by customs officials when they arrive at Piarco Airport, the long delays in checking passports, the completely arbitrary determination of the length of stay, and the lengthy interrogations to which almost everyone is subjected by the officials, indicating a cynical, or at any rate indifferent attitude toward tourism. For example, when during one of these interrogations I expressed my interest in carnival, the official asked why I did not go to Rio de Janeiro.

Also typical of the tourist climate on Trinidad is the situation in which unsuspecting visitors may end up if they make the trip to the famous pitch lake, one of the tourist attractions of the island. My own experience and a number of newspaper reports from the period 1985–8 indicate that they are likely to become involved in a war between authorized and non-authorized guides, who attack one another with stones and bottles to gain the right to take tourists round the site. The victorious party in the fray orders the visitor to follow him, and will not take 'no' for an answer.

Another case relates to an elderly American couple who landed in Trinidad for a day on their Caribbean cruise. No doubt with the pleasant memories of the warm welcome given to tourists on Aruba or Barbados still fresh in his mind, the man wanted to take a picture of an innocent scene in one of the streets of Port of Spain. A street vendor seized him by the throat and demanded the roll of film 'since he had given no white man permission to take pictures of him' (*Express*, 20 February 1986). Nor will tourists feel at ease if they experience what I have experienced on various occasions in the busy shopping streets in the centre or in Queen's Park Savannah, where someone hisses as you pass by: 'Go home you fucking whitey!' or words to that effect.

Peter O'Connor (*DE*, 13 February 1987) has provided a good portrait of the general atmosphere in Trinidad (which he has nicknamed 'Paranoia') in a comparison with Barbados. He begins by noting that tourism in Trinidad is still regarded as a threat to national identity. After recounting how a Trinidadian taxi driver does his best to address the newly arrived tourist in an American accent, he continues:

> In Barbados, tourism is like in other Caribbean islands, the major money earner, yet citizens of Barbados are proud and independent – speak Bajan

among themselves and to the visitors. Politeness is not regarded by a Bajan as servitude, and therefore the whole society benefits from the fact that visitors are made to feel welcome. No one speaks to visitors in a 'yankee' accent – as a proud Bajan would consider this foolish mimicry to be a form of servitude. However, in Paranoia, which possesses greater cultural diversity and magnificent cultural innovation, the attitude towards tourism totally suppresses the spread or export of the rich culture. The unfounded, never substantiated, fear of tainting a local culture infects the attitude of the government and people of Paranoia.

The second weapon in the large-scale tourist campaign, the Carnival Champion programme, was aimed at what the advertisements called the 'visitors'. The chairperson of the Tourist Board had stated in an interview that the campaign was intended for the 5 000 or so Trinidadians who were 'returning for the season' (*TG*, 19 January 1988), but this was not explicitly stated in the text of the advertisements. When I reported to the Tourist Board as an interested 'visitor', the first reaction was one of surprise, but afterwards they were prepared to explain how I could become a Carnival Champion. The woman who spoke to me trotted out a carefully rehearsed text which left no room for questions from me. I would receive a promotional package containing video and sound recordings, folders about the country and carnival, and 'stunning full colour posters'. 'Everything you need to convene group sessions in your home or club, and to deliver professional, persuasive presentations to encourage vacationers to choose Trinidad and Tobago', as she repeated from the text of the advertisement. My efforts would form part of a complicated competition with as first prize an all-in holiday in Trinidad and Tobago. When I expressed my interest in the package, I was told that it would cost US$125. The advertisements had not said a word about this. I declined. Later the price suddenly dropped to US$40, which brought the credibility of the action into disrepute. The government had already followed a pricing policy of this kind – arbitrary and counter-productive as regards promoting tourism – in 1985, when, under pressure of a serious financial deficit, the price of a visa extension was raised overnight from TT$5 to TT$200 (*TG*, 27 January 1985). A little while later the measure was reversed in an equally drastic fashion.

The errors in the Tourist Board's perception of tourists and its estimate of their motivation and financial resources were clearly revealed by the low level of success of the campaign. A few months later a report appeared in the paper (*TG*, 15 May 1988) that only fifty people had taken up the offer to become Carnival Champions (Van Tulder 1989: 45).

Notes

1   'The staged folk dance celebration is an example of what I will call cultural objectification', Handler (1988: 14) writes in his book *Nationalism and the Politics of Culture in Quebec*. He continues: 'I initially took the idea from Bernard Cohn, who has written of Western-educated intellectuals in India who "have made [their culture] into a 'thing' " and "can stand back and look at themselves, their ideas, their symbols and culture and see it as an entity".'

2   The plans of a Dutch television station (Veronica) to broadcast the series in the Netherlands ran up against similar opposition from the ANC representatives in Amsterdam. A member of the film division of the Dutch television station concerned told me that, as a result of this protest, 'Shaka Zulu' could not be screened in 1987, as planned, but broadcasting had to wait until 1990. The ANC's main objection was that, as a South African cultural product, Dutch government policy necessitated a ban on the series. It was this aspect, and not the content of the series, which bothered the ANC, my informant told me.

3   According to Davidson (1984: 163), the first clash with the English was under the Zulu king Cetshwaio, Shaka's successor.

4   During the 1993 carnival filming was not allowed during the two main days of the festival in the streets of Port of Spain (this ban applied to both film and video cameras). The National Carnival Committee placed watchers along the route of the masquerade procession to make sure that no one tried to film it. Taking photographs, however, was allowed (oral information from Graham Mayo).

7 | The spirit of Canboulay: the socio-cultural autonomy of carnival

How to judge the carnaval parade? If the audience of the celebration is not he who makes it, but rather the class for whom it is set up, whose should the aesthetic values be? Should they be popular? Should they be middle class? Should they be those of the intellectual elite which sits as official judge? This is not clear. The day that it is, the judgements will lose the atmosphere full of polemic and distrust which predominates today.

(Da Távola on the Brazilian carnival, cited in Taylor 1982: 301)

In this chapter attention is focused on the open character of carnival through a description of the various components of the festival. The fading away and disappearance of boundaries between what were originally class-bound socio-cultural spheres provides an opportunity for entirely new forms of exchange and confrontation between opposite orientations. It is not the social, political or organizational dominance, but the cultural ambivalence of the Creole middle class, with the carnival competition as an important mediating instrument, which has safeguarded the festival from the superficiality which has occurred in other areas of society as a result of the process of middle-classization. Carnival has therefore retained its function as a forum for the national debate on Trinidad's search for its own identity, unimpeded by the fact that the festival is utilized for purely propagandist, political and national ends too. Above all those middle-class groups which have an interest in preserving the myth of 'truly one nation, all ah we is one' want to present carnival as the great national conciliator. It is a viable myth, but there are also factors involved which might expose it. The festival is susceptible to numerous highly ambivalent expressions which are not always pleasing to the government; they mostly refer to Trinidad as a nation, but they are not the result of a (propagandistic) representation of society as a peaceful social and cultural unity without any problems.

The exotic idyll is disturbed

In his discussion of carnival on the Caribbean island of Antigua, Manning (1978: 198–9) gives two reasons adduced by those who regard it as a packaging of culture intended to titillate white visitors with the sensuous delights of the native way of life. First, the festival was launched partly on the initiative of the government and the world of industry and commerce in 1957 as part of an attempt to set up a major tourist industry. Second, the baroque and colourful extravagance of the festival corresponds to the popular image of what tourists like to see. The tonal emphasis of carnival is one of hedonistic and luxurious entertainment and the display of abundance and showy consumption, which form the basis of the Caribbean illusion as expressed by tourism promoters.

Closer examination of carnival in Antigua, however, reveals that it has developed independently of the tourism promotion plan. The carnival public consists almost entirely of Antiguans, West Indian visitors and a growing number of black Americans. Only a small number of the white Americans and Canadians who visit the island come for carnival and witness the official Parade of Bands, and they are absent from the competition shows in Carnival City, where the atmosphere is more informal and chaotic and the public consists of active participants engaged in heated debates on their personal favourites instead of passive spectators. If they came into closer contact with this carnival, most of these tourists would find it menacing rather than entertaining. Black identity as the cohesive ideology of carnival in Antigua is not conducive to being packaged as part of an innocent presentation of native culture. 'Indeed, the black militant orientation of Carnival runs counter not only to the image built by tourism promotors but to the government's moderate, rather complacent nationalism', concludes Manning (1978: 199).

Leaving aside for the time being all the actual differences between the two situations which will prove to be very important for the development of my argument, one could say pretty much the same of the Trinidad carnival. The post-war efforts by the Tourist Board and NCC set up by the government have not managed to turn the carnival into an innocent tourist attraction. This conclusion led Errol Hill (1983: 36) to comment:

> There is one aspect of the carnival that has always made me feel proud; that is, in a world that is prone to prostrate itself (I almost said 'prostitute itself') before the tourist dollar, the Trinidad carnival has remained inviolate. No part of the festival should be altered or adjusted to accommodate tourists. This is our celebration. The people had fought for it, earned it, treasured it. Visitors are welcome – most of them are fellow West Indians anyhow – provided they are prepared to accept all the crazy but glorious inconsistencies and unpredictabilities that go along with our festival.

But matters are not that simple. 'The people' can certainly be credited with the heroic achievement of keeping carnival out of reach of commercialism and tourism, but one should not lose sight of the socio-economic factors which, as has been pointed out, helped to give the festival its present shape and which were prompted by different, less noble motives. For example, if the lack of economic necessity and the fact that very few tourists show an interest are taken into account, the statement that 'the people had fought for it' takes on a different aspect. In Antigua, as we shall see, the tourist industry plays a real and overwhelming socio-economic role; in Trinidad, on the other hand, the idea of tourism is a vague term referring to the future, and especially to the preferences, expectations and desires which result from the process of middle-classization. If we bear this difference in mind, then Hill's comment becomes more acceptable, for present-day carnival still offers enough scope for cultural and ideological expressions which refuse to be bound by the limitations which certain sectors of society would like to impose on the festival in the name of tourism. These limitations are strongly characterized by the morality and aesthetic of a middle-class lifestyle, including the nationalism which the government is so keen to promote.

This situation is reflected in the various components of the carnival. It is hardly surprising that it is those aspects of the programme whose content and organization are in the hands of the NCC that display the greatest influence of tourist and middle-class lifestyles. Vice versa, in those areas where the NCC and related organizations such as the Downtown Carnival Committee are only responsible for the preconditions for certain events, or have no share in them at all, those elements of the carnival repertoire will tend to predominate with which representatives of the lifestyles referred to above claim to have little in common, and which (to use Manning's terminology) tourists are likely to experience as alarming rather than entertaining. These elements include all kinds of expressions of militant Black Power and pan-African nationalism, as well as incidents and events which may be viewed as racist and sexist, and calypso presentations containing messages of social criticism or political satire. This should not be taken to imply that one of the carnival segments is completely free of the expressions and events which determine the organization or mood for the other segment. The inner strength of carnival, as we shall see, lies precisely in the fact that themes and expressions which originally belonged to a specific socio-cultural domain are diffused to some extent among the more-or-less distinct social echelons of the festival. The point here, however, is to stress the tendencies or shifts of emphasis which result from particular organizational frameworks. It is not just the events themselves, but also the social areas in which carnival takes place which some people, especially those from the world of the middle class, prefer to avoid and which they do not regard as suitable for tourists. This sensitivity is clearly demonstrated in the reactions to Rudder's visit to the Desperadoes' panyard in Laventille (see page 217–8).

On the borderline between cosmos and chaos: crumbling boundaries between traditional socio-cultural areas

Dimanche Gras

Of the category of the components of carnival in which the NCC predominates, the most pronounced cases are the Dimanche Gras show on Sunday evening, and the Parade of the Bands on Mardi Gras in the Savannah. The Dimanche Gras show in particular, which includes the finals of the King and Queen of the Masquerade Bands competition and the calypso competition, leading to the coronation of the Calypso Monarch of the Year, is a tightly run, programmatically organized show in which little is left to chance. Production, direction, decor and presentations are modelled on the American world of showbiz. These official carnival contests alternate with acts by local entertainers and comedians and a dance company, which puts on a middle-class interpretation of the African cultural legacy. Choreography and staging are inspired by cinematic romanticism of the Tarzan genre, accompanied by the deafening rhythm of drums and the piercing sound of brass instruments that mimic the trumpeting of elephants with their long-drawn-out blasts. Associations with the 'dark continent' are evoked by a group of dancing girls with torches. Wearing slave bangles on their arms and ankles, they are dressed in bikinis decorated with jute strands to give the whole an exotic flavour. A limbo act is performed in their midst by a man dressed in a similar 'jungle' attire, to the light of their torches and accompanied by pounding drumbeats. The limbo dance, which is said to have originated in Trinidad, is praised as a native attraction in the tourist folders, but it is not practised today anywhere on the island. The Hilton Hotel regales its guests with a limbo show from time to time. The invisible master of ceremonies, whose voice is heard over the loudspeakers between acts, addresses the relatively orderly audience in impeccable English, and there is a clear distinction between the spectators in the seats and the participants on stage. The programme meets the organizers' demands in exuding an atmosphere of respectability which they expect to appeal to the average tourist, even though broken from time to time by eruptions of lively enthusiasm. These are concentrated mainly in the North Stand, which is popular among the less well-to-do classes because of the lower price of admission there. Outbursts of spontaneity are concentrated in that part of the show when the calypso final is held. The presentation of the calypso singer and the text of the song may provoke an unruly atmosphere, which is the exact opposite of what the organisers want. Their intention, after all, is that the spectacle should run smoothly, in line with the image of carnival that the NCC propagates – but more on that later.

Panorama

Though just as highly organized as the Dimanche Gras show, the programme of the Steelband Panorama Finals is a good deal more chaotic and the atmosphere less formal, thanks to a number of factors which the NCC does not control. As the steelbands wait their turn or move slowly forward (ten or twelve of the hundred or so competing orchestras reach the final), forming a queue stretching a long way from the grounds of the Savannah stadium, the spirit of the traditional rebel street carnival seems to make its way into the festival organized by the NCC. During the hours of waiting, the bands, each numbering between eighty and a hundred players, rehearse the music that they will presently be performing on stage, surrounded by tens or even hundreds of fans. A carefree party mood is already in the air long before the actual stage performances, and it is very different from the neat and regulated ceremony that the organizers would like to see. The fans are there not only to lend the band enthusiastic moral support, but also to push the mobile platforms from time to time on which the various sections of the music group have taken their place. When the time to go on stage has come, all these platforms are pushed up onto the elongated stage with slopes on both sides in a triumphal procession, while the musicians continue their rehearsal undisturbed. At the same time, the band which has just been on is cheered (or jeered) off the stage by its fans. It is particularly at moments like these that the distinction between performers and spectators collapses and the stadium is overtaken by a mood of friendly anarchy.

The stands also present a different picture from that of the pompous Dimanche Gras show. Since the programme is long (the preliminary rounds and final may well last as long as six or eight hours), the members of the public are squeezed between cool boxes and shopping bags full of things to eat and drink. The scene as a whole is reminiscent of a massive picnic: the eating, talking, singing and dancing picnickers indulge in self-satisfied amusement which sometimes overshadows the entertainment for which they have come. The popular calypso hits which boom out of the public address system every time there is a gap between steelband acts are just as capable of stirring the audience into a frenzy as the performance itself. My impression is that, compared with the Dimanche Gras show, the lower class and lower-middle class are better represented, or at any rate set the tone, at the Panorama spectacle. This is in accordance with the social origin of the steelbands and their loyal fans. Their style and community spirit represent the culture shared by Creole neighbourhoods such as Belmont, Laventille and East Dry River. While many regard these districts as embodying the soul of carnival, and the NCC and the Tourist Board pay them propagandist lip-service, the real feelings of these middle-class organizations toward them are suspicion and fear.

Calypso tents

The lower and lower-middle classes also dominate the scene among the public which attends the calypso tents. Apart from one, government-sponsored exception, these tents are in the hands of private entrepreneurs. Even more emphatically than during the steelband contests, these theatres provide scope for all kinds of carnival expressions which run counter to the taste and norms of those social groups which feel more at home in the middle-class setting. In 1987 there were nine tents in Trinidad and Tobago, which presented a total of around one hundred and eighty calypsonians. An NCC jury visits all the theatres in the weeks preceding the carnival weekend and chooses twenty-four candidates for the semi-final. Seven of these go on to the final to compete against the ruling Calypso Monarch (the winner of the previous year). The competition thus begins in the tents, which open their doors in January, but that does not mean that the repertoire is limited to the calypso genre that comes close enough to the dominant fashion to be selected for the finals.

The charm of these theatres lies precisely in the fact that they offer an extremely wide range of calypso entertainment. The artists revive the original spirit of the calypso by giving vent to their feelings and opinions about political scandals and social injustices, and the programme is full of sexual innuendo and *double entendre* in text and gesture. The oldtimers are skilled at rejuvenating their dated *kaisos*, incorporating all the classical ingredients of *picong* and *fatigue*. Their capacity to improvise, which stood them in good stead during the heyday of the Calypso wars, still commands respect from the audience. The Chinese singers Rex West and Ping Pong Pow manage to raise a laugh with practically the same acts every year. With their deliberately clumsy style of delivery and the way they mimic the gestures of a calypsonian, they fulfil the caricatural role of the joker which has apparently become the lot of the Chinese minority in the relations between the races. Their act also serves to confirm the firmly held conviction on the part of sectors of the public and of calypsonians themselves that this style of singing is a prerogative of the blacks.[1] It is acceptable to make fun of the 'peculiarities' of the Chinese in that very area where Indians and Creoles are extremely wary of one another in public in order to avoid racial tensions. The Chinese aspirations to take part in the calypso circus are realized in buffoonery, while Indian calypsonians, such as Drupatee, are eager for their calypso interpretations to be taken seriously, and this is reflected in the reactions of the public too. Warner (1993: 285, 286) notes that

> ... it was not until the emergence of Drupatee in the late 1980s that one heard anything close to an authentic Indian 'voice' in calypso.... Drupatee released a calypso that went a long way toward breaking down racial and gender barriers.... What Drupatee captured was the growing interpenetration of black/Creole and Indian music as she made no attempt to disguise her Indianness, even playing to the stereotype of the Indian female who cannot dance ('wine') like the other Trini women.

Chinese and gays are also the perpetual butts of the repertoire of sexual jokes delivered by the master of ceremonies. They are portrayed as stupid and naïve, and the audience is in stitches when the MC mimics their 'funny way of talking'.

Despite the influence of North American stylistic elements, in particular in the presentation and dress of MCs and calypsonians, and despite the up-to-date musical arrangements and texts which are required for successful participation in the competition, the calypso tents have retained a good deal of their original character. They still offer a platform for all those who feel the need to ventilate moral or political feelings or convictions which, even though they may be 'below the diameter of bourgeois respectability' as far as the average twentieth-century members of the middle class are concerned, still hold some degree of appeal for them. However, it is not always a treat for prominent representatives of the middle class – such as political leaders of the country whose position obliges them to put in an appearance (a large proportion of their electorate is gathered there) – to venture into the lion's den. A newspaper report (*DE,* 19 January 1988) with the caption 'Calypso crowd not too happy with ministers' contains an account of a visit by the Premier and a couple of ministers to Spektakula Forum in Henry Street. The mood in the tent is described as follows:

> Patrons reacted with marked animosity during Saturday's show and strong criticism could be heard throughout the Forum, when MC Tommy Joseph announced that the Prime Minister was in the audience. The crowd could not, apparently, contain its anger and shouted negative remarks at the Prime Minister and company. MC Tommy Joseph appealed to the crowd to be quiet. Minutes after the MC managed to control the crowd the uproar started again when calypsonian Smiley came on stage and sang his 1988 composition, 'Robbie and Georgie' [first names of the Prime Minister in office and his predecessor] a strong social commentary on the 'peculiarities' of the politicians. The crowd reacted by cheering everytime Smiley criticised

a politician. Smiley was encored five times with heavy stamping of feet, clapping of hands and shouts of 'Vote Them Out'.... The crowd's reaction to the government officials continued in the second half of the programme. Through it all the prime minister and his entourage sat quietly and took the crowd's obvious dissatisfaction in stride.

Despite the campaigns of the Tourist Board, very few tourists visit the calypso tents. It is standard practice for the MC to welcome foreigners, even though there is hardly a single one to be seen in the tent. The programme makes no concessions whatever to the (supposed) taste or expectations of the tourists. The calypsonians mainly sing their songs in the dialect of Trinidad. The MC speaks the same dialect when he cracks his jokes between the acts, and they all bear on local situations and events. Foreigners usually have difficulty in following them and miss the point, which once prompted an MC to remark: 'We have a lot of visitors in the tent tonight. When you don't understand the jokes, just laugh when they [the Trinidadians] laugh.'

Although a considerable number of the visitors are middle class, the atmosphere in the tents is largely determined by members of the black lower and lower-middle class. The latter are certainly not the bearers of the social and cultural values which the broad front of middle-class groups would like to see represented in carnival and which are supposed to appeal to tourists. The calypso tents provide people with a freedom and a sense of sharing the same values which is hardly tempered, if at all, by the presence of outsiders, and they are no longer afraid of the danger of playing into the hands of the prejudice of others. This can be seen from a joke which an MC told during one of these performances: A good spirit appears to a black civil servant in his office and tells him he can make three wishes. The black's first wish is to be able to stay in Miami for the rest of his life. His wish is immediately granted. His second wish is to be white, and this is granted too. His last wish is not to have to work any more and ... he is a black civil servant sitting behind his desk again! This form of poking fun at oneself is not intended for the ears of the middle class or the tourists, but both groups can still enjoy it and will not feel ill at ease in an atmosphere of this kind.[2]

This is a sector of carnival which Manning describes for the Antiguan situation as informal, chaotic and menacing rather than amusing, as can be seen from the Denyse Plummer affair. This singer 'with a white complexion' (as physical appearance is commonly referred to on the island) was born and bred in Trinidad, and she already had a long career as a singer behind her when she suddenly emerged as a calypsonian in 1986. Her song 'One Love' immediately took her to the Calypso Monarch Semi-Finals, held in Skinner Park in San Fernando. The following is an excerpt from her calypso:

> *This country is a love country*
> *Love is the key*

From African to Chineeman
All that is we
Any race that comes to mind
In this place you bound to find
A multimix society with a fix on unity
The secret is one love.

During her performance she was surrounded by children of various 'races', waving the flag of Trinidad and Tobago as a living expression of this unity. However, when she appeared on stage in Skinner Park and began to sing the song, she was bombarded with bottles and all kinds of paper darts. The hostile audience unrolled banners with slogans like 'Go back to South Africa' and 'White People Do Not Sing Calypso'. She was forced to stop in the middle of her act and find a refuge with the panic-stricken children. The newspapers were disgusted by this 'outburst of racism'. An editorial in the *Express* (4 February 1986), for instance, stated: 'Carnival, calypso or steelband is not the sole enclave of any one sector of the community and one of the proud boasts of this country has been the ability to meld its varied races into one homogeneous nation'.

All the same, the incident was not entirely unexpected. The public was dissatisfied with the choice of the twenty-four semi-finalists. Rumour had it that the jury of the NCC (still called CDC at the time) had applied different criteria instead of the usual musical and lyrical ones, and that it had been instructed to choose at least one candidate from its own tent. The CDC was also supposed to have instructed the jury not to choose singers who went in for hard-hitting political comments. Thus the young and extremely popular calypsonian Cro Cro was believed to have been kept out of the final, even though he had been one of the most successful candidates in the preliminary rounds. The public was annoyed by the exclusion of Cro Cro and vented its anger by holding up placards with the slogans 'CDC we pay for the best, so why not pick the best' and 'Quacks and Invalids' (a reference to Chalkdust's calypso with that title from the same year). However, this could not all be blamed on Plummer, and indeed it was not directly connected with her. I suspect that she was the target of all these frustrations because her unusual (white) physical appearance was associated with the unpopular, establishment-run NCC. The incident also served to express another feeling: the association of calypso with black identity. As a columnist of the *Sun* (7 February 1986) put it:

> Calypso is only black people thing. Since time immemorial. Simply because calypso is inherently African and only black people here and in other parts of the Caribbean have cared about the art form to do anything about it, to propel it to 'acceptable levels'. Now that it has reached that pinnacle of

acceptability others are getting on the band wagon.... Plummer appears to have no trouble crooning American pop songs. It is a clear statement as to how she perceives herself; culturally different from me, yet we come from the same, small island, presumably. And that is the crux of the matter. Plummer is representative of a segment of the society who seek to uphold these perceived differences.

Two years later Plummer was immensely popular with her hit 'Woman is Boss', and Cro Cro won the calypso competition, which once again caused a furore. We shall come back to Cro Cro later.

Jouvert Morning

In a comparison of the various components of the carnival festival, the Dimanche Gras show and Jouvert Morning (the opening of the carnival in the early hours of Lundi Gras) can be seen as polar opposites in a number of respects. Dimanche Gras is an expression *par excellence* of the carnival aspirations produced by the middle class and propagated by government bodies such as the Tourist Board and the NCC. Using quasi-cosmopolitan symbols, as expressed in the glitter and glamour of the North American show styles, the spectacular performance gives shape to the island's own romanticized image as it is found nowadays in the stereotypes of tourism as a carefree tropical paradise. From this perspective, carnival is reduced to innocent entertainment, a stage show which must not be allowed to shock anyone in any political, social or sexual way. Although the calypso finale in particular may cause considerable ripples on this smooth surface, art and culture are supplied in a highly processed form to a public that is assumed to be aloof from the inner streets of Port of Spain. This district is the original setting where spontaneous forms can still be found that are a far cry from the sterile shows which they have become. It is this originality and spontaneity that characterize Jouvert Morning, which means something like 'the dawn'. This part of carnival bears little or no relation to the show genre, but is the ideal opportunity to participate fully without any restraint. It is a time of freedom, camaraderie and boisterous enjoyment, in which an expressive mood is created reminiscent of Turner's (1969) 'communitas'.

After the definitive prohibition of the Canboulay procession of the Jamettes in 1884, this was replaced by Jouvay (Hill 1972: 86). 'Obscene' joking in the spirit of Dame Lorraine still occupied pride of place. Dressed in rags, sheets, banana leaves and the like, the carnival revellers presented striking caricatures of top-ranking government officials and politicians in the colony. Men dressed as women and dancing women in men's clothes made fun of the relations between the sexes. Others wore nappies and swigged from a feeding bottle filled with rum in a parody of childhood, or wore primitive exotic dress to parody ethnic characteristics (Stewart 1986: 302). In addition, up to the end of the nineteenth century the streets were filled with strange figures from folklore and mythology, such as the *soucouyant*, a witch who turns into a vampire-like creature at night; *diablesse, loup garou, Papa Bois*; and *Phantom*, a tall, monstrous man who camouflages himself with branches and leaves and blocks the road to travellers (Hill 1972: 86). When belief in these figures declined, their representation in the masquerade disappeared too. New creations emerged between the turn of century and the 1930s, which often lived a life of their own independently of the bands, such as Death, Pirates, Clowns, Red Indians, Robbers and Pierrots. There were also scenes of magistrates wearing wigs and lawyers with their clerks who held hearings on the street corners, and Baby Dolls, women in short skirts with masses of ribbons and frills, who carried a big doll in their arms, approached men who were suspected of being the fathers, and asked them for money 'to mind the chile' (Carr 1975: 68).

Nowadays many steelbands leave their panyards in the dead of night on Sunday and make for the city centre, followed by a rapidly growing procession of revellers. The bands run into one another on street corners, decide who goes first, get in one another's way, and eventually mingle with a crowd of people singing and dancing 'cooolll' regardless, who soon take over all the streets and squares of the city area of Port of Spain. Jouvay masquerade bands and enormous trucks with live bands and DJs, squeezed with their electronics between walls of loudspeakers, try to force their way through to the route which will bring them past the spectators in the stalls specially erected for the occasion. There is no room for individual manoeuvring in the darkened streets; everyone is forced to follow the collective, steady rhythm coming from the nearest source of music. Whether they like it or not, everyone is borne on the rhythmic wave which runs through the crowd, back to back and belly to belly. The masquerade bands have none of the spectacular visual effects of the bands which will dominate the streets in the daytime on Monday, and especially on Tuesday. The costumes are not as carefully made, but their satirical power is much greater.

This parade, traditionally known as Ole Mas (from Old Masquerade) is marked by a large degree of freedom for personal expression. For instance, a fake film team covered with black grease paint suddenly emerges from the procession of fools, and with a lot of fuss starts filming the real TV cameras from behind a cardboard camera mounted on a tripod. Then it pans to the Minister of Culture on the stand, who is doing her best to appreciate it. She is specially dressed for the occasion in a pair of jeans, a T-shirt and a beret. The revellers usually wear home-made costumes instead of ones made by official designers, and they poke fun at current political and social issues or bring to life the fantastic carnival figures of the past in a grotesque way. The bands, with names like Barbarians, or Kids in Hell, include large numbers of musicians who accompany themselves by banging spoons or knives on bottles, biscuit tins, buckets or wheel hubs. Their bodies are cosmetically smeared with greasy substances, soot, paint and light brown mud. It is as if the gates of hell have been set wide open to release the most bizarre creatures into the world and to scare bystanders to death. There is an aggressive, erotically charged atmosphere, boosted by generous doses of alcohol and ganja, which seem to bring some people into a state of trance. Someone suddenly falls to the ground, wriggling and snorting, sometimes assuming the stealthy gait of a wildcat about to pounce on its prey. Bystanders in the band have to lend a hand to try to control the wild contortions of the body. The mood seems to change gradually as the day breaks. The massive chaos dies down as the steelbands, music floats and masquerade bands form a single, long procession which winds its way slowly over Independence Square. The spell which held everyone in its thrall in the dead of night has been broken; daylight is too revealing.

Jouvert Morning is an unmistakable part of the official festival, but it also has the eccentric characteristics of an anti-carnival or shadow carnival, which seems to set itself up against the pervasive middle-class values which have permeated the festival at all levels up to a certain point. Although a growing number of members of the middle class are involved in Jouvay as spectators and participants, only a few of my middle-class friends took part in it. Considerable cultural value is attached to this carnival event, but people prefer to keep a safe distance from confrontations which are regarded as shocking. There are a striking number of prostitutes on the streets during Jouvay, who come from the murky and poky dens on the waterfront. Often drunk and scantily clad, they take part in carnival intensely by unsteadily clinging to every man they bump into. A police officer need not bat an eye-lid when one of them in a skimpy bikini emerges from the crowd to spread her legs and lean against him, but not everyone likes to be approached in this way.

The anarchy of Jouvert Morning is continued in a light, relaxed form on Monday afternoon, when after a couple of hours of relative quiet the revellers and steel bands reappear in the streets of the city. The individual, pluriform outfits have given way to collective, uniform ones to distinguish the various sections of the masquerade bands from one another, but the band members still lack the discipline to comply fully. They take the liberty of detaching themselves from their place and dress nonchalantly in the costume they have bought with highly colourful and glittering materials, leaving the finest or most impractical parts at home. It is not until Mardi Gras that the masquerade bands, accompanied by steelbands and music floats, move in a long procession to the Savannah, where they display themselves to the public and the jury as a well-organized group dressed in full array.

The cultural homelessness of the Creole middle class as guarantee of the festival's expressive autonomy

Studies of carnival in various places in the world emphasize the group-binding aspects of the festival. For instance, research on carnival in Santiago de los Caballeros (Dominican Republic) led Gonzalez (1970: 328–42) to the conclusion that the event is a demonstration of intra-class identity and solidarity. It works as a mechanism that marks off the boundaries between classes and ethnic groups. Very little intermingling takes place as the various classes in the city take part in the festivities. This is diametrically opposed to the popular notion that carnival is the destroyer of social barriers *par excellence*. The carnival studied by Gilmore (1975: 331–44) in Southern Spain does provide an instance of something of the kind, but the festival in question is strictly confined to the lower class. Ritualized conflict during carnival has a paradoxical effect on intra-group solidarity and identity within this class. It promotes social interaction, confirms group norms, clarifies group boundaries and characteristics, and creates a community spirit which gives those involved a feeling of self-respect. Kinser's (1990) historical research on the carnival in New Orleans demonstrates that black associations such as the Mardi Gras Indians still compete with others from the same social background for valuable and prestigious prizes today. In this way they confirm their class identity and separate place in a festive event which is still dominated by a white economic and political power structure (see also M.P. Smith 1990: 11–32).

Trinidad carnival is different from these examples. The way the Trinidadians are involved in carnival as spectators and participants only reflects the traditional ethnic and class divisions to a certain extent. These divisions are to be found particularly in the composition of the masquerade bands. In theory, anyone can join the band of his choice, but in practice the situation is different. Both the members of the elite/middle class and those of the lower class organize their own bands. As a result of the specific relation which exists in Trinidad between difference in skin colour and the division into social classes (even within the wider boundaries defined by 'race'), the lower-class bands are dominated by members of the black population, while the elite/middle-class bands consist mainly of people of mixed blood and whites ('Trinidad Whites' or 'French Creoles'), besides an increasing number of well-to-do Indians, Portuguese, Chinese and Syrians, who feel an affinity with their Afro-Creole counterparts on the basis of their common middle-class lifestyle. This cultural and ethnic homogeneity means that there is strong cohesion, loyalty and class solidarity within the lower-class bands. They often consist of relatives, friends and individuals from the same circle who maintain a personal relation with the band leader or organizer. This tight structure implies that the lower-class bands are usually limited to a maximum of three or four hundred members. It is precisely because of the lack of these factors conducive to both cohesion and social demarcation that the middle-class bands can expand to become large-scale, ethnically heterogeneous and loosely structured conglomerates. Each of the three largest masquerade bands – those of Edmond Hart, Raoul Garib and Peter Minshall – has a membership of between two and three thousand. These are thus largely middle-class in composition.

However, carnival is the only annually recurring festival in which the different classes meet and interact in various ways. The description given earlier in this chapter of the several components of carnival shows that class consciousness still plays a part in the composition of the public, but the traditional social divisions have lost their rigidity. It is rather the case that the degree and nature of the participation by various social groups in various parts of the carnival give the differences between the social strata a changed emphasis. Thus, in terms of organization, participation and the composition of the public, the Dimanche Gras show is regarded by most Trinidadians as an elite/middle-class affair, even though both passive and active participation by the lower class and lower-middle class can certainly not be considered insignificant. At the other end of the social spectrum, while the calypso tent is traditionally regarded as a phenomenon belonging to the socio-cultural domain of the lower class, changes in social attitudes and the composition of the public have given the tents a popularity which is by no means confined to that class alone. Similarly, although it can be seen from my descriptions of Dimanche Gras, Panorama, calypso tent and Jouvert Morning that each component of carnival attracts a larger public from a particular class and embodies its values, expressions and traditions more explicitly than the others, one can no longer refer to the Trinidad carnival as a public festival marked by social and cultural components that are divided by clear-cut boundaries.

The predominant influence of the middle class in the last few decennia and the penetration of society by middle-class attitudes and values have undoubtedly had a homogenizing effect on public interest and participation in carnival. While on many social fronts this situation reveals a cultural and social levelling out or equalizing, carnival has still retained its cultural heterogeneity and variety to a large extent. In view of the significant influence of the middle class and its tendency to view the festival in a monolithic way, as expressed in its desire to present carnival as a sterile tourist attraction, this is a remarkable fact. However, it is not the middle class as a homogenizing factor, but the specific cultural position of this class within the dynamic field of social relations, that explains why carnival has not been entirely absorbed by the general social process of middle classization. This can be illustrated by a brief analysis of the historical development of two important components of carnival which have already been mentioned.

The difference between Jouvert Morning and Mardi Gras in terms of style, mood and aesthetics can be understood in the context that existed at the end of the nineteenth century. At that time carnival developed as a result of the class division of society at two levels: as a wild and always potentially violent festival of the lower class, filled with local beliefs and practices taken from local mythology and folklore – a strong undercurrent, according to Lewis (1968: 31–2) of Shango, bamboo-tamboo, Canboulay, and secret Negro cults; and as a carnival of pomp and splendour, set in a formal decorum, in line with a European cultural tradition in which the upper classes and the white elite felt at home. The Creole middle class occupied an ambivalent position *vis-à-vis* the two carnival styles. As we saw in Chapter 3, its members were driven by a deep desire to be accepted by the white elite as their equals. They suffered from the discrimination of that elite, which refused to acknowledge these aspirations. On the other hand, this coloured class had an original affinity with the cultural heritage of the black lower classes, although they did not wish to be identified with them socially. They regarded an invitation to attend a ball in the higher echelons of society as a proof of social success, for it offered them the opportunity to move in the social circles to which they aspired, albeit for a brief moment. However, they were also attracted by the forbidden pleasures which the spontaneous festivities of the black lower class had to offer. They joined in the revels in the streets, they organized masquerade bands and demonstrated their support of the stick-fighter's ritual. With its two currents, carnival reflected the ambivalence in which the middle class was caught, but at the same time it represented the main cultural context in which this ambivalence could be creatively and expressively experienced. This separation of the levels of carnival persisted more or less until the 1950s, although the middle class began to play an increasingly active role in those components of carnival which were the traditional preserve of the upper classes and the colonial elite. Although they continued to take part in Jouvay, the members of this class devoted special attention to the Carnival Queen Contest, which was held during the Dimanche Gras show, and to the Mardi Gras procession.

This process of cultural appropriation acquired its definitive form with the political independence of Trinidad in the early 1960s. From then on the Creole middle class dominated these carnival events. Their old aspirations to measure up to the upper classes and the white colonial (administrative) elite, which had largely disappeared by now, continued to colour new forms of expression which were adapted to suit the changed times. The original, ambivalent position of the middle class, however, and its disguised or at least embarrassed sympathy for the cultural values of the lower class, with which it is historically connected, guarantee the survival of the spirit of the two carnivals in the present festival.

While the dominance of the middle class, combined with the process of middle-classization, has a primarily homogenizing effect on carnival as a social event, the culturally ambivalent position of this class (its penchant for foreign, quasi-colonial values, as well as its realization that carnival, calypso and steelband are the major symbols of the national culture of Trinidad) has a diversifying effect on the components and themes of the contemporary carnival. As a result, the festival is more or less free of the general levelling or equivalence of creative, artistic and political expressions which has gained so much ground in society at large. The reason why this is so with regard to carnival is primarily connected with the special historical relation of the middle class with the festival and with the organizational structure of the contemporary Trinidad carnival as a competition, which makes it particularly receptive to cultural ambivalence. This is an important point, which will be explained in more detail later on.

This ambivalence does not mean that all kinds of carnival expressions are approved of by the middle class, but that there is still enough room within the festival for events which it does not welcome, or at any rate to which it does not pay lip-service. A newspaper report and commentary (from the respectable *Express*) on the tumultuous 1970 carnival (on the eve of the Black Power disturbances and a mutiny within the army) indicates that the position of carnival as a forum for rebellious expression and establishment reaction without official repercussions has hardly changed at all in the last hundred years (*Express,* 15 February 1970, cited in Oxaal 1982: 220):

> The marchers carried huge portraits of Eldridge Cleaver, the Black Panther leader; the late Malcolm X, Carmichael, and others. There was also a caricature of Prime Minister, Dr. Eric Williams, looking somewhat like a pig. And there were lots of slogans, mainly calling for solidarity among the black people of the world. 'King Sugar' recreated the hardships suffered by the workers in the sugar industry from slavery and indentureship up to the present day. The message the band was trying to put over was scrawled on its banner – 'Black blood; black sweat; black tears – white profits'.
> ... The mere proliferation of socio-political protest bands may not mean much, but a lot will depend on the form the protests take. What will happen, for example, if the authorities feel that the bands are going too far in their protests, and ban them? Legislation may even be introduced to stop this kind of mas'.

The lack of such measures can of course be accounted for by the traditional argument that it is better for such provocative events to be held at fixed times; as long as they are encapsulated, some degree of control in the festival is guaranteed. However, I believe that other motives play a role as well. The fact that certain groups from the Creole middle class largely dominate the organizational framework of the carnival for political and nationalist reasons does not necessarily imply full control over the content. What applied to the festival a few decades ago still applies today: despite the artistic endeavours of representatives of the middle class, many of the carnival scenes, ideas, creations and expressions are derived from the world of the black lower class – 'the view from the dunghill', as Lewis expresses it. The cultural homelessness of the middle class makes it to some extent dependent on the cultural production of the lower class. As a Trinidad journalist with an impeccable middle-class background put it: 'The Trinidadian middle class has not been able to create anything of lasting value, and it therefore has to be parasitic on the culture of the working class' (Eriksen 1990: 33). Still, as we have seen, it is not just a question of parasitism. It is also a traditional affinity (or barely disguised sympathy) with the values of the black lower class, which ensures that the middle class is still receptive to certain expressions of carnival. All these factors form the ambivalent attitude of the middle class which in the last resort boils down to attempting to confer respectability on carnival while displaying an understanding of the need to maintain the original, traditional carnival values.

The confrontation of the middle class with its own ambivalence

This ambivalence of the middle class not only determines its attitude to carnival but has a divisive effect in its own ranks with regard to all kinds of issues and incidents connected with the festival. When in 1988 the Minister for Sport, Youth and Culture, Jennifer Johnson, proposed moving the carnival from the Savannah to the national stadium on the periphery of Port of Spain, her suggestion met with heavy criticism. It would be the end of the spontaneous street carnival which forms a historical and symbiotic whole with the happenings in the Savannah. Such far-reaching centralization would give the government an unacceptable degree of control over carnival and would make the event (even more of) a sterile folklore spectacle instead of a popular festival. The calypsonian Singing Francine, whose songs are generally a reflection of the feelings of the black lower class, voiced these criticisms in her calypso song 'Cultural Controversy':

... But for now lady Minister
don't move the mas' from the Savannah
Leave things as they are and don't get me mad
I strongly object the removement
to stadiumize we carnival
and so does all the people of Trinidad

Chorus: *Move the mas' from the Savannah? No way!*
Jessica you will cause riot I say
We mas' in the Savannah must stay!
Jessica, you're crazy.

There were also protests against the minister's proposals from the members of the middle class itself. Despite their desire for an orderly festival without unexpected incidents or scandals, many of them felt that this move would extinguish the true spirit of carnival. In 1987, during the carnival seminar organized by the Ministry of Culture, similar ideas to those of the Minister had also been voiced, and they met with a similar lack of response among the majority of middle-class participants in the seminar. Genuine revellers, whether they come from the lower or the higher strata of society, regard the Savannah as the sacred territory of carnival and the heart of the national culture which must be left intact. After the wave of criticism had washed over her, Jennifer Johnson stated that she had never meant it like that (*Sunday Punch*: 13 March 1988).[3]

The annually recurring discussion on morality within carnival reveals in a different way the conflicting values of the middle class. Negative reports in the press about the alleged 'smut and vulgarity' of calypso lyrics and above all about the appalling display of sex and eroticism in the masquerade processions provoke an equally strong barrage of support. It is as if the antagonists from the middle-class camp keep one another in perfect balance. This can be illustrated by the furore caused by the presentation of Peter Minshall's masquerade band Jumbie on the stage of Queen's Hall in 1988. This was a preview for special guests and the press of a number of prototype costumes which were to be displayed to the public at large a few weeks later during carnival. The fact that one of the male models wore nothing but a g-string under his carnival costume, which did little to hide his body anyway, caused a commotion not so much among the audience on the spot as among those who saw a couple of photos in the paper. Moral indignation was whipped up this time by TV personality June Gonsalves, followed by a flood of commentators, senators, high-ranking church dignitaries, spokeswomen for the Rape Crisis Centre and the Mothers' Union of the Anglican Church, Bible believers and concerned students from St Mary's College. The tone and argument of Gonsalves's commentary in the paper, under the heading 'Is nothing private in T+T?', are typical of the reactions to such instances of 'moral degeneration' in society:

> The editor: If you really think about it, hardly a day passes without an opportunity to stand up and be counted on some issue of importance – issues which effect our way of life, our principles and our ideals. I want to protest vigorously about the lewd pictures of members of Peter Minshall's 1988 Carnival band, which appeared on pages one and five on Friday, January 15. I believe it is my civic responsibility to let this talented bandleader know that what we really need in our country now are well-rounded human beings, not necessarily brilliant by any means, but people with the ability to think clearly and rationally, who will eventually put into practice what is necessary to make Trinidad and Tobago a better place to live.
>
>   You see, I care passionately about my country and its people. I care about the young generation and the example that we adults set before them. Bare bottoms and revealing vaginas have their place (they already desecrate our beaches), but what message are you giving to the young when you show them a horde of non-thinking half naked people, wining and rubbing bouncing derriéres across a Savannah stage and on our streets? Trinidad has already become a place where private property is no longer private, must this also apply to the private parts of the human body? By the way, isn't there a law about indecent exposure? Are our women in particular and our masqueraders in general so bewitched, bewildered and brainwashed by Peter Minshall, that they are incapable of resisting the most arrant nonsense, all in the name of carnival? God help us.

Designer and band leader Peter Minshall's laconic response was that he had not designed naked bodies. He left that up to God, and he was bound to confess that God had made a pretty good job of it. 'It is between people themselves and their God to decide how or in what way they wish to display His good work. I am their artist, not their moral arbiter', he concluded (*DE*, 26 January 1988). Sympathizers emphasized that carnival was above all a question of art and creativity, not the fixation on the almost bare bottom of some male model.

Both parties continue to attack one another right up to the carnival; the excitement dies down immediately afterwards; and the glowing embers blaze up again with a similar scandal the following year. It is the same old story: protest and a call for action are ineffective, nothing changes. Since the criticisms are mainly voiced by the middle class and are generally aimed only at the carnival behaviour of the middle class itself and not at the Jamet-like activities of the lower class (which are equally frequent throughout practically all the components of carnival and which came under such heavy fire from the middle class in the past), the recurrent pattern seems to indicate a tussle on the part of the middle class with its own ambivalence. More than any other event of the year, carnival forces the middle class to confront its own divided nature, which inevitably leads to controversy, the dramatic presentation of the problematic and insoluble ambiguity which is characteristic of its culture and morality. Controversy is inextricably connected with the function of the Trinidad carnival. The Trinidad columnist Wayne Brown (*DE*, 28 January 1988) writes:

> If, as in the past, both sides content themselves with cussing each other, until Carnival is over and the controversy fades, then another chance for us to become the subjects rather than the objects of our own lives will have been wasted – and the controversy will arise again; and again; and again.

The conflicting loyalties of the jury

While the Creole middle class thus largely dominates the organizational framework of the carnival festival for political and nationalist reasons, the mutually antagonistic value complexes which determine its socio-cultural position guarantee the persistence of a diversity of cultural expressions within the festival. This equivocal attitude on the part of the middle class can be seen not only from the above examples, but also from the manner in which NCC carnival policy itself takes shape. The NCC's endeavour to streamline the organization of the carnival contest (as its main function) is at odds with the social, cultural and aesthetic motives which guide the judgements of the jury, itself the creation of this very commission. During the last thirty-five years, the commission has managed to transform the majority of the adult and children's competition shows into a stage culture whose evident restrictive character provides opportunities to control the events, to discipline them and to purge them as far as possible of all moral aspects which do not conform to the 'respectable' image for tourist consumption that the commission, in line with government policy, is out to achieve. According to the NCC regulations as laid down in the *Guide to Participation 1986*, contestants are expected to follow all the instructions of the producer or stage director of the show in which they take part; otherwise they are excluded entirely from the competition. Exclusion is also the penalty for those who wear a costume which is considered to be substandard. Immediate disqualification follows if a masquerade band which has been allowed to take part in the competition appears on stage with a presentation which can be regarded as obscene or in any other way offensive. While the commission does all it can to preserve the festival from distasteful elements and incidents, however, the criteria observed by the jury sometimes lead it to rate carnival events and expressions very highly which appear to be diametrically opposed to these norms and which are bound to result in minor or major social controversies of a generally moral and/or political character.

The jury, whose composition is in the hands of the NCC, is clearly middle-class by nature. It is therefore reasonable to suppose that it will endorse many of the objectives of the commission. All the same, many of the members of the jury have earned their reputation in the artistic and creative world of carnival, which may explain their higher level of sympathy for or affinity with controversial carnival expressions. However, it is not just the attitude or frame of reference of the jury which is responsible for the fact that the NCC-organized carnival is still characterized by aspects which are frowned upon by the middle class. It is the character of the carnival competition itself, the pressure of public opinion, and the extent to which the public has a say, which force the jury to make choices, even when they do not entirely correspond to the jury's own motivation or taste. The clearest illustration of this is provided by the 'choice' of the Road March of the year. This is the calypso song which is performed most often during Mardi Gras, whether live, or electronically from trucks which ride in the procession, or in an arrangement by the steelbands which head the procession, to accompany the dancing and singing members of a masquerade band during their parade through the city to the Savannah. Keeping a tally of the road marches at various points in the city and in the rest of the country ensures that the most popular song makes its own way to the top. Calypsos of this kind generally consist of a short, repetitive text involving sexual *double entendre* (which generally creates a stir), an ear-catching melody, and a driving rhythm. 'Suck me, soucouyant, suck me' was the message of Crazy's winning Road March in 1985, and two years later Road March King Mighty Duke sang:

> *If I only hold you tonight is thunder*
> *Ah giving you thunder*
> *Ah going to make you tell me 'surrender'*
> *Ah giving you thunder*
> *Ah giving you whole night*
> *You prancing up whole night*
> *You dancing up whole night*
> *You poking me whole night*
> *Provoking me...*

In the Road March competition the task of the jury is confined to counting the number of times a song is performed and announcing the winner; it is the taste of the carnival public which decides everything.

Even in those aspects where the jury does have more say, it still has to take factors into account which guide its choice in a particular direction. After all, the cultural production is still largely in the hands of the black lower class, and it is all the more compelling because of the lack of an alternative cultural source of inspiration for the (ambivalently sympathetic) middle class. New steelband arrangements and calypso compositions are developed and tried out in panyards and calypso tents, which are traditionally the socio-cultural domain of the lower class. This is where the arbiters of the taste of carnival culture are to be found, surrounded by like-minded associates and fans from their own class, who have also received the warm interest of a select, carnival-minded public from the higher social circles for years. After weeks of preparation and fertile interaction between the creators and critical connoisseurs, the presentations arrive in the preliminary rounds of the formal competition, already knocked into shape and pre-sorted. These preliminary rounds are held all over the island where the sophisticated influence of the urban middle class is hardly perceptible and public opinion is largely determined by the 'view from the dunghill'. The jury can hardly turn a blind eye to the extremely expressive way in which the emotionally involved public indicates its preferences during these presentations.

This is true of the steelband competition, but it is probably even truer of the way in which the calypsos for the final are selected. (The situation is different in the case of the masquerade competition. There is only one adjudication of the bands on Mardi Gras, without any previous selection.) Week after week, hundreds of calypsos – in 1987 there were 397, sung by 299 calypsonians (*TG*, 18 February 1987) – are presented to the public during numerous performances in parks, stadiums and calypso tents. The public makes no attempt to disguise its opinion, and at this stage in the contest the jury is under great pressure from the encouragements and comments which the public never fails to express. In particular, during the jury's daily visits to the tents as part of their official assignment, it is virtually impossible to adopt an objective point of view amid the critical reactions of the public as an unfailing gauge of the popularity of a calypso song. Of course, the jury's own taste will affect its decisions, and given its sympathy with original carnival expressions, this may well correspond to the taste of the public. However, if it deviates too far from public opinion, or even if rumours are enough to give public opinion the impression that this is the case, the jury forfeits its credibility. This loss of face can lead to unpleasant incidents (such as the Denyse Plummer affair), which may cast a blemish on the image of carnival as the celebration of national unity.

This is the setting, largely determined by 'the social classes at the bottom of the West Indian social compost' (Lewis 1968: 28), which forms the solid and broad foundation of the pyramid structure of the competition. But that is not all. With the cultural production of the black lower class on the one hand, and the ambivalent stance of the culturally homeless Creole middle class which controls the organization of the festival on the other, the competition functions both as a mediatory instrument between divergent socio-cultural orientations, and as an engine which transports the expressive values and creations from 'below' through the various (and no longer clearly defined) socio-cultural echelons of carnival to the official NCC platforms. This guarantees the cultural autonomy or internal dynamic of carnival, which refuses to be straitjacketed by government bodies such as the Tourist Board and the NCC.

'Burn Dem'

The Caribbean illusion as propagated by the government and tourist promoters may be seriously disrupted by expressions of black identity as one of the cohesive factors of the original carnival ideology. In 1987 Black Stalin was Calypso Monarch of the Year with his hit 'Burn Dem'. This song successfully shattered the illusion and brought the spirit of Canboulay to life in the Savannah stadium. This was not the first commotion in the musical career of Black Stalin, whose musical messages at the very least evoke a mood which appeals to the racial sentiments of the black population. He had already pulled it off with 'Caribbean Man' in 1979. In the 1987 carnival, writes Keith Smith in the *Sunday Express* (15 March 1987), 'he burnt up the Savannah stage, bringing 10,000 people to their feet, singing with his fiery denunciation of people whom he felt had wronged the African race'. In 'Burn Dem' he joins St Peter at the gate of heaven to make sure that the wrong people are not allowed in. Drake, Raleigh, Rhodes, Victoria, Mussolini, Ian Smith, Columbus, Thatcher, Reagan must all be denied entry. Black Stalin (whose stage name has an ironic ring in this company!) impatiently urges Peter to throw them all into the fires of hell. The following is an excerpt from the text:

> *Peter you doh know*
> *The pressure that I undergo*
> *From these mad men and women*
> *Ah feel the full weight*
> *Of they hand*
> *They make dey oppress law*
> *They never care about the poor*
> *Peter these people had they day*
> *Well now is the time for Stalin to play.*

Refrain: *Why this is my time for burning*
> *Ah burning and ah burning and ah burning*
> *Peter keep the fire blazing*
> *Blazing, blazing, blazing.*

Peter look the
English woman
Who on South Africa
Refuse to put sanction
Burn she, burn she
Peter ah jest do care
What you do but
Reagan going in the fire too
Burn he, burn he.

Leroy 'Fathead' Williams, 1987

During his performance in the final, Black Stalin was dressed in a cloak which fell in capacious folds, decorated with a pattern of hellish yellow flames against a fiery red background. His rasta locks were tucked into a gigantic beret made of the same material. Gesticulating wildly, his cloak billowing around him, he ran from one end of the stage to the other, which was fenced off by figures dressed in red with blazing torches. Rockets and fireworks were launched from different parts of the stadium, which had been darkened for the occasion, and their flares seemed to underline the grim message of the calypsonian. The public went out of their minds. Thousands of people stood up and danced, cheered and chanted with their clenched fists raised 'burn them!' 'He woke the whole Savannah to life, and set the people to mutiny and rage', wrote chronicler Michael Anthony (1989: 483) in his report of the event. Indeed, it showed every sign of turning into a riot, which, despite the dominant festive mood, would not have been equally palatable to every 'outsider'. As I stood in the press area right in front of the stage, one of the Trinidad photographers suddenly burst into a sort of Indian war-cry with appropriate dance steps. As he thrashed his arms wildly about him, pushing or kicking away anyone who tried to calm him down, he screamed: 'Yeh, yeh, burn dem, burn all the focking whities! I hate dem, I hate dem, burn dem!' His spasm was over as suddenly as it had begun and he went back to work as if nothing had happened. One of the close associates of Black Stalin described the scene when the newly crowned monarch reappeared on stage with the winner of the previous year, David Rudder, to receive the ovations of the public (*DE*, 15 March 1987):

> He gone up on the stage with Rudder. The people start to run on and a policeman telling them to cool it and the crowd responding threateningly: 'We go bun all yuh!' Well, the police now decide he not interfering with that so he call me and tell me: 'Yuh better go up there and take him out!'. Well as he tell me that, I just run through the crowd and pull him out, telling the people: 'All yuh move!'

Black Stalin's act and the reactions of the public at least create an electrifying mood which is closer to the original popular festival than the glamour spectacle envisaged by the organizers of Dimanche Gras. All the same, the two settings are not impervious to one another. It may be useful for analytical purposes to make the distinction, but reality, as it has developed from the cultural dualism and the special function of the competition as an important carnival mechanism, points to a greater unity, in so far as the inability of the two moods to merge is only sustainable by the fact that they support and influence one another; their relation to one another is one of intonation rather than detonation. The tension created in this situation is precisely what is characteristic – and perhaps even essential – for the ability of the present-day Trinidad carnival as a national happening to survive.

Cro Cro's provocation: the guarantee of success

While this example is indicative at the performance level of the rebellious atmosphere which is subtly combined with typical middle-class aspirations in every carnival, the affair involving the calypsonian Mighty Cro Cro the following year illustrates that the festival still provides a stage for the dramatic presentation of controversies generated by the value orientations in society which have already been described. In 1986, the indignant public claimed that Cro Cro had been excluded from the final by the NCC jury because of the political content of his calypso. Two years later, in 1988, he was crowned Calypso Monarch of the Year by the same jury. This time, the presentation and calypso lyrics were even more controversial, unleashing a social debate on a hot topic which lasted for weeks.

Cro Cro brought the excitement of the spectators in the Grand Stand and the North Stand to fever pitch with his biting condemnation of the policy of the NAR government, which had taken over from the PNM in 1986. Under the slogan of 'One Love', a number of Creole and Indian parties and movements had formed a mammoth alliance which was overwhelmingly successful in its attempts to convince the electorate of the viability of a multi-racial government coalition. Once the crushing victory had been won, however, a power struggle broke out between the three leaders of the NAR – Robinson, Panday and Hudson-Phillips – which inspired Cro Cro's song 'Three Big Bo Rats Can't Live in One Hole'. (The words of the song continued: 'And I remember when they hug, like three turtle dove fooling the public and calling "one love" '). This frank criticism was in tune with current political developments and met with a favourable reception in broad circles, but it was completely outstripped by the furore caused by Cro Cro's next hit, 'Corruption in Common Entrance Exam'. This calypso criticizes the procedure of the entrance examination to so-called prestige schools. His claim is that it is corruption and nepotism, with colour and class as the main criteria, and not the intelligence and capacity of the pupil, which are the decisive factors in selection. The controversial calypso opens:

> *Me ain't tainting vie*
> *And me ain't trying to protect my child*
> *But corruption is a constant annoyance*
> *For now too long in Common Entrance*
> *You don't have to be intelligent that is a lie*
> *Your father must be of good esteem with complexion high*
> *Your child could be bright like a poor bulb from Laventille*
> *Forget 'Holy Name Convent' and 'Bishop Anstey'.*

Cro Cro goes on to name a number of rich and well-known families in Trinidad whose children are supposed to have enjoyed special privileges in the entrance examinations, concluding with the refrain: 'It looks like there's a high class in the class'. Cro Cro then sings that you need connections with the Ministry of Education if you want your child to be considered for one of the prestige schools instead of having to go to school in one of the Junior Secondary Schools with a bad reputation:

> *Before 'Common Entrance' last year*
> *I'm liming on Independence Square*
> *A woman was shopping but I called her on the pavement*
> *I see a uniform of the 'Holy Name Convent'*
> *I say woman how did your child pass for that school*
> *She say she connection cool and she ain't no fool*
> *She say she husband is on the staff and she start to laugh*
> *She say, Cro Cro, inside the whole ministry is maf*
> *Their parents know where they're going long before they rise.*

Finally, the calypsonian advises poor black parents to change the surname of their children:

> *So change your children's surname and don't be a fool*
> *If you want your children to go to a brand new school*
> *You see, you're not a local white*
> *You ain't got big money*
> *So your child can't go to QRC [Queen's Royal College],...*
> *Because black hen chicken are designed for the Junior Sec.*

Cro Cro's song was introduced by a sketch which illustrated his message in an extremely suggestive way. In this satirical skit, fellow calypsonian Short Pants played a schoolteacher who conducted the entrance exam in his class. He favoured a white and an Indian pupil, neither of whom knew the answer to an extremely simple piece of arithmetic, above two black children who did know the right answer.

'Corruption in Common Entrance' set a lot of tongues wagging and prompted a discussion which exposed a wide range of socially sensitive issues. Under the headline 'Calypso corruption', an editorial in the conservative *TG* (3 March 1988) summed it up as follows:

> No calypso in recent years has so outraged the sensibilities of so many people in the country, and been based on such a brutalisation of the truth. No calypso has called so many names of individuals and made such grievous charges against them. No calypso has made such open charges of racial discrimination or done as much to provoke racial antagonism in the country. No other has taken the calypsonian's traditional freedom of expression so far into the license of character assassination and abuse of identifiable ethnic groups in a multi-ethnic society.

Perhaps the newspaper is exaggerating, loyal as it is to the tradition of commentators who want the most recent carnival to outshine all its predecessors in both positive and negative terms. After all, Cro Cro was not the first calypsonian to incur the wrath of the authorities and the public. Black Stalin with his 'Caribbean Man' was earlier, and Mighty Sparrow had been taken to court and given a (symbolic) fine for his denigrating comments on the restless public in the North Stand in Queen's Park Savannah (*DE*, 1 March 1988). Lord Shorty, recently dubbed Ras Shorty I, underwent a similar experience in 1974 after singing a song ('The Art of Making Love') in the carnival stadium which many people regarded as obscene (*DE*, 2 March 1988). Still, it is true that Cro Cro's provocative calypso stirred the blood of supporters and opponents of the entrance system. Education officials and pressure groups who felt that the message was aimed at them put up a vigorous defence. People whose surnames had been seized on in the calypso demanded compensation. The racial tensions which were always present beneath the surface were reawakened. The fact that an Indian girl was presented as being unable to count to five in the sketch with Short Pants led some Indian organizations to set up a Committee against Racism in Calypso. Managers of calypso tents, record stores, and radio and television stations which continued to advertise Cro Cro's song were threatened with legal action (*TG*, 29 February 1988). In turn, the political organization National Joint Action Committee, the Calypsonians Association, and the Committee in Defense of Culture (specially created on the spur of the moment) came up with their counter-reactions. The Communication Workers Union labelled the whole affair a class issue (*DE*, 22 February 1988):

... the most vociferous attacks and criticisms have come from the mouthpieces of the upper-middle and ruling classes in our society.... Once more the ruling class was attempting to stifle the voices of the people whose political and social views are popularly expressed through the medium of calypso.

The old call to restrict the freedom of calypsonians to express their opinions echoed again. 'Shockingly', wrote the *TG* (3 March 1988) in its editorial, 'the National Carnival Commission completely abdicated its responsibility to examine this song or to give guidelines to a rather immature calypsonian.' A Presbyterian minister claimed that Cro Cro should be prosecuted for slander (*TG*, 4 March 1988). Romesh Mootoo, mayor of San Fernando and chairman of the local carnival committee, called upon the Procurator General, Selwyn Richardson, to investigate whether legal measures could be taken to protect individuals, groups and society as a whole against such mockery and divisive commentaries (*TG*, 5 March 1988). Mootoo also cast doubts on the competence of the jury, joining those critics who claimed that Cro Cro had been selected without first asking whether the calypsonian had done enough 'research' before drawing such bold conclusions (*TG*, 6 February 1988). On the other hand, writes political commentator Selwyn Ryan, 'A calypso is, after all, a calypso, and not a doctoral thesis, though Sparrow has been given a honorary doctorate for his contribution to calypso' (*DE*, 21 February 1988).

For a moment it looked as though the government might intervene when the Indian Minister of Education, Clive Pantin, stated his intention of taking steps against the calypso 'Corruption in Common Entrance', which he called 'extremely libellous' (*DE*, 27 January 1988). In an interview, Cro Cro said that he had expected reactions of this kind from that sector of society. What surprised him, however, was the fact that the same minister invited him to sing the calypso in his ministry a week later (*DE*, 25 February 1988). Cro Cro defended himself against all this commotion by appealing to the supreme being, as senator Myers had so successfully done: 'When I am on stage I move with God, so I know that although some of my lyrics would hit some people hard, they would also project a true message to many others' (ibid.). It is difficult to say whether supernatural forces were at work, but it is a fact that the (black) Minister for Sport, Youth and Culture, Jennifer Johnson, who did not agree with Cro Cro, did not intend to intervene: 'I am not a censor and I don't believe the ministry should act as a censor to calypsonians. The people should do that' (the *Sun*, 4 March 1988). And so the discussion had gone full circle.

The contributions of Black Stalin and Cro Cro, as well as some of the other carnival manifestations described in this chapter, demonstrate that the festival has retained a rebellious potential or a social critical bent. This is not confined to the lowest social regions of the festival, but regularly surfaces within the context of the deliberately domesticated middle-class presentations of native culture. The romanticized middle-class image of Trinidad as a carefree tropical paradise according to the stereotypes intended for tourist consumption, which contains a number of the aspirations of this class and is expressed in its purest form in the Dimanche Gras show, comes irrevocably under pressure every year from expressions, events and incidents which are more likely to alarm than to entertain the tourists. The fact that this regularly occurs is not so much the result of the inability of the carnival organization to suppress such expressions or to hold them in check; it is rather the result of a subtle interaction between ambivalent forces which act, deliberately or not, on the Creole middle class and on society as a whole, influenced as it is by the process of middle-classization.

Carnival itself is born and shaped by this cultural and ideological dualism, which has played a prominent part in various guises throughout the entire history of Trinidad. At the same time, despite attempts by certain social groups to annex and domesticate the festival, it has managed to secure a place for itself which guarantees an autonomous cultural reflection of this dualism. That it has done so is due to the ambivalent socio-cultural relations between the black lower class and the Creole middle class in particular, and to the mechanisms inherent in carnival itself, such as the mediatory function of competition. The following chapter will deal in more detail with this dualism in both a general Caribbean and a particular Trinidadian perspective, as well as specifying the properties of carnival which contribute to this process and which will prove to be significant for the construction of a national identity.

Notes

1   These 'other' groups exist 'on the margins of the calypsonian's consciousness', as Rohlehr (1990: 494) writes. 'Since the [black] calypsonian generally perceives himself as an insider, a man in the know and at the forefront, groups seen to be on the margins are rarely presented as sanely ordered within themselves, but as eccentric, unsophisticated, weird and comical'.

2   Nevertheless, outsiders should not be overhasty in concluding from this example of self-mockery that they can also take liberties. An American tourist from New York who assumed that everything was allowed during carnival joined a masquerade procession dressed as a blackamoor. The black grease paint on his face soon gave away the fact that he was white, and he barely had the chance to enjoy the carnival role reversal for a couple of minutes before the crowd threatened to molest him. He was forced to dive into a chemist's and remove his carnival disguise as fast as he could.

3   In 1993 the government decided to move a number of carnival events, such as the calypso competition and the Dimanche Gras show, to the national stadium after all. The main argument was that the new location was better equipped for satellite transmission. In response to strong social protest, the government was forced to announce that the move was only an experiment (Graham Mayo, personal communication).

8 | Carnival as a vehicle in the quest for national identity

The concept of 'game' as such is of a higher order than that of seriousness. For 'seriousness' endeavours to exclude 'game', while 'game' is quite capable of incorporating seriousness.

(Johan Huizinga, *Homo Ludens*)

Present-day carnival has not become a broken-winged festival, an innocent tourist attraction to uphold a lost folk tradition, as some critics of the festival tend to assume. Carnival is deeply anchored in and interwoven with socio-cultural processes which concern the entire society. Placed in historical perspective, carnival has successively belonged to the social and cultural domain of different groups or classes in society which accordingly placed different accents on the expression of dominant values and subordinated counter-values. Especially after World War II, these contesting values have increasingly merged into one carnival, run but not entirely ruled by the Creole middle class. Carnival, with its symbolic and ambiguous potential, dramatizes, depicts and generates diverging Caribbean sets of values within the context of its own autonomous dynamics, but confesses no preference. The impartiality of the festival and thus its ability to give a form of 'meta-comment' on Trinidad within the performance of a kind of collective psycho-drama, guarantees its exceptional vanguard position in the struggle towards a national identity in a society which, at the same time, retains a great social and cultural variety.

In mapping the contours of the Trinidad carnival, the account of the genesis and development of calypso, steelband and masquerade in particular will have made it clear that carnival is a cultural form. However, the fact that the carnival festival was initially an expression of the status and domination of the planter elite before becoming the expressive instrument to register the protest and resistance of the black population confers a socio-political dimension on this cultural phenomenon as well. Both the cultural and the socio-political dimensions have come in for a good deal of discussion in the course of the present study; at various points they were juxtaposed for clarity's sake, even though they are both tightly interlocked, which – in a transcultural comparison – accounts for the intrinsic meaning of carnival as a universal phenomenon.

The question of the meaning of the present-day Trinidad carnival falls within the historical line that I have traced. I shall therefore begin by drawing attention to the views of the Trinidad-born writer and anthropologist John Stewart (1986: 289–315), because he offers a characterization of carnival and puts forward a number of theses which overlap to some extent with the thrust of my own analysis, while at the same time allowing me to contrast his vision with mine and to provide a more balanced picture.

Is this still a carnival?

Although carnival never took place in an atmosphere of political neutrality, Stewart considers that the festival is becoming increasingly politicized today. While in the past the festival provided a framework for the alternating possibilities of reflection and rebellion, it has now developed into an extension of a process of mitigation which Stewart (1986: 291) calls 'moderating', and to which he adds 'modernising' in parenthesis (see too Manning 1983: 11). This process corresponds to the predominant aim of the current political authorities: they sustain the image of a society which has risen above racial, social and cultural division, manipulating the beliefs and feelings of the public to legitimate their own power and influence. There is nothing unique about this procedure in itself, but the historical and socio-cultural circumstances of this strategy in relation to carnival make the whole a special Trinidadian phenomenon.

Under the supervision and guidance of the National Carnival Commission, whose members are usually also members of, or have some other close relation to, the ruling political party, the annual festival becomes an exercise in 'cultural patriotism' (Stewart 1986: 306). Stewart emphasizes the virtual disappearance of the street carnival and the related cultural traditions, such as the steelband parade on Lundi and Mardi Gras. These have been replaced by a tightly organized carnival competition, resulting in more-or-less stage-directed events which practically dominate the festival. These somewhat static stage performances have increased enormously within carnival. Under the patronage and control of the ruling Creole middle class the festival has grown to become a massive spectacle, a top-rate public attraction. Spontaneous participation has virtually disappeared from the festival and there is only little contact possible between the actors on stage and the spectators.[1]

Stewart supports his thesis with the fact that a growing number of Trinidadians spend the carnival weekend abroad (Barbados, Miami) or on the island beaches far from the mêlée in Port of Spain, which seems to have been specially created for the tourists. These foreign visitors hardly have to leave their hotels. Calypso singers, masquerade groups and small steelbands play at parties and create an artificial carnival atmosphere of exemplary manifestations, while television carries extensive coverage of the various competitions in the city. The visitor who experiences this for the first time will find the colourful people, costumes, music, dancing, drinking and eating, and the occasional meeting with a reveller pleasant enough, without noticing anything of the 'tensions and contradictions which are operative within carnival', according to Stewart (1986: 311). Now that we have reached the point of being prepared to take the writer at his word when he claims that the Trinidad carnival has degenerated into nothing more than an empty tourist attraction (though he reports occasional popular protests against this tendency) he refers to tensions and contradictions within the festival. His whole argument takes a strange turn at this point, revealing a serious contradiction in his approach to carnival. Stewart provides us with a one-sided and selective picture of the festival in the first instance, which he takes to be a mere shadow of its meaningful past, but then he goes on to attribute a wealth of anthropological meanings to the universal phenomenon of carnival. The question therefore arises: can we justify calling the Trinidad festival a carnival at all?

The anthropological meaning of the Trinidad carnival

To explain the meaning of present-day carnival after his portrayal of it, Stewart (1986: 312–13) interprets the festival as a ritual, citing with approval the words of Geertz (1983: 40) that 'any particular ritual dramatizes certain issues and mutes others'. It is precisely the changes in what is dramatized over the years which enable carnival to retain its dominant position in the local culture of Trinidad better than any other institutional form. In the light of the examples provided by Stewart, this mechanism was thus not only operative in the past, but it still is today. The changes oscillate between the poles of social ideality and social reality, with a tendency to avoid extremes. Where underlying tensions as a fundamental part of everyday social relations are powerfully expressed in carnival also, the festival degenerates from ritual to rebellion or chaos. Vice versa, where too much emphasis is laid on an ideal of harmonious integration, as he argues is the case with modern carnival, a similar loss of ritual vitality occurs. The people of Trinidad want an easy-going experience of the tensions between ideal and reality, balance and excess, tolerance and restriction. This experience is rooted in a system of paradoxes which connects socially determined oppositions at both community and individual level. Important social criteria such as 'race', colour, class, wealth and power are simultaneously reinforced and criticized as principles of social organization by carnival. A certain tendency may gain ascendancy from time to time, but a dominance of this kind inevitably elicits a counter-tendency. The essence of the carnival experience, as Stewart (1986: 313) concludes, still remains the tension between constraint and licence.[2]

The attention Stewart draws to certain conditions which determine carnival as ritual is hard to reconcile with his previous argument that carnival has become a spineless festival of entertainment lacking in any internal dynamics. He outlines two more or less mutually exclusive images of carnival and suggests that they are connected, but he does not establish a clear link between the festival, that he takes to be completely under the control and supervision of the Creole middle-class government, on the one hand, and its function as a platform for all kinds of socio-cultural force fields, on the other. Stewart's more theoretical reflections on carnival as a general socio-cultural phenomenon have an impressive depth, although he refuses to attribute these values to the phenomenon in the Trinidad situation. However, it is only demonstrating the connection between the two, no matter how difficult that may be, that enables us to do justice to carnival as it is manifested today. In what follows I shall try to make this connection.

The dynamic-ritual role of carnival in relation to its social context

The analysis of the Antigua carnival by Manning (1978: 191–204) yields insights which attribute a whole ritual dynamic of its own to Stewart's carnival as a moribund folk festival. Before following Manning's argument, it is necessary to modify a number of Manning's key concepts to make them applicable to the Trinidad carnival. These key concepts are summed up by Manning (1978: 192) at the beginning of his study: 'I will view the Antigua Carnival as a symbolic response to such antithetical forces as black consciousness and nationalism, on the one side, and the demands of a foreign dominated, tourist-oriented economy to the other.' We are therefore concerned with the key concepts of black consciousness and nationalism, on the one hand, and a tourist-oriented economy, on the other.

The population of Antigua consists for the most part (93 per cent) of descendants of African slaves. The rest is composed of a few descendants of the former ruling class of planters, together with a number of Arab and Portuguese entrepreneurs. The Antigua carnival is held on the first Monday and Tuesday in August in commemoration of the abolition of slavery on 1 August 1834. The festival is thus to a large extent shaped by an ideological expression of black consciousness, which not only reinforces feelings of insular identity, but also rejoins the Afro-Caribbean cultural awareness at the regional level. The tourist industry has developed enormously since the early 1960s. In the wake of other Caribbean islands, the government provided tax and settlement facilities for foreign hotel project developers, legalized casino gambling, and gave high priority to infrastructural services for the demanding North American visitors who were accustomed to a life of luxury. By the end of the decade tourism accounted for 90 per cent of the Antiguan national income (Manning 1978: 197). Carnival was launched in 1957 as an initiative by government and commerce as part of the attempt to set up a major tourist industry. The travel literature portrays the festival as a tourist attraction *par excellence*, a baroque, 'tarted-up' extravaganza, tailored to suit the taste of the average big spender.

Trinidad, on the other hand, is a pronounced multi-racial society. Black consciousness does play an important part in the regulated carnival expressions under the control and supervision of the NCC, in which pride of place is occupied by a nationalistically coloured philosophy of 'One love' or 'All o' we is one', but as a result of the mitigating effects of the presence of other ethnic groups, it is voiced in a less pronounced way than in Antigua and other Caribbean islands. A consequence of this is that the experience of a regional Afro-Caribbean cultural awareness is more problematic. The Trinidad carnival is characterized by 'a rather smug chauvinism' (Manning 1978: 196). To illustrate, in 1977 an Antiguan singer seemed likely to win the Road March title in Trinidad with his song 'Tourist Leggo'. Calypsonians and carnival organizers from Trinidad did everything within their power to get the 'foreigner's' song removed from the contest (Dunstan 1978: 324). In 1986 the NCC (still called CDC at the time) tried to make the Calypso March Competition open to citizens of Trinidad alone (*TG*, 9 February 1987).

The fact that Stewart describes the Trinidad carnival as a soulless tourist attraction is bound to cause surprise in the light of the economic and ideological position occupied by tourism in this society. As we have already seen, the overabundant flow of oil dollars prevented the government from seeing any need to set up a tourist industry until recently. Besides, the oil boom had put Trinidad society in the luxurious position of being able to allow itself a nationalistic ideology which could portray and reject tourism as a new form of colonial servitude. This state of mind still determines the almost xenophobic relation of the Trinidadians to foreigners or tourists which forms one of the major obstacles to the development of tourism now that the oil revenues have been drastically curtailed.

What Stewart is actually referring to when he describes modern carnival is the profound influence on certain aspects or elements of the festival of what Lewis (1968: 33) calls the process of Americanization of the carnival complex, reinforced, I would like to add, by the materialistic consumer neurosis of the oil boom period. Trinidad has been seriously orientated for a long time towards the North American economy and culture, earning it the reputation in the region as the East Caribbean centre of glamour, fashion and abundance. The presentation of the Dimanche Gras show as an element of the carnival which is intended to appeal most strongly as a grand production to the taste of the white North American tourist goes back, as I have already argued, to the 1950s, and developed under the influence of the American military presence during World War II and the popularity of Hollywood film spectacles in the post-war period. Dimanche Gras is a spectacle which corresponds to the middle-class Trinidadians' aesthetic, experience and perception of their surroundings as stimulated by these North American influences, a perception ultimately derived from a historical receptivity to exotic colonial or quasi-colonial values. As the most important and prestigious carnival attraction, the show is attended for the most part by Trinidadians and their fellow patriots who now live in North America or the UK, plus a smattering of Afro-Caribbean visitors from the region. The chairperson of the Tourist Board, Allan Clovis, stated that around 40 000 visitors come to Trinidad each year during the carnival period (*DE*, 19 January 1988). However, the number of whites among the audience is negligible, and this is equally true of Mardi Gras when the masquerade bands file past the long and narrow stage in Queen's Park Savannah. What takes place during Jouvert Morning and on typical carnival sites such as the panyard, mas camp and calypso tent, happens almost entirely out of sight of the white North American and Afro-Caribbean tourists. Data from the Trinidad and Tobago Central Statistical Office indicate that 78 270 (42 per cent) of the total number of 187 090 visitors in 1985 came from the North American continent (USA plus Canada), while 73 300 (39 per cent) came from the Commonwealth Caribbean itself. That these are mainly Afro-Caribbean relatives and friends who go 'home' for their holiday rather than white North American tourists can be seen from the fact that only 18 100 of the total number of visitors were classified as 'hotel holiday visitors', as against 109 370 'private home holiday visitors'. It is also noteworthy that 34 970 (47.7 per cent) of the total number of visitors from the Caribbean came from Guyana. These are not tourists, but mainly small-scale commercial travellers (the total number of 'business visitors' is 56 360!), who offer wares from Trinidad on the flourishing black market in their own country.

Now that the differences between the situations of the two islands are clear, the application of Manning's key concepts or premises to Trinidad can be formulated as follows: the Trinidad Carnival can be viewed as a symbolic response to such antithetical forces as the struggle for Creole identity and nationalism, on the one side, and the process of Americanization, to the other. Following Manning, it is important to add in the case of Trinidad that the specific character of the carnival only emerges properly if the process of Creole identity and nationalism is coupled with an ideological expression through the symbolism of various genres of entertainment, masquerade themes, fashion styles and public behaviour, and the process of Americanization is coupled with an orientation towards abundance, glamour and hedonism.

These two processes seem to be in conflict. The movement towards Creole identity inspires cultural pride and national self-esteem, while the North American 'imitation syndrome' (Manning 1977: 274) – the assumption of all kinds of expressions of North American culture – might be expected to produce the opposite effect. 'There is a conflict here', writes a commentator in the *Sunday Guardian* (1 March 1987), 'in our trying to be an independent nation while we continue indiscriminately to consume foreign cultural values.' Carnival is a cultural symbolization of this paradox.

I can echo Manning's conclusion on Antigua (1978: 199) in summarizing the situation in Trinidad: while carnival contains cultural themes that are related to both Creole nationalism and Americanization, it is not dominated by either of these two influences; it is neither an advertising gimmick nor a piece of propaganda for either of them, but a ritual with a symbolic autonomy of its own. What then is the underlying significance of carnival if it is more than Stewart's picture of a 'venture in cultural patriotism' manipulated by the government for the sake of a handful of foreign tourists?

Manning (1978: 199–202) shows how two well-known anthropological perspectives can throw light on the dynamic-ritual role of carnival in relation to its social context. The emphasis in carnival on the theme of the ideological expression of Creole identity and hedonistic glamour (as a theme of Americanization) recalls Turner's theory (1964: 30) that the power of ritual is derived from the coincidence of opposites. Ritual symbolism, he claims, has both ideological and sensory or tonal poles of meaning. The two poles are mutually implicated in the active social field (although rather than poles, I would prefer to speak of dimensions or components to emphasize their coherence; the term 'pole' places too much emphasis on their mutual exclusiveness). An exchange of meaning takes place which enriches the ideological element with an appeal to what is perceived by the senses, while vice versa this appeal is enhanced by the attribution of ideological legitimacy. It is obvious how this theory applies to carnival. On the one hand, Creole consciousness is enhanced with stylistic and sensory attractiveness; on the other hand, this attractiveness is regarded as part of the Creole cultural order. Previously the tonal symbols of glamour and luxurious style in the carnival tradition were taken from the social world of the white planter class. Today these tonal symbols are derived from the North American way of life. Through the exchange of ideological and sensory meanings in carnival, the material abundance of the North American way of life is symbolically introduced to a native context or native expressive idiom.

With respect to the connection of native ideological concepts with metropolitan material attractions, Manning claims, it is hard to ignore the parallel between carnival and classic revitalization movements, especially those of the cargo-cult type, the second anthropological perspective. Colonized peoples have often reacted to the confrontation with the prosperity and power of metropolitan countries by reaffirming their own culture in disguises taken from the metropolitan world of representations. Worsley (1959: 122) demonstrates that one of the main stimuli for the Melanesian revitalization movements was the black North American soldier, who embodied the idea that a person of their own colour could allow himself the level of prosperity and comfort which had been the exclusive preserve of the white world until recently. Perhaps this helps to explain the popularity of black American stylistic orientations in carnival. They combine *par excellence* an assertive awareness of racial identity with a conspicuous display of abundance.

Manning goes on to pose the crucial question of whether the carnival fantasy creates a temporary relaxation or liberation from the dominant social order, which takes over again as if nothing had happened when the party is over. In other words, is carnival a 'ritual of rebellion' (Gluckman 1959), or does it exert a long-term progressive influence? Manning considers that the latter is true of Antigua and the majority of other Caribbean islands which have undergone rapid change and which are deliberately searching for an order and identity of their own. Here (carnival) fantasy is more than just representation. Manning cites Turner's (1977) distinction between liminal and liminoid ritual, which is more orientated towards the meaning of symbols than in Gluckman's theory. Liminal ritual, especially common in pre-industrial societies, reverses the social structure with the result that its values are reaffirmed. Liminoid ritual, which occurs in modernizing societies, produces a new, creative cultural *Gestalt* (Wallace 1956: 265) which can serve as a model for social change. Manning (1978: 201) considers that the new *Gestalt* which Turner sees emerging from the liminoid genre is equivalent to what Wallace regards as the result of the process of revitalization: 'a reformulated "mazeway image" that offers a new but nativistically oriented understanding of society and culture in a period of change'.

Manning (1978: 202) wishes to regard the analogy between carnival and cargo cult as a panoramic metaphor, a comprehensive concept, which offers a general perspective on the Antigua carnival and its relation to the field of social processes in which it is set. He stresses the need for caution in making specific comparisons. Unlike the classic cults, carnival is neither religious nor millenarian, although Naipaul (1970: 32–4) suggests that carnival fantasy has a certain millenarian character.[3] Its rites are exuberant rather than ecstatic, the festival does not have any prophets (though it has culture heroes enough), and its devotees are a collection of aficionados rather than members of a cult in the usual sense of the word. What appeals to Manning in the revitalization concept, however, is that it makes it possible to relate the phenomenon of mass tourism to other forms of colonial influence.

Nevertheless, there are serious objections to the application of the concept of revitalization to the situation in the Caribbean in general, and to Trinidad in particular. Wallace (1956: 265) defines a revitalization movement as a 'deliberate, organized, conscious effort by members of a society to construct a more satisfying culture'. He thus emphasizes the intentional, abrupt and simultaneous way in which changes take place and are transformed into a new *Gestalt*. Manning (1978: 278–9) describes Wallace's concept of 'mazeway reformulation' as the 'synthesis of a new image of society and culture following a period of distortion generally produced by acculturative pressures.' The abrupt, planned way in which carnival has been introduced on Antigua seems to correspond to the accounts provided by Manning and Wallace, but it is still questionable whether one may legitimately speak of carnival as a reaction to rapid change, and to a disruptive period as a result of the pressure of acculturation which directly preceded the festival.

Also debatable is the extent to which the Caribbean is the scene of a clash between existing (authentic) cultural systems, on the one hand, and a sudden invasion of foreign influence, on the other, for what characterizes this region is a process of synthesis of diverse internal and external cultural values that extends throughout its entire history. These are changes of the kind which Wallace (1956: 265) describes as *not typical* of revitalization movements:

> ... they do not depend on deliberate intent by members of a society, but rather on a gradual chain-reaction effect: introducing A induces change in B; changing B affects C; when C shifts, A is modified; this involves D... and so on *ad infinitum*. This process continues for years, generations, centuries ...

The Trinidad carnival is an example of this type of process of change. The unique feature of the festival is the fact that it spans the entire British colonial and post-colonial history of the island and is intimately connected with political, economic, social and cultural developments. Its expressive charge has constantly reflected these developments and helped to shape them. It therefore did not serve to revive native culture at a specific moment in history. The originality of Trinidad carnival contributes to a growing pan-Caribbean cultural awareness in the region and as such it was seen as a model for the many 'new' carnivals which have been introduced during the last few years, particularly on the English-speaking islands, and as a result of the economic necessity to attract tourists. But that does not mean that these carnivals can be written off as tourist gimmickry, as Lewis (1968: 30) claims. While there are thus difficulties in the application of the concept of revitalization in this context, Manning makes it clear that Turner's concept of 'polarization of meaning' and the liminoid character of ritual certainly can help to reveal an important function of carnival in the Caribbean which raises the festival above the level of a hollow tourist attraction which Stewart emphasizes so much. The Trinidad carnival pre-eminently draws its autonomous force as a dynamic popular festival from these ritual mechanisms.

Unlike the situation elsewhere in the Caribbean, the conflicting symbolic orientations which play a role within this carnival are stimulated by and interwoven with socio-cultural processes with a much longer history. This means that the tension between the process of Americanization, on the one hand, and the striving for Creole nationalism or Creole identity, on the other, is too recent to provide a complete picture. The rich field of carnival expressions is further complicated by the 'native' dichotomy of values of reputation and respectability (given theoretical underpinning by Wilson – 1969) which is connected with the historically moulded, extremely heterogeneous composition of classes and 'races' within Trinidad society. This implies a much broader repertoire of meanings, values, themes and motives than Manning attributes to the Antigua carnival.

The ruling class and other ideas

Stewart is not the only one to see the modern Trinidad carnival virtually as a reminiscence or remnant of what was once a valuable secular ritual. Cohen (1980: 71) uses the same kind of vocabulary: since Independence the Trinidad festival is a national, government-coordinated, middle-class-dominated affair aimed at tourists, in which the participants are men and women from divergent ethnic, religious and other social groups – 'a festival of polyethnic, inter-class, national integration, fully controlled and supervised by the government' (1980: 83). As we have seen, this simplified picture does not do justice to reality. It is probably motivated by the author's attempt to place greater emphasis on the social dynamics of a different carnival (the Notting Hill Carnival in London, described in the article from which I am quoting). In a different article he writes on that carnival (1982: 34):

In London towards the end of the 1960s and certainly in the 1970s, on the other hand, [i.e. by comparison with the Trinidad carnival] it served as a medium for expressing and organizing protest, resistance and counteraction, first on the part of a working-class section, consisting of both white and black groups, later on the part of West Indians only.

Cohen (1982: 23–4) develops a view which, though not conceived for that purpose, can be very useful to qualify both his and, *mutatis mutandis*, Stewart's overstated emphasis on the dominant role played by the Creole middle class in the Trinidad carnival. To this end he cites Marx's well-known aphorism that the ideas of the ruling class are the dominant ideas in any period (see also J.M. Taylor – 1982: 303 – on the Brazilian carnival). This dictum is founded on the assumption that the masses are prepared through various techniques of education, persuasion and mystification not only to accept the dominant culture, but also to express it, thereby indirectly maintaining the entire politico-economic system that dominates and exploits the very same masses. Such a monolithic view required revision of the study of subcultures, which had developed among the various sections of the subordinate classes as a response and reaction to the dominant culture. In his book *Marxism and Politics*, from which Cohen also quotes, Miliband (1977: 53–4) claims that one should take into account the many-sided, ongoing challenge to the ideological preponderance of the 'ruling class' and the fact that this challenge, despite the difficulties and defeats it experiences, can entail a gradual erosion of that preponderance. The discussion on hegemony and class consciousness must reckon with the idea of a struggle which is fought simultaneously on a number of fronts. 'The ideological terrain is by no means wholly occupied by "the ideas of the ruling class"; it is highly contested territory' (Miliband 1977: 54).

With this qualification of the position of the ruling class and its ideas in mind, we can obtain a clearer picture of the relation between the Creole middle class and carnival. In connection with the Brazilian carnival, J.M. Taylor (1982: 301–11) argues that the middle class has largely appropriated elements of popular culture deriving from the working class: 'They adopt and promote concepts and symbols which represent the dominant groups' interpretation of the concepts and symbols of the subordinated or marginal groups whose support they are seeking' (1982: 310).[4] Elsewhere Taylor refers to a revitalization of spontaneous carnival as a protest against the commercial festival of the middle-class strata (see Turner 1983: 124). There is no such 'shadow carnival' in Trinidad, unless the Jouvert Morning festivities are to be seen in this light. The middle class exercises enormous influence on the festival, but it has not annexed it in politico-cultural terms or turned it into an exclusive forum for its own ideas. The influence of the middle class should be seen, as Cohen (1980: 65) understands it for certain social groups in connection with the London carnival, 'as a process by which a collectivity mobilises, revives, modifies, creates and integrates *various cultural symbolic forms derived from different cultural and artistic traditions* to deal with changing economic-political conditions' (emphasis added).

The Creole middle class is steward of carnival as a cultural property. It controls the arena in which the various values and ideas of society (including those of the Creole middle class itself, of course) are dramatized as theatrical expressions of contesting idea and value complexes. All kinds of themes are utilized which, though often related to politico-cultural nationalism and the effects of the Western economy (two aspects which are firmly embodied in the Creole middle class), are not entirely in its service as a sort of promotion and propaganda machine.

As a symbolic instrument, carnival has been contested over the years by various interests and social forces. As a cultural and artistic spectacle, it has always maintained an intimate, dynamic relation with the political order and the struggle for power. Its symbolic form contains the capacity for political articulation, sometimes leading to rituals of rebellion with a collective catharsis, and in the last instance as a mechanism for the maintenance of the status quo; at other times leading to protest, resistance and violence. These expressions are not in conflict with the traditional significance of carnival. On the contrary, carnival as an annually recurring festival with its fun, satire, and excess of eating, drinking and sex is a tremendous experience for many people. That is what makes it so easy to understand the manipulation and control of the festival by political interests. Cohen (1980: 81) formulates this 'ambiguous unity of cultural and political significance', as he calls carnival, as follows:

> Despite the crucial part played by politics in shaping the structure of the carnival event, it would be futile to try to explain, or rather explain away, the cultural in terms of the political. On the contrary, cultural symbols and the communal relationships they generate and sustain are so powerful in their hold on people that political groups everywhere, including the state, always attempt to manipulate them in their own interests.

The internal autonomy of carnival, the arena which is only managed by the Creole middle class in Trinidad, leads Da Matta (1984a: 225–8) to call the festival 'a rite without a patron'. Although his argument is based on the Brazilian version, he is nevertheless referring to certain transcultural aspects of carnival. Programmed meetings of a collective character, on the other hand, are connected with an individual, a theme or a purpose. A religious procession, for example, is an act of devotion to a saint whose birth, death or suffering are commemorated. The same applies to military parades which focus on the heroic deeds of a regional or national hero, or to demonstrations protesting against alleged abuses or injustices involving persons or things. If a ritual has a theme or owner, the theme or owner becomes the focal point, providing the motive, significance and unity.

But who owns carnival? Da Matta (1984a: 225) says that the reply people give is 'Each plays Carnival as he can' ('to play mas' in Trinidad), because 'Carnival belongs to everybody.' Carnival is perhaps the only national festival without an owner. All social situations have an owner in Brazil, either a specific person or a saint, or failing that, a hero or even some abstract social domain or other. A specific code always has to be imposed to ensure that the situation can be understood and classified. 'In Carnival', Da Matta writes (1984a: 227), 'the law is to have no law. This is the inverted ideology of the festival.' This does not mean that there are no rules or regular procedures in carnival. The general principle of this lawlessness corresponds to the refusal to see the festival as the exclusive property of a group, segment or social class. This guarantees the plural character of the festival and offers participants the opportunity of exercising an extremely high level of social creativity. If sexual alliance (rather than sex) were celebrated, the institution of marriage would be the owner or patron. If carnival was the festival of wealth (rather than luxuriance), it would have a social class as theme. Da Matta adduces these and other arguments to show that carnival does not have an owner. 'It appears, therefore, as an immense social screen, where multiple visions of social reality are projected simultaneously' (1984a: 228).

The point here is that it cannot be denied that the Trinidad carnival, particularly since Independence, has assumed the character of a festival of national allure with the latent and manifest function of symbolizing the unity of an ethnically and culturally heterogeneous population. It is also the case that the leadership and ideology of the Creole middle class form the driving force behind it. Nevertheless, it would betray a monolithic point of view (as the objections to Marx's dictum correctly point out) to dismiss the Trinidad carnival like that. Behind this formal representation of the situation – to which, with a measure of popular adaptation, the (Creole) Tourist Board and the National Carnival Committee will certainly subscribe – lies the fact that the Trinidad carnival still balances precariously between the affirmation of established values and ideas and their rejection.

Like the Notting Hill Carnival (as analysed by Cohen), and despite Stewart's doubts, the present-day Trinidad carnival is still what Miliband (1977: 53–4) refers to as a 'contested event'. Stewart and Cohen suggest that the organization, theme and expression of the contemporary Trinidad carnival have suppressed those very mechanisms which characterize the festival as a typical socio-cultural phenomenon. These mechanisms, which lend the festival its internal dynamics, are recognized in historical perspective; cause and effect, which seem to present themselves automatically within such a perspective, appear to facilitate such a view. However, the process and its inherent changes disappear from the scene as a frozen picture of the present-day festival is allowed to displace diachronic analysis. Miller (1991: 326; 1994: 123–4) raises a similar objection to Stewart's position in discussing the fact that nowadays 80 per cent of the participants in masquerade bands are women (except for Jouvert Morning), whereas the proportion was the reverse until the 1950s. Although he expresses admiration for the clear and detailed summary of the development and political context of the Trinidad carnival provided by Stewart, he accuses the latter of representing a male point of view in seeing this over-representation by women, who buy their tailored costumes, dance 'pretty Mas' and join the tourists with a glass of beer in their hand, as a degeneration of the 'authentic' carnival of *Jabjab* and Dragon, so that many Trinidadian men have lost interest in this new, state-dominated, artificial version. Miller (1994: 123–4) writes: 'What he [Stewart] takes as the end to certain oppositional Carnival themes may, however, turn out to be simultaneously a beginning for new themes ... from political emancipation to gender emancipation.'

In 1920 the eminent French writer Jean-Richard Bloch wrote an essay entitled 'Carnival est mort. Premiers essais pour mieux comprendre mon temps'. In 1965 the Spanish ethnologist Julio Caro Baroja echoed his words: 'El Carnaval ha muerto'. That is exactly what people were saying about pilgrimage when Turner began to study the phenomenon in the early 1970s (Turner 1983: 104). He soon discovered that millions of people, sometimes under the guise of tourism, still follow the pilgrimage routes of the world's major religions. Carnival is certainly not dead in the Brazil Turner describes; and rumours of its demise elsewhere – in Trinidad, New Orleans or Germany – are terribly exaggerated.

Dramatization of values and counter-values

Wertheim (1964: 23–37), who advises us to detect tensions and conflicts in society 'as possible agents in future change' (ibid.: 35), calls a synchronic account fundamentally inadequate because conflicting value systems can only be grasped in their historical development. I fully support this view; the attention I have paid to the history of carnival was intended particularly to trace the dynamic process of this festival. Any description of a given society must take account of deviant value systems as fundamental elements in the structure of social life. Every society has its hidden or open forms of protest against the dominant hierarchy. In general it is possible to distinguish a more-or-less dominant set of common values, for otherwise a society would lack sufficient coherence to exist at all. Behind the dominant theme, however, there always lie distinct value systems which to a certain extent belong to determinate social groups and which function as counterpoints to the main melody.

Following Wertheim's approach, I regard the Trinidad carnival today as a dramatic and symbolic reflection of dominant values and counter-values in society. As Manning (1983: 6) puts it: 'Celebration is a "text", a vivid aesthetic creation that reflexively depicts, interprets and informs its social context.' Others who have written on carnival, for example Cohen (1980; 1982; 1993),[5] Da Matta (1977; 1984), Lavenda (1980; 1985) and Le Roy Ladurie (1981) also regard the festival as a text on the internal relations within a community and the way it defines itself *vis-à-vis* the outside world. Although Geertz (1983: 23) warns against the easy use of analogies which are nowadays fashionably borrowed from the humanities ('society is ... a serious game, a sidewalk drama, a behavioral text'), one is bound to make the comparison with his own (1974: 26) masterly analysis of the Balinese cockfight as a 'metasocial commentary': 'a story they tell themselves about themselves'. In a similar vein, Turner (1982: 104) writes of theatre in the broadest sense of the word as 'a play a society acts about itself', significantly adding that it is not just a 'reading' of (societal) experience, but an interpretive performance of that experience. Abrahams (1983: 98, 107–8) also stresses this last point in his comparative study of Christmas and carnival on the Caribbean island of St Vincent. He considers that these festivities do not reveal an unequivocal concept of the social order, but that they are interpretations of the polarizations of conflicting attitudes and lifestyles. This 'performance complex' functions neither as an aesthetic alternative to life, nor as a direct reflection of reality, but as a stylized dramatization of certain key everyday expressive customs and moral concerns of the participant group or groups. Abrahams refers also to Geertz's analysis of the Balinese cockfight. Such intense cultural displays are neither imitations of a specific pattern of Balinese life nor an expression of it, but rather 'an example of it, carefully prepared' (Geertz 1973: 451). Similarly, within the social transition of Trinidad, which can be characterized as a process of decolonization, struggle for independence, nationalization or modernization, carnival as a 'performance complex' has its own internal and autonomous dynamics. This dynamic force implies that people's ideas about themselves and their society are not passive reflections, but are actively moulded. In connection with 'saturnalia or carnival morality', Huizinga (1955: 13–15) writes:

> The action stands for a cosmic activity, not purely as representation, but as identification. It repeats that event. The cult brings about the effect that is represented in the action. Its function is not pure imitation, but contribution or participation. It is 'helping the action out'.

If my account of carnival is to be set within this context, it is important to recognize the dominant values and counter-values within Trinidad society, as well as their connection with and their symbolic-dramatic fashion translation into the organization, form and content of the festival. In a nutshell, the festival is a complex product wrought by two centuries of history in which it has successively undergone the cultural and ideological influences of the white planter elite, the black lower class, and the Creole middle class. This process, as we have already seen, has conferred on the festival a hybrid cultural baggage. Numerous divergent elements, facets and themes which potentially sink into the background or come to the fore in turn guarantee an ongoing flexible receptivity to react and respond to current social issues. The old values and ideas from the various cultural domains to which the festival belonged in the past have at last combined under the auspices of the dominant Creole middle class, muted and transformed into forms and manifestations which can represent contemporary social conflicts and problems. These conflicts and problems lack the inevitable romantic glamour which is conferred on the past, but they are essentially of sufficient significance to warrant inclusion in a sociological analysis and – because it is not clear from what we experience today what will turn out to be historically valuable – they cannot be dismissed as mere trivialities. Stewart's account of the Trinidad carnival as a lifeless tourist attraction lays him open to criticisms of this kind.

Of course, values do not hang in the air; to a certain extent they belong to particular social groups. There is no further need to argue that the dominant values in Trinidad are the values which are accepted and expressed by a large part of the Creole middle class. We are here concerned with values and counter-values, which implies a relation between them: they are inter-related as mutual opposites. For example, the way members of the middle class want to turn carnival into a festival to promote tourism elicits counter-reactions from their own ranks or from other social groups who see things differently. Or again, members of the middle class in particular take umbrage each year at the behaviour of women in the carnival processions, while other people (artists, intellectuals, calypsonians, panmen and members of the lower class) consider these objections to be hypocritical and puritanical. Other hot topics include the threat to the position of the steelband by the rise of DJs and modern-life music; the disputed criteria and taste of the juries in the various competitions; the level of acceptance of reggae and soul within the 'native' festival; alleged racist incidents on the part of the public or calypso singers; the acceptability of an implicit or explicit political message in a masquerade performance or calypso text; and the claim that some people lay to carnival as a purely African heritage.

This is only an arbitrary selection from the numerous conflicts which occur at various ideological, moral and aesthetic levels as contemporary expressions of deep-lying, contradictory sets of values. The considerable attention that I have paid to the historical development of calypso, steelband and masquerade and its implication with the favourable or unfavourable aesthetic and moral interference of the elite, lower class and middle class, has already revealed the contours of divergent value complexes – a line of argument which was continued in the impressionist description of the present-day carnival in the previous chapter.

Conflicting orientations and the struggle for national identity

The year that carnival comes and goes without some major controversy will be the year that it ceases to be of more than marginal interest to the national psyche, some sort of tourist entertainment, perhaps, and no longer this society's essential mirror and milestone.

(Wayne Brown in *DE*, 28 January 1988)

Carnival creates an opportunity for social engagement and communication between the members of a society in a manner which transcends the existing ethnic and cultural boundaries. Though the festival is predominantly the product of Creole society, its current ideological influence extends much further than the social groups to which the term can be applied. At this level the Indians are equally affected, a group which actually participates in the festival, albeit warily.

I have called carnival an arena in which contesting values and ideas are dramatized. The festival forms a system of paradoxes which are both self-critical and creative at the same time; it is its own subject and object, where culture is the platform for symbolic struggle for power and legitimation of the social order, simultaneously confirmed and rejected. Having this ambiguity as its most important characteristic – 'posing a contradiction within a unity of form' (Cohen 1982: 37) – makes carnival so suitable to express dominant and oppositional ideologies within society. That is why carnival is the only large-scale festival in Trinidad which rises to a certain extent above the divisions which have been discussed in the present work and which are summarized in the two theses on page 191; the festival does not choose sides.

As we have seen, Cohen's article 'Drama and Politics in the Development of a London Carnival' (1980: 83) tackles the question of the nature of the relation between culture and politics (or power relations). In this connection, he argues that culture in general is expressed in terms of symbolic forms and representations which by definition are ambiguous and thus refer at the same time to political and existential questions. For example, it is this ambiguity which confers effectivity on the symbols of kinship and ritual in the expression of political interests and organizations in both pre-industrial and industrial societies. Once the symbols are reduced to purely political or existential questions, they become one-dimensional signs, devoid of impact or social function. There is an ongoing dialectical, dynamic connection – Cohen (1974; 1982: 37) calls it 'two-dimensional' – between symbolic expression and power relations: 'Like a grand joking relationship, carnival expresses both alliance and enmity, both consensus and conflict, at one and the same time'. In other words, carnival is an ambiguous symbolic creation which both camouflages and mystifies ambiguity. Cohen (1982: 37) emphasizes that if carnival is to remain carnival, there must be a balance between what he calls 'the potentialities of carnival for articulating both hegemonous and opposition political formations'. He considers both orientations to be present in every carnival. If the balance tips definitively in favour of one of the two forms of expression, carnival ceases to exist and we find ourselves faced with a completely different genre – a political rally as performed in a totalitarian state, or the opposite, a political demonstration against such a system (Cohen 1982: 37).

In this connection, the Brazilian anthropologist Roberto da Matta (1977) makes clear the extraordinary position of carnival in his article 'Constraint and License: A Preliminary Study of Two Brazilian National Rituals', in which he analyses the role and meaning of rituals within the context of the complex Brazilian society mainly on the basis of two cultural events: Carnival and Independence Day (*Dia da Patria*). He comes to the conclusion that the two events can be understood as distinct discourses which bear on the same reality, essential aspects of which are expressed by each of them in its own special way. Thus Independence Day witnesses a reaffirmation of the social hierarchy, where uniforms symbolize specific social realities which operate at all levels of social life. Carnival, on the other hand, effects a dissolution of the system of social roles and positions by means of the important mechanism of symbolic inversion (1977: 253–4).[6]

As the major transcultural aspect of carnival, this mechanism has the capacity to enlarge the conceptual repertoire and thereby remove the existing oppositions from their embeddedness in everyday life, making culture and society more transparent for its members and even providing a basis for change. Symbolization (like ritualization), in Da Matta's discussion (1984a: 213–15) of the capacity of carnival to create a space within which the 'everyday' opposition between the home and the street can be suspended, means fundamentally the dislocation of an object (person, thing or value), or the operation of social roles outside their original domains. It is a process that sharpens awareness of the nature of the object, and of the qualities of its original domain, and its adaptation to a new locality. Da Matta considers it important to pay attention to the process of dislocation, because everything suggests that this is how we can exaggerate (or reinforce), reverse (or disguise by a change of position) and neutralize (reduce or eliminate) properties of objects. Inspired by the work of Mary Douglas (1966) in which she elaborates the idea of 'dirty as an object out of place', Da Matta (1984a: 213) claims that dislocation of objects is responsible for scandals, scenes, dramas and dirtiness, 'since they provoke an acute consciousness of the interference of one domain in another.' This makes us aware of fundamental processes and social spheres, he considers. As a counterpart to what Littlewood (1984: 713) writes about the prophetic or messianic Mother Earth movement on Trinidad, in which the prophet or messiah personifies the normative antithesis, the carnival festival sharpens awareness of one's own potentialities and powers and offers a more critical insight into the relativity of the social system. The rigidity of the original pattern of oppositions, as it occurs in social reality, is weakened, which can lead to greater ideological autonomy with regard to specific environmental and political determinants and thus probably to more internalized values. The festival can thus be of importance for the promotion of a politico-cultural nationalism by making it clear that the orientations and contradictions referred to form a part of and may be an expression of a developing native cultural order.

Carnival does not solve the national problems, but it does provide a forum where the various expressions of the socio-cultural heterogeneity of Trinidad are combined in an unusual but more or less spontaneous and harmonious fashion. This atmosphere of *communitas* creates the illusion or translates the ideal of national identity. What is more, as a powerful and eloquent social statement, the festival provides those cultural attributes by which this ideal can be experienced as a tangible reality by the people of Trinidad. 'Trinidad; the Rainbow that is Real' is the slogan which the Tourist Board propagates. Nowhere is the colour spectrum of the rainbow as bright as in carnival. 'Our carnival is the greatest show on earth, sir!' the Indian taxi driver proudly announces, even though he would not spend his time in town during the Creole Bacchanal for any money in the world.

To what extent carnival reflects social reality and acts as the driving force or as the avant-garde in initiating certain processes which are able to transcend the contradictions and divisions is difficult to determine with any exactness. It is important to repeat that carnival is not *a priori* a promoter in the service of these processes. It is a ritual with its own symbolic autonomy, characterized by contradictory relations with the instrumental and the expressive, the constrained and the exuberant, the serious and the light-hearted, and the themes of consensus and conflict. Not only does carnival itself illustrate or dramatize divisions and conflicting orientations in its own symbolic charge. The festival is followed every year by a form of broad social discussion which focuses directly or indirectly on burning social issues and connects them, justifiably or not, with carnival. Religious bodies, political parties, school and medical spokespersons, the tourist board, educators, moralists, artists and the media all participate in every possible way in this discussion, which in many respects repeats the previous year's debate. Carnival discourse and social discourse overlap as a reflection and interpretation of and as information about the situation in society. During this time of the year, when its 'own' culture is being celebrated by the steelband, calypso and masquerade, society engages in self-criticism.

Both discourses – the central (or internal) discourse and the peripheral (or external) discourse – have to a large extent determined the content of my account of modern carnival. The hybrid nature of the actual situation prevents the two spheres from being distinguished completely, and elements of reputation and respectability often run through them both. The way in which I have arranged the material was determined by a number of salient themes on which I have hung the corresponding spheres, and nothing more. In line with Turner's view (1970: 26) that symbols often refer to something hidden, it would be better for the reader to go to Trinidad on his or her own quest and to become absorbed in the dizzying, elusive audio-visual spectacle of carnival. My own experience of the adventurous journey through the festival that has to be celebrated is best formulated by Ronald Grimes (1982: 231):

> A public celebration is a rope bridge of knotted symbols strung across an abyss. We make our crossings hoping the chasm will echo our festive sounds for a moment, as the bridge begins to sway from the rhythms of our dance.

Notes

1   Stewart is in good company with his view of the alleged demise of carnival. In his reading of Rabelais's representation of medieval European Carnival, Bakhtin (1968: 7) remarks:

> In fact, carnival does not know footlights, in the sense that it does not acknow-ledge any distinction between actors and spectators. Footlights would destroy a carnival, as the absence of footlights would destroy a theatrical performance. Carnival is not a spectacle seen by the people; they live in it, and everyone participates because its very idea embraces all the people.

2   It is surprising that Stewart does not mention Cohen (1982) or Da Matta (1977) in this account, for his argument, language and terminology correspond closely to theirs. It is equally remarkable that B.E. Powrie's article 'The changing attitude of the coloured middle class toward carnival' (1956) is also ignored by Stewart, as I know of no other

work in which the relation between the Trinidad carnival and the middle class, which Stewart stresses so much, is referred to as explicitly.

3   In *Power to the Caribbean People*, he has the following to say about the Trinidad carnival:

> During the war an admiration for Russia – really an admiration for 'stylish' things like Stalin's mustache and the outlandish names of Russian generals, Timoshenko, Rokossovsky – was expressed in a 'Red Army' band. At the same time an admiration for Humphrey Bogart created a rival 'Casablanca' band. Make-believe, but taken seriously and transformed; not far below, perhaps even unacknowledged, there has always been a vision of the black millennium, as much a vision of revenge as of a black world made whole again.

4   Oliven (1984: 103–15) also pays special attention to the phenomenon in Brazilian society of the appropriation of cultural manifestations belonging to certain social groups by others and their transformation into national symbols.

5   Cohen's 1993 study entitled *Masquerade Politics: Explorations in the structure of urban cultural movements*, can be considered as a comprehensive compilation of his research of recent years concerning the Notting Hill Carnival.

6   Babcock (1978: 14) defines symbolic inversion as 'any act of expressive behavior which inverts, contradicts, abrogates, or in some fashion presents an alternative to commonly held cultural codes, values and norms be they linguistic, literary or artistic, religious, or social and political'.

Bibliography

Abrahams, R.D. 1979, 'Reputation vs. Respectability: A review of Peter J. Wilson's concept', *Revista/Review Interamericana*, 9: 448–53.

—— 1983, *The Man-of-Words in the West Indies: Performance and emergence of Creole culture*. Baltimore/London: Johns Hopkins University Press.

Alonso, A.M. 1990, 'Men in "Rags" and the Devil on the Throne: A study of protest and inversion in the carnival of post-Emancipation Trinidad', *Plantation Society in the Americas: Carnival in Perspective*, 73–120.

Angrosino, M.V. 1989, 'Identity and Escape in Caribbean Literature', in P.A. Dennis and W. Aycock, *Literature and Anthropology*, 113–32. Austin: Texas Tech University Press.

Annual Economic Survey 1986, Port of Spain: Central Bank of Trinidad and Tobago.

Anthony, M. 1982, *Profile Trinidad: A history survey from the discovery to 1900*. London/Basingstoke: Macmillan.

—— 1985, *First in Trinidad*. Port of Spain: Circle Press.

—— 1986, *Heroes of the People of Trinidad and Tobago*. Port of Spain: Circle Press.

—— 1989, *Parade of the Carnivals of Trinidad 1839–1989*. Port of Spain: Circle Press.

Babcock, B.A. (ed.) 1978, *The Reversible World: Symbolic inversion in art and society*. Ithaca/London: Cornell University Press.

Bakhtin, M. 1968, *Rabelais and His World*. Cambridge/Massachusetts/London: MIT Press.

Baptiste, O. (ed.) 1988, *Women in Mas'*. Port of Spain: Inprint Caribbean.

Bennett, H.L. 1989, 'The Challenge to the Post-Colonial State: A case study of the February Revolution in Trinidad', in F.W. Knight and C.A. Palmer, *The Modern Caribbean*, 129–46.

Best, L. 1968, 'Outline of a Model of Pure Plantation Economy', *Social and Economic Studies*, 17(3): 283–326.

—— 1990, 'The Principle of Politics: Wiser than Gulliver', *Trinidad and Tobago Review*, 12 (11 and 12): d.

Black, J.K., Blutstein, H.I., Johnston, K.T., McMorris, D.S., 1976, *Area Handbook for Trinidad and Tobago*. Washington DC: Foreign Area Studies (FAS) of the American University.

Blood, P.R. 1988, 'Is Being Boss All?' in O. Baptiste, *Women in Mas'*, 33–9, 56.

Boissevain, J.A. 1968, 'The Place of Non-Groups in the Social Sciences', *Man (n.s.)*, 3/4: 542–56.

Braithwaite, L. 1954, 'The Problem of Cultural Integration in Trinidad', *Social and Economic Studies*, 3(1): 82–96.

—— 1960, 'Social Stratification and Cultural Pluralism', in V. Rubin, *Social and Cultural Pluralism in the Caribbean*, Annals of the New York Academy of Sciences, 83(5): 816–31.

—— 1974, 'Problems of Race and Colour in the Caribbean', *Caribbean Issues*, 1: 1–14.

—— 1975, *Social Stratification in Trinidad*. Kingston: University of the West Indies (1st edition 1953).

Brana-Shute, G. 1979, *On the Corner: Male social life in a Paramaribo Creole neighborhood*. Assen: Van Gorcum.

Brereton, B. 1979, *Race Relations in Colonial Trinidad 1870–1900*. Cambridge: Cambridge University Press.

—— 1981, *A History of Modern Trinidad 1783–1962*. Kingston/Port of Spain/ London: Heinemann.

Broek, A.G. 1985, 'Kaito-Kaiso-Caliso-Calypso', *De Nieuwe West-Indische Gids*, 3/4: 291–6.

Brown, L. 1984, *West Indian Poetry*. London: Heinemann.

Burke, P. 1978, *Popular Culture in Early Modern Europe*. New York: Harper Torchbooks.

Carr, A. 1953, 'A Rada Community in Trinidad', *Caribbean Quarterly*, 3: 36–54.

—— 1956, 'Pierrot Grenade', *Caribbean Quarterly*, 3/4: 281–314.

—— 1975, 'Carnival', in M. Anthony and A. Carr (eds), *David Frost Introduces: Trinidad*: 57–72. London: André Deutsch.

Clarke, L. 1978, 'Masks and Mas', *Trinidad Carnival*: 84–5. Port of Spain: Key Caribbean Publications.

Cohen, A. 1974, *Two-Dimensional Man*. London: Routledge & Kegan Paul.

—— 1980, 'Drama and Politics in the Development of a London Carnival', *Man (n.s.)*, 15(1): 65–87.

—— 1982, 'A Polyethnic London Carnival as a Contested Cultural Performance', *Racial and Ethnic Studies*, 5(1): 23–41.

—— 1993, *Masquerade Politics: Explorations in the structure of urban cultural movements*. Oxford/Providence: Berg.

Cowley, J. 1996, Carnival, Canboulay and Calypso: Caribbean traditions in the making. Cambridge: Cambridge University Press.

Cox, H. 1970, *Het narrenfeest*. Bilthoven: Ambo.

Crocker, J.C. 1982, 'Ceremonial Masks', in V.W. Turner, *Celebration: Studies in Festivity and Ritual*, 77–87. Washington DC: Smithsonian Institute Press.

Crowley, D.J. 1956, 'The Traditional Masques of Carnival', *Caribbean Quarterly*, 3/4: 192–223.

—— 1956a, 'The Midnight Robbers', *Caribbean Quarterly*, 3/4: 263–74.

—— 1957, 'Plural and Differential Acculturation in Trinidad', *American Anthropologist*, 59: 817–24.

—— 1973, 'Cultural Assimilation in a Multiracial Society', in L. Comitas and D. Lowenthal, *Slaves, Free Men, Citizens: West Indian perspectives*: 277–85, New York: Anchor.

DaMatta, R. 1977, 'Constraint and Licence: A preliminary study of two Brazilian national rituals', in S.F. Moore and B.G. Meyerhoff, *Secular Ritual*: 244–65. Assen: Van Gorcum.

—— 1984, 'On Carnival, Informality, and Magic; A point of view from Brazil', in E.M. Bruner, *Text, Play and Story: The construction and reconstruction of self and society*: 230–46. Washington DC: American Ethnological Society.

—— 1984a, 'Carnival in Multiple Planes', in J.J. MacAloon, *Rite, Drama, Festival, Spectacle: Rehearsals towards a Theory of Cultural Performance*: 208–40. San Francisco: Institute for Contemporary Studies.

Davidson, B. 1984, *Een groots continent: Afrika (Africa: History of a Continent)*. Haarlem: Rostrum.

De Leon, R. 1988, *Calypso, from France to Trinidad: 800 Years of History*. San Juan: General printers of San Juan.

Deosaran, R. 1987, 'The "Caribbean Man": A study of the psychology of perception and the media', in D. Dabydeen and B. Samaroo, *India in the Caribbean*: 81–118. London: Hansib/University of Warwick.

De Verteuil, A. 1984, *The Years of Revolt; Trinidad 1881–8*. Port of Spain: Paria Publishing.

Devisch, R. 1978, 'Carnaval als algemeen menselijk verschijnsel: Een semantisch antropologische benadering', *Volkskunde* 79(1): 4–18.

Dirks, R. 1987, *The Black Saturnalia: Conflict and its ritual expression on British West Indian slave plantations*. Gainesville: University Presses of Florida.

Douglas, M. 1966, *Purity and Danger: An analysis of concepts of pollution and taboo*. New York/Washington: F.A. Praeger.

—— 1973, *Natural Symbols: Explorations in cosmology*. Harmondsworth: Penguin (1st edn 1970).

Dunstan, R.D. 1978, 'St Lucian Carnival: A Caribbean art form'. Unpublished PhD thesis, State University of New York.

Eastman, R. 1986, 'Calypso and the Church', *Paper presented to the Seminar on the Calypso*, 1–24. St Augustine: University of the West Indies.

Elder, J.D. 1966, 'The Evolution of the Traditional Calypso of Trinidad and Tobago: A socio-historical analysis of song-change'. Unpublished PhD thesis, University of Pennsylvania.

—— 1988, *African Survivals in Trinidad and Tobago*. London: Karia Press.

Eriksen, T.H. 1990, 'Liming in Trinidad: The art of doing nothing', *Folk*, 32: 23–43.

Espinet, R. 1987, 'David Rudder: From the belly of the bamboo', *Trinidad and Tobago Review*, 11–13.

Fanon, F. 1967, *The Wretched of the Earth*. Harmondsworth: Penguin (1st edn 1961).

Geertz, C. 1973, 'Thick Description: Toward an interpretive theory of culture', in C. Geertz, *The Interpretation of Cultures*, 3–30. New York: Basic Books.

—— 1974, 'Deep Play: Notes on the Balinese cockfight', in C. Geertz (ed.), *Myth, Symbol and Culture*, 1–37, New York: Norton & Company (1st edn 1972).

—— 1983, *Local Knowledge*. New York: Basic Books.

Gilmore, D. 1975, 'Carnaval in Fuenmayor: Class conflict and social cohesion in an Andalusian town', *Journal of Anthropological Research*, 31(4): 331–49.

—— 1987, *Aggression and Community: Paradoxes of Andalusian culture*. New Haven/London: Yale University Press.

Glazier, S.D. 1983, *Marchin' the Pilgrims Home: Leadership and decision-making in an Afro-Caribbean faith*. Westport, Connecticut/London: Greenwood Press.

Gluckman, M. 1954, *Rituals of Rebellion in South-East Africa*. Manchester: University Press.

—— 1959, *Custom and Conflict in Africa*. New York: The Free Press.

Gonzalez, S. 1975, *Steelband Saga: A story of the steelband, the first 25 years*.

Grimes, R. 1982, *Beginnings in Ritual Studies*. Washington DC: University Press of America.

Halpin, M. 1979, 'Confronting Looking-Glass Men: A preliminary examination of the mask', in N.R. Crumrine, *Ritual Symbolism and Ceremonialism in the Americas: Studies in symbolic anthropology*, Part 1, 41–61.

Hamner, R.D. (ed.) 1977, *Critical Perspectives on V.S. Naipaul*. Washington DC: Three Continents Press.

Handelman, D. 1977, 'Play and Ritual: Complementary frames of meta-communication', in N.J. Chapman and H. Foot, *It's a Funny Thing Humour*. London: Pergamon.

—— 1979, 'Is Naven Ludic? Paradox and the communication of identity', *Social Analysis*, 1: 177–91.

Handler, R. 1988, *Nationalism and the Politics of Culture in Quebec*. University of Wisconsin Press.

Herskovits, M.J. and F.S. 1947, *Trinidad Village*. New York: A.A. Knopf.

Hill, D.R. 1993, *Calypso Calaloo: Early carnival music in Trinidad*. Gainesville: University Presses of Florida.

Hill, E. 1971, 'Calypso', *Jamaica Journal*, March: 23–7.

—— 1972, *The Trinidad Carnival: Mandate for a national theatre*. Austin: University of Texas Press.

—— 1976, 'The Trinidad Carnival; Cultural change and synthesis', *Cultures*, 3(1): 54–86.

—— 1983, 'The History of Carnival', *Paper presented to the Seminar on the Social and Economic Impact of Carnival*: 6–39. St Augustine: University of the West Indies.

Hobsbawm, E. and Ranger, T. (eds) 1983, *The Invention of Tradition*. Cambridge: Cambridge University Press.

Hodge, M. 1974, 'The Shadow of the Whip: A comment on male-female relations in the Caribbean', in O. Coombs, *Is Massa Day Dead?*: 111–18. New York: Anchor Press.

—— 1987, 'People: Examining the stereotypes of Trinidad & Tobago's multi-ethnic society', in E. Saft, *Trinidad and Tobago*: 69–82.

Hoetink, H. 1967, *The Two Variants in Caribbean Race Relations: A contribution to the sociology of segmented societies*. London/New York/Toronto: Oxford University Press.

—— 1973, *Slavery and Race Relations in the Americas: Comparative notes on their nature and nexus*. New York/Evanston/San Francisco/London: Harper and Row.

Holder, W.R. 1990, 'Naipaul and the Rebels without Conscience', *Trinidad and Tobago Review*, 12 (11 and 12): 18.

Hollis, C. 1941, *A Brief History of Trinidad under the Spanish Crown*. Port of Spain: Trinidad and Tobago Government Printer.

Hope, K.R. 1986, *Economic Development in the Caribbean*. New York/Westport/Connecticut/London: Praeger.

Huizinga, J. 1955, *Homo Ludens: A study of the play elements in culture*. Boston: Beacon Press (1st edn 1938).

James, C.L.R. 1973, 'The Middle Classes', in D. Lowenthal and L. Comitas, *Consequences of Class and Color: West Indian perspectives*: 79–92. New York: Anchor Books.

—— 1973a 'The Mighty Sparrow', in D. Lowenthal and L. Comitas, *The Aftermath of Sovereignty: West Indian perspectives*: 372–81. New York: Anchor Books.

Jha, J.C. 1985, 'The Indian Heritage in Trinidad', in J.G. LaGuerre, *Calcutta to Caroni: The East Indians of Trinidad*: 1–18. St Augustine: University of the West Indies (1st edn 1974).

John, D. 1988, 'Women in Mas', in O. Baptiste, *Women in Mas'*: 5–7, 90–2, 95–6.

Johnson, K. 1983, 'The Social Impact of Carnival', *Paper presented to the Seminar on the Social and Economic Impact of Carnival:* 171–207. St Augustine: University of the West Indies.

—— 1987, 'Political and Economic Beginnings', in E. Saft, *Trinidad and Tobago*: 38–45.

—— 1987a, 'Forged from the Love of Liberty', in E. Saft, *Trinidad and Tobago*, 54–62.

Joris, L. 1992, *Zangeres op Zanzibar en andere reisverhalen*. Amsterdam: Meulenhoff/Leuven: Kritak.

Kasinitz, P. 1992, *Caribbean New York: Black immigrants and the politics of race*. Ithaca/London: Cornell University Press.

Kinser, S. 1990, *Carnival, American Style: Mardi Gras at New Orleans and Mobile*. Chicago/London: University of Chicago Press.

Klass, M. 1961, *East Indians in Trinidad: A study of cultural persistence*. New York/London: Columbia University Press.

—— 1973, 'East and West Indians: Cultural complexity in Trinidad', in L. Comitas and D. Lowenthal, *Slaves, Free Men, Citizens: West Indian perspectives*: 286–98. New York: Anchor Books.

Knight, F.W. and Palmer, C.A. (eds) 1989, *The Modern Caribbean*. Chapel Hill and London: University of North Carolina Press.

LaGuerre, J.G. 1975, 'Afro-Indian Relations in Trinidad: An assessment', *Social and Economic Studies*, 25(3): 291–306.

—— 1982, *The Politics of Communalism*. Port of Spain Pan-Caribbean Publications (2nd edn).

—— 1988, 'Race Relations in Trinidad and Tobago', in S. Ryan, *Trinidad and Tobago: The Independence experience 1962–1987*: 193–206. St Augustine: University of the West Indies.

—— 1991, 'Leadership in a Plural Society: The case of the Indians in Trinidad and Tobago', in S. Ryan, *Social and Occupational Stratification in Contemporary Trinidad and Tobago*: 83–112. St Augustine: University of the West Indies.

Laurence, K.O. 1963, 'The Settlement of Free Negroes in Trinidad before Emancipation', *Caribbean Quarterly* 9: 26–52.

Lavenda, R.H. 1980, 'From Festival of Progress to Masque of Degradation: Carnival in Caracas as a changing metaphor of social reality', in H.B. Schwartzman, *Play and Culture*: 19–30. New York: Leisure Press.

—— 1985, 'Festivals and Carnivals', in H.E. Hinds and C.M. Tatum, *Handbook of Latin American Popular Culture*: 191–205. London: Greenwood Press.

Leach, E.R. 1970, *Political Systems of Highland Burma*. London: Athlone Press (1st edn 1954).

—— 1976, *Culture and Communication: The logic by which symbols are connected*. Cambridge: Cambridge University Press.

Leigh Fermor, P. 1984, *The Traveller's Tree: A journey through the Caribbean islands*. Harmondsworth: Penguin (1st edn 1950).

Le Roy Ladurie, E. 1981, *Carnival in Romans: A people's uprising at Romans 1579–1580*. Harmondsworth: Penguin (1st edn 1979).

Lewis, G.K. 1968, *The Growth of the Modern West Indies*. New York: Modern Reader Paperbacks.
—— 1983, *Main Currents in Caribbean Thought*. Baltimore/London: Johns Hopkins University Press.
—— 1985, 'The contemporary Caribbean: A general overview', in S.W. Mintz and S. Price, *Caribbean Contours*: 219–50. Baltimore/London: Johns Hopkins University Press.
Lieber, M. 1976, 'Liming and Other Concerns: The style of street embedments in Port of Spain, Trinidad', *Urban Anthropology*, 5(4): 319–34.
—— 1981, *Street Scenes: Afro-American culture in urban Trinidad*. Cambridge: Schenkman Publishing.
Littlewood, R. 1984, 'The Imitation of Madness: The influence of psychopathology upon culture', *Social Science and Medicine*, 19(7): 705–15.
Liverpool, H. 1973, *From the Horse's Mouth*. St Augustine: University of the West Indies.
—— 1986, *Kaiso and Society*. Minneapolis: Meyers Printing.
López de Villegas, C. 1980, 'Identity and Environment: Naipaul's architectural vision', *Revista/Review Interamericana*, 2: 220–9.
Lynch, K. 1960, *The Image of the City*. Cambridge: M.I.T. Press.
MacDonald, S.B. 1986, *Trinidad and Tobago: Democracy and development in the Caribbean*. New York/Westport/Connecticut/London: Praeger Scientific.
Maharaj, N. 1990, 'In Trinidad kijkt men niet verder dan vandaag; De carnavaleske couppoging van Abu Bakr', *NRC-Handelsblad*, 30 July.
Mandle, J.R. and J.D. 1988, *Grass Roots Commitment: Basketball and society in Trinidad and Tobago*. Parkersburg: Caribbean Books.
Manning, F.E. 1977, 'Cup Match and Carnival: Secular rites of revitalization in decolonizing, tourist-oriented societies', in S.F. Moore and B.G. Meyerhoff, *Secular Ritual*: 265–82. Assen: Van Gorcum.
—— 1978, 'Carnival in Antigua: An indigenous festival in a tourist economy', *Anthropos*, 73(1/2): 191–204.
—— 1983, 'Cosmos and Chaos: Celebration in the modern world', in F.E. Manning (ed.), *The Celebration of Society; Perspectives on contemporary performance*: 3–30. Bowling Green (Ohio): Bowling Green University Popular Press Canada.
Márquez, R. 1989, 'Nationalism, Nation and Ideology: Trends in the emergence of a Caribbean literature', in F.W Knight and C.A. Palmer: *The Modern Caribbean*: 293–340. Chapel Hill/London: University of North Carolina Press.
Maslow, A.H. 1943, 'The Authoritarian Character Structure', *Journal of Social Psychology*, 18, 401–11.
Matthews, B. 1952, *Crisis of the West Indian Family*. Port of Spain: University of the West Indies.
Mendes, J. 1985, *Cote ce, Cote la: Trinidad and Tobago dictionary*. Port of Spain: Syncreators.
Miliband, R. 1977, *Marxism and Politics*. New York/Toronto/London: Oxford University Press.
Miller, D. 1991, 'Absolute Freedom in Trinidad', *Man*, 26(2): 323–41.
—— 1994, *Modernity, An Ethnographic Approach: Dualism and mass consumption in Trinidad*. Oxford/Providence: Berg.
Mills, T. 1987, 'Port of Spain: The unruly and cosmopolitan capital', in E. Saft, *Trinidad and Tobago*: 125–44.

280   *Trinidad Carnival*

Mintz, S.W. 1959, 'The Plantation as a Socio-Cultural Type', in *Plantation Systems of the New World*: 42–9. Social Science Monographs No. 7, Washington DC: Pan American Union.

—— 1967, 'Caribbean Nationhood in Anthropological Perspective', in S. Lewis and T.G. Mathews, *Caribbean Integration: Papers on social, political and economic integration*: 141–55. Río Piedras: Institute of Caribbean Studies.

Naipaul, S. 1985, *Black and White*. London: Abacus (1st edn 1981).

Naipaul, V.S. 1958, *The Suffrage of Elvira*. London: André Deutsch.

—— 1970, 'Power to the Caribbean People', *New York Review of Books*, 3 September: 32–4.

—— 1975, *Guerrillas*. London: André Deutsch.

—— 1977, *The Mimic Men*. Harmondsworth: Penguin (1st edn 1967).

—— 1981, *The Loss of El Dorado*. Harmondsworth: Penguin (1st edn 1969).

—— 1981a, 'The Killings in Trinidad', in *The Return of Eva Perón*: 11–92. Harmondsworth: Penguin (1st edn 1980).

—— 1982, *The Middle Passage*. Harmondsworth: Penguin (1st edn 1962).

—— 1982a, *Miguel Street*. Harmondsworth: Penguin (1st edn 1959).

—— 1983, *A House for Mr Biswas*. Harmondsworth: Penguin (1st edn 1961).

—— 1985, *Finding the Centre*. Harmondsworth: Penguin (1st edn 1984).

—— 1994, *A Way in the World*. London: Heinemann.

Nazareth, P. 1977, '"The Mimic Men" as a Study of Corruption', in R.D. Hamner, *Critical Perspectives on V.S. Naipaul*: 137–52.

Nooteboom, C. 1993, *De koning van Suriname*. Amsterdam: Rainbow.

Nunley, J.W. 1988, 'Masquerade Mix-Up in Trinidad Carnival: Live once, die forever', in J.W. Nunley and J. Bettelheim (eds), *Caribbean Festival Arts*: 85–116, Seattle/London: University of Washington Press.

Oliven, R.G. 1984, 'The Production and Consumption of Culture in Brazil', *Latin American Perspectives*, 40 (1): 103–15.

Oxaal, I. 1968, *Black Intellectuals Come to Power: The rise of Creole nationalism in Trinidad & Tobago*. Cambridge, Massachusetts: Schenkman.

—— 1971, *Race and Revolutionary Consciousness: An existential report on the 1970 Black Power revolt in Trinidad*. Cambridge, Massachusetts: Schenkman.

—— 1982, *Black Intellectuals and the Dilemmas of Race and Class in Trinidad*. Cambridge, Massachusetts: Schenkman.

Paxton, J. (ed.) 1990, *The Statesman's Year-Book 1988–89*. London/Basingstoke: Macmillan.

Pearse, A. 1956, 'Mitto Sampson on Calypso Legends of the Nineteenth Century', *Caribbean Quarterly*, 3/4: 250–62.

—— 1971, 'Carnival in Nineteenth Century Trinidad', in M. Horowitz, *Peoples and Cultures of the Caribbean*: 528–52. New York: Natural History Press.

Pires, B.C. 1988, 'What Wining are they Talking about?', in O. Baptiste, *Women in Mas'*: 47, 50, 52–4.

Powrie, B.E. 1956, 'The Changing Attitude of the Coloured Middle Class Toward Carnival', *Caribbean Quarterly*, 3/4: 224–32.

Procope, B. 1956, 'The Dragon Band or Devil Band', *Caribbean Quarterly*, 3/4: 276–88.

Quevedo, R. 1983, *Atilla's Kaiso: A short history of Trinidad calypso*. St Augustine: University of the West Indies.

Rique, R. 1983, 'Women in Mas': They Come out to Play', *People in Carnival*, March 1983: 35–6.

Rodman, H. 1971, *Lower-Class Families: The culture of poverty in Trinidad*. New York/Toronto/London: Oxford University Press.

Rohlehr, G. 1969, 'Calypso and Morality', *Moko*, 6(4), January 1969.

—— 1971, 'Calypso and Politics', *Moko*, October 1971: 7–18.

—— 1974, 'History as Absurdity; A literary critic's approach to "From Columbus to Castro" and other miscellaneous writings of Dr Eric Williams', in O. Coombs, *Is Massa Day Dead?*: 69–109. New York: Anchor Press.

—— 1983, 'An Introduction to the History of Calypso', *Paper presented to the Seminar on the Social and Economic Impact of Carnival*: 40–120. St Augustine: University of the West Indies.

—— 1985, 'Man Talking to Man': Calypso and social confrontation in Trinidad from 1970 to 1984', *Caribbean Quarterly*, 31(2): 1–13.

—— 1986, 'Calypso Sensorship: Historical', *Paper presented to the Seminar on the Calypso*, 1–76. St Augustine: University of the West Indies.

—— 1990, *Calypso and Society in Pre-Independence Trinidad*. Port of Spain: Gordon Rohlehr.

Rubin, V. 1960, 'Cultural Perspectives in Caribbean Research', in V. Rubin (ed.), *Caribbean Studies: A symposium*: 110–22. Seattle: University of Washington Press (2nd edn).

—— 1962, 'Culture, Politics and Race Relations', *Social and Economic Studies*, XI: 433–55.

Rubin, V. and Zavalloni, M. 1969, *We Wish to be Looked upon: A study of the aspirations of youth in a developing society*. New York: Teachers College Press.

Saft, E. (ed.) 1987, *Trinidad and Tobago*. Singapore: APA productions.

Samad, I. 1990, 'The Myth of Martyrdom', *Trinidad and Tobago Review*, 12 (11 and 12): 2.

Samaroo, B. 1985, 'Politics and Afro-Indian Relations in Trinidad', in J.G. LaGuerre, *Calcutta to Caroni: The East Indians of Trinidad*: 77–92. St Augustine: University of the West Indies (1st edn 1974).

Segal, D.A. 1993, 'Race' and 'Colour' in Pre-Independence Trinidad and Tobago', in K.A. Yelvington, *Trinidad Ethnicity*: 81–115.

—— 1994, 'Living Ancestors: Nationalism and the past in postcolonial Trinidad and Tobago', in J. Boyarin, *Remapping Memory: The politics of timespace*: 221–39. Minneapolis/London: University of Minnesota Press.

Simon, P. 1975, 'Steelband', in M. Anthony and A. Carr, *David Frost Introduces: Trinidad*: 99–110. London: André Deutsch.

Simpson, G.E. 1962, 'The Shango Cult in Nigeria and in Trinidad', *American Anthropologist*, 64: 1204–19.

—— 1964, 'The Acculturative Process in Trinidadian Shango', *Anthropological Quarterly*, 37: 16–27.

Singh, H.B. 1969, 'V.S. Naipaul: A spokesman for neo-colonialism', *Literature and Ideology*, 2: 71–85.

Singh, K. 1985, 'Indians and the Larger Society', in J.G. LaGuerre, *Calcutta to Caroni: The East Indians of Trinidad* 33–60. St Augustine: University of the West Indies (1st edn 1974).

—— 1988, *Bloodstained Tombs: The Muharram Massacre 1884*. London/ Basingstoke: Macmillan.

Smith, M.G. 1965, *The Plural Society in the British West Indies*. Berkeley: University of California Press.

——— 1967, 'Foreword', in L. Despres, *Cultural Pluralism and Nationalist Politics in British Guiana*: vii–xxi. Chicago: Rand McNally.

——— 1971, 'Institutional and Political Conditions of Pluralism', in L. Kuper and M.G. Smith, *Pluralism in Africa*: 27–65. Berkeley: University of California Press.

——— 1974, *Corporations and Society*. London: Duckworth.

——— 1984, *Culture, Race and Class in the Commonwealth Caribbean*. Mona: University of the West Indies.

——— 1991, 'Pluralism and Social Stratification', in S. Ryan, *Social and Occupational Stratification in Contemporary Trinidad and Tobago*: 3–35. St Augustine: University of the West Indies.

Smith, M.P. 1990, 'New Orleans' Carnival: Culture from the underside', *Plantation Society in the Americas: Carnival in Perspective*: 11–32.

Smith, R.T. 1956, *The Negro Family in British Guiana*. London: Routledge & Kegan Paul.

Stewart, J. 1986, 'Patronage and Control in the Trinidad Carnival', in V.W. Turner and E.M. Bruner, *The Anthropology of Experience*: 289-315. Illinois: University of Illinois Press.

——— 1989, 'The Literary Work as Cultural Document: A Caribbean case', in P.A. Dennis and W. Aycock, *Literature and Anthropology*: 97–112. Austin: Texas Tech University Press.

Taylor, J.M. 1982, 'The Politics of Aesthetic Debate: The case of Brazilian carnival', *Ethnology*, 21(4): 301–11.

Taylor, R.L. 1978, *Art, an Enemy of the People*. Hassocks: The Harvester Press.

Tourism Surveys 1986, including extract from 'The Imperatives of Adjustment' Draft Development Plan. Research and Planning Unit of the Trinidad and Tobago Tourist Board.

Tulder, A. van 1989, 'Het carnaval en de Calypso op Trinidad: de sociaal-politieke betekenis in historisch perspektief. Unpublished MA thesis, University of Amsterdam.

Turner, V.W. 1964, 'Symbols in Ndembu Ritual', in M. Gluckman, *Closed Systems and Open Minds*: 20–51. Chicago: Aldine.

——— 1969, *The Ritual Process: Structure and anti-structure*. London: Routledge & Kegan Paul.

——— 1970, *The Forest of Symbols: Aspects of Ndembu ritual*. Ithaca: Cornell University Press (1st edn 1967).

——— 1974, *Dramas, Fields, and Metaphors: Symbolic action in human society*. Ithaca and London: Cornell University Press.

——— 1977, 'Variations on a Theme of Liminality', in S.F. Moore and B.G. Meyerhoff, *Secular Ritual*: 36-53. Assen: Van Gorcum.

——— 1978, 'Comments and Conclusions', in B.A. Babcock, *The Reversible World*: 276–96.

——— 1982, *From Ritual to Theatre: The human seriousness of play*. New York: Performing Arts Journal Publications.

——— 1983, 'Carnaval in Rio: Dionysian drama in an industrializing society', in F.E. Manning, *The Celebration of Society: Perspectives on contemporary performance*: 103–25.

——— 1983a, 'The Spirit of Celebration', in F.E. Manning, *The Celebration of Society: Perspectives on contemporary performance*: 187–92.

Vogt, R.C. 1975, *'The Development of a Sense of Political Community in a Plural Society: Nation building in Trinidad'*: Unpublished PhD thesis, State University of New York.

Wallace, A. 1956, 'Revitalization Movements', *American Anthropologist*, 58: 264–81.

Warner, K. 1983, *The Trinidad Calypso: A study of calypso as oral literature.* London/Kingston/Port of Spain: Heinemann (1st edn 1982).

—— 1993, 'Ethnicity and the Contemporary Calypso', in K.A. Yelvington, *Trinidad Ethnicity*: 275–91.

Warner-Lewis, M. 1984, 'Yoruba Songs from Trinidad.' Mona: University of the West Indies, unpublished manuscript.

Weller, J.A. 1966, 'A Profile of a Trinidadian Steelband', *Phylon (Quarterly)*, 22: 68–77.

Wertheim, W.F. 1962, *East-West Parallels: Sociological approaches to modern Asia.* The Hague: W. van Hoeve Ltd.

Williams, E. 1960, 'Race Relations in the Caribbean', in V. Rubin, *Caribbean Studies: A symposium*: 54–60.

—— 1982, *History of the People of Trinidad and Tobago.* London: André Deutsch (1st edn 1963).

Williams, L. 1987, 'Burn Dem, Sung by Black Stalin', in *1987 Carnival and Calypsoes.* Port of Spain.

Wilson, P. 1969, 'Reputation and Respectability: A suggestion for Caribbean ethnology', *Man (n.s.)*, 4: 70–84.

—— 1970/71, 'Caribbean Crews: Peer groups and male society', *Caribbean Studies*, 10(4): 18–34.

—— 1973, *Crab Antics: The social anthropology of English-speaking Negro societies of the Caribbean.* New Haven/London: Yale University Press.

Winer, L. 1986, 'Socio-Cultural Change and the Language of Calypso', *Nieuwe West-Indische Gids*, 60 (3/4): 113–48.

Winkler, J.J. 1990, *The Constraints of Desire: The anthropology of sex and gender in ancient Greece.* New York/London: Routledge.

Wood, D. 1986, *Trinidad in Transition: The years after slavery.* Oxford/New York/Toronto: Oxford University Press (1st edn 1968).

World Bank 1988, *A World Bank Country Study. Caribbean countries: Economic situation, regional issues, and capital flows.* Washington DC: World Bank.

Worsley, P. 1959, 'Cargo Cults', *Scientific American*, 200 (May): 120–2.

Wyndham, F. 1971, 'V.S. Naipaul', *The Listener*, October 7: 461–2.

Yelvington, K.A. (ed.) 1993, *Trinidad Ethnicity.* London/Basingstoke: Macmillan.

Index